Frank O'Hara Now
New Essays on the New York Poet

Frank O'Hara Now

New Essays on the New York Poet

Edited by

ROBERT HAMPSON *and* WILL MONTGOMERY

LIVERPOOL UNIVERSITY PRESS

First published 2010 by
Liverpool University Press
4 Cambridge Street
Liverpool
L69 7ZU

Copyright © 2010 Liverpool University Press

British Library Cataloguing-in-Publication data
A British Library CIP record is available

ISBN 978-1-84631-231-1 cased
     978-1-84631-233-5 limp

Typeset in Monotype Dante by
Koinonia, Manchester
Printed and bound in Great Britain by
Bell and Bain Ltd, Glasgow

Contents

Contents

3 The Work of Others

List of Illustrations

In the chapter by Nick Selby:

Abbreviations

AC Frank O'Hara, *Art Chronicles* (New York: George Braziller, 1975)

AN *Amorous Nightmares of Delay: Selected Plays*. (Baltimore, MD: Johns Hopkins University Press, 1997)

CP *The Collected Poems of Frank O Hara*, ed. Donald Allen (New York: Alfred A Knopf, 1972)

PR *Poems Retrieved*, ed. Donald Allen (Bolinas, CA: Grey Fox Press, 1977)

SS *Standing Still and Walking in New York*, ed. Donald Allen (Bolinas, CA: Grey Fox Press, 1975)

Acknowledgements

The editors thank the following individuals and institutions for permission to reproduce the images listed below.

Cover image: Philip Guston, *Frank*, 1955, pencil on paper, 8 1/2 × 11. Collection: Bill Berkson, San Francisco.

Jackson Pollock, *Bird Effort*, 1946. © the Pollock-Krasner Foundation Ars, NY and DACS, London 2010. Peggy Guggenheim Collection, Venice (Solomon R. Guggenheim Foundation, NY).

Norman Bluhm and Frank O'Hara, *This is the First…*; *Bang*; *Noël*; *May!* (all 1960). Grey Art Gallery, New York University Art Collection, Gift of Norman Bluhm.

Guy Debord and Asger Jorn, facing pages from *Fin de Copenhague*, 1957. © Donation Jorn, Silkeborg/billedkunst.dk. Photograph: Lars Bay.

Stills from Alfred Leslie's film *The Last Clean Shirt*, 1964. © Alfred Leslie.

Photograph of Grace Hartigan at her kite-flying party, 1952 and photographic contact sheet for *Masquerade*, 1954. Grace Hartigan Papers, Special Collections Research Centre, Syracuse University Library. The estate of Grace Hartigan.

Joe Brainard and Frank O'Hara, *I Grew this Mustache…*, 1964. Collection: Bill Berkson & Constance Lewallen, San Francisco.

Joe Brainard, *Good'n Fruity Madonna*, 1968. Collection: Peter R. Stern. The estate of Joe Brainard. Courtesy of Tibor de Nagy Gallery, New York.

Jasper Johns, *In Memory of my Feelings – Frank O'Hara*, 1961. © Jasper Johns/VAGA, New York/DACS, London 2010. Collection: Museum of Contemporary Art, Chicago. Partial gift of Apollo Plastics Corporation. Courtesy of Stefan T. Edlis and H. Gael Neeson. Photography © Museum of Contemporary Art, Chicago.

Jasper Johns, *Memory Piece (Frank O'Hara)*, 1961–70. © Jasper Johns/VAGA, New York/DACS, London 2010. Collection of the artist.

The editors gratefully acknowledge permission to cite:

From *The Collected Poems of Frank O'Hara* by Frank O'Hara, edited by Donald Allen, copyright © 1971 by Maureen Granville-Smith, Adminstratrix of the Estate of Frank O'Hara, copyright renewed 1999 by Maureen O'Hara Granville-Smith and Donald Allen. Introduction copyright © 1971 by Alfred A. Knopf, a division of

Random House, Inc. Used by permission of Alfred A. Knopf, a division of Random House, Inc.

Excerpts from 'River', 'Poem [There I Could Never Be a Boy]', 'For Grace, After a Party', 'Meditations in an Emergency', 'Radio' from *Meditations in an Emergency* copyright © 1957 by Frank O'Hara. Used by permission of Grove / Atlantic Inc.

Excerpts from 'A Step Away from Them', 'Image of the Buddha Preaching', 'The Day Lady Died', 'Adieu to Norman, Bon Jour to Joan and Jean-Paul', 'Personal Poem', 'Steps', 'For the Chinese New Year & for Bill Berkson', and 'Mary Desti's Ass', from *Lunch Poems,* copyright © 1964 by Frank O'Hara. Reprinted by permission of City Lights Books.

'Variations on a Theme of Kenneth Koch After his Variations on a Theme by William Carlos Williams', 'Love', and 'Just for Now' (Pierre Reverdy, trs. Frank O'Hara), from autograph manuscripts in the Kenneth Koch Archive of the New York Public Library. By permission of the Henry W. and Albert A. Berg Collection of English and American Literature, The New York Public Library, Astor, Lenox and Tilden Foundations.

Excerpts from the subtitles to the film *The Last Clean Shirt*; collaborative artworks produced with Norman Bluhm and Joe Brainard; poems published by Grove / Atlantic and City Lights listed above; manuscript material listed above; material from *Art Chronicles, Amorous Nightmares of Delay: Selected Plays, Poems Retrieved* and *Standing Still and Walking in New York*. By permission of Maureen Granville-Smith, Administratrix of the Estate of Frank O'Hara.

Excerpts from the work of John Ashbery, copyright John Ashbery; used by permission of Georges Burchardt, Inc., and Carcanet Press, for the author; all rights reserved.

'Auberge' by Pierre Reverdy. By permission of Editions Flammarion; Patricia Terry's translation by permission of Wake Forest University Press.

Thanks also to Bill Berkson, Olivier Brossard, Jinny Colby.

Introduction

Robert Hampson and Will Montgomery

Frank O'Hara's reputation today is higher than at any time since his death. His poetry appeals to many different kinds of reader and writer, and he is unique in commanding admiration across the schismatic world of contemporary poetry. His writing is both read and taught widely on both sides of the Atlantic. There are, we think, many reasons for this popularity, both intrinsic and extrinsic to the poetry. For one thing, there is the grace and wit of his best-known poetry, which has chimed with a postmodern celebration of irony, pastiche and playfulness. There is also his relationship with the art world, and the evocation of 1950s' New York in his poetry, which attracts readers to his work.[1] More recently, his poetry's engagement with sexuality has also attracted critical attention.[2] Other aspects of his work, however, such as the role of moods of boredom or aggression, or his interest in art forms such as music or dance, or his political engagement, have received rather less attention. In assembling this volume – the first collection of essays on O'Hara for almost two decades – we have sought to broaden the scope of the critical response to a body of work that we identify as uneasier, more challenging and more uncompromising than some previous accounts would allow.

O'Hara's halcyon days in New York, which coincided with a crucial time in the development of American art, have become hard to separate from the work. Indeed, the figure of this gregarious and charming O'Hara – Larry Rivers declared in his funeral oration that at least 60 people in New York considered him their best friend – has been associated with his writing in a way that is quite unusual in contemporary literary studies. In part this derives from the recurrent references to friends in his poetry and the evocation of a specific New York 'coterie' culture. Two recent studies of O'Hara – both very strong – ground themselves in complex ways in O'Hara's relationships with his peers, whether conceived as 'coterie' or

---

1 It is significant that one of the early, indeed foundational studies of O'Hara's work was Marjorie Perloff's *Frank O'Hara: Poet Among Painters* (Austin: University of Texas Press, 1977; reprinted Chicago and London: University of Chicago Press, 1998).

2 See, for example, Hazel Smith, *Hyperscapes in the Poetry of Frank O'Hara: Difference, Homosexuality, Topography* (Liverpool: Liverpool University Press, 2000).

'friendship'.[3] It is true that the life is obtrusively present in the poems, yet criticism of less substance than that of Shaw or Epstein has sometimes struggled to free itself from anecdote and reminiscence, as if the chatty, witty voice that speaks in many of O'Hara's best-known poems defined the writings' intellectual horizons. Sometimes, it is as if we – as dazed and star-struck readers and writers – would like nothing more than to be his friend too.

One book that has been influential in the reception of O'Hara over the years has been *Homage to Frank O'Hara*, co-edited by two of the poet's friends, Joe LeSueur and Bill Berkson. This collection of reminiscences, short critical pieces, and images has proved a key resource for critics, offering many lively first-hand impressions of the social and aesthetic environment in which the poetry was produced. It is worth pausing to wonder, however, whether a readership, scholarly or otherwise, would ever pay so much attention to the circumstances of John Ashbery's existence in the '50s and '60s. Sometimes it seems as if the sociability of O'Hara's writing steers readers into a particular style of reading. Those famous first-name references to O'Hara's friends and associates often have the effect of drawing the reader towards a mode of vicarious involvement in the events, moods and encounters of the remarkably dynamic circle that the texts memorialize. We might, however, ask whether the evident wit and effervescence that shapes this sociability exists alongside other less fully explored qualities. And we could also consider whether the abrupt end to the life story, like that of O'Hara's beloved James Dean, lends a seductive, but ultimately questionable glow to the foregoing and eternally youthful life. O'Hara's early death has had the paradoxical effect, it may be argued, of injecting his life into the writing in ways that it does not always invite. The memorials and *Festschriften* that untimely death elicited have coloured both life and work with the pathos of unfulfilled potential.

Another factor that has shaped the reception of O'Hara's foreshortened oeuvre has perhaps been the pre-eminence of the *Lunch Poems*, published in 1964 in the popular Pocket Poets series by City Lights. As John Wilkinson remarks in an essay in this volume, 'the mass-market edition of *Lunch Poems* [has] come to signify Frank O'Hara to the wider poetry readership'. There have, it is true, been several correctives to this version of O'Hara but, nonetheless, the 'I do this, I do that' manner that is evident in the best-known poems of this (actually rather diverse) volume is the O'Hara that has gained widest currency. This is O'Hara the wit, the raconteur, the poet of the dazzling surfaces of city life and the voluble witness to the intense social and aesthetic activity of the 1950s' New York art scene. This is the accelerated O'Hara who dashes off poems at work, at a party or while watching TV, only to stuff them later, as Ashbery's introduction to the *Collected Poems* attests,

---

3 See Lytle Shaw, *Frank O'Hara: The Poetics of Coterie* (Iowa: University of Iowa Press, 2006); Andrew Epstein, *Beautiful Enemies: Friendship and Postwar American Poetry* (New York: Oxford University Press, 2006).

into 'drawers and cartons and half forget them' (*CP*, vii).[4] This is the O'Hara who irritated Robert Lowell by reading at Wagner College a poem he had written on the Staten Island ferry on his way to the event.[5] 'Often,' begins O'Hara's evidently self-penned blurb to *Lunch Poems*, 'this poet, strolling through the noisy splintered glare of a Manhattan noon, has paused at a sample Olivetti to type up thirty or forty lines of ruminations…'. This image of insouciant genius, apparently so careless of his talents, has proven attractive to generations of readers and writers, O'Hara's immediate successors among them, and has perhaps veiled the writing's more demanding qualities.

What, however, if O'Hara is only sometimes so insouciant, only sometimes so sociable? What if the writing is, in other words, rather more strenuous in its ambition than O'Hara's cultivated flippancy sometimes suggests? If, for example – as Daniel Kane's essay in this book demonstrates – O'Hara took such great care to fillet his past work for the subtitles he contributed to Alfred Leslie's film *Last Clean Shirt*, might he not have been at times rather more attentive to its importance than the sock-drawer stories imply? And might we not find in the work an unfriendly O'Hara, a bored O'Hara, a melancholic O'Hara, a politicized O'Hara – perhaps even a disturbingly sober O'Hara?

One can only speculate what might have happened had O'Hara had Ashbery's chance to develop the many pathways opened up by his writing of the '50s and '60s. Perhaps, like that of his friend Barbara Guest, his work would have taken shape as a sceptical counterpoint to the late-twentieth-century North American poetic avant-garde. And, as Andrea Brady speculates in her essay on 'Second Avenue', 'perhaps his I-do-this *Lunch Poems* would have been viewed as a temporary aberration' in a body of work more notable for its 'use of violent imagery, pop-art personae, super-ficial anecdotalism, non sequiturs and absurdism'. Perhaps his relationship with the art world would eventually have accommodated a response to tendencies such as minimalism, process art or performance art. We worry, in any case, that O'Hara's reputation is in danger of calcifying around the urbane and charming persona that speaks in his poems in a way that does not do justice to the manifold challenges of those poems.

We did not, however, assemble this volume in an aggressively revisionist spirit. We do not mean to pitch this collection as a salutary corrective to decades of supposed misreadings. Yet, in our reading, our conversations and our teaching we have found that the O'Hara that is so widely known and loved is often not quite the same O'Hara that we, in our separate ways, have loved. The wit, rapidity and surface energies of the writing, going on its nerve as it does, is greatly admired by us. The O'Hara who celebrates the speed and varied opportunities of the city – cultural, sexual and commercial – is a vitally important figure in that twentieth-century

---

4 See also Diane di Prima's account of finding O'Hara's poems scattered all over the poet's flat and rescuing unique copies of poems from drawers. Cited in Perloff, *Poet Among Painters*, p. 115.

5 Brad Gooch, *City Poet: The Life and Times of Frank O'Hara* (New York: Alfred A. Knopf, 1993), p. 386.

reorientation of poetry towards the urban. However, we have also found ourselves drawn to an O'Hara who is receptive to the unsettling legacy of modernism. This is an O'Hara who embraces filth and abjection with Nietzschean zest, who is thrilled by the possibilities of montage, who swoons at Cage and Feldman as well as at Rachmaninov and the New York City Ballet, who embraces the new independent cinema as well as Hollywood comedies, who can break his lines and his syntax in deceptively violent ways, who preserves in his writing a knotty relationship with Pound, Surrealism and 'old' Europe as well as with the New World consumerist ephemera that floats in the frothy tides of his poems. This is an O'Hara, too, who spurns year-zero American isolationism, reading beyond modernism through Romanticism to the Renaissance. The brash dismissal of history – Europe, in other words – that was common to many artist contemporaries of O'Hara was not shared by the poet.

In his biography of O'Hara, Brad Gooch describes the beginning of O'Hara's friendship with Ashbery, in their last days at Harvard. Their rapidly developing conversation was animated, Gooch notes, by a love of high *and* low culture – the second Viennese school one minute, Daffy Duck the next – in an eclectic, plural-istic inclusiveness.[6] In much O'Hara criticism, we contend, the first half of that dyad has been somewhat overlooked, the challenge of contemporary composi-tion ditched for the sprawling energies of American popular culture. At one time, the pop-culture references clearly seemed refreshingly iconoclastic – a counterblast against the constraints of high modernism in its 'academic' form; now, reading and writing in conditions in which popular culture has become entirely hegemonic, we are impelled to recover a fuller O'Hara. It is, at least, worth considering that the pressures and exigencies of such models as Schoenberg perhaps never vanished from O'Hara's writing.

All the above is not to say that we wish simply to replace surface with depth, or low with high, or to claim O'Hara for yet another articulation of a supposedly modernist aesthetic over a tarnished and now discredited postmodernism. None of these substitutive manoeuvres would do justice to the diversity, complexity and strangeness of the writing. We do, however, want to suggest that O'Hara is not as easily assimilable – or indeed as friendly – as he might appear. His poems can be difficult and recalcitrant, their surface fluency concealing obdurate lacunae and hesitation. O'Hara's cheerfulness is the cheerfulness of one who has encountered and embraced suffering. The ready wit often conceals doubt and uncertainties.

It was important to us, from the outset, that the collection should reflect the engagement with O'Hara's work currently taking place on both sides of the Atlantic. This reflects our sense that O'Hara's reception in the UK remains, despite the work of a number of British scholars – Geoff Ward, Mark Ford, Hazel Smith, and William Watkin – under-documented. This, in turn, was prompted by our

---

6 Gooch, *City Poet*, p. 137.

awareness of O'Hara's impact on the writing of the post-war modernist tradition in British writing, the early years of which are sometimes, though not without controversy, referred to as the 'British Poetry Revival'.[7] O'Hara was important to many of the poets who established themselves in the 1960s and 1970s, admired by writers as different as Lee Harwood, John James, J. H. Prynne and Barry MacSweeney. His influence was felt by a later generation of writers – Geoff Ward, John Wilkinson, and Robert Hampson, for example – and is important now to younger poets such as Redell Olsen, Keston Sutherland and Andrea Brady (and to emerging poets younger than them). The existing critical coverage of O'Hara does not successfully account for the appeal of his poetry to such writers. Although it did not occur to us until the commissioning process was complete, we feel it is no accident that, with the exception of Will Montgomery, Brian Reed and Nick Selby, all those who have contributed to the volume are poets as well as critics.

In our desire to produce a response to O'Hara that had a transatlantic dimension, we invited a number of British writers as well as figures such as Lytle Shaw, Brian Reed, Richard Deming, Andrea Brady, and Daniel Kane, who would allow us to present a sampling of voices that speak American, if not quite O'Hara's American. Yet, even as we attempted to draw in established and emerging voices from both sides of the Atlantic, the interpenetration of our poetic cultures ensured that references to this side or that side became hard to sustain. As the essays came in, we did not feel that we were negotiating two entirely different 'traditions' of response to O'Hara. Wilkinson, a poet associated with the Cambridge nexus of writers, has in recent years been based in the US. The American poet and critic Andrea Brady, on the other hand, who studied with Kenneth Koch at Columbia (and was for two years his assistant), has lived and worked in the UK for more than a decade. Daniel Kane, too, is an American exile in England.

Marjorie Perloff's early book on O'Hara firmly established him as a 'poet among painters'. This aspect of O'Hara's life and work cannot be ignored. Essays in our collection consider O'Hara alongside Norman Bluhm, Jasper Johns, Robert Motherwell and Grace Hartigan, but they do so in ways that seek to complicate our understanding of the relationship between different art forms. In addition, we also wanted to examine O'Hara's affinities with music, dance and film – areas of activity that have been insufficiently explored to date. O'Hara's engagements with these forms, which sometimes involved collaborations, were often the site of a testing and critiquing of the limits of the apparently self-sufficient personae that emerge in some of his poems.

From diverse starting points, a number of our contributors consider issues relating not just to O'Hara's presence in his own work but to the very question of embodiment as it is played out in the writing. Others investigate the strangely

---

7 See Eric Mottram, 'The British Poetry Revival, 1960–75', in Robert Hampson and Peter Barry (eds.), *New British Poetries: The Scope of the Possible* (Manchester: Manchester University Press, 1993), pp. 15–50.

nihilistic versions of democracy that come into being – paradoxically or not – as the lyric selves posited by O'Hara's poetry self-destruct and disperse. Others still encounter in O'Hara a debt to a splenetic version of Romanticism. In such cases we can ask ourselves: what thickets of history, responsibility and commitment shadow the apparently untrammelled speakers of O'Hara's poems? What are the circumstances and limitations of this obsessively iterated freedom? Why is it, to put it another way, that 'joy seems to be inexorable' (*CP*, 340)?

In dividing our book into three sections – 'City', 'Selves', 'The Work of Others' – we have attempted to address some of the interlocking scenes of O'Hara's work: his sense of the city; the versions of selfhood that emerge in the writing; and his encounters with artists working in different disciplines. These are, of course, familiar ways of approaching O'Hara's work, and we hope that the continuities with the existing criticism can thus be noted. Yet neither O'Hara's writing nor the critical discourse it gives rise to in our collection settles comfortably within such categories. The reader will notice many cross-flows and incipient conversations between essays from the three sections. As these connections emerge, it will be clear that other categories – embodiment, for example, or Europe, or freedom – make similarly strong claims on the reader's attention.

The first section, 'City', begins with an essay by Geoff Ward, whose book *Statutes of Liberty* (1993, reprinted 2000) was decisive in inaugurating a new level of scholarly conversation about the writing of O'Hara and his poet friends. Ward's essay in this volume focuses on New York: he considers the warping of historical perspective that follows 9/11 and the demise of the New York that hosted the various New York Schools. This New York, in Ward's view, was 'founded and terminated by acts of war', book-ended by the Second World War and 9/11. Ward pays particular attention to O'Hara's late long poem 'Biotherm (for Bill Berkson)', discussing the implications of its 'broken and looped phrasings' for the very notion of relationship in O'Hara's work.

Lytle Shaw has written probably the most valuable monograph on O'Hara's work, *Frank O'Hara: The Poetics of Coterie* (2006). In his essay for this volume, Shaw addresses the crisis in 'gestural' painting of the late 1950s in the context of O'Hara's collaboration with Norman Bluhm: the *Poem-Paintings*. Shaw places these works provocatively alongside the gestural aesthetics of Situationism, arguing that the 'realization of gesture in urban situations' practised by the Situationists in Europe was analogous to O'Hara's practice of 'productively debasing poetry'. Like Ward, Shaw seeks to reconsider O'Hara's relationship to Abstract Expressionism, particularly the influential conservative version advanced by professional art critics. In 'French Frank' Rod Mengham considers O'Hara's relationship to Europe from a different perspective. Noting O'Hara's apparent endorsement of a typically isolationist view of the US, he then reads the poetry for its encounter with French poetry, particularly the writing of Pierre Reverdy. In Mengham's view, O'Hara's long-standing affinities with French poetry enable a poetic undermining of the heroic, freedom-loving individualism embodied in Cold War accounts of artists such as Jackson Pollock.

A notion of 'freedom' is integral to Andrea Brady's essay, an extended examination of O'Hara's 'Second Avenue' that poses searching questions about the nature and legacy of O'Hara's writing. Brady considers the distractedness of O'Hara's poetic voice in 'Second Avenue' and interrogates Charles Bernstein's category of 'anti-absorptive' writing – writing that frustrates the reader's desire for unselfconscious immersion in the text. She discusses the limitations of O'Hara's distractedness, positioning the poetry's apparent textual freedoms as part of a tyrannical insistence on surface that leads ultimately to a kind of ethical shortfall.

David Herd also tackles the theoretical scope of O'Hara's poetics as he addresses the trope of the 'step' in O'Hara. By this he means several things: O'Hara's own gait as he walked the city streets; the prosodic unit; and a variant of the Heideggerian 'leap'. Reading O'Hara through William Carlos Williams, Herd asks how O'Hara's prosody might, in Simon Jarvis's influential formulation, be thought of as a mode of cognition. For Herd, an apprehension of 'measure' in the writing enables us to comprehend the intellectual work that the poems achieve with such deceptive sure-footedness.

The Polish poet and scholar Tadeusz Pióro explores O'Hara's relationship to modernism, building his argument around two ideas in O'Hara's writing: its relationship to the totemic modernist category of novelty, and its allied investment in a kind of *ennui* or Baudelairean spleen. Pióro finds that, in its scepticism about the 'new' and, in particular, in countenancing states of boredom, O'Hara's writing can be read against the grain of prevailing accounts of the intellectual and emotional tenor of the work. As with several of our contributors, Pióro is keen to stress O'Hara's relationship to European antecedents. In addition, Pióro's presence in the volume reflects the profound influence of O'Hara on Polish poetry since the mid-1980s.[8]

Our second section, on subjectivity in O'Hara, begins with a discussion of O'Hara's *Odes*. These were published as a book by the Tiber Press in 1960, but, as John Wilkinson argues, they have not been sufficiently understood as a discrete grouping in O'Hara's *oeuvre*. Wilkinson attributes to the *Odes* the ability to simultaneously inhabit and parody several traditions. In particular, he discusses O'Hara's skewed adaptation of the writing of Shelley in the context of ideas of death and memorialization. A mixture of bathos and the sublime, in Wilkinson's view, replaces a monolithic notion of selfhood with a 'flickering montage of part-identifications' that has a radically democratic potential. Ideas of identification and the self are explored in striking ways by Keston Sutherland, whose essay is grounded in a 'close

---

8 See Tadeusz Pióro, Rod Mengham and Piotr Szymor (eds.), *Altered State: The New Polish Poetry* (Todmorden: Arc, 2003).

reading' of a single poem by O'Hara, 'For Grace, After a Party'. This close reading is itself a questioning of the implications of the idea of close reading. Sutherland means more than is habitually understood by the term, pursuing, by means of Keats, Reverdy and queer poetics, an investigation of the peculiar form of intimacy that is enacted in the encounter between poet and reader. In Sutherland's view, the 'limit' of solitude is probed by the illocutionary act of the poem. As he demonstrates, this occurs in especially self-conscious and intense ways in 'For Grace, After a Party', as it tests the borders of 'closeness'.

Richard Deming, like Sutherland, builds his argument around a single poem. He focuses on the social implications of O'Hara's extraordinary poem 'Hatred', written in 1952. This poem, almost anomalous in O'Hara's *oeuvre* for its mixture of vitriol and violence, paradoxically enacts, in Deming's account, a specifically ethical vision of the poet's relationship to the social. Reading through Whitman, Deming argues that 'Hatred' amounts to 'an indictment of an entire age'. For Deming, the social is intrinsically affective, a space in which 'contesting and complementary values and meanings' are present. This, he suggests, opens the possibility of an appraisal of the relationship between affect and ethics in O'Hara's writing: through a demanding encounter with the passion of hatred, the reader of the poem is rendered self-conscious about his or her necessary ethical investments. Another younger scholar, Josh Robinson, is one of several contributors for whom the issue of embodiment in O'Hara's writing is important. Robinson is particularly interested in breath and the specific articulation of the breath that is laughter. Robinson explores the relationship between laughter and mirth in the context of aesthetic theory, discerning in O'Hara's poetry a kind of laughter that can withstand the critiques of laughter-as-entertainment advanced by the Frankfurt School. O'Hara's poems, he argues, induce a particular range of bodily responses in their readers, constituting together a singular and singularly valuable form of embodied aesthetic experience.

Our final section is devoted to O'Hara's interactions with other artists. In his detailed account of Alfred Leslie's *The Last Clean Shirt*, Daniel Kane brings a new perspective to bear on O'Hara's relationship to film, which is typically seen in the context of his enthusiasm for Hollywood. Kane discusses O'Hara's involvement with Leslie and the burgeoning filmic counterculture of the New American cinema. He elucidates O'Hara's cannibalizing of his own texts to produce the subtitles for the film and shows how, thus recontextualized, O'Hara's words draw into their orbit not the uptown gallery scene, but the Lower East Side world of Ginsberg and the Beats. In so doing, Kane unearths a grubbier, more seditious O'Hara, for whom playfulness and camp are shadowed by an investment in the emerging counterculture.

Another important relationship of O'Hara's that has received insufficient attention to date is that with the painter Grace Hartigan, a close friend who took on the role of muse in several of his poems. Redell Olsen draws a parallel between Hartigan's use of photography in her painting process and O'Hara's use of paintings (often by Hartigan) in his writing. Each involves an engagement with posing, masks, and self-staging performance. Olsen argues that posing was important to Hartigan and O'Hara, both as a means of negotiating social and political tensions and, in their work, as an interface or mediation between experience and art.

Will Montgomery explores the relationship between O'Hara and the New York school of composers, seeking to complicate accounts of O'Hara's musical affinities. In particular, he is interested in Morton Feldman, who twice set to music O'Hara's 'Wind', a short poem dedicated to the composer. O'Hara wrote the sleeve notes for Feldman's first long-player and at one point considered collaborating with Feldman. Montgomery notes the equivocal notion of freedom that is developed in 'Wind' and explores the poem's relationship to the much longer 'Ode to Michael Goldberg ('s Birth and Other Births)'. He finds in O'Hara and Feldman, each of whom had an intense affiliation with the art and artists of Abstract Expressionism, a mode of working that does not sit easily with the liberatory ambitions of gestural art.

Brian Reed argues for a proprioceptive recognition of the body's role in O'Hara's writing. As for David Herd, the body moving in space is held to represent an analogue of the movement of the poem. Like Lytle Shaw, Reed discusses the nature of the 'gestural', but, where Shaw approaches O'Hara's poetry through the 'urban situations', Reed's analysis draws on the phenomenology of dance as it unfolds in several of O'Hara's poems. Reed mobilizes a version of intermedia theory to develop a nuanced account of the presence of other art forms in O'Hara's writing.

The final essay of the collection, by Nick Selby, broaches issues of memorial and intimacy as they emerge in the work of Jasper Johns and in the collages O'Hara produced with Joe Brainard. For Selby, the body becomes the primary site of an ironically elegizing poetics that 'unpicks […] the textual stitches in which authenticity and feelingness might be located'. O'Hara, in this view, writes a radical form of lyric poetry that activates qualities of 'feelingness' in the guise of memory and elegy at the same time as it exposes the very poetic ruses through which that affect is represented.

In entitling our book *Frank O'Hara Now* our intention is to offer some suggestions as to why O'Hara's work should still remain so important to us more than four decades after his death. We are pleased that, although some common threads are discernible in the essays and across our subdivisions, we are presenting some rather divergent analyses of O'Hara's significance. In these divergences lie some of the reasons for the continuing challenge presented by O'Hara's writing. The essays in this volume collectively make the case for an argumentative and non-consecutive O'Hara, one whose fluency is always imperilled, whose charm cohabits with spleen, and one whose commitment to the everyday in speech and experience is everywhere shadowed by the hallucinatory.

1
City

'Housing the Deliberations': New York, War, and Frank O'Hara

Geoff Ward

I

Frank O'Hara's 'Ode: Salute to the French Negro Poets' is a characteristically dashing and passionate poem, throwing in its lot with the late Aimé Césaire, whose varied activities spanned Surrealist poetry and practical politics. Across these 'shifting sands', O'Hara's account of 'trying to live in the terrible western world' attempts to make the West liveable by looking outside it, yearning for an other that can be recognized, but recognized *as* other, and not be subsumed or contained:

> the only truth is face to face, the poem whose words become your mouth
> and dying in black and white we fight for what we love, not are (*CP*, 305)

If the cut to the emotional chase is typical of O'Hara's warmth and readiness to articulate personal risk, so is the quieter and ultimately more troubled acknowledgment of the difficulties inherent in the 'love we bear each other's differences'. The more one dwells with this poem, the more its orientation veers away from the explicit themes of its title, and turns inward to America and to O'Hara's own life. Words 'become' your mouth, grace it and heighten your and their attractiveness; but as they in a different sense become your mouth you are instantly in language already used and therefore loaded, in danger, in the political, in 'categorically the most difficult relationship', a compulsion to seek the other which is an ineluctable part of 'our nature' and yet one fraught with the potential for misunderstanding or violence. O'Hara is driven to the intertwining of risk and trepidation, as the deliberately overblown reference to Whitman ('my great predecessor') undermines American exceptionalism from the outset, while the mock-Jacobean phrasing of 'here where to love at all's to be a politician' ironizes self-absorption while remaining true, here in New York, in 1958, to the intense layerings of Frank O'Hara's life.

Clearly O'Hara's homosexuality is the main autobiographical site for his disquiet over what can and cannot be said without risk, may and may not be yearned for with any realistic expectation of a happy outcome. The third part of this essay will be concerned with his last long poem, 'Biotherm', a work anchored in his friendship with the poet Bill Berkson. Though they were evidently not features of the poets' friendship, aggression, frustration and obscenity are hallmarks of this problematic text, which attempts to wrest value in the form of poetic innovation from rupture and abrasion, while still acknowledging, and finding no salve for, the sheer difficulty of human relationship. What is other is what is desired; but what is other, being other, spells conflict and discord. Where the Ode invokes the wider international world in order ultimately to address interpersonal frustrations, 'Biotherm' crosses the same political/personal terrain from the opposite direction, anchoring in interpersonal tensions a poem which is ultimately as attentive to the macro-aggressions of the Cold War period.[1]

If you make your way to Manhattan's southern tip in Battery Park City, and look out over the river facing the Statue of Liberty, you have to lean on poetry for support, if only because words by both Whitman and O'Hara were sculpted into the railings by Siah Armajani at the end of the 1970s, when this landfill extension of the island grew from the excavation of the site of the World Trade Center. To turn and look behind at this point is of course to see a very different view from the one that dominated the skyline between 1979 and 11 September 2001. This essay is also about the relationship between these views of New York, much altered by macro-aggression, and Frank O'Hara's changing places – past, present and predictive – in its history. The New York School, the coterie of O'Hara, John Ashbery, James Schuyler and others, in complex ways attached to/disengaged from the post-1945 New York art world the better to project itself, the world of Abstract Expressionism, then Warhol and Pop Art, was an enterprise that pictured Manhattan in glowing colours as *the* City, the intricate maze that made modernity fun, pollution excusable, and an ant-heap existence exciting. In what ways, post-9/11, has that image of the vibrant art-capital been bulldozed, historicized, or gained reinforcement from being pushed back in time towards myth? And what is the final relationship, the final balance of powers, between O'Hara's Romantic and his more riven New Yorks, the respective contexts of the lightest *Lunch Poems*, but also 'Biotherm'?

One immediate effect of 9/11, for any reader of American writing, was that texts changed their meanings overnight. The sundry canons shifted, are still rippling with aftershocks. The title of O'Hara's late poem 'Enemy Planes Approaching' suddenly lost its cartoon-like two-dimensionality in order to hint at a prophetic mode that the poem itself can now neither deliver nor shake off. Earlier texts changed too; Henry James' *The American Scene* is a particular case in point. James is troubled by the new New York of 1906, 'this huge jagged city', but his criticisms of its rampant commercialism and lack of cultural depth are, as he is forced to concede,

---

1 O'Hara, of course, had direct experience of the machinery of macro-aggression, serving in the US Navy between 1944 and 1946. When he entered Harvard in 1946 it was through the GI Bill, designed to help in the education of returning service personnel. See 'Ode to Michael Goldberg ('s Birth and other Births)' for material on O'Hara's Navy period: 'when someone you love hits your head and says "I'd sail with you any/ where, war or no war"/ who was about/ to die a tough blond death' (*CP*, 294–95).

rendered petty by the scale of its overt and simple triumph. 'This was just the ache of envy of the spirit of a society which had found there, in its prodigious public setting, so exactly what it wanted. One was in presence, as never before, of a realized ideal and the childlike rush of surrender to it'. Thus far, this is a recognizably Jamesian reaction to a recognizable New York. Abruptly, in endeavouring to step back from surrender and the City, James mobilizes the vocabulary of fundamentalist religion. The endlessly circulating, mesmerized hoards 'became thus the serene faithful, whose rites one would no more have sceptically brushed than one would doff one's disguise in a Mohammedan mosque'.[2] In the shadow of 9/11, this East–West metaphor is suddenly more charged than charming. The surreal image of the Master escaping detection in some form of burka reminds us that a later New York, and the possibility of later, catastrophic encounters between East and West, were encrypted in what James termed the 'gilded and storied labyrinth', but brought to sharp legibility only when, in the events of 9/11, it was seemingly too late to address peacefully what O'Hara warned is 'categorically the most difficult relationship'.[3]

Such blips and swerves of meaning are inevitable effects, ceaselessly changing, of any self-aware reading activity, that, taking place over time, becomes inflected by history. More arresting is a text that seems to predict more exactly, because it does so politically, the fateful events of 9/11. The following may appear at first sight to have been written around the close of the twentieth century:

> The subtlest change in New York is something people don't speak about much but that is in everyone's mind. The city, for the first time in its long history, is destructible. A single flight of planes no bigger than a wedge of geese can quickly end this island fantasy, burn the towers, crumble the bridges, turn the underground passages into lethal chambers, cremate the millions… because, of all targets, New York has a certain clear priority. In the mind of whatever perverted dreamer might loose the lightning, New York must hold a steady, irresistible charm […] [T]his riddle in steel and stone is at once the perfect target and the perfect demonstration of non-violence, of racial brotherhood, this lofty target scraping the skies and meeting the destroying planes halfway, home of all people and all nations, capitol of everything, housing the deliberations by which the planes are to be stayed and their errand forestalled.[4]

In fact, this apparent premonition of Bin Laden and the planes comes from a short book called *Here is New York*, written by E. B. White in 1948. In White's postwar-prewar musings, we find a reminder that the city of Jackson Pollock, of Willem de Kooning, of the multitude of writers, painters and others who so densely populate the *Collected Poems* as to make it the most detailed – and the most optimistic –

---

2 Henry James, *The American Scene* (1907) (New York: St Martin's, 1987), p. 105.

3 There is of course a tradition of explorers adopting Muslim disguise, including the somewhat un-Jamesian figures of Richard Burton and R. B. Cunninghame Graham.

4 E. B. White, *Here is New York* (New York: Harper, 1949), pp. 50–53.

evocation of an artistic milieu in the history of Anglophone poetry, Frank O'Hara's New York, was founded, terminated and contextualized by war. The New York School is centred in the years of the Cold War, and bookended first by the Second World War, and then by whatever name history will give the ongoing conflict which brought down the Towers. O'Hara's vitality, his radiant and enabling optimism, the boundless confidence in his city and his century, are unquenchable aspects of his poetic and other identities which are frequently the attributes readers latch on to first, and continue to like best. I am not attempting here to undermine those attributes, but to point out the less frequently noticed importance of pressure and aggression along the whole personal/political spectrum, as crucial factors in both New York's and O'Hara's sense of themselves.

II

The fall of France to the Nazis toppled Paris from its pre-eminence as art capital of the world, bringing immigrant Surrealists such as André Breton and Max Ernst, along with other post-Impressionist artists and, as importantly, artist-teachers, to Ellis Island. Their influence, in combination with the impact of psychoanalysis, again boosted by the flight of the European intelligentsia, would impact on Pollock, and other emerging artists needing to raise their sights, so as to produce Abstract Expressionism. This was the Triumph of the Avant-Garde, to recycle the subtitle of an important study by Irving Sandler, named 'balayeur des artistes' by O'Hara in his 'Adieu to Norman, Bon Jour to Joan and Jean-Paul' (*CP*, 328). Pollock could now preserve all his bohemian credentials as a paint-spattered, bar-wrecking genius while appearing on the cover of *Life* magazine. His work, decried by the square press for its abandon and opacity, was simultaneously reproduced in the brochures advertising identikit suburban houses sold by Tarrytown Homes Inc. to up-and-coming ad execs in the New York region.[5] In this context of acceleration and ambivalence in the career transitions of artists such as Pollock, Rothko and de Kooning, E. B. White's premonition of an attack on New York attains an extra resonance. New York, 'home of all people and all nations, capitol of everything, *housing the deliberations* by which the planes are to be stayed' (my emphasis). This is more than a pointer to the United Nations, or a pious hope that the USA's new dominance would bring wisdom to world-leadership. Deliberations as to where, not when or whether, America was to house the cultural stores and emblems of its coming victory had been the subject of high-level, covert discussion since at least 1943. Millionaire gallery owners and influencers such as Caresse Crosby and James H. White duly made their pitch, and the New York School was in a locational sense very nearly the Washington School.[6] Ellis Island won it for New York. The

5 See Serge Guilbaut, *How New York Stole the Idea of Modern Art: Abstract Expressionism, Freedom, and the Cold War* (Chicago: University of Chicago Press, 1983), p. 185.
6 Guilbaut, *How New York Stole the Idea of Modern Art*, p. 217, n. 20.

definitive account of economic, propagandist and other factors in the shaping of the avant-garde's relationship to the shouldering state is still Serge Guilbaut's 1983 account, *How New York Stole the Idea of Modern Art*. Yet for all its bloodhound footnoting and detailed argument, Guilbaut's exposure of the politics behind the art-politics mentions Frank O'Hara only once, and then with utter disdain, as one of the dandies and hangers-on whose aesthete's criticism, *rechauffée* and served up endlessly, constitutes 'the tragedy of American modern art history'.[7] It ought to be possible to use Guilbaut's authoritative research as one building-block in a more nuanced modelling of the housed deliberations, O'Hara's professional roles, and the relationship of his poetry to both, not least because of the critical and political deliberations the poetry itself houses behind a generally bright surface.

In his *New Art City: Manhattan at Mid-Century*, Jed Perl writes of O'Hara's employment in the Museum of Modern Art that 'O'Hara had never exactly planned to have a curatorial career at the museum – it had just sort of happened', a loose assertion of precisely the kind Guilbaut set out to unpick.[8] There is admittedly some serendipity in O'Hara's rise from sales assistant at the front desk to associate curator in MoMA at the height of the Cold War, becoming on the way a key exponent of, and player in, the Museum's and Alfred Barr's story about the relationship between Matisse and other, mainly French painters, and the new American painting. In this cultural narrative the latter could be shown to have learned from, equalled and at least arguably 'surpassed' its predecessors, at least in its gestural freedom, a flagship therefore for the American project in opposition to black-and-white Soviet conformities. A consummate insider when it came to the daytime workplace and the night-time art scene, O'Hara knew also how to stand off in order to see more clearly. All accounts of his career stress this crucial element of an outside perspective that, while it led some to view him as an untrained maverick, ultimately aided his progress as both curator and poet.[9] He is the other 'balayeur des artistes' named in his signature poem 'Adieu to Norman…', adept at abrading creatively the boundaries of friendship, influence, art, poetry and the museum, a blurring assisted by the alcoholic tilt of the time, and the thought implicit in the *Collected Poems* that while the poems (to re-use John Ashbery's terms, from his Introduction) were 'big, airy structures' (*CP*, ix), reminiscent therefore of the more glamorous skyscrapers, it is New York itself which is the masterwork big enough to contain all aspects of these lives and works and days.

Hero-worship of the city itself is a vivid feature of 'Walking', in which O'Hara is first pictured dropping his hot dog into a fountain at the Seagram Building while brushing a cinder from his eye, this self-deprecating vignette on a theme of obstructed vision abruptly turning into a wide-angle paean to the city: 'the country

---

7 Guilbaut, *How New York Stole the Idea of Modern Art*, p. 9.

8 Jed Perl, *New Art City: Manhattan at Mid-Century* (New York: Vintage Books, 2005), p. 414.

9 See the many reminiscences gathered in Bill Berkson and Joe LeSueur (eds.), *Homage to Frank O'Hara* (Bolinas: Big Sky, 1978), particularly Waldo Rasmussen's 'Frank O'Hara in the Museum'.

o good for us/ there's nothing/ to bump into…', as the wind airlifts the now ecstatic poet to the Narrows and an aerial view of 'New York/ greater than the Rocky Mountains' (*CP*, 476–77). However, it is, significantly, blurred vision, collision, bumping and resistant surfaces that generate this final image of freedom. Likewise 'Steps', a love poem addressed to the city, begins 'How funny you are today New York/ like Ginger Rogers in *Swingtime*', and ends famously 'oh god it's wonderful/ to get out of bed/ and drink too much coffee/ and smoke too many cigarettes/ and love you so much'. Yet these freedoms are made creative by lockdown and friction:

> all I want is a room up there
> and you in it
> and even the traffic halt so thick is a way
> for people to rub up against each other
> and when their surgical appliances lock
> they stay together
> for the rest of the day (what a day) (*CP*, 370)

The initial para-quotation from a song in *My Fair Lady* mutates into a surreal encounter of persons and artifice, and artificial bits of persons, that, although cartoon-like and therefore at one level conceding its unreality, contains again this insistence that edginess, abrasion and bumping-into are vital signs that 'in a sense we're all winning/ we're alive'. The later, less optimistic poem 'Biotherm' will insist that 'that is important (yeah) to win (yeah)' but then on the next page opine wearily 'I don't think I want to win anything I think I want to die unadorned' (*CP*, 437–38). In the 'Steps' of 1960 we are not yet at the dark cruces of O'Hara's last long poem, finished in early 1962, but edginess, competitive assertion and friction are still central to the dynamic of even the most upbeat poems.

Confirmation of the importance of frustration and duplicity to even the most positive aspects of O'Hara's poetry can be located outside as well as within his own work. The blurring and abrading of worlds is something that clearly stayed with Allen Ginsberg, writing as O'Hara's elegist in 'City Midnight Junk Strains' (1966). This poem, not only one of Ginsberg's finest but one of the finest modern poems on the death of a poet, explodes magnificently the customary assumption that elegies are really about the elegist. Instead Ginsberg captures a series of contiguous but edgily different O'Haras, including the sharply dressed professional of 'Poem [Khrushchev is coming on the right day!]', that with the photograph by Fred McDarragh of the curator poet stepping through the revolving door of MoMA would become our shared image of him:

> Poet of building-glass
> I see you walking you said with your tie
> flopped over your shoulder   in the wind down 5th Ave
> under the handsome breasted workmen

> on their scaffolds ascending Time
> & washing the windows of Life
> – off to a date with Martinis [...][10]

Ginsberg catches the importance of constriction; the tie, the punning 'scaffolds' on which O'Hara's hope that he might speak his desire across class and heterosexist lines dies (a sadness that rests in beautifully placed conjunction with the Time/ Life workmen as an unwitting gay chorus); and the way the capitalist sign-system turns time and life into glassed offices and brand names, setting reflections on mortality on a par with the market leader in Italian vermouth. Elsewhere in the poem, Ginsberg draws pointed distinctions between O'Hara and those with whom he mixed – 'your boys', Ivy League 'collected gentlemen' – noting that in complex distinction from their automatic upward mobility 'you mixed with money/ because you knew enough language to be rich', a deft conflation of O'Hara's ability to get on in the workplace because of his skills of persuasion, with a traditional sense of poetry retaining a semi-hidden value beyond market price. To Ginsberg, clearly, O'Hara's occupation of a position of influence was not something that had just sort of happened. A later, jokey imaging of a naked Ginsberg and O'Hara strumming harps in Heaven is immediately dismissed as 'boring' because as Ginsberg notes, 'Someone uncontrolled by History would have to own Heaven'. There is no escape from the control of temporality and history knowable to us. The first destroys, while the second is busy sorting us into genres. Ginsberg's elegy tries to mitigate the degradation of his memory of O'Hara from life-narrative to *post mortem* fragmentation, by selecting images from the recollected life that the poems composed by the living poet had already in effect proposed as their author's memorial. He attempts to counterbalance the random accident of O'Hara's premature death by shoring up the image-bank of his friend, which the latter had been able in some measure to control. There is no airbrushing or idealization here, because at the same time his poem warns against any attempted simplification of O'Hara's artfully tangled selves.

Forty is 'only half a life', as Ginsberg puts it. Not that O'Hara's later work lacks a premonitory sense of diminished returns. Written following a diagnosis of venereal infection, 'Song [I am stuck in traffic in a taxicab]' is a great poem about refusing to bow to the inevitable, if only because of the inevitable's terrible vulgarity: 'how I hate disease, it's like worrying/ that comes true' (*CP*, 361), as in a more aggressive way is 'For the Chinese New Year & For Bill Berkson' – along with 'Biotherm' O'Hara's angriest poem, as is borne out by the one available recording:[11]

> no there is no precedent of history no history nobody came before
> nobody will ever come before and nobody ever was that man
>
> you will not die not knowing this is true this year (*CP*, 393)

---

10 Allen Ginsberg, *Collected Poems 1947–1997* (New York: HarperCollins, 2006), p. 465.
11 CD, *The Voice of the Poet: Frank O'Hara* (New York: Random House Audio, 2004).

This knuckleduster of a koan resists paraphrase. Suddenness, speed of transition, was hugely important to O'Hara, not just as a modernist device to do with preferring collage to continuity, but as expressing one of the ways life makes itself felt. The abrupt airlift to the Narrows in 'Walking' is an instance of such suddenness, in the optative mode, where here suddenness is the killer punch. Among the possible implications is an intuition that we are finally only in the here and the now, our cherished constructions of connectedness exactly that, strategies of false consolation. (This dark existentialism, characteristic of the time and of some of the European writers O'Hara championed, is one thread in the skein of his thinking.) If you were to die in a state of 'not knowing' in this or any subsequent year, you would possess neither knowledge nor life – not, on the face of it, a happy position to occupy. If you were not to die 'not knowing' the facts of our condition this year, then you would admittedly be granted a stay of execution, but one whose consolatory value would be somewhat eroded by the fact that you might or might not die the year after, not knowing when we will die being part of the bind we're in. And so a guarantee that 'you will not die not knowing this is true this year' may be the least worst fortune cookie on offer, its message invalidated, however, by the fact that if as speaker you know that our true condition is one of saccadic disconnect, then you are hardly in a position to promise anything certain to yourself, let alone Bill Berkson. The anger that leads to such knotted formulation is perhaps more the point than the distinct philosophical strands that can be made visible by untying the loops. 'That's not a cross look it's a sign of life' (*CP*, 353). We *fight* for what we love, not are. There is warmth in anger, and therefore the possibility of love. In 'Biotherm' Wallace Stevens will be dismissed because 'I don't get any love from Wallace Stevens no I don't' (*CP*, 439).

III

In 'Biotherm' there isn't much love around in any dependable form. In fact there is in multiple senses no dependable form, except artistically in the torn and shifting surfaces of collage, and politically in the form of Cold War bad behaviour:

> [...] and at the
> most recent summit
> conference they
> are eating string
> beans butter
> smootch slurp
> pass me the filth
> and a coke pal
> oh thank you (*CP*, 442)

The tension is further reinforced by references to nuclear tests in the Nevada desert. The poem is full of filth and expressions of disgust; 'spitting', 'grizzly odors', 'belches', 'fart', 'bullshit', 'lice', 'a shitty looking person', 'a case of clap', 'ugh'. 'The ditch is full of after dinner', into which unsavoury ferment the poem gleefully plunges. Examples are everywhere; in a birthday compliment to the close friend, the best the poet can manage in terms of eulogy is: 'you put the shit back in the drain/ and then you actually find the stopper' (*CP*, 443).

'Biotherm', the longest example of O'Hara's late style, seems intent on uncorking every drain in sight. There is a nervy vitality in the poem ('vitality nellie arty ho ho that's a joke pop' [*CP*, 441]), but not one that can be separated from a sourness and bile quite contrary to the vibrancy and genial qualities of the bulk of the *Collected Poems*. The jokes are unwilling to amuse, or even complete themselves:

> take off your glasses
> you're breaking my frame
> sculptresses wear dresses (*CP*, 441)

This seems to want to play around 'boys don't make passes at girls who wear glasses', which wasn't funny anyway, but doesn't do anything more than reminiscently break the frame. Threats are issued frequently: 'perhaps you'd better be particularly interested' (*CP*, 437), as are insults; 'you are the biggest fool I ever laid eyes on' (*CP*, 443), 'you god-damned fool you got/ no collarbone you got no dish no ears' (*CP*, 437), the Surrealist extensions doing little to mute the spleen that animates this last long poem. Elsewhere poetic devices and the conventions of rhyme are burlesqued, but with a deliberate flatness (or worse) in contrast to O'Hara's usual verve: 'vass hass der mensch geplooped/ that there is sunk in the battlefield a stately grunt/ and the idle fluice still playing on the hill/ because of this this this this slunt' (*CP*, 440). The apparent nonsense word 'slunt' was in fact a vicious conflation of 'slut' and 'cunt', coined by O'Hara's friend the painter John Button.[12] It is as if everything were known now, but nothing now worth knowing. The lines that follow are more witty:

> it's a secret told by
> a madman in a parlor car
> signifying chuckles
>   *Richard Widmark*
>   *Gene Tierney*
>   *Googie Withers* (*CP*, 440)

However, the echo of *Macbeth*, a play hardly lacking in claustrophobic relationships, darkness and failed attempts to scrub filth clean, does little to lift the tension. Neither does the likely reference to Richard Widmark's first screen success as the

12 This is stated by Bill Berkson in the 'Glossary' to *Biotherm* in his *Companion to Biotherm*, which accompanies O'Hara, *Biotherm [For Bill Berkson]* (San Francisco: Arion, 1990), pp. 16–24, at p. 18.

psychopathic, chuckling killer in *Kiss of Death* (1947).[13] That the sound and fury of an angry poem might signify nothing is a constant, gnawing threat that the incessant recourse to proper names holds forcibly at the centre of the poem. That those names themselves might come to mean nothing is a new departure for a poet so previously intent on naming his artistic contemporaries in the context of canonical preferences so as to merge both. Much labour has been devoted to the unpacking of the cultural and other references. Bill Berkson, to whom the work is dedicated, has published a commentary on the poem, though a number of references remain inaccessible.[14] Brad Gooch, O'Hara's sole biographer to date, also puts in a considerable amount of detective work, retrieving references to Marlene Dietrich in *A Foreign Affair*, arguably relevant to the 'complex courtship' of Berkson by the poet, which included a flight to Rome.[15] Other instances sourced by Gooch, such as a lunch engagement on 4 January 1962 at a restaurant called *Quo Vadis* with the composer Gian Carlo Menotti, are relegated like Berkson's dead-ends to the 'impossibly private'.[16] Even when not impossibly private, many of the references in the poem are so glancing as to make reference itself, private and public, a main issue. It is hard to see any significance in the choice of some, beyond say a certain movie having been on late night TV while O'Hara was hammering at the keys. 'I could have had all of wrestling in London in my hand' (*CP*, 440), spoken, again by Richard Widmark in *Night and the City*, is an odd moment from an oddly cast movie, signifying nothing beyond itself, perhaps, except that beyond one thing is... the next. The *Collected Poems* are replete with emphatic critical judgments that do not change.

Joe Brainard writes of O'Hara attacking Andy Warhol one day and then defending him to the death, the next; but one somehow doubts that he would have swung as wildly on Pollock or de Kooning.[17] O'Hara's poems house certain key critical deliberations which are part of his wager with posterity. But in 'Biotherm' judgment has evolved in a new direction, one less interested in depth and selection, but more minded to view art (and everything else) as part of an always mobile tapestry, a depthless montage. This makes the poem less sunny and convivial than many of its predecessors. But if it is something like this that led Joe LeSueur to describe 'Biotherm' in negative terms as 'poetry concerned with poetry [...] clever, dry, experimental, obscure [...] nothing to move and stir the reader', it is also what gives the work its grit and interest, in many ways anticipating the digitization of information in the present day.[18] More definitively Cold War in style is the deflated and

---

13 As pointed out by Berkson in his 'Glossary', p. 19.
14 'Companion to "Biotherm"', in O'Hara, *Biotherm*.
15 Brad Gooch, *City Poet: The Life and Times of Frank O'Hara* (New York: Alfred A Knopf, 1993), p. 384.
16 Gooch, *City Poet*, p. 383.
17 Joe Brainard, 'Frank O'Hara', in Berkson and LeSueur (eds.), *Homage*, pp. 167–69, at p. 167.
18 Joe LeSueur, *Digressions on Some Poems by Frank O'Hara: A Memoir* (New York: Farrar, Straus and Giroux, 2003), p. 238.

desperate thought, latent throughout the poem, that the mushroom clouds aren't going to be picky and spare the paintings of Jackson Pollock but not the films of Richard Widmark, or vice versa. If this goes up, i.e. down, it all goes down, i.e. up.

This is both flattening, to put it mildly, and yet in a terrible way liberating. All the negatives can be seen as positive aspects to the poem's overall question of 'whatdoyoumeanandhowdoyoumeanit' (*CP*, 445). Bill Berkson observes of 'Biotherm' that:

> It makes sense that if most of the events in 'Biotherm' center on the 'meeting' of personal pronouns, the connections between them should be continually reinvented instead of grammatically enforced. Fragments converse across indents and silences.[19]

This is also the case for reading the poem as a precursor to Language poetry, its use of 'found' materials locating it alongside experimental poems such as 'Europe' in John Ashbery's *The Tennis Court Oath* (1962). This approach gains support from the poem's opening:

The best thing in the world   but I better be quick about it
better be gone tomorrow
                                        better be gone last night and
                                next Thursday better be gone
better be
                                always   or what's the use the sky
            the endless clouds trailing we leading them by the bandanna, red (*CP*, 436)

This principle of mobility means that, rather than looking for a depth and validation in the use of allusions, it is precisely their transience which gives them a lively role across as well as inside the new up-down-across spaces, surges and silences of 'Biotherm'. In a recent study of O'Hara, Lytle Shaw goes further, arguing that the imploded monumentality of a poem that can reference, glancingly, such a 'vast number of cultural artifacts' values transience so highly that 'the very statement of this principle must itself get interrupted in order to remain "true" to itself'.[20] Shaw's argument is illustrated by his deconstruction of a slew of references early in the poem to a 'Universal-International release' entitled 'Practically Yours' (*CP*, 437), a nest of citations which turn out to be invented, a collage of deliberate misattribution: 'none of the people mentioned was in the movie *Practically Yours*, and only one is even an actor'.[21]

This puts 'Biotherm' into an intriguing and interrogative relationship to O'Hara's earlier poetry, even putting into question the methods of such signature pieces as 'A Step Away From Them'. At one level, that poem of 1956, like many of the 'I do this, I do that' pieces, anticipates the transient verbal traffic of 'Biotherm' by

---

19 As given in Lytle Shaw, *Frank O'Hara: The Poetics of Coterie* (Iowa City: University of Iowa Press, 2006), p. 75.
20 Shaw, *Frank O'Hara: The Poetics of Coterie*, p. 76.
21 Shaw, *Frank O'Hara: The Poetics of Coterie*, p. 77.

its juxtaposition of urban, lunchtime snapshots: the 'dirty / glistening torsos' of 'laborers' (resurrected perhaps by Ginsberg in his elegy for O'Hara), the 'bargains in wristwatches', 'cats playing in sawdust', Times Square signs, 'blonde chorus girl' and other vibrant, glimpsed moments, human and other (*CP*, 257). The poem and its siblings from the 1950s build on techniques pioneered by the anti-metaphysical modernism of William Carlos Williams.[22] At one point, all serendipitously, 'everything ... honks', leaving open to us one way of reading reality as saccades, metonym, fragmentary happenstance, and another as self-orchestrating, finally led to coherence, however provisionally. The poem is for the most part determinedly light and bright, wearing its heart, if not on its sleeve, then in O'Hara's pocket, in the form of 'Poems by Pierre Reverdy' (*CP*, 258). The implication is both that New York's endlessly deep spaces can readily and safely carry a poet, carrying another poet's poems, in which there will be other worlds evoked, to where all need to go; and that, at the same time, that there is no safety, and no necessarily extended life for these honks and glimpsed moments, painters and librettists, if the poet's word-Kodak is not there to snap them. An interest in posterity is active in the poem. However, it is not yearned for, but rather questioned. Recalling the recent deaths of Bunny Lang and John Latouche and Jackson Pollock, O'Hara asks 'is the / earth as full as life was full, of them?' (*CP*, 258) A large shadow has trodden on the poem's sunlit spaces, but is soon banished by new, transient thoughts; then 'back to work'. It is up to the reader to determine the balance of light and dark, and the consequences for reading texts, lives and the city. This is O'Hara's generosity, his creation of a poem in which the moving parts can be further moved and re-balanced by reading. The risk undertaken by 'Biotherm' is one of moving on to a poetry of signs whose openness to fleeting micro-data is so emphatic that it begins to critique the earlier poetry. This critique potentially discloses a level of authorial guidance in the choices available to readers of the 'I do this, I do that' poems that might make their apparent openness relative, a property of stage-machinery now starting audibly to creak. It is a risky move, and one that allies O'Hara to modernism, not in any comfortable library-bound sense, but in the sense that what is avant-garde destroys by superseding its predecessors, including the author's own work. The *via negativa* of an ultra-modernist vanguardism is bound intimately to the personal negativity in 'Biotherm'.

This negativity is not in any simple, autobiographical way directed at Berkson by O'Hara. Berkson concedes in his 'Companion to "Biotherm"' that '[the] basic plot of "Biotherm" is a portrait of two, the poet (Frank) and the addressee (me), with some love poetry included'. He qualifies this by noting the fluidity and multiplicity of voice in the text, and goes on to suggest a complex relationship behind and around the poem, albeit not one that could be tied down generically:

---

22 I have written about this poem and others by O'Hara at greater length in *Statutes of Liberty: The New York School of Poets* (Basingstoke: Macmillan, 1993; new edition Palgrave / St Martin's, 2001).

There was no sex involved. (If Frank spent any time 'trying to make me', as the poem at one point suggests, he never let me know it.) But, besides our intimacy, there was the 'camp' element, that attitude which was supposed to be strictly of gay provenance but which I enjoyed and courted [...]

In response to a mild enquiry from John Ashbery as to 'what was really going on between us', Berkson recalls announcing 'I am a woman in love' in a Garboesque accent, but dismisses this with hindsight as 'rhetorical flippancy'.[23] The important thing vis-à-vis 'Biotherm' is less the flickering intricacies of the relationship in life than its capacity to mobilize O'Hara's feelings of frustration, of things not going anywhere, and of failure to get what is exciting about otherness and what is simply irreconcilably other, into a liveable ratio. The negativity is articulated in broken and looped phrasings and collage that supply a compensatory freedom and innovation that the originating feelings failed to supply in life. Confirmation of this way of reading the poem may be found in the copious illustrations to the poem supplied by artist Jim Dine for the 1990 edition, which includes Berkson's commentary. Human figures are depicted through whirling and knotted tubular lines that both delineate and constrict them; a male figure undressing another human figure could equally be strangling it; squid- or octopus-like forms writhe throughout; an eye stares wildly from the centre of a heart; and the final image is of a pincushion St Sebastian. According to publisher Andrew Hoyem's note to the 1990 edition, Dine 'suggested "Biotherm" as the poem of O'Hara's that had most excited him [...] The poem signified for Dine a literary equivalent to his own disjunctive impulses in visual art'.[24]

'Biotherm' is then a qualified triumph of the disjunctive, but one which still has a lyric side. The poem sets up passages of 'lyrical' encounter, only to have them explode into cartoon or self-deconstruct. That doesn't stop them from being among the most engaging passages in the poem, but it does mean that they are not what they first seem. A passage which begins by tying the addressee down as Berkson by naming his book, *Saturday Night*, unties itself in a farcical sketch of a botched seduction attempt:

> hey! help! come back! you spilled your omelette all over your pants!
> oh damn it, I guess that's the end of one of our meetings (*CP*, 440)

Except, that is, for the fact of a line break before the two quoted, which releases Berkson as addressee from what follows. Any new line, or break, spells the end of one of the poem's 'meetings'. The discursive shifts are compelling and quite new in the poetry while twisting earlier approaches in fresh directions:

---

23 Berkson, 'Air and Such: An Essay on *Biotherm*', in 'Companion to *Biotherm*', pp. 8–15, at pp. 10–11.
24 Andrew Hoyem, 'Publisher's Note', in 'Companion to *Biotherm*', pp. 3–7, at p. 5.

why are you melancholy
if I make you angry you are no longer doubtful
if I make you happy you are no longer doubtful
what's wrong with doubt (*CP*, 443)

We expect from a reading of the earlier O'Hara to see anger and happiness elevated because of their warmth, but it's doubt that wins because doubt means more new data impinging in an unpredictable field. In this sense the ditch is full of after dinner, the past, so let's get out of the ditch, even if the cost is the vertigo of unpredicted change:

> [...] I'm dying of loneliness
> here with my red blue green and natch pencils and the erasers
> with the mirror behind me and the desk in front of me
> like an anti-Cocteau movement (*CP*, 441)

In Cocteau's *Orphée*, Orpheus dives through mirrors of mercury to reach the realm of Heurtebise, death, and cryptic poetry coming through the radio, like a proto-Jack Spicer movement. The desk, by contrast, has erasers and pencils on it, but no metaphysics about or in it. Once again the bumped-into, the constraining work-tool, life's hard furniture, are the agents of freedom more than deep spaces without resistance, which may only lead to forms of death.

> where you were no longer exists
> which is why we will go see it to be close to you how could it leave (*CP*, 440)

These lines, another angry koan, insist on a disjunction in the field of data recorded and generated by poetry which, if played out in life, would be incompatible with the fidelity and ties of affection based on continuity. The optimistic artistic agenda of the poem, if it were to operate in the emotional sphere, would be antithetical to relationship. These matters do not reach a resolution in 'Biotherm', which is the braver for both resisting closure, and refusing to enter into a method for producing art which sidesteps its implications for the rest of life.

O'Hara's great poem 'In Memory of My Feelings' had concluded with a coldness that the poet judged necessary to the making of poetry, the killing of emotion's ghosts, to save 'the serpent in their midst', the snake in the leaves of grass (*CP*, 257). 'Biotherm' takes this to its logical conclusion, mirroring something the composer Morton Feldman also sensed, writing of Frank O'Hara that, 'secreted in O'Hara's thought is the possibility that we create only as dead men'.[25] To prize the illusionism of art, its coldness, most of all perhaps when all seemed impro-vised from the warmth of desire, enthusiasm, even anger. To bend the ear of the outer world. You could do it better, if you were in New York. You could do it best

---

25 Morton Feldman, 'Lost Times and Future Hopes', in Berkson and Le Sueur (eds.), *Homage*, pp. 12–14, at p. 14.

if you said you *were* New York. That is what Frank O'Hara dared; gambling that his metrophiliac identification with the mountainous island would carry a certain version of both into history.

What follows is not by O'Hara, but by John Ashbery. It is excerpted from a Dream Journal that he kept briefly as a student at Harvard in the 1940s:

> June 15, 1947. I was at a meeting in what was apparently the living room of a certain brick house in Memorial Drive, Cambridge. It was run by the communists and apparently the meeting was about the professor. Someone was trying to win me over to the communist side, I being neutral. Suddenly policemen with machineguns entered, and I was looking at the front of a house. People in the house thrust long poles through the windows and with them lifted up a facsimile of the house against the house; as a protection, I guess. Machine guns were fired and the person who had been trying to win me over shouted "Go home!!" I escaped through the French windows and ran over the bridge... This dream was partly suggested by an article I had been reading on the beating of Jews by their fellow students in Roumania in 1938.[26]

Ashbery the poet would indeed 'escape by the French windows' of Surrealism, the work of Reverdy and Roussel, maybe also by the 'bridge' of Hart Crane, and certainly, through the attentions of Harold Bloom and others, reach an accommodation with 'the professor'. But the intricate specifics of this Cold War dream remind us of the intricacies of a wider social history, and group allegiance, as well as the world of poetry. The facsimile house, with its false front, recalls simultaneously the paintings of the Surrealist René Magritte, clandestine wartime resistance, and the false front of the 1940s' homosexual poet in a pre-Stonewall era. Ashbery's as yet unwritten future seems latent in the dream, triggered by reading about anti-Semitic incidents on the eve of an earlier war. But here we revert to the instability of the text moved by history to highlight this and downplay that, apparent signs and echoes that may just be accidental.

New York, the realized ideal of publicity and commercialization that so fascinated and repelled Henry James, would, in the aftermath of the Second World War, image hubris to E. B. White, whose speculations that the towers might burn would come true half a century later. In between, Frank O'Hara was of his time, ahead of it, writing it, influencing and at work in it. On 11 September 2001, the poet Charles Bernstein wrote of crossing and observing Manhattan on the day the post-war era ended. He titled and ended his account with an echo of O'Hara:

> This could not have happened. This hasn't happened.
>
> This is happening.
>
> It's 8:23 in New York.[27]

---

26 Notebook from box 31 of John Ashbery papers, Houghton Library, Harvard University. © John Ashbery 2010. All rights reserved. Used by permission of Georges Borchardt, Inc. for the author.

27 Charles Bernstein, *Girly Man* (Chicago: Chicago University Press, 2006), p. 19.

While the poetry of Frank O'Hara does not in any direct let alone uncanny way predict what happened, it houses and articulates deliberations of which an act of war is one possible conclusion, just as acts of war had helped shape the world O'Hara wrote and occupied. The breadth of understanding and strength of his poetry make it, like Auden's 'September 1st 1939', apt and braced for such a time, but able also to look beyond, to a world more fortuitous:

for if there is fortuity it's in the love we bear each other's differences (*CP*, 305)

Gesture in 1960:
Toward Literal Situations

Lytle Shaw

Decay sets in when someone suddenly
stops singing and life becomes a
bad reproduction of Jackson Pollock's
beautiful *Bird Effort* in a magazine
that folded. Where will we go
when we have truly moved, when life
says, 'Look, you're new, be calm'
and angrily we leave and die.
> – Frank O'Hara (*PR*, 184)

Clearly the principal domain we are going to replace and *fulfil* is poetry, which burned itself out by taking its position at the vanguard of our time and has now completely disappeared.

> – Guy Debord[1]

My first epigraph is the last stanza of 'University Place', a poem O'Hara composed on 27 March 1959, the night before he left his New York apartment at 90 University Place for one on East Ninth Street close to Avenue A.[2] O'Hara had lived on University Place since February 1957 – minutes from what would become

---

1 Guy Debord, 'Preliminary Problems in Constructing a Situation', in Ken Knabb (ed. and trans.), *Situationist International Anthology* (Berkeley, CA: Bureau of Public Secrets, 1981), pp. 43–45, at p. 44. A previous version of this essay was published in *New York Cool: Painting and Sculpture from the NYU Art Collection* (New York: Grey Art Gallery, 2008). My thanks to the exhibition's curator, Pepe Karmel, to the Grey's curator, Lynn Gumbert, and to Lucy Oakley for the invitation and the aid.

2 The poem is a riff on the topics that will occupy O'Hara for the summer and fall of 1959, perhaps the highpoint of his career: the eerie absence after a singing voice stops (as in the famous last line of 'The Day Lady Died' [*CP*, 325], composed 17 July, ending 'and everybody and I stopped breathing'); the rhetorical questions about identity in the face of corrosion and death of 'Adieu to Norman, Bon Jour to Joan and Jean Paul' (composed 7 August [*CP*, 328]); apostrophes to contemporaries (the poem begins 'Oh Alice Esty! we are leaving/ University Place the day after/ your concert') which also open 'Naphtha' ('Ah, Jean Dubuffet', 3 September 1959 [*CP*, 337]); and the pervasive decay of 'Joe's Jacket' (10 August 1959 [*CP*, 329]). But O'Hara perhaps thought it, itself, was a bad reproduction of a Frank O'Hara poem and so never sent it out. The one older poem it seems to riff on is 'A Step Away From Them' (16 August 1956 [*CP*, 257]).

29

the Grey Art Gallery and what already was the famous Cedar Bar.[3] Mostly because of the Cedar Bar (which was on the west side of the Street, between 8th and 9th Streets) University Place had been linked to the early days of Abstract Expressionism, and then, by the late 1950s, to the second-generation abstract painters with whom O'Hara was most closely associated. In fact, from 1955, when he began formally at the Museum of Modern Art, until 1966 when he died after being struck by a jeep on Fire Island, O'Hara was in contact not only with most artists associated with both generations of abstract painting, but also with an array of neo-realists, assemblagists and sculptors pursing widely different practices.[4] He either wrote about or curated exhibitions that included Norman Bluhm, Louise Bourgeois, Helen Frankenthaler, Robert Goodnough, Adolph Gottlieb, Philip Guston, Al Held, Alex Katz, Elaine de Kooning, Willem de Kooning, Seymour Lipton, Conrad Marca-Relli, Robert Motherwell, Louise Nevelson, Kenneth Noland, Philip Pearlstein, Robert Rauschenberg and Richard Stankiewicz.[5] While in some cases (Bourgeois, Nevelson, Noland, Pearlstein) the interaction was either mediated by the museum or a comparatively minor mention in O'Hara's prose, in the others the relationships were so close as to cause distress to other artists, art historians and curators. 'Under suspicion as a gifted amateur,' as his colleague at MoMA Waldo Rasmussen put it, O'Hara 'didn't have the credentials of art history training or a long museum apprenticeship to support his claim to direct exhibitions. His very closeness to the artists was questioned as a danger to critical objectivity.'[6] Painter John Button suggests that O'Hara had to 'rely more on his own fine sensibility than on professional skills'.[7] The musician Virgil Thomson went even further, suggesting that just as the French modernist painters had benefited from the blurbs of poets to

---

3 See Joe LeSueur, 'Four Apartments', in Bill Berkson and Joe LeSueur (eds.), *Homage to Frank O'Hara* (Bolinas: Big Sky, 1988), pp. 46–56, at p. 53.

4 After working at the museum's front desk from late 1951 until early 1954, O'Hara joined the International Program at MoMA in 1955 – first as a special assistant to its director, Porter McCray. In 1960 O'Hara became Assistant Curator; in 1965 Associate, and in 1966, the year of his death, Curator. Even before he was appointed Assistant Curator, however, O'Hara was selecting works for exhibitions. Exhibitions O'Hara directed at MoMA included retrospectives of major artists associated with Abstract Expressionism including Franz Kline, Robert Motherwell and David Smith. Before his death O'Hara was scheduled to curate both Willem de Kooning and Jackson Pollock retrospectives at MoMA. For a more detailed timeline of his activities at MoMA see *AC*, 158–61.

5 O'Hara had repeated involvement with most of these artists; I mention here, however, only those who appear infrequently in his exhibitions or writings: he discusses Elaine de Kooning's work in 'Nature and New Painting'; Richard Stankiewicz was included in *Modern Sculpture USA* (1965) and mentioned in 'Art Chronicle II' (*SS*, 135); Pearlstein is mentioned on the same page; Stankiewicz also appeared in four exhibitions at MoMA during O'Hara's tenure: *Sixteen Americans* (1959); *Recent Sculpture USA* (1959); *The Art of Assemblage* (1961); *Hans Hofmann and His Students* (1963). None of these, however, was under O'Hara's direction. Nevelson was included in *Modern Sculpture USA* (1965); Marca-Relli was included in *Documenta 11* (1959).

6 Waldo Rasmussen, 'Frank O'Hara in the Museum', in Berkson and LeSueur (eds.), *Homage*, pp. 84–90, at p. 86.

7 John Button, 'Frank's Grace', in Berkson and LeSueur (eds.), *Homage*, pp. 41–43, at p. 42.

whom they would give paintings, so those contemporary painters endorsed by the Museum of Modern Art could now depend on a plug from their own official poet: 'Poets write the best advertising copy in the world'.[8]

Biographical closeness, lack of professional training, graft – these (along with outrageous comparisons) were the features that prominent critics such as Clement Greenberg and Michael Fried seized on in order to rule out the interpretations of post-war American painting put forward by the poets (including O'Hara) who were associated with the journal *Art News*.[9] If one could simply clear the field of those 'men and women who are in no way qualified for their profession', Michael Fried suggested in his 1965 catalogue essay 'Three American Painters', then, finally, modern painting could receive the professional treatment it deserves.[10] And while I want neither to recuperate all of the art criticism produced by these poets, nor to rescue O'Hara's 'objectivity', I think it is clear that he developed, especially in his poetry, a critical language for gestural painting that has no parallel among other critics. O'Hara suggested provisional social contexts for gestural painting – from Hollywood lexicons of masculinity and violence to international Cold War debates about 'freedom' – that, far from exhausting the painting in reductive iconographic readings, instead opened it experimentally to culture in ways no other critics pursued. And in this sense O'Hara did anticipate later revisionist accounts.[11] He went further, however. Often it was as if what he loved about Abstract Expressionist painters was a kind of camp spectacle: tortured subjectivity (mostly masculine) inventing and reinventing itself, through painterly gestures, within a flimsy Hollywood set: 'Richard Burton/ waves through de Kooning the/ Wild West rides up out of the Pollock' ('Favorite Painting at the Metropolitan' [*CP*, 423]). O'Hara's readings of Pollock and de Kooning revel in the excessive, melodramatic qualities of a masculine subjectivity pushing the limits of its 'freedom'. O'Hara describes Pollock's *Number 12, 1952,* for instance (a painting that went to Europe as part of

8   Thomson says: 'I used to complain to Edwin Denby about his working for the Museum […] It was just like those French poets. They all wrote blurbs about modern painters and got paid off in pictures. The Picasso gang were all plugged by poets. I don't say incorrectly, but they were. Poets write the best advertising copy in the world. Now the Museum of Modern Art was very busy keeping up the prices of the pictures in its trustees' collections. They were back and forth to Paris all the time. As a matter of fact they used to get Paris writers to do catalogues for them for awhile. And then they found Frank, this flexible Irishman who could push the opinions they wanted pushed' (Brad Gooch, *City Poet: The Life of Frank O'Hara* [New York: Knopf, 1993], p. 296). One might read O'Hara's poem 'Commercial Variations' (*CP*, 85) as a response to such a charge.

9   See Greenberg's 'How Art Writing Earns its Bad Name' in *The Collected Essays and Criticism, Volume 4: Modernism with a Vengeance, 1957–1969*, ed. John O'Brian (Chicago: University of Chicago Press, 1986), pp. 135–44.

10 This essay is reprinted in Fried's *Art and Objecthood* (Chicago: University of Chicago Press, 1998), pp. 213–65, at p. 214.

11 I develop this reading in my *Frank O'Hara: The Poetics of Coterie* (Iowa City: Iowa University Press, 2006). Chapters three to six deal with O'Hara's art writing; chapters four and five focus especially on his writings about Abstract Expressionism.

Figure 1 Jackson Pollock, *Bird Effort*, 1946.

the 1958–59 *New American Painting* exhibition) as a 'big, brassy gigolo of a painting; for the first time the aluminum paint looks like money, and the color is that of the sunset in a technicolor Western'. To return to 'University Place', then, if O'Hara was in 1959 leaving the immediate neighbourhood of the Cedar Bar, he was in no way leaving the world of gestural painting that centred around it.

It is customary, when mentioning O'Hara or the Cedar Bar, to wax nostalgic for New York's art and poetry worlds of the 1950s: after all, this was a moment when inexpensive rents made it possible for artists to have part-time jobs and live in

Manhattan; when there were few enough of these artists that they knew each other (if they cared to); when most exhibitions were reviewed, when most reviews were still critical and even polemical, and when 'art' still meant the manageable history of two media – painting and sculpture. Over the next decade all of this would, of course, change: first performances and happenings; then Pop Art, Minimalism, Earthworks, Conceptualism, and institutional critique – all of it intersecting at various (though certainly not all) points with the political concerns of the New Social Movements of the 1960s.

However, I have not quoted O'Hara's 'University Place' to evoke yet again the Eden of 1950s' painting. I am interested, instead, in the concerns – the fears, even – that emerge from his poem. For although these, too, are foreign to the art world of 2010, their foreignness may complicate the Edenic picture of the 1950s. 'University Place' begins with one of O'Hara's famous apostrophes: 'Oh Alice Esty! we are leaving/ University Place the day after/ your concert' (*PR*, 183). The address to this singer and art patron then frames the awkward and somehow depressing silence after music that begins the final stanza. Casting his metaphor across media ('Decay sets in when somebody suddenly/ stops singing') O'Hara is concerned not just with a kind of general existential decay that follows creative outbursts, but with the more specific problem of how artists might follow in the wake of a bravura cultural performance like Jackson Pollock's.

And yet *Bird Effort* (Figure 1) is, at least initially, a strange choice for Pollock's representative performance. Not a drip painting, it is one of the last gestural abstractions he made before his classic, fully abstract period. In fact, *Bird Effort* is one of the few Pollocks in which the treatment of totemic abstractions resembles Willem de Kooning's handling. And it was de Kooning's gestural idiom, far more than Pollock's drips, that left a formally legible trace on the second-generation gestural painters with whom O'Hara was closely associated. At least to ungenerous critics, de Kooning, that is, seemed to generate a great number of 'bad reproductions'.[12] This charge was levelled, in various ways, at many of O'Hara's closest friends including Mike Goldberg, Norman Bluhm, Grace Hartigan, Alfred Leslie, and even Larry Rivers.[13] My point is not that O'Hara was secretly saying de Kooning by selecting this Pollock, but rather that in saying and meaning Pollock he nonetheless chose the Pollock of a certain kind of gesturalism that – unlike the drip paintings – others could and did imitate.

12 Consider de Kooning's remark about why he values Rubens: 'For creating a style and working in it with complete conviction and reckless abandon' (in Selden Rodman, *Conversations with Artists* [New York: Capricorn, 1961]), p. 104.

13 'De Kooning and Pollock's return to figuration,' Paul Schimmel, for instance, asserts, 'had an immediate impact on the artists now associated with Figurative Expressionism, including Grace Hartigan, Lester Johnson, Alex Katz, George McNeil, Jan Müller, Fairfield Porter, Larry Rivers, and Bob Thompson, among others'. See Paul Schimmel, 'The Faked Gesture: Pop Art and the New York School', in Russell Ferguson (ed.), *Hand Painted Pop: American Art in Transition, 1955–1962* (Los Angeles/New York: Museum of Contemporary Art, Los Angeles/Rizzoli, 1992), pp. 19–66, pp. 20–21.

By the late 1950s both critics and artists had condensed their sense of these 'bad reproductions' (of de Kooning especially) into a two-word term: 'Tenth Street'. Irving Sandler notes, for instance, that by 1956 Clement Greenberg had already 'waged war on gesture painting'. That year, Greenberg 'announced at The Club that "Tenth Street painting" or "de Kooning style painting" had become "timid, handsome, second generation [...] in a bad way"'.[14] Though Tenth Street might also have been remembered for the emergence of artist-run galleries including Hansa and Tanager, the term came to suggest only something that was perceived about many of the artists who showed in those galleries: that they were committed to a beleaguered and derivative gesturalism, one increasingly entrenched in the face of rapid shifts in the New York art world. This was not a generous reading; nor was it O'Hara's – but it was an influential, even dominant, one.[15] Even within gestural painting there is more variation and invention than Greenberg suggests; and in fact artists in general responded to the legacy of Abstract Expressionism through a much wider and richer vocabulary than Greenberg allows. But rather than survey the range of these responses – Stella's, Noland's and Agnes Martin's rather disparate versions of what Greenberg called 'post-painterly abstraction', Rauschenberg's and Stankiewicz's equally dissimilar projects of assemblage, Katz's and Bourgeois's approaches to figuration, Frankenthaler's stains – I want to use O'Hara's 1960 collaboration with Norman Bluhm, *Poem-Paintings*, to suggest how the two sought to amplify and perhaps thereby recode what was to many at the time the seemingly exhausted project of gestural abstraction.[16] While Rauschenberg and Stankiewicz each in different ways, for instance, participated in a move toward 'real' materials, toward the use of the same urban detritus that would soon generate the literal environments of happenings and performance, O'Hara and Bluhm held on to classic gestural abstraction only to reframe it, with poetry, in a more explicitly urban environment – pushing the Tenth Street aesthetic literally into the street. Ultimately it is the attempt to ground gesture in empirical locations that I want here to examine, linking O'Hara's project (both in *Poem-Paintings* and more generally) with his role at MoMA as an exporter of gestural painting to the Cold War world, and especially to Europe, where avant-garde artists and theorists like the Situationists pursued a more thoroughly articulated and programmatic

14 Irving Sandler, *A Sweeper-Up After Artists: A Memoir* (New York: Thames and Hudson, 2003), pp. 231–32. Sandler provides a blow-by-blow of how gestural painting developed into a 'new academy' in the late 1950s. The title for Sandler's memoir, we might note here, comes from O'Hara's description of him as a 'balayeur des artistes' (*CP*, 329) in his poem 'Adieu to Norman, Bon Jour to Joan and Jean-Paul'.

15 One thing that was importantly different about that art world – in addition to all of the quaint and attractive features with which I began – is that the question of historical succession was planted centrally in every artist's mind. Whether one was committed to abstraction or not, no-one imagined his or her work as existing independent of some kind of historical argument. The art world was, in short, pre-pluralist.

16 The term 'post painterly abstraction' was introduced by Greenberg in 1964. See 'Post Painterly Abstraction', in *The Collected Essays and Criticism, Volume 4*, pp. 192–97.

project of realizing gesture in urban situations, of, as Debord put it, replacing and fulfilling poetry by bringing it into the streets.

First, then, a brief word about O'Hara's larger project of productively debasing poetry, of puncturing the measured, myth-centric lexicons of tired mid-century modernism.[17] This he did by incorporating in his work an array of contemporary idioms, found languages, and a pantheon of recent and as-yet-unauthorized references (New York artists, dancers, composers, Hollywood stars, obscure friends, cult modernists) – all arranged often below the range of acceptable poetic address (in flat non-artistic tonalities) or above it (in non-lyrical syntactic disruptions that seem to obliterate the idea of a 'speaker').[18] This formal debasement, which is in play in various ways throughout O'Hara's career, often gets explicit thematic amplification. Perhaps the most powerful instance of this is his 1952 poem 'Commercial Variations', which urges New York artists to embrace their status as world parvenus (owners of a 'silver mine' when gold 'has become the world standard look' [*CP*, 85]) rather than trying lamely to justify their post-war power, wealth and nascent cultural dominance. 'I know what I love,' the poem's larger-than-life, theatricalized spokesman advises 'Belle of Old New York', 'and know what must be trodden under foot to be vindicated' (*CP*, 86): at once myths of American exceptionalism and the would-be transparent and neutral language, poetic or art historical, that might convey them.[19] In its collision of tonalities, lexicons and fragments of provocative rant, this poem (like 'Easter' (*CP*, 96), 'Second Avenue' (*CP*, 139) and other poems concerned with debasement) is at once a statement about and an enactment of treading forms under foot.[20] Similarly, O'Hara's 1952 poem 'Easter' begins:

> The razzle dazzle maggots are summary
> tattooing my simplicity on the pitiable.
> The perforated mountains of my saliva leave cities awash
> more exclusively open and more pale than skirts.
> O the glassy towns are fucked by yaks

The context of this bizarre opening is less an empirical place than a series of ambushed literary values: summary is attacked by explosive maggots; simplicity finds itself tattooed onto torsos; speech sputters into saliva while transparency gets

17 See, for example, the Eliot-influenced work represented in Donald Hall, Robert Pack and Louis Simpson (eds.), *New Poets of England and America* (New York: Meridian Books, 1957).

18 The idioms and proper names are everywhere in O'Hara's work; poems that seem to make use of found or appropriated language are a bit less common. A few of these latter include: 'Spring's First Day' (*CP*, 245); 'Four Little Elegies' (*CP*, 248); 'A Whitman Birthday Broadcast with Static' (*CP*, 224) 'My Day' (*PR*, 208); 'F.O.I.' (*CP*, 411); 'Summer Breezes' (*CP*, 412); 'FYI (Prix de Beaute)' (*CP*, 424); 'Biotherm' (*CP*, 436); 'At the Bottom of the Dump There's Some Sort of Bugle' (*CP*, 478); 'The Green Hornet' (*CP*, 484); 'Cheyenne' (*CP*, 489).

19 As elsewhere, O'Hara is here careful to imagine forms of cultural or social succession that do not rely on heterosexual reproduction: it is from 'Sodom-on-Hudson' (*CP*, 85) that this advice emerges.

20 See for instance 'My Heart' (*CP*, 231), 'Ave Maria' (*CP*, 371), 'Ode on Necrophilia' (*CP*, 280), and 'Ode to Joy' (*CP*, 281).

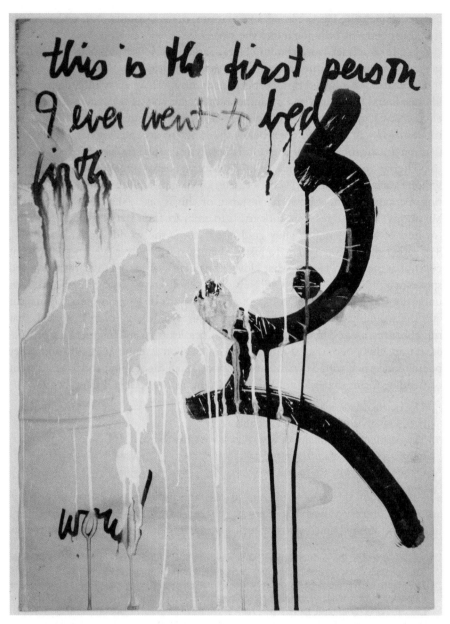

Figure 2 Norman Bluhm and Frank O'Hara, *This is the First…*, 1960.

humped by yaks. Early poetry such as this is often written off as O'Hara's apprenticeship in Surrealism – valuable primarily for the later, more personal voice it is
seen to engender. In fact, O'Hara used his experiments in Surrealism consciously to
test the limits and possible contexts of voice and person, or what he understood in
the context of painting as 'gesture'. This last project is taken up most compellingly
in O'Hara's 1953 poem 'Second Avenue', where (in a poem similarly characterized
by formal debasements) he imagines contexts or interpretive frames for Abstract
Expressionist gesture that include not merely the familiar existential struggles, but
also the 'inadmissible' contexts of American cars, Hollywood violence, and Cold
War ideology. O'Hara was obviously an enormous fan of gestural painting. Still, his
interpretation could be seen as provocatively debasing dominant models of gesture
as purely existential or formal, just as his poems could be seen as treading violently
on the limited domain set aside by mid-century modernists for poetry.

For some time now art historians have been rethinking the would-be absolute
divide between the all-over, gestural, anti-referential Abstract Expressionist artwork
of the 1950s and the taped-off, consumer-culture-referencing Pop of the early 1960s.
In fact de Kooning employed proto-Pop images as early as 1950 and many of the
Pop artists began their careers doing painterly work. Rather than a simple refusal
of gesture, what seems more to have changed in the artwork of the late 1950s is
an attitude *towards* gesture. In a catalogue essay for his groundbreaking 1992–93
exhibition *Hand-Painted Pop*, Paul Schimmel describes this transition as one from
a 'conviction among painters that a gesture could be pure and unencumbered,
and reveal nothing but itself and the action of making a picture' to a stance in
which 'that existential freedom' soon began to be 'caricatured, copied, reproduced,
appropriated, synthesized, and finally drained of conviction'.[21] But if this recoding
of gesture, this draining of conviction (often through the introduction of literal
language or linguistic puns enacted through objects) was already emerging in the
mid-1950s' works of Robert Rauschenberg and Jasper Johns, how does this affect
our view of a 1960 collaboration like O'Hara and Bluhm's *Poem-Paintings* (Figure
2), with its gestural swirls of paint overlaid with (or sometimes spilled over) short
oblique poems in large cursive letters?[22] Is *Poem-Paintings* a baroque, belated, and
perhaps slightly desperate claim to gestural immediacy? Is it, more pointedly, a kind

---

21 Schimmel, 'The Faked Gesture', p. 19.
22 The collaboration is usually described as consisting of 26 *Poem-Paintings*, 22 of which are now in the
collection of New York University (see for instance Berkson and LeSueur [eds.], *Homage*, p. 124).
According to Bluhm, though, there must have been 27 pieces initially, until one was destroyed;
he writes: 'I didn't give them all to NYU. I gave one to the Metropolitan Museum of Art. That
was the biggest mistake I made, because they've never hung it up. It's just sitting in their storage
somewhere. I gave one to Leroi Jones, which got destroyed in a fire, and one to Tom Hess. Helen
Hess has that one now. And I gave one to Bill Berkson and kept one for myself – *Haiku*, which
is in Vermont' (in John Yau and Jonathan Gams, '26 Things at Once: An Interview with Norman
Bluhm', which initially appeared in *Lingo* 7 and is now reprinted online at www.cultureport.com/
cultureport/artists/bluhm/index.html (last accessed 1 June 2008).

of counter-reformation intensification of gesturality at the moment of its seeming dissolution?

This suspicion has, I have to admit, kept me away from writing about this piece for many years. O'Hara's other collaborations tend not to press this kind of question: *Stones*, done in 1957 with Larry Rivers, has a kind of refreshing awkwardness that reminds one of (but does not try to become) children's art.[23] Written characters here are not offered as large gestural analogues to painterly strokes and spills, but as blocky print commentary within an all-over field of figure fragments, linear doodles, and areas of overlaid chalky colour. Similarly successful, O'Hara's cartoons and comics with Joe Brainard playfully *détournent* the language of illustration; likewise O'Hara's collages with Brainard offer oblique and playful captions for multivalent visual fields they cannot possibly hope to summarize in their brief spans. This tension produces the humour in the work, as does the tension between conventional cowboy narratives and queer recodings in some of the cartoons. More generally, O'Hara's collaborations with both Rivers and Brainard succeed in part through the *contrast* between written language and images: *Poem-Paintings* seems, on the contrary, to assert the poem's graphic embodiment as a large-scale gestural event on a par with Bluhm's swirls and splashes of black and white gouache and ink – the writer's lyric interior scrawled out in quadruple calligraphic scale against a blotchy Ab-Ex background.

But perhaps this is less an attempt by O'Hara to make his own writing *like* a gestural painting than, as in his art writing, a way of concretizing and contextualizing gesture, of grounding it in immediate circumstances. The poet and artist might be seen as consciously debasing gestural painting, in a sense, by literalizing it. What if we saw *Poem-Paintings* as fragmentary notes and graffiti that asserted literal contexts for gestures – the city as one, a small, tight-knit social circle as another? Asked by Marjorie Perloff about the collaboration, Bluhm says that each of the pieces 'grew out of some hilarious relationship with people we knew, out of a particular situation'.[24] Bluhm sketches some of these to Perloff: Kenneth Koch picking up a woman with enormous feet, Bluhm's father's crashing a plane, or French slang Bluhm learned in Paris. Even in comparison to O'Hara's often-fragmentary poems, however, *Poem-Paintings* give us few details about such situations. In fact, the writing is so fragmentary that Perloff claims (in an otherwise positive assessment of the collaboration) that 'few of the *Poem-Paintings* contain real poems'.[25] Perhaps she has in mind single-word poem-paintings, like *Bust* or *Bang* (Figure 3) or poems with only brief, elliptical phrases: 'Let's wait and see / what happens / it could be / a golf ball' or '!noël / apples / light / fires / dances.'[26]

---

23 This seems to have been a result both of Rivers' doodles and of O'Hara's having to write backwards for a lithographic plate.

24 Marjorie Perloff, *Frank O'Hara: Poet Among Painters* (Austin: University of Texas Press, 1977), p. 107.

25 Perloff, *Poet Among Painters*, p. 108.

26 Bluhm, however, suggests that 'the words are more important than the gesture. Basically, we tried to keep the art as just a gesture [...] not an illustration of the poem.' See p. 214 for *Noël*.

Figure 3 Norman Bluhm and Frank O'Hara, *Bang*, 1960

Though one could certainly argue that much of the most significant poetry of the 1950s and 1960s puts pressure on the distinction between 'real poems' and various smaller units of composition,[27] Perloff's reading brings to light two crucial features of the poem:[28] the idea of nested social references that, although generative in the production of the work, cannot be fully recuperated by later readers; and the related process of radical fragmentation that makes even what *is* offered point beyond itself. The kind of particularity mentioned in the anecdotes above reminds one of the crucial charges of coterie in O'Hara's reception history: O'Hara's frequent use of obscure proper names, in particular, has brought the charge, even by his supporters, that his writing is in fact *intended* only for those referenced in it.[29]

It is true that O'Hara's writing, like his collaborative artwork, insists on an internal frame of reference – a scene of production and reception – that severs the work from the fiction of a universalized audience. In an interview with John Yau and Jonathan Gams, for instance, Bluhm stresses both the spontaneous and intersocial aspects of working on all of the tacked up *Poem-Paintings* at once: this 'meant that we would have different connections with different poem paintings. Each one was different. Frank would write something on a sheet of paper while I was in another part of the studio, making a gesture on the paper. It was all instantaneous, like a conversation between friends.'[30] Such conversations are typical in O'Hara's works; but they are obviously designed to be overheard. Rather than a finalized destination, this frame is better conceived as a representation of the shifting social formation out of which the work emerges, before it is disseminated beyond it.

The dialogic aspect of *Poem-Paintings* is immediately evident. Some of O'Hara's one-word poems – *Bang, Bust* – read almost like sound-effects or captions for painterly gestures. If this is a crass literalization of action painting, it is perhaps no crasser than Warhol's 'piss paintings' or Paul McCarthy's performances, *Whipping a Wall and a Window with Paint* (1974) or *Inside Out Olive Oil* (1983). Conversely, one effect that working in relation to gesture has for O'Hara is to liberate him from 'the poem' as a unit of composition. In this sense, the short, elliptical phrases operate as an unexpected truncation of the category of poetry: lines and fragments seemingly severed from larger contexts. Here O'Hara works with riff

---

27 Perloff herself explored this in her later criticism.

28 Concrete poetry in particular. A large international cross-section of such work from the 1950s and early 1960s was collected by Emmett Williams in his *Anthology of Concrete Poetry* (New York: Something Else, 1967). This included work from, among others, Bob Cobbing, Augusto de Campos, Haroldo de Campos, Ian Hamilton Finlay, Eugen Gomringer, Ernst Jandl, Decio Pignatari, and Gerard Rühm.

29 Gilbert Sorrentino makes this point most explicitly, arguing (in what is in fact a generally positive review of *Lunch Poems*) that O'Hara's poems are 'messages to a personal cosmopolitan elite, which apparently consists of O'Hara and his immediate friends'. 'From "The New Note"', in Jim Elledge (ed.), *Frank O'Hara: To Be True to a City* (Michigan: University of Michigan Press, 1990), pp. 15–16, at p. 15.

30 Yau and Gams, '26 Things at Once', n. p.

fragments, the line or small line cluster excised from its more familiar frame. At times, however, these multivalent riffs are recontained, even 'illustrated', by their juxtaposition with Bluhm's gestures: 'There I was minding my own business when' – big Bluhm splash – 'buses always do that to me'. Similarly (but now in reverse) when O'Hara's handwriting is at its largest, taking up the entire picture plane with continuous writing overlaid with light painterly drips, the effect is of a kind of period diary page that the graphic designer (in preparation for a book cover) has rendered in Photoshop's new 'Abstract-Expressionism' treatment.[31] A gaudy picture of a writer's 'interior'? Perhaps, but it helps to see moments like this in relation to O'Hara's conscious anatomization of such conventions – as in his poem 'L'amour avait passé par là': 'they have painted the ceiling of my heart/ and put in a new light fixture' (*CP*, 333). If the subjective interior is here theatricalized, other *Poem-Paintings* like *Chicago* might be said to theatricalize an intersubjective space, thereby approaching the status of multi-voiced graffiti. In this one an all-capitals text reads: 'YOU YOURSELVES MUST BURN THE FAGGOTS YOU HAVE BROUGHT'. Inside this appears: 'There I was an hour late for lunch – it was Oct 9,/ 1960, Cedar bar feeling/ terrible on Sunday'. There it is, the phrase 'Cedar bar' – literally inside a painting – complete with homophobic action painters (or self-reliant, if retro, fire-builders?) bellowing in the background. This does indeed mark a baroque moment in the history of Abstract Expressionism, true enough. And yet the voices that rattle through the poem do not so much own and advertise their collective cosiness in the Cedar as scrawl conflicting messages on its john door.

This graffiti effect reminds one of the particular version of urbanism in O'Hara's work in general and in his reading of Abstract Expressionism in particular: O'Hara sees de Kooning's paintings 'roaring through fluttering newspapers' (*CP*, 285) and in the line 'stunning collapsible savages' (ibid.) seems to compare them to billboards or scaffoldings. The poems 'Commercial Variations' and 'Second Avenue', like many other shorter O'Hara poems, both develop their highly playful and heretical readings of Abstract Expressionism by collapsing certain aspects of the painting on to the city, and vice versa. O'Hara's notes to his poem 'Second Avenue' recall a visit to see one of the Woman paintings in de Kooning's studio; this in turn generates a new perception of the city that leads back into the poem via 'a woman I saw leaning out a window on Second Avenue with her arms on a pillow [...] influenced by de K's woman (whom he thinks of, he once said, as "living" on 14th St)' (*CP*, 497). What is interesting about passages like this is that the drive to read abstraction in relation to immediate urban contexts coincides, paradoxically, with a disruptively multivalent sense of how gestural painting's gestures might be framed interpre-

31 'I'm so tired from all the parties, it's like January! And the hangovers on the beach – they're fun too – and you at least get to wear your Christmas presents'. This one is presented like a blown-up page from a journal, filling the paper edge to edge, with white gestural spots flung along the left side running vertically.

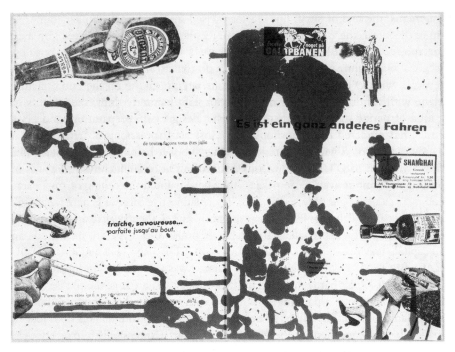

Figure 4 Guy Debord and Asger Jorn, facing pages from *Fin de Copenhague*, 1957

tively. Though O'Hara is an urbanist, he never reads social space as a singular or ultimate interpretive horizon.

At times, however, his urbanist impulse does take on a comparative cast, as when he considers New York in relation to Paris. O'Hara's poem 'Adieu to Norman, Bon Jour to Joan and Jean-Paul' (*CP*, 328), written on 7 August 1959, before a goodbye lunch with Norman Bluhm, is, at one level, about the movement of gesture painters (Bluhm, Joan Mitchell) between Paris and New York. At a larger level 'Adieu' deals, thematically, with establishing and maintaining both personal and national identities – French and American – within the cultural capitals of the two countries. And yet these very identities were being affected by O'Hara's trips back and forth to France promoting Abstract Expressionism for the Museum of Modern Art. The poem evokes the secure value of established French writers – 'René Char, Pierre Reverdy, Samuel Beckett it is possible isn't it' (*CP*, 329) – as a kind of charm that could somehow activate and galvanize, could improperly canonize merely through touch, the then-unknown names of O'Hara's friends, his coterie. But O'Hara's operation here becomes even stranger if one remembers that at precisely this moment the causal lines of influence and prestige between the United States and France were, in fact, beginning to work in the opposite direction:

on the heels of the blockbuster 1958 exhibition *The New American Painting*, which O'Hara had helped to organize, Abstract Expressionism was colonizing not just France but all of Europe. Gesture had become an American export; O'Hara a field representative.[32]

Obviously European artists were not simple consumers who lacked critical faculties. And yet whether or not they embraced American gestural painting, its rise to prominence tended to mark their practices.[33] Take, for instance, Guy Debord and Asger Jorn's 1957 book, *Fin de Copenhague* (Figure 4), completed just before the formation of the Situationist International – a book that is worth examining in this context, too, as a collaboration between a painter and a writer that engages the language of gesture. As 'art', gestural painting would – like all other art – seem to come under Situationist censure. That is, even if Debord helped artists such as Jorn, Constant Nieuwenhuys, and Giuseppe Pinot-Gallizio with their careers, the Situationists as a group famously rejected the category.

Poetry, however, was a different story – and one that has been less analysed. Let me return to my epigraph: 'Clearly the principal domain we are going to replace and *fulfil* is poetry, which burned itself out by taking its position at the vanguard of our time and has now completely disappeared'. We are familiar with the related claim, among artists of the late 1950s, that art could only be continued by a turn to literal environments – a claim from which the Situationists were extremely careful to distinguish themselves. Distrustful of any expansion of art that retains the category, the Situationists felt more comfortable staging the transcendent aspect of their project in the domain of poetry. Why is 'poetry' so

32 Let us consider what the Situationists would have known about American Abstract Expressionism, and what O'Hara himself might have had to do with their knowing it. In both *Art Chronicles* and *The Collected Poems* the editors assert that the blockbuster 1958–59 exhibition *The New American Painting* was 'the first exhibition of American Abstract Expressionism circulated in Europe'. Both *Art Chronicles* and *The Collected Poems* call *The New American Painting* 'the first exhibition of American Abstract Expressionism circulated in Europe 1958–59' (*AC*, 158–59; *CP*, xiv). In fact, though, Europeans had been exposed regularly to Abstract Expressionism, not merely in the United States' representation at the Venice Biennale (since 1948, when de Kooning was shown) but also in circulating exhibitions including *Modern Art in the United States* (July 1955 to August 1956), which – in addition to displaying prints, architecture, industrial design, typography, photographs and film – also presented 108 paintings and 27 sculptures selected by Dorothy C. Miller. In Paris the show was titled '50 Ans d'art aux États-Unis' and ran from 30 March to 15 May 1955. As the MoMA archives tell us, the painting, sculpture, and print sections, in combination with one or more of the other sections were shown thereafter as *Modern Art in the United States: Selections from the Collections of the Museum of Modern Art* in Zurich, Barcelona, Frankfurt, London, the Hague, Vienna and Linz, and Belgrade. This show included 12 Abstract Expressionists: Baziotes, Gorky, Guston, Hartigan, de Kooning, Kline, Motherwell, Pollock, Rothko, Stamos, Still, and Tomlin. For more on this, see Eva Cockcroft, 'Abstract Expressionism, Weapon of the Cold War', in Francis Frascina (ed.), *Pollock and After: The Critical Debate* (London: Routledge, 2nd edn, 2000), pp. 147–54.

33 What is significant for our purposes is that while in 1957 Europeans such as Debord and Jorn might have seen some Abstract Expressionist work, their sense of it as a dominant style would most likely not have emerged until at least after *The New American Painting*. O'Hara himself, that is, had a direct role in changing the meaning of gesture in Europe.

often a figure for the great beyond? Here, the result is that the Situationists must claim two new and structurally inaccessible meanings for poetry: first, it is the authentically lived and unrepresentable experience of a Situationist activity, such as their *dérives* – the improvisatory walks the Situationist staged in cities, following their desires into unexpected zones and encounters and hoping thereby to remake social space; second, poetry names the future social totality of which the *dérive* is an anticipatory fragment: the post-revolutionary world in which it will be possible to live such poetry, everyday life having been totally reconfigured. The problem is neither their practice nor their goals but rather the status of poetry relative to both. What I mean, then, about poetry being paradoxically inaccessible for the Situationists is not, of course, a matter of its difficulty: rather poetry, *as a category*, is neatly contained first inside a private experience and second inside a utopian future. As Vincent Kaufmann writes of the Situationists' version of the poetic: 'Poetry is always at least the figure of revolution. It is the revolution in absentia, its shadow; it evokes its absence while repeating its promise'.[34] Debord expands on this in *Panegyric*. Claiming that he too grew up in the streets, he continues: 'After all, it was modern poetry, for the last hundred years, that had led us there. We were a handful of people who thought it necessary to carry out its programme in reality, and certainly to do nothing else'.[35]

Though it has become a commonplace that the Situationists were attempting to *live* poetry – a recent book on Debord is subtitled *Revolution in the Service of Poetry* – few critics have asked what this meant literally... for poetry. Instead, references to 'poetry' in Situationist criticism are almost invariably claims about the authentically real – the domain of irrecuperable and singular experience, like that presumably had on Situationist *dérives*. Let us return to *Fin de Copenhague*.

The materials for the book, which includes English, Danish, French and German text, are supposed to have been pilfered on a single trip to a newsstand during a trip to Copenhagen. Encountering a series of expressivist drips juxtaposed with advertising images of commodities (liquor, cars, cigarettes, tasteful crackers, tropical vacations), sometimes in the process of being consumed, at other times just as iconic images, one might initially see these features as neatly paired: Abstract Expressionsism, forced down the French public's throat like Hollywood movies under the Marshall Plan, was a kind of fake spontaneous freedom that – like travel, cars and booze – was part of the spectacle rather than a useful critique of it.[36] Andrew

---

34 Vincent Kaufmann, *Guy Debord: Revolution in the Service of Poetry*, trans. Robert Bononno (Minneapolis: University of Minnesota Press, 2006), p. 177.

35 Guy Debord, *Panegyric*, Vol. 1, trans. James Brook and John McHale (London: Verso, 2004), p. 22.

36 These films came as part of the 1946 Bluhm–Brynes accord that jump-started the post-war French economy by wiping out war debt and lending large sums of American cash. As Serge Guilbaut notes, 'the film clause in the treaty stipulated that French theaters would be required for at least two years to show no more than four French films per quarter (rather than the nine per quarter preciously allowed). The American film industry thus killed two birds with one stone. It got rid of French competition, and it knocked down the old quotas, thus allowing American films to take over the French market.

Hussey describes the excised phrases as 'set against a red and blue background in the then fashionable style of a Jackson Pollock "action" painting'. 'Other texts,' he continues, 'sneeringly celebrated the joys of alcohol'.[37] Such an understanding of a secure ironic distance from Abstract Expressionist gesture and liquor would also seem to underlie Simon Sadler's claim that the book 'satirized the empty heart of the spectacle'.[38] But is it right to assume that Jorn, who had after all studied with or worked for both Léger and Le Corbusier, had a purely negative and ironic relation to gesture by 1957?[39] One recent Jorn catalogue goes so far as to suggest that all of Jorn's 'inkblots' are found.[40] But their similarity to his paintings and drawings would seem to belie this – as would the process of illustration used in Jorn's next collaboration with Debord, *Mémoires*, in which Debord seems to have given Jorn a series of collages on top of which Jorn drew various lines and splatters.[41]

It seems more accurate to suggest that *Fin de Copenhague* sets up a relay between Jorn's gestural drips and various cultural contexts, between acts of spontaneity and the decors that might activate or deaden them. Now while there is in Debord's writing an obvious drive toward replacing artistic gestures with social ones in real time and real space, with turning poetry into the street, I want to suggest nonetheless that in *Fin de Copenhague* Jorn's painterly gestures stand in for this force that is to be liberated, this seemingly unrepresentable act that is always, for the Situationists, literally realizing itself. In his 'Preliminary Problems in Constructing a Situation' Debord is insistent on the idea of gesture: a situation 'is composed of gestures contained in a transitory decor. These gestures are the product of the decor and of themselves. And they in turn produce other forms of decor and other gestures.'[42]

The European market was now wide open, and Hollywood was in a good position to capitalize on the situation, since it was prospering (between 1939 and 1944 the Americans had made 2,212 films, while the French film industry was practically shut down). Furthermore, Hollywood films were offered at unbeatable prices, since their production costs had already been recouped on the American market. It was not, then, only a matter of taste (French public preferring American movies) but a question of market structure which doomed the French film industry.' *How New York Stole the Idea of Modern Art*, trans. Arthur Goldhammer (Chicago: University of Chicago Press, 1983), p. 137.

37 Andrew Hussey, *The Game of War: The Life and Death of Guy Debord* (London: Jonathan Cape, 2001), p. 119.

38 Simon Sadler, *The Situationist City* (Cambridge, MA: MIT, 1998), p. 17.

39 Jorn studied with Leger in 1936 and worked for le Corbusier in 1937 on the Palais des Temps Nouveaux at the 1937 Paris Exhibition.

40 Here is how the catalogue for a recent Jorn exhibition shown in Denmark, Holland and Germany, *Asger Jorn* (Ishoj: Arken, 2003), describes *Fin de Copenhague*'s Situationist strategies: 'First of all, working collectively was a subversion of the role of the artist as a creative genius. The Situationists claimed that all aesthetic products are created within and by a situation in society. They therefore used the already-existing images of society in their aesthetic stance – not necessarily in order to create works of art, but to apply their critical, artistic approach to the rest of society. *Fin de Copenhague*'s collage of newspaper-cuttings and ink blots was not only an aesthetic manifestation but also a political criticism' (p. 124).

41 The reissue of *Mémoires* (Paris: Editions Allia, 2004) makes this clear by displaying Debord's collages.

42 Debord, 'Preliminary Problems in Constructing a Situation', p. 43.

Critics tend to take Debord at his word here, seeing 'gesture' in a purely social format – even when Debord is collaborating with Jorn. But what is interesting to me about Situationism is the fact that even in negating art for the real, art becomes the inescapable figure for this negation.

Similarly, if the Grants, Black and White, or White Horse Cellar Whisky, the Tuborg beer bottles or text from Dubonnet ads are 'ironic' citations of administered leisure, the irony is more complex than negation. Alcohol was also, famously, fuel for the very *dérives* charted by the Situationists. Debord in fact devotes an entire chapter of the first volume of *Panegyric* to rhapsodizing on how '[w]ines, spirits, and beers [...] became essential and [...] marked out the main course and the meanders of days, weeks, years'.[43] The point is not simply that the Situationists celebrated alcohol, but that *it too* seems to have held for them the power of *détournement*, making and remaking maps out of quotidian experience. And these experiences are at the heart of the Situationists' version of authenticity: 'Two or three other passions [...] have been more or less continuously important in my life. But drinking has been the most constant and the most present'.[44] Indeed we might say that drinking is itself central among the Situationists' multivalent gestures – its powers being one sense of Jorn's drips and splatters.[45]

Back, then, to Paul Schimmel's remark about how the 'existential freedom' previously associated with gesture began, by the late 1950s, to be 'caricatured, copied, reproduced, appropriated, synthesized, and finally drained of conviction'.[46] Despite the aesthetic of appropriation, *Fin de Copenhague* might, in fact, be positioned *against* this transformation – aligned, that is, with an older sense of gesture as the domain of existential freedom.[47] And yet the Situationists were explicit in their rejection of action painting. As Jorn put it, 'The conception of art implicit in *action painting* reduces art to an act in itself, in which the object, the work of art, is a mere trace, and in which there is no more communication with the audience. This is the attitude of the pure creator who does nothing but fulfil *himself* through the

43 Debord, *Panegyric*, Volume 1, trans. James Brook (London: Verso, 2004), p. 29.

44 Debord, *Panegyric*, Volume 1, p. 29. See also Jean-Luc Nancy, *Being Singular Plural* (Stanford, CA: Stanford University Press, 2000), p. 53: 'The Situationist critique continued to refer essentially to something like an internal truth (designated, for example, by the name "desire" or "imagination"), the whole concept of which is that of a subjective appropriation of "true life", itself thought of as origin proper, as self-deployment and self satisfaction. In this, Situationism demonstrates the nearly constant characteristic of the modern critique of exteriority, appearance, and social alienation – at least, since Rousseau.'

45 One contests the spectacle, then, not simply by negating its administered equation of leisure and booze, but rather by giving leisure no opposite for which booze would be a reward, and by living this rerouted full-time leisure in public, spontaneously.

46 Schimmel, 'The Faked Gesture', p. 19.

47 In 1963 the Situationist International announced a desire 'to negate "Pop art" (which is materially and "ideologically" characterized by *indifference* & dull complacency)' (quoted in Sadler, *The Situationist City*, p. 19).

materials for his own pleasure.'[48] Action painting's gesture, in this reading, would operate centripetally, not centrifugally, projecting one always toward the subject and not toward culture or the social. If we accept such a reading provisionally (though it is worth noting that O'Hara provided compelling terms for seeing action painting in precisely the opposite way), then we might wonder how one would contextualize a Situationist gesture. How, that is, would it achieve 'communication with the audience'? While it is common to cite the 'public' or 'urban' nature of city maps, what the Situationists *did* to maps insists precisely on the idea of the irrecuperable personal trace – the itinerary through the map, and more importantly the experience of its terrain, that is not available. As Vincent Kaufmann says: 'It is up to the reader to discover what kind of social behavior such a map points to, the life it traces in legend, to reconstruct the wanderings and driftings of Debord and his accomplices'.[49] Even if one is interested not so much in Debord's experience but in how his maps might be exemplary, how they might introduce strategies to rearrange, appropriate, recode urban space, the Situationists' idea of 'poetry' paradoxically presents a roadblock to this reading: poetry, to repeat, is the transcendent and necessarily inaccessible realization of one of these maps – either in the form of the Situationists' own private, or everyone's utopian future, experience. As such, the poetic operates not as a domain of defamiliarizing linguistic devices or alternative meaning-making machines, but as a promise of subjective and social realization that can always occur only off-stage. Like their concept of unitary urbanism, which took any urbanist intervention short of social revolution as reformist, so they practise what might be termed a 'unitary poetics'.

Basically what I'm arguing is that while Debord problematically *idealized* poetry, insisting that the Situationists' provisional microsociety could not be represented (that their maps could only index the subjectively quarantined 'poetry' the members claimed to experience as a harbinger of things to come), O'Hara in fact productively *debased* poetry (as he did Abstract Expressionist gesture), rejecting its normative referential assumptions in order to figure his own micro-society in all of its continual flux. On this score, as a theory of what poetry is or can do, I side unequivocally with O'Hara – even if *Poem-Paintings* is far from his best realization of these concerns, if its literalizing, socializing, and debasing of gesture is tentative (and quickly undone by Bluhm's later, far more heroic, practice). Linked to the rest of O'Hara's work, however, its seemingly throwaway spontaneity in fact opens it to comparison, as I've been suggesting, with a work like *Fin de Copenhague*.

Obviously the result of much more conscious theorization, nonetheless *Fin de Copenhague* participates in the Situationists' slumming in poetry. But release the word 'poetry' from its bondage, in the work of the Situationists, to subjective interiors, offstage group activities, or future totalizations – *détourne* their own descriptive

48 Asger Jorn, 'Detourned Painting', in *Asger Jorn*, p. 118.
49 Kaufmann, *Guy Debord*, p. 104.

language, that is, and the Situationists continue to offer an almost endless array of tools, especially for experimental urbanisms.

Still, the would-be spontaneity of painterly gesture and whiskey are ambivalent – not simply negative – terms in *Fin de Copenhague,* at once symptomatic and liberatory – and this is part of what makes them rich. Through juxtaposition with actual maps and concretely arranged or deformed text passages, painterly drips, splatters, and splotches become themselves analogies for maps. The 'grounding' of gesture is far more specific and articulate (if also various and playful) than in *Poem-Paintings*, where (outside both the codex form and the language of print) handwritten commentaries reframe a more limited lexicon of splatters. In fact, most specialists on the Situationists will no doubt sniff at this comparison with a seemingly 'spontaneous' and untheorized work. But this is largely from having misread, or more likely not read, O'Hara.

Given O'Hara's heretical interpretation of Abstract Expressionism – a fan who, with amped-up enthusiasm, turns the work into queer Hollywood cowboy parodies, Cold War spy thrillers, sidewalk stains, and billboard ads – it makes sense to see *Poem-Paintings* not merely as a late, baroque homage to the embattled authenticity of gestural forebears, but rather as an awkward coterie realization of action painting that puts pressure on its vocabulary by oddly specifying its context. To literalize art and writing's production within the contexts of concrete relationships and larger social formations, to raise these contexts to the status of alternative kinship structures (groups that make and consume their own culture while at the same time offering it not just as a commodity, but as a do-it-yourself example, to audiences beyond) – this is the power of a productive rather than symptomatic version of coterie.

French Frank

Rod Mengham

'Why so many references to France?', asked the critic Susan Holohan in an essay on Frank O'Hara's poetry published in 1973.[1] In the thirty-six years since she posed the question, literary critics have produced no substantial answer. One of the most significant collections of essays on O'Hara's work, edited by Jim Elledge, is entitled *Frank O'Hara: To Be True to a City*, and the city does not need to be specified – because O'Hara is regarded as the New York poet *par excellence*, the most indigenous, perhaps, of the New York School comprising poets such as Ashbery, Schuyler, Guest and Koch. O'Hara's work is immersed in, saturated with, the sights and sounds, the street names and references to personalities, of the New York of the 1950s and 1960s. And yet, looking through the more than five hundred pages of the *Collected Poems*, it is striking how often New York references are supplanted by French references, how often the space that these poems explore seems to be simultaneously French and American, how often meditations on New York City end up being displaced by reveries about Paris. Frank O'Hara in New York is drawn constantly towards the imaginative exploration of Paris.

Paradoxically, when he is in Paris, the reverse is true:

> Frank and I happened to be in Paris at the same time in the summer of 1960. I was staying there with my family and had been very busy with the Guide Bleu looking at every placard on every building I could find. And I had located the 'bateau lavoir' where Picasso and Max Jacob had first lived and where they had held all those studio parties with Apollinaire and Marie Laurencin. And across the street was a very good restaurant. I suggested that we have lunch there, our party included Grace Hartigan and her husband at the time, Robert Keene. We had a 'marvelous' lunch, much wine and talk and we all congratulated ourselves on being in Paris at the same time – a continuation of the Cedar St Bar, where we had formerly and consistently gathered. After lunch I suggested that we cross the street to the 'bateau lavoir', a discovery of mine and one I thought would intrigue Frank. Not at all. He did go across the street, but he didn't bother to go into the building. 'Barbara,' he said, 'that was their history

---

1 Susan Holohan, 'Frank O'Hara's Poetry', in Robert E. Shaw (ed.), *American Poetry Since 1960: Some Critical Perspectives* (Manchester: Carcanet Press, 1973), pp. 109–22.

and it doesn't interest me. What does interest me is ours, and we're making it now.'[2]

This anecdote of Barbara Guest's illustrates two factors in the post-war shift in American attitudes towards French culture. It suggests first of all that a fascination with the Paris/New York axis is not an idiosyncrasy of O'Hara's, but is a shared preoccupation. It might in fact be the key to understanding American culture and cultural relations during the late 1940s and the 1950s. And the second factor it draws attention to is an emerging tendency to attempt to negate French modernism and to put in its place an independent, autonomous American art that does not acknowledge its roots in, or its affiliations to, French modernism. What is unusual about Guest's anecdote is that it reflects in the conversation of O'Hara what is to become the ideologically dominant response to the problem of America's cultural, and actually political, relations with Europe during the aftermath of the Second World War, even though O'Hara's writing pulls in a very different direction. What is specifically interesting about O'Hara's stance towards these issues is his apparent doubleness: because in his poetry and criticism there is a tendency that counteracts the above denial that *their* history could be a part of *our* history. O'Hara sitting in the Paris café gives voice to the shared American mood of his time; O'Hara the writer is much more often drawn towards slyly, enthusiastically, insistently, stressing how 'we' should still try to inhabit the space marked out by French culture; a space filled with the concerns that are proposed by French poetry, and for O'Hara, by the poetry of Reverdy in particular.

Paradoxically, what leads me to frame O'Hara's work in this way is the awareness that anyone who reads his work soon acquires a sense of how important to O'Hara's poetry are developments in the sphere of painting. The relevant art historical background is provided by Serge Guilbaut in his provocatively entitled *How New York Stole the Idea of Modern Art* (1983), which examines how and why the perceived centre of international modernism shifts from Paris to New York in the years after the Second World War.[3] Guilbaut's controversial thesis is that American Abstract Expressionism is conscripted not only by politically motivated art critics but even by government itself as the cultural wing of an all-out campaign to achieve American supremacy in the new and developing Cold War situation. In a Europe understood to be politically weakened and susceptible to the lure of Communist ideology, where the symbolic cultural centre is a Paris that houses a merely residual modernist movement perceived to be lacking in vitality, there is scope for, and a need for, a new initiative in the arts that will give America the opportunity of taking the lead, just as it is already doing in all other forms of international relations.

---

2 Barbara Guest, 'Frank and I happened to be in Paris...', in Bill Berkson and Joe LeSueur (eds.), *Homage to Frank O'Hara* (Bolinas: Big Sky, 1978), p. 77.

3 Serge Guilbaut, *How New York Stole the Idea of Modern Art: Abstract Expressionism, Freedom, and the Cold War* (Chicago: University of Chicago Press, 1983).

Guilbaut's case is documented in considerable detail: he measures the impact of the Smith-Mundt Act, passed in January 1948, which was designed to expand the Information and Cultural Program; he brings out the significance of the call made in the US Senate in March 1950 for a 'world-wide Marshall plan in the field of ideas'; he demonstrates Presidential involvement in and approval of this project; and he shows how some of the most prominent and authoritative commentators of the cultural scene effectively join forces to promote a specifically American ideology. Guilbaut argues that Clement Greenberg, Harold Rosenberg and Irving Sandler – to name the most famous – converge in their efforts to create a perception of Abstract Expressionism as a strong, independent and distinctively American art possessing the qualities that will enable it to combat totalitarianism. Clement Greenberg, in his elevation of Jackson Pollock to the status of heroic leader of the Abstract Expressionist movement, stresses, in a direct contrast with what he sees as the failures of Jean Dubuffet's painting, Pollock's violence, force and spontaneity.

What is celebrated by all these writers as the source of the new power of American art is its stress on individualism, and specifically the freedom of the individual, guaranteed paradoxically by the evidence that can be found in Abstract Expressionist paintings of psychological insecurity, anxiety and neurosis. Leslie Fiedler writes in *Partisan Review* in 1948 of the 'importance of the individual, his aloofness, his independence of ideology, and his new vocabulary of "freedom, responsibility, and guilt"'.[4] Arthur Schlesinger proclaims, in *The Vital Center* in 1949, the necessity of anxiety: 'Against totalitarian certitude, free society can only offer modern man devoured by alienation and fallibility'.[5] Insecurity is regarded as proof of the existence of freedom of choice. What all these writers emphasize is not the abstract side of Abstract Expressionism, but the expressionist side. In the face of all those energetically worked surfaces of paint they see only testimony to a psychological depth. And this is an emphasis that O'Hara is consistently opposed to. As curator at the Museum of Modern Art in New York and as art critic, reviewing the works of Abstract Expressionist painters, O'Hara concentrates on technique, on surface elements, avoids depth psychology and even quietly introduces a critical genealogy that gives Jackson Pollock, no less, an indebtedness to French Surrealism.

O'Hara's stance is very much part of a rearguard action, and this can be seen in his direct involvement with the exponents of and products of American Abstract Expressionism; but it is especially clear in his poetry. In what follows, I offer discussions of two poems which actively invite the reader to think of how a counter-example to American ideology might be found in a return to France, in a restoration of the links that O'Hara maintains with the work of French poets such as Reverdy.

The first of these poems, 'Adieu to Norman, Bon Jour to Joan and Jean-Paul', with its hybrid French and English title, includes many references to Paris landmarks

4 Guilbaut, *How New York Stole the Idea of Modern Art*, p. 187.
5 Arthur M. Schlesinger, Jr, *The Vital Center: The Politics of Freedom* (Boston: Houghton Mifflin, 1949), p. 57.

and personalities in the course of shrugging off reasons to be anxious in a bravura performance of sustained insouciance. The whole poem is a playful response to Samuel Beckett's *L'Innomable* [*The Unnamable*], which first appeared in 1952 and was published in English translation in 1959, the year in which O'Hara's poem was written. The celebrated dilemma of Beckett's ending ('I can't go on, I'll go on') is here cheerfully overwritten by O'Hara's insistence on rhythmic unstoppability and sentimental resilience:

> and surely we shall not continue to be unhappy
> we shall be happy
> but we shall continue to be ourselves everything continues to be possible
> René Char, Pierre Reverdy, Samuel Beckett it is possible isn't it
> I love Reverdy for saying yes, though I don't believe it (*CP*, 329)

The poem contains fourteen uses of the word 'continue', building up enough momentum to make its repetition seem potentially endless, in marked contrast to Beckett's much more disturbing tension between the alternatives of continuance and termination. The whole question of what it means to 'be ourselves', and to continue to be so, is the occasion of anxiety and even of fear in Beckett's text, but in O'Hara's poem it prompts a hedonistic abandon and the kind of proteanism that is elaborated on definitively in 'In Memory of My Feelings' (*CP*, 252–57). The world of the Beckettian solipsist, which rests on a basis of psychological depth, is replaced by a carefree skimming over the surfaces of what continues in the day-to-day world; the universal scope that many readers have assigned to the fiction of the Paris-dwelling Irish author is replaced by specifically local forms of behaviour and concerns of the moment, pinpointed on the maps of both New York and Paris. The ideologized version of Abstract Expressionism, meanwhile, which sees grandeur in the artist's isolation and locates meaning in the presence of neurotic individualism, is represented as effectively as anywhere else in the writings of Irving Sandler. His book *The Triumph of American Painting* (1970) suggests by its title the inflated nature of the claims made for Abstract Expressionism, endowing it with a pomposity that is undercut peremptorily by the gossipy confidentiality of O'Hara's aside:

> and Irving Sandler continues to be the balayeur des artistes
> and so do I (sometimes I think I'm 'in love' with painting) (*CP*, 329)

The switch from English to French might suggest something fancy, something at least moderately exotic, but 'balayeur' actually means 'sweeper-up', undermining the pretentiousness that O'Hara himself is allergic to, and reassigning Sandler to the same condition that O'Hara occupies – one of refusing to take himself too seriously. In circumventing the depth psychology and the triumphalism of a Sandlerian emphasis, O'Hara is rejoining an alternative tradition in American culture – one that could be regarded as a more native tradition. His poem generates an atmosphere that sustains everything without discrimination; it has a generosity of attention and an all-inclusive tendency of the kind that can be seen in the work of Whitman, Carl Sandburg, William Carlos Williams. It has a celebratory vulgarity, and it cherishes the quotidian, which makes it entirely appropriate that the temporal scale O'Hara is operating with in this poem, as in so many of his poems, is precisely diurnal. The poem starts with a reference to the time – around mid-day – like so many other poems by O'Hara, such as 'The Day Lady Died':

> It is 12:20 in New York a Friday
> three days after Bastille day (*CP*, 325)

Here also the reader is being reminded of the Paris–New York axis. Both poems are part of a group of so-called 'lunch poems' some of which were published under that title: every day the poet takes lunch, and every lunch-time he writes a poem; writing a poem is simply a function of the diurnal cycle – it is one of those things that continues, that recurs day by day. The diurnal rhythm has important implications for the question of what continues and what does not. Every day brings a different set of contingencies to be open to, to be receptive to, to respond to, and by extension, to adapt to and be changed by. Every day brings the possibility of change as well as continuity, the possibility of not being yourself, of transforming into something else – every day has a revolutionary potential; every day a Bastille day.

Of course, it is paradoxical that this return to a native American tradition should be mediated by a series of references to France ('Why so many references to France?'). O'Hara is reviving the links with the repressed antecedent of his contemporary American culture – Parisian modernism; in fact, he is reading contemporary American culture through French poetry, and it is specifically in the poetry of Pierre Reverdy that he finds something exceptionally significant that he can make use of in his attempt to resist the triumphalism attached to American art.

Reverdy is a key figure in the other O'Hara poem I want to look at in some detail, so it is important to demonstrate how his own poetic procedures and concerns might be exemplary for O'Hara's practice. A significant degree of overlap between the poetic thinking of Reverdy and O'Hara can be seen in a poem such as 'Auberge':

> Un oeil se ferme
>
> > Au fond plaquée contre le mur
> > la pensée qui ne sort pas
> >
> > Des idées s'en vont pas à pas
>
> > On pourrait mourir
> Ce que je tiens entre mes bras pourrait partir
>
> > Un rêve
> L'aube à peine née qui s'achève
> > Un cliquetis

Les volets en s'ouvrant l'ont abolie

Si rien n'allait venir

Il y a un champ où l'on pourrait encore courir
       Des étoiles a n'en plus finir
Et ton ombre au bout de l'avenue
       Elle s'efface

On n'a rien vu
De tout ce qui passait on n'a rien retenu
Autant de paroles qui montent
Des contes qu'on n'a jamais lus
           Rien

Les jours qui se present à la sortie
       Enfin la cavalcade s'est evanouié

En bas entre les tables où l'on jouait aux cartes[6]

At first glance, there may seem to be as many dissimilarities as similarities, especially with regard to the movement of the poem, which in Reverdy is much more cautious and meditative than in O'Hara. But in its own way, Reverdy's writing shows a fidelity to the quotidian that is as fundamental as the equivalent commitment in O'Hara. For Reverdy, this seizure of the everyday is influenced, appropriately, by developments in the visual arts at the time of writing. He follows Cubism in rejecting symbolism in favour of a renewed attention to the ordinary objects of the physical world. But he also reveals an interest in the influence of the cinema on the cultivation of effects of simultaneity in modernist experimentation. In 1913, Blaise Cendrars published *Premier Livre Simultane*, at the same time as Robert Delaunay was formulating the principles of 'Simultaneism' in painting.[7] This allowed for the presentation of different events taking place at the same time in different places, creating a dynamic effect very close to one of the goals of O'Hara's writing.

6 Patricia Terry's translation ('Inn'), published in Pierre Reverdy, *Selected Poems*, selected by Mary Ann Caws, edited by Timothy Bent and Germaine Brée (Newcastle upon Tyne: Bloodaxe, 1991), runs as follows: 'An eye closes// Deep inside and flat against the wall/ the thought which doesn't go out// Ideas step by step go their way// Death could happen/ What I hold within my arms could slip away// A dream// Dawn at its birth dies out/ Annulled in a clatter/ Of opening shutters// If nothing were going to come// There's a field where we could still run/ Unlimited stars/ And your shadow where the avenue ends/ Vanishes// We have seen nothing/ Of all that was passing we have held on to nothing/ So many words rising/ Stories we never read/ Nothing// The days in a rush for the exit/ At last the cavalcade has faded out// Down there between the tables where they played cards.'

7 See Robert Delaunay, 'Simultaneism in Contemporary Modern Art, Painting, Poetry', in Mary Ann Caws (ed.), *Manifesto: A Century of isms* (Lincoln, NE: University of Nebraska Press, 2001), pp.160–63.

Jean Schroeder, in her monograph on the French poet, judges that Reverdy's 'preferred leitmotif' consists of 'the wanderings of an anonymous traveller whose objective and destination are never clearly defined'.[8] This could be taken almost as a blue-print for the way that O'Hara is drawn repeatedly in his poetry to effect a kind of *dérive* around and across the streets of New York, and – simultaneously in the imagination – among the *environs* of Paris, as well. 'Auberge' conjures up the exploration of a virtual space, which is simultaneously the space of a dream ('Un rêve'); most of the moving about is accomplished by thoughts and words, rather than by an anonymous traveller. In O'Hara, the poet-as-walker and his reveries are equally mobile. In fact, the later poet maintains an equilibrium between the claims of the virtual and the real, whereas Reverdy, as in 'Auberge', was often tempted to engage the virtual in a displacement of the real.

In the early twentieth century, there was a greater programmatic urgency in the opposition to naturalist priorities in literature. Reverdy's essay 'Sur le Cubisme' advocates the delineation of form rather than of anecdote,[9] and this emphasis corresponds to the organizing principles of his own poetry, which is structured by recurring elements that bind the text together through patterns of sound rather than points of reference. In 'Auberge', consonance is very clearly a primary focus for the writing, which forms long chains of assonantal echo-effects:

> 'contre', 'vont', 'On', 'l'ont', 'l'on', 'On',' 'on', 'contes', 'qu'on', 'l'on';
> 'pourrait', 'pourrait', 'n'allait', 'pourrait', 'passait', 'jamais';
> 'mourir', 'partir', 'venir', 'courir', 'finir';
> 'plus', 'bout', 'vu', 'retenu', 'lus';

and this list catches only the most obvious parallels. As the first of these assonantal chains indicates, this poem also provides no fewer than five examples on one page of a crucial feature of Reverdy's procedures, his systematic use of the pronoun 'on'. Anthony Rizzuto argues that 'on' appears more than any other pronoun in Reverdy's work. Its frequency draws attention not only to itself but also to the absence of 'je' as the main point of reference.[10] The insistence on using 'on' in place of 'je' is part of the effect that Reverdy is striving to create in accord with his statement in 'En Vrac': 'La personnalité d'un auteur, son apport durable, non sont pas du tout dans ce qu'il a pu avoir de plus surprenant, de plus déroutant de prime abord. C'est, au contraire, cela qui vieillit le plus vite et devient insignifiant ou insupportable. Ce qui dure, c'est ce qui peut, de lui, devenir le plus commun, le plus général'.[11]

---

8 Jean Schroeder, *Pierre Reverdy* (Boston: Twayne, 1981), p. 9.

9 Pierre Reverdy, 'Sur le Cubisme', in Pierre Reverdy (ed.), *Nord-Sud* 1 (15 March 1917), pp. 5–7.

10 Anthony Rizzuto, *Style and Theme in Reverdy's 'Les Ardoises du toit'* (Tuscaloosa, AL: University of Alabama Press, 1971), pp. 41–47.

11 Pierre Reverdy, *En Vrac* (Monaco: Editions du Rocher, 1956), p. 33. 'The personality of an author, and his lasting contribution, do not reside in his apparent capacity to be especially surprising, or especially idiosyncratic. On the contrary, it is that which grows obsolescent the most quickly,

Reverdy's concept of authorship is orientated towards the dispersal of the individual personality, in a process of assimilation to whatever is most typical in the individual's experience. Both Reverdy and O'Hara work towards the refusal of access to a confessional dimension in their poetry. O'Hara's flamboyantly confidential asides and his impulse towards gossip go hand-in-hand with the avoidance of the heroic manner attributed to Abstract Expressionism together with the assumption of unique psychological depth. From the second line of 'Auberge' onwards – 'Au fond plaquée' [In the veneered depth] – Reverdy plays relentlessly on the relationship between surface and depth, and the exploration of space generally in the poem questions the status of clear demarcations between depth and surface, inside and outside, entry and exit: 'Si rien n'allait venir' [If nothing was going to come]. The clear separation of points in a deep space that might be envisaged behind the linguistic surface – as behind the picture plane in a painting – is constantly obscured as the reader becomes absorbed instead in the oxymoronic play of the phrasing.

In the essay 'L'Emotion', Reverdy proposed a radical rethinking of poetry's relationship to the articulation of emotion, arguing that it was the business of the poem not to relay emotion but to generate it.[12] The poem should not be concerned to communicate a pre-existing emotional reality, to which it gives sole access, but from which, by the same token, the reader is ultimately barred. The poet should rather convince the reader that the only emotion worth having is that which is produced entirely by the experience of reading the poem. This proposition is very close to the central idea in O'Hara's mock-manifesto 'Personism':

> Personism has nothing to do with philosophy, it's all art. It does not have to do with personality or intimacy, far from it! But to give you a vague idea, one of its minimal aspects is to address itself to one person (other than the poet himself), thus evoking overtones of love without destroying love's life-giving vulgarity, and sustaining the poet's feelings towards the poem while preventing love from distracting him into feeling about the person. (*CP*, 499)

This diversion of emotion away from persons and towards poems, coupled with an insistence on downgrading the role of the poet in relation to the poem, moving the focus away from self-expression and towards interaction with the reader – 'It puts the poem squarely between the poet and the person' (*CP*, 499) – is recommended in a text that is diametrically opposed to the register of canonizing pomposity associated with contemporaneous discourse on Abstract Expressionism.

The full range of preoccupations shared with Reverdy can be seen in a poem written in 1956, the same year as publication of the French poet's commonplace book, *En Vrac*. This is 'A Step Away From Them', one of O'Hara's best known 'lunch

---

becomes meaningless and intolerable. That which lasts, is whatever he has within him that can become the most commonplace, the most generalized'. My translation.

12 Pierre Reverdy, 'L'Emotion', in *Nord-Sud* 8 (October 1917), pp. 3–6.

poems', remarkable for its internationalism, for its reminder of America's radical openness to the impact of other cultures, counterpointing a black bystander with a blonde chorus girl, Coca-Cola with papaya juice, and then gathering together Giulietta Massina, Federico Fellini, passing Puerto Ricans, a poster for 'Bullfight', three American artists and the inevitable French poet, Reverdy himself. What motivates this internationalism is quite precisely not the kind of exploration of individual psychological depth that can be represented as having universal value, but something that is perhaps much more characteristic of American cultural tradition, its consumerism. Everything is available in New York, everything is seemingly offering itself up for the poet to write about, not because of American cultural superiority, but because of American economic superiority. The poet's ability to sample other cultures is of a piece with his readiness to investigate bargains in wristwatches, and there is a knowingness about this in the writing. It is particularly revealing that the reference to Reverdy at the end of the poem comes soon after a commemoration of Jackson Pollock:

> There are several Puerto
> Ricans on the avenue today, which
> makes it beautiful and warm. First
> Bunny died, then John Latouche,
> then Jackson Pollock. But is the
> earth as full as life was full, of them?
> And one has eaten and one walks,
> past the magazines with nudes
> and the posters for BULLFIGHT and
> the Manhattan Storage Warehouse,
> which they'll soon tear down. I
> used to think they had the Armory
> Show there.
> A glass of papaya juice
> And back to work. My heart is in my
> pocket, it is Poems by Pierre Reverdy. (*CP*, 258)

Pollock, elevated to the status of virtual patron saint of the ideologized version of Abstract Expressionism, assumed to be the chief exemplar of heroic individualism, is here conflated with two minor artists with very different profiles, and incorporated into a phrase that becomes the crux of the poem, presenting as it does a mild conundrum for the reader. One can well imagine a critic such as Clement Greenberg finding ways of exaggerating how Pollock was 'full of life', but O'Hara turns this familiar phrase around and strips Pollock of his individualism, celebrating instead how life in general was enriched almost in equal measure by these three artists, drawing attention through the reversal of the expected phrasing to the linguistic surface of his poem rather than hinting at any unplumbed depths.

The reference to Reverdy is prepared for eight lines earlier by a very conspicuous use of the impersonal pronoun 'one', in a line whose deliberate clumsiness makes the connection with the French poet's regular deployment of 'on' seem unavoidable. And the reader is forcibly tugged back up to the linguistic surface by the phrasing of the last two lines, which uses enjambment to effect a torque on the idiomatic expression 'wearing one's heart on one's sleeve'. The allusion to this phrase is in itself an initial move away from emotional depth or intensity in favour of surface display, but in substituting 'pocket' for 'sleeve' O'Hara is going further, attaching his poem to the locus of consumerist spending power. His stage-managed confusion over the location of the original Armory Show (in February 1913) also neatly correlates the American art scene with consumerist pressures. The fact that 'Reverdy' is actually the last word in the poem sets the final seal on O'Hara's refusal of spurious depth, on his blockage of confessionalism, underlining the purpose for which his poetry has recruited so systematically 'all those references to France'. Reverdy turns out to be the specifically un-American pivot around which these poems turn, playing with a contemporaneous American register of psychological profundity and parodying it, framing it with various deflationary measures, not in a simple embrace of the surface as opposed to the depth but in a process of complicating the relations between them.

Distraction and Absorption
on Second Avenue

Andrea Brady

How can we read Frank O'Hara's 'Second Avenue'? Its length and associative belligerence, its radical and sometimes electrifying shifts from recognizably O'Haran conceits (flight, breath, sexual intimacy, and the multiplicity of the poetic persona) to absurdist propositions, all make this poem extremely difficult to grasp. O'Hara justifies his own evasiveness, describing 'the kiss and the longing to be modern and sheltered and different/ and insane and decorative as a Mayan idol too well understood/ to be beautiful' (*CP*, 141). *Il faut être absolument moderne.* To remain a beautiful 'idol', different, insane, decorative, the poet must be careful not to be 'too well understood'.[1] The poem's beauty resides in its erotic power, its clinging to displacement (longing) and surface (the decorative). That desire not to be 'understood' may seem to anticipate Charles Bernstein's thesis that non-absorptive poems produce 'artifice, boredom,/ exaggeration, attention scattering, distraction,/ digression', and intense self-consciousness in the reader.[2] Indeed, Bernstein's description of the anti-absorptive poem as 'not to describe or incant but to be/ the thing described' recalls O'Hara's own assertion about 'Second Avenue', that 'I hope the poem to *be* the subject, not just about it' (*CP*, 497).[3] However, where Bernstein links absorption to Romanticism and reverie, this essay will suggest that O'Hara uses strategies of distraction – pulling the text, poet and reader, apart – in order to protect the autonomy of the poet and to guard against exegetical strategies which might peer below the surface of both poem and poet. O'Hara's poetic personae, dressed in aleatory costumes, perform in an illusionary theatre meant to discourage the reader from considering the poet's individuality. However, that performance can have the opposite effect, drawing attention to the autonomous artist directing proceedings from behind the curtain. The anxiety to avoid interpretation and to create an anti-absorptive poem makes it very difficult to read 'Second Avenue' without becoming distracted by its distraction, its madly decorative

---

1 On the relation of this image to O'Hara's writing on Pollock, see Lytle Shaw, *Frank O'Hara: The Poetics of Coterie* (Iowa: University of Iowa Press, 2006), chapter 5.
2 Charles Bernstein, 'Artifice of Absorption', in *A Poetics* (Cambridge, MA: Harvard University Press, 1992), p. 29.
3 Bernstein, 'Artifice of Absorption', p. 25.

surface. This also means that readers are forced to construct an alternative herme-neutic strategy for dealing with this text; and in doing so, they resist its impulses and (if we are to believe the notes O'Hara wrote to the poem for a magazine editor [*CP*, 495–97]) its intentions.

'Second Avenue' seems a rebarbative achievement, recoiling from sentimen-tality but also from the reader. The few critics who have attempted to account for it have attributed its obfuscating modernity to O'Hara's associations with painters: O'Hara, in this view, is imitating graphic abstraction textually. However, visual and verbal materials exact different forms of attention to a total object whose structural resources are either simultaneously displayed or progressively unfolded. While a painting's surface can be examined in its constituent parts or materials or zones, or absorbed in its entirety, it unfurls its layers of meanings and qualities within the elapsing immediacy of the gaze. A poem, by contrast – especially one of this length – emerges consecutively, motivating the search for consecutive meanings, for argument. 'Second Avenue' repels critical arguments. This is not because it is simply a chronicle of modernist adventurers in surface and temporariness: rather, it is the consummate example of the 'instantaneous quality' of O'Hara's poetry that John Ashbery celebrates in his preface to the *Collected Poems* (*CP*, vii). But the ubiquity of potentially figurative language in the poem, which seems teasingly to invite psychoanalytic interpretation, means that its materiality of signification can never be free of symbolic potential. In 'Second Avenue', close reading can string together the poem's accidental preoccupations; these seem to illuminate specific features of O'Hara's practice and interests in the 1950s. But close reading relies on the elimination of a great deal of textual 'noise' – reading strategies which the poem, and O'Hara's notes on the poem, explicitly discourage.

I'm not alone in finding this poem difficult; in his preface Ashbery declares it a failure, an obfuscating and finally unsatisfactory pleasure that O'Hara would learn by experimentation to abandon. However, the frequency with which O'Hara quotes from the poem in his subtitles for the 1964 Alfred Leslie film *The Last Clean Shirt* suggests that the text continued to resonate with O'Hara for at least a decade. And compared to O'Hara's late work, 'Second Avenue' is not uncharacteristic in its use of violent imagery, pop-art personae, superficial anecdotalism, non sequiturs and absurdism. Had O'Hara lived longer, perhaps his 'I do this' *Lunch Poems* would have been viewed as a temporary aberration in an *oeuvre* constituted by what Ashbery refers to inaccurately as his 'French Zen' period.

A few critics have aligned this poem with O'Hara's French and Russian predilections, with the influence of Surrealism, Dadaism, Futurism (in particular the poem's dedicatee Mayakovsky);[4] or they have compared it to Cubist, Abstract

---

4 Marjorie Perloff, 'Transparent Selves: The Poetry of John Ashbery and Frank O'Hara', *Yearbook of English Studies* 9 (1978), pp. 171–96.

Expressionist or action painting.[5] Certainly, the poem reflects on painterly technique: O'Hara declares that 'I emulate the black which is a cry but is not voluptuary like a warning,/ which has lines, cuts, drips, aspirates, trembles with horror' (CP, 150). The black solid with its lines, cuts, drips, and aspirations are visual approximations of a warning cry; the description could apply to O'Hara's text, with its poetic lines, collage technique, references to breathing and occasional trembles. 'Second Avenue' also refers explicitly to the painting of Grace Hartigan and of Willem de Kooning.[6] It invokes a 'he' who 'had an autocratic straw face like a dark/ in a de Kooning where the torrent has subsided at the very center/ of classicism' (CP, 148–49), going on to compare the classical order with the 'whirlpools' of modernism. This is one of many comparisons of the text to water, this time water threatening to suck the reader or viewer under in its centripetal force. I'll return to the importance of water in 'Second Avenue' shortly. But these painterly associations do not explain what O'Hara actually *does* in the poem; they just give his activities a genealogy. Moreover, they neglect to account for O'Hara's decision to replace the painter de Kooning as the poem's dedicatee with the poet Mayakovsky. That replacement suggests that 'Second Avenue' is contending with specific challenges to modernism in *poetry*, inspired in part by the confrontation between representation and abstraction which the Russian Futurist staged with such passion and violence.

'Second Avenue' consists of 11 sections of unequal length, all of unrhymed verse. Published in 1960, it was written in April and May 1953, while O'Hara was living on East 49th Street. Larry Rivers maintains that it was 'written in my plaster garden studio overlooking that avenue' (CP, 529), but Joe LeSueur identifies it as dedicated to the place where '[we] did so much of our shopping, eating out, and movie-going'.[7] O'Hara, in his notes to the poem, asserts that 'actually everything in it either happened to me or I felt happening (saw, imagined) on Second Avenue'. Like Mayakovsky and de Kooning, O'Hara says, he wanted to create a work 'as big as cities where the life in the work is autonomous (not about actual city life) and yet similar' (CP, 497).[8] O'Hara suggests that the poem is both *about* the city (which supplies its experiential content) and *not about* the city but about the poetic imagination that occupies it. A record of actual or psychic events, 'Second Avenue' is primarily a portrait of subjectivity within the particular conditions of urban modernity.

5   David L. Sweet, 'Parodic Nostalgia for Aesthetic Machismo: Frank O'Hara and Jackson Pollock', *Journal of Modern Literature* 23.3/4 (Summer 2000), pp. 375–91; Brad Gooch, *City Poet: The Life and Times of Frank O'Hara* (New York: Knopf, 1993), p. 223.

6   Terence Diggory, 'Questions of Identity in Oranges by Frank O'Hara and Grace Hartigan', *Art Journal* 52.4 (Winter 1993), pp. 41–50.

7   Joe LeSueur, *Digressions on Some Poems by Frank O'Hara* (New York: Farrar, Straus and Giroux, 2003), p. 34.

8   Compare O'Hara's Statement for *The New American Poetry* (CP, 500): 'I am mainly preoccupied with the world as I experience it [...] What is happening to me, allowing for lies and exaggerations which I try to avoid, goes into my poems. I don't think my experiences are clarified or made beautiful for myself or anyone else; they are just there in whatever form I can find them.'

This might lead the reader to expect that the poem was fractured by the same fault lines of desire, repression, social performance and intimate revelation which structure individual personalities, a structure yanked out of shape by the distractions of the city and unbidden perceptions, conditioned by the associative instabilities of language. However, O'Hara works to keep the poem at arm's length from psychologically, socially or philosophically coherent realities. He argues in the notes that 'I have a feeling that the philosophical reduction of reality to a dealable-with system so distorts life that one's "reward" for this endeavour (a minor one, at that) is illness both from inside and outside' (*CP*, 495). The poem portrays reality prior to systematizing reduction, in order to avoid physical and mental illness which (he argues) is the inevitable consequence of classificatory thinking. In this way, his project does bear comparison with Tristan Tzara's 'Dada Manifesto' of 1918, which, in the translation by Ralph Manheim which was published in an edition by Robert Motherwell two years before O'Hara began work on 'Second Avenue', describes psychoanalysis as 'a dangerous disease' that 'puts to sleep the anti-objective impulses of man and systematizes the bourgeoisie'.[9] O'Hara's poem resists analysis and psychology: at one point O'Hara offers the comparison 'Pseudo-aggressive as the wife of a psychiatrist. Beating off' (*CP*, 149). Masturbation is a means of resisting diagnosis and dealing with aggressive impulses, as well as defeating the sexual desires of her psychiatrist-husband. But the qualifier 'pseudo-' indicates that her aggression is a performance. I'll return to the poem's confrontational use of sexuality later, but here I want to suggest that the rejection of analysis is commonly a way of protecting rather than avoiding 'illness'; and in 'Second Avenue', the rejection of the analytic perspective becomes a compositional principle designed to protect the autonomy and 'anti-objective impulses' of the poet.

In addition to its violent rejections of psychoanalysis, 'Second Avenue' seeks to outwit hermeneutic analysis generally. O'Hara doesn't want to allow readers to make anything of his poem: it is to unfold immediately and without repercussions. In his notes, O'Hara describes 'the verbal elements', the anecdotes, as 'intended consciously to keep the surface of the poem high and dry, not wet, reflective and self-conscious' (*CP*, 497). The poem is dry, anti-absorptive: attention beads up and drips away from its lacquered surface. A contrast with painting is useful: when the paint is still wet, the painting can still be worked, revised and reshaped; a dry matt painting is no longer receptive of marks or revisions. By keeping his poem 'dry', O'Hara prevents the reader from intervening in the making of the text's meaning. This differentiates his intentions (if not his text) from the emphasis on the reader as participant producer in such later developments as Language poetry, but also raises the question of what the reader is actually meant to do with this text.[10] It

9 Tristan Tzara, 'Dada Manifesto 1918', trans. Ralph Mannheim, in R. Motherwell (ed.), *The Dada Painters and Poets* (Boston: Harvard University Press, 1989 [New York, 1951]), pp. 76–82.

10 Bruce Andrews articulates one of the central themes of Language poetry when he writes, 'writing is clearly produced by the central activity of reading. Reading becomes the first production, rather

situates its reader very specifically. His desire to stay 'high and dry', O'Hara says, is the source of the 'obscurity' of the 'relationship between the surface and the meaning' in 'Second Avenue'. The symbolic geography of surface and meaning or reflection locates the 'you' – philosopher, critic, reader searching for cognizable content, practising

> This thoroughness whose traditions have become so reflective,
> your distinction is merely a quill at the bottom of the sea
> tracing forever the fabulous alarms of the mute (*CP*, 139)

The poem displaces this valueless work in the depths of the sea among sedimented meanings with an insistence on surface. However, although it disparages specific forms of reading, including investigative attention, close reading and psychoanalysis, the poem does not offer a model of appropriate reading. Instead, the reader is expected to have already failed, following behind the text's outrageous speed, tracing the 'alarms of the mute' like a pair of ragged claws at the dark bottom of the sea. This expectation of failure is symptomatic of a sadistic relation to critics and readers throughout O'Hara's work – O'Hara's violent delight in humiliating the reader with his or her own insufficiency is apparent in 'Second Avenue' and in many other texts, a point to which I'll return shortly.

The lack of reflection O'Hara aims for is not easily achievable, however: a simple assertion of wet/dry will not accomplish it. For all its techniques of distraction and speed, the poem is not capable of outpacing self-consciousness. O'Hara knows this, and remarks on it in the poem's frequent references to the sea. The speaker describes himself as an 'oceanographer of a capricious promptness/ which is more ethical than dismal' (*CP*, 141–42), and again as 'a limp hand [...] which [...] is capable of resigning from the disaster it summoned ashore' (*CP*, 146). In the first case, the poet as oceanographer is either characterized by capricious promptness or engaged in mapping it. The poet's capricious lexical choices attempt to protect the spontaneity ('promptness') of his outflow. In the second case, the 'ethical' vigilance of the oceanographer has been reduced to a 'limp hand', able only to surrender responsibilities for the general disaster that it has evoked: or more specifically, that it has brought 'ashore', out of the oceanic depths on to dry land. In another instance, the speaker is a nun trembling with erotic excitement at a movie premiere, who is rescued from the 'projection' of her fantasies on to the big screen for public viewing because 'a tidal wave has seized the theatre' (*CP*, 140). The tidal wave, threatening to overturn the ocean and invert depth and surface, transports her to Siam. The

---

than consumption – not a relay of an author's vain transcriptions of a representational content. Reading operates the text, is a rewriting, a new inscription.' 'Code Words', in Bruce Andrews and Charles Bernstein (eds.), *The L=A=N=G=U=A=G=E Book* (Carbondale and Edwardsville: Southern Illinois University Press, 1984), p. 55. On the influence of O'Hara on Language poetry, see Geoff Ward, 'Language Poetry and the American Avant-garde', British Association for American Studies Pamphlet 25 (1993), http://www.baas.ac.uk/resources/pamphlets/pamphdets.asp?id=25.

speaker is also 'drag[ged...] beneath the Bering Sea' (*CP*, 140); imposed meanings threaten to drown him in the sea which might unclothe him (bare) and birth him (bearing). Later, when the poem seems to fail, 'I can only enumerate the somber instances of wetness' (*CP*, 140), or account for its reflections and so accede to a conventional and 'sombre' idea of the poem as a signifying practice.

To escape from these seas filled with desire, affect and psychological depth, O'Hara repeatedly refers to flight. The Futurist dream of acceleration is epitomized in an anecdote about a pilot, who smells the sweetness of lightning 'over the zoo of the waves'; 'The sea looked like so many amethyst prophets and I,/ hadn't the cannery sent forth perfume? would never go back' (*CP*, 143). The sea far beneath the pilot is hard and gorgeous, as he escapes forever from the 'cannery' trap of a life drenched with aromatic self-consciousness. Then again, 'Sunday came, the violet waves crusted./ The sand bristled and with its stinging flashes we dove/ screaming into the rocks where pythons nestled and brooded' (*CP*, 148). There is safety on the high, dry land; but if we are cast ashore by the random motion of the waves, we may find ourselves bitten and stung by pythons. Navigating the passage from symbolic depth to anti-signifying surface requires careful self-location and defensiveness.

But O'Hara's notes on 'Second Avenue' entail a contradiction. O'Hara says he wants to avoid reflection, but nonetheless, he asserts that the poem is 'intended consciously': so it is the product of reflection, intention and deliberation. These contradictory impulses produce a tension in the poem between a deliberately fashioned structure and an associative drive which must work fast to avoid being set in the concrete of analysis. That tension forces 'Second Avenue' into a dramatically perpetuated present tense. Although there are a few moments of recollection or narrative markers of the past, such as 'I recall...', the poem strains to keep up its presentness, as if anything drawn from the past has already fallen prey to the classificatory sickness of memory. For example, the poem briefly gets stuck with the remark 'The past, the sensations of the past. Now!' (*CP*, 146). Describing how invention ground briefly to a halt, O'Hara exposes the effort of maintaining spontaneity. But this effort is exposed only to commemorate the excitement of the poem's resumption 'Now!', as the floodgates of the imagination open again suddenly. Between them is the silence of stalled composition, a silence which – O'Hara says elsewhere – 'returns you to the open fields/ of blandest red honey where the snake waits' (*CP*, 141): like the shoreline crawling with pythons, the fields of honeyed speech and bland abundance are also places where the snake of temptation, of sexual and rhetorical poison, lurks.

The conclusion of 'Second Avenue' asserts boldly that 'You've reached the enormous summit of passion/ which is immobility forging an entrail from the pure obstruction of the air' (*CP*, 150). Rather than relying on the mechanical transcendence of the airship, you arrive at the poem's conclusion through arduous self-exertion. The poem as a 'summit of passion' and expression of high feeling has overcome the obstruction of immobility, creating a channel for the relief of wastes out of the obstructed air itself – out of the surroundings, the city, the poet's experiences. At once a sardonic description of the text as both trail and entrail, and a subversive indication of the zone of pleasure, this anal image at the 'summit' or end of the poem marks the poem's desire not to disappear into ethereal and metaphysical transcendence through flight. It also recalls Tzara's 'Dada Manifesto', in which Tzara describes how '[m]arried to logic, art would live in incest, swallowing, engulfing its own tail, still part of its own body, fornicating within itself, and passion would become a nightmare tarred with Protestantism, a monument, a heap of ponderous grey entrails'. The poem's eschewal of logic threaten to turn the whole of the city, the whole of its own field of operations, into a self-consuming anti-referential artefact, its 'entrail' stuffed in its mouth.

Perhaps O'Hara's insistence that the poem is the product of conscious reflection is a means of claiming back the textual revelations of the unconscious which his associative technique liberates. To avoid literary analysts taking his poem as a compendium of unconscious drives and anxieties, O'Hara asserts their status as verbal objects deliberately manipulated across the poetic surface.[11] If so, how are we to read lines like this one: 'a mammoth/ unstitched from the mighty thigh of the glacier, the Roaring Id' (*CP*, 147)? The prehistoric which has been 'unstitched' from the thigh draws on the mythic story of the origin of Dionysus, the god of wine, madness and freedom from care. Eleutherios embodied combines with the mammoth escaping from the prehistoric ice of the id, awake and roaring. But the mammoth has not liberated itself: it has been 'unstitched', the threads deliberately unpicked by an external agent, by the poetic archaeologist working on the surface.

The 'roaring Id' of 'Second Avenue' speaks of sexuality, violence, depravity and filth. 'Fangs' sink 'upon my brazen throat' (*CP*, 140); children 'bereaved of their doped carts' discover 'priests with lips like mutton in their bedrooms at dawn!' (*CP*, 141); 'snow said, "and doesn't your penis look funny today?!" I jacked "off"' (*CP*, 144); angels are 'discharged for sodomy' (*CP*, 146); and a 'piratish elderly girl' dances past, 'her fan up her ass' (*CP*, 145). These images deface the traditional poetic topoi of childhood innocence, natural pleasance, religion and the beauties of art. On the one hand, they confirm the particular conditions in which O'Hara can evoke artistic illumination: 'your lamp will never light without dirt' (*CP*, 140), he declares. On the other, they revolt specifically against patriarchal prohibitions on his sexuality which O'Hara quotes in the poem: 'My father said, "Do what you want but don't get hurt,/ I'm warning you. Leave the men alone, they'll only tease you"' (*CP*, 148). O'Hara's text can't stop returning to the site of sexual pleasure. 'Steven farted./ He dropped his torpedo into the bathtub' (*CP*, 146). The torpedo is both the child's bath toy, and a metaphor for shit. Here, O'Hara combines references to

---

11 On the links between O'Hara, action painting and the unconscious, see Sweet, 'Parodic Nostalgia for Aesthetic Machismo', pp. 375–76.

anal pleasure and to water: the bath water, or the ocean where the torpedo is fired. Although the torpedo in the bath might also recall Bloom's 'languid floating flower' in the 'Lotus Eaters' episode of *Ulysses*, it is more typical of the poem to fixate on the rectum rather than the anus or the penis as locus of sexual curiosity and delight. The rectum is the body's underground, a place of darkness and wetness. 'Second Avenue' repeatedly displaces the attraction and repulsion of its depths: 'going underground is like discovering something in / your navel that has an odor and is able to fly away' (*CP*, 139–40). Penetrating the surface *is like* discovering something in your navel: the displaced anal cavity releases something which 'can fly away', something autonomous whose flight removes the strangeness of discovery and of its 'odour'. The poem repeatedly lingers on sexual odours: '"You come to me smelling of the shit of Pyrrhian maidens!' (*CP*, 145), 'a whole harem / of swaying odors and caravanserai grit' (*CP*, 145), and 'your languorous black smells' (*CP*, 147). We stink of sex and shit, the poetic dominator assures us, but still we comply, trying to follow the confusing poetic instructions. Later, the poem attacks the reader who 'suddenly got an idea of what black and white poetry / was like, you grinning Simian fart, poseur among idiots / and dilettantes and pederasts' (*CP*, 148). A 'grinning Simian fart', the critic has little feeling for the text, its black and white complexities, but he or she stinks of attitude, and keeps company with 'idiots, dilettantes and pederasts': critical insufficiency is equated with stupidity and a sexual desire driven to prey upon defenceless children. This sexualized attack on the critic corresponds to what I've identified as a sadistic attitude towards his readers. It is also, interestingly, an instance in which O'Hara's aggression towards those who would undermine his desires for superficiality fuses with his anger towards the patriarchal figure who tries to prevent him from mucking about with men.

So, the poem consists of multiple levels: the underground, the ocean, 'high and dry' land, and the heavens. If the underground represents self-consciousness and reflection, it is also an erotogenic zone and a place of burial. But despite his declared preference for surface as the space of life, the depths – associated with criticism, sexuality and mortality – are also places of great attraction. The struggle to escape them can be horrific: 'whose strangeness crushes in the only possible embrace, / is like splintering and pulling and draining the tooth / of the world, the violent alabaster yielding to the sky' (*CP*, 141). The attempt to take flight requires a violent extraction that splinters the tooth of the world. Mortality threatens when no plane can be found: 'No airship casts its shadow down the Road / of the Golden Arm, over which is folded the Canal / and the Shroud' (*CP*, 142). In another scene, children watch a disastrous air show: 'And the simple yet exquisite pertinence of that race / above the airfield, those tubby little planes flopping / competitively into the wind sleeve.' They crumble into giggles 'at each flaming accident', showing no compassion for the pilot's risks and glorious death (*CP*, 143). The poet's self-liberating flight is also a dangerous escapade, requiring heroism and self-exposure. Another figure 'remembered / the many tasks done and forgotten and famous which, / as a pilot, he had disdained, trusting to luck always' (*CP*, 143). There is a reference to Lindberg – '"and then bowed forth screaming 'Lindy Has Made It!'"' (*CP*, 145). While pilots rely on their mechanical gear, the poetic persona can liberate himself from gravity through acceleration. This produces a conflation of poetic risk and heroism with self-destruction and suffering which is typical of O'Hara's poetic personae. The speaker complains that 'I suffer accelerations that are vicarious and serene' (*CP*, 140), as if the poem's 'accelerations' of image and movement are painful.

Acceleration is also a means of avoiding boredom. The poem urges time, language and image into rapid motion; and motion is counterpoised to 'paralysis', an artistic and emotional condition which threatens to halt the flight from the underground and to reduce the poem to a still life. Strong feeling itself can be paralysing and can silence the poetic imagination: 'And then the paralyzing rush / of emotion, its fists caught in Venetian blinds, silent' (*CP*, 148). The Surrealist or Dadaist arrays of objects in his text require an intuitive response, one which moves quickly to keep pace with the exchange of signifiers while retaining a sense of their general emotive drive. As O'Hara writes, 'Except that you react like electricity to a chunk of cloth, / it will disappear like an ape at night' (*CP*, 144). The cloth of the text vanishes from view unless you respond 'like electricity': current, flowing, full of vital force without which the poetic mechanism would grind to a halt. The 'paralytic' is also invoked in a series of lines which are central, in my view, to the poem's depiction of its own activity.

> The houses look old, viscous, and their robes bear
> massive pretenses to anxiety, the animal's dream
> of successiveness, the paralytic's apprehension of germs,
> and then, fleeing! the dancer's nestling into kelp
> and the condemned man's amusement at versatility,
> the judge's ardent approximation of harrowing languor
> in which the pelt of the whole city moves forward as a flame. (*CP*, 142)

Here, we see O'Hara shifting through multiple personae or objects, from houses to robes, to animals, paralytics, dancers, condemned man and judge. These personae are 'enumerated' or listed as temporary stopping-points in the poem's 'fleeing' from those forces which would arrest it: age, viscosity, anxiety, germs, kelp (an entangling sea-plant?), condemnation, languor, even versatility. There is a sense that only a condemned man could be amused at the versatility of which the poem itself is constituted, perhaps because no change is forthcoming which will save him. Perhaps O'Hara, the heroic and daring poetic pilot, is also that condemned man, laughing at his own imaginative versatility.

These personae are exchanged within the city, which is fast changing like a flame. Syntactically, it is not clear if their relation is based on that location or on anxiety: if their attributes are characteristic of their 'pretenses to anxiety' (another qualification which emphasizes performance, like 'pseudo-aggressive'). What the taxonomy achieves however is a distraction from any specific persona as the agent of the poem's development; these identities are exchangeable, ceding each to the next without protest but all embedded in the 'pelt' of the city, its furry hide and its rapid motion. Francis Picabia wrote along similar lines in 1923 of his desire 'to invent, to imagine, to make myself a new man every moment, then forget him, forget everything. We should be equipped with a special eraser, gradually effacing our works and the memory of them. Our brain should be nothing but a blackboard, or white, or better, a mirror in which we would see ourselves for a moment, only to turn our backs on it two minutes later. My ambition is to be a man sterile for others.'[12] Like Picabia, O'Hara's personae are products of invention and forgetting, a refusal of reflection and a desire to be 'sterile for others', to reduce the reader's potential for gain through co-making of the poem's meaning. O'Hara decrees that 'I want listeners to be distracted, as fur rises when most needed/ and walks away to be another affair on another prairie' (*CP*, 145). The distracted reader shows no commitment to determining the significance of any moment, but simply 'walks away' to another affair, another attraction.

So 'Second Avenue' could be described as a catalogue of distractions assembled to alleviate boredom, to transport the reader syntactically away from the stultification of reflection and analysis or the sedimentation of buried and symbolic meanings. Certainly it is a distracted and distracting text. This is not to say that its mind is elsewhere, that the poet or the reader is induced to turn from it to the world beyond: that would suggest a symbolizing operation. Rather, it is absorbed (as a text, by the reader) in its own distracted state. When I use the words 'distraction' and 'absorption', I am not referring only to the condition of the poet or reader in their encounter with the text, but also to qualities manifested by the text itself. On the one hand, there is little use in reconstructing the distraction or absorption of the poet as categories for his poetic labour; that would centre the composition in irrecoverable subjective states. We are reminded of the futility of such manoeuvres by O'Hara himself, with his misleading revelation that everything in the poem 'Second Avenue' 'either happened to me or I felt happening (saw, imagined) on Second Avenue'. In fact, the geographic location gives no insights at all into the text. On the other hand, if we apply the condition of distraction or absorption to the poem itself, then we risk subjectivizing it, imposing a pattern of attentions, deliberations, susceptibility and free associations on the art object itself.

Rather, we might think of the distraction and absorption of 'Second Avenue' as transactional properties, emerging from the friction that builds up between a poet who refuses to surrender his autonomy to analysis or reflection, a poem whose associative speed encourages the reader to accelerate over possible significations while wholly immersed in the textual present, and a reader whose daily habits of

12 Francis Picabia, 'Francis Merci!', in Lucy R. Lippard (ed.), *Dadas on Art* (Englewood Cliffs, NJ: Prentice-Hall, 1971), p. 171.

information-gathering necessitate the development of skills in the rapid discrimination of useful from useless text. A reader establishes patterns and illusions of consecutiveness through selection – in my case, the selection of images of sea, flight, sexual pleasure and the underground, from a text full of other possibilities. 'Second Avenue' teases me about my capacity to make such analytic discriminations. It contrasts with those poems which fixate on a single object, achieving meditative composure and self-absorption by refusing to engage with the other discursive and material frames in which the object is located. Such a willingness to ignore the complicities of the textual material turns such attentive poems into conservative repositories of specificity, and are just as controlled and controlling as O'Hara's circumlocuted text.

A poetics of absorption might be produced from the poet's willingness to expose herself in a moment of poetic intensity to the uninterrupted flow of associations, desires and vectors which themselves take over the poem's order. This seems to be O'Hara's mode in 'Second Avenue': wilful self-exposure to the desire to write, withholding a set of objects or references which might facilitate argument and consecutiveness in order to allow the poem to shape itself by chance. But chance entails repetition; and within those chance operations, repetition leads to the emergence of certain fields of semantic possibility. O'Hara struggles to contain those possibilities, simultaneously disavowing reflection and analysis, and imposing the most stringent form of analysis: one in which his materials are not allowed to be anything other than surface. The problem with a poetics of absorbed distraction, or distracted absorption, of this kind, is that it transforms the poem into an assemblage of fragments whose status in their original (material or language) context is associated with argument, complicity, social or political signification, but which within the almost utopian freedom of the poem are relieved of such entanglements by the professed triviality and automaticity of associations. Such a text also turns the reader into a distracted consumer of alienated situations and contexts not dissimilar to the arrays of optionality offered by the site map, but the ethical habits of selective gathering are not replaced by other forms of advanced attention; instead, the reader is restrained by the tyranny of superficiality into respecting the poet's autonomy, without enjoying any of her own. In that case, freedom is a site of consumption of authorial choices devoid of the ethics of selection, devoid of history or context. If there is anything positive about such freedom, it is that it is illusory.

Stepping Out with Frank O'Hara

David Herd

My interest here is in how the poet thinks. I want to consider how, in what manner, he or she might be thought to know things.[1] I say 'he or she' because to some extent I want the argument to bear generally on poetry. Specifically, though, I'm talking about Frank O'Hara, about how he thinks, and even as I begin to do so I am aware of sounding cumbersome. Here is an example of how O'Hara thinks, from 'Personism: A Manifesto':

> Too many poets act like a middle-aged mother trying to get her kids to eat too much cooked meat, and potatoes with drippings (tears). I don't give a damn whether they eat or not. Forced feeding leads to excessive thinness (effete). Nobody should experience anything they don't need to, if they don't need poetry bully for them. I like the movies too. And after all, only Whitman and Crane and Williams, of the American poets, are better than the movies. As for measure and other technical apparatus, that's just common sense: if you're going to buy a pair of pants you want them to be tight enough so everyone will want to go to bed with you. There's nothing metaphysical about it. Unless, of course, you flatter yourself into thinking that what you're experiencing is 'yearning'. (*CP*, 498)

This is impossible to follow – not that you can't track its meaning, but that you don't want to have to, you don't want to come after it. O'Hara has stolen the show and quite likely what you're experiencing already is yearning. In one sense, of course, you don't have to follow it. 'Personism' is a mock-manifesto. It presents a movement, as O'Hara says, he founded one day after lunch. You can take 'Personism' or leave it. 'There's nothing metaphysical about it.' To follow it, in the name of commentary, is to sound cumbersome. And yet nonchalance is part of the allure, and anyway the thinking of 'Personism' is too quick to let it go. So you go back to O'Hara's manifesto, you try to work out what it thinks. And then, because it's so sure of itself, you try to work out *how* it thinks, something you can only hope to do with any success at all (failure) if you keep in mind the need to be light-footed.

1 I wish to thank colleagues in the Departments of English at Edinburgh and Kent, where this chapter was first presented as a research paper, for their help in developing the ideas presented here.

O'Hara gives us the metaphor of light-footedness for free. Speaking about how poems are made he offers the manifesto's presiding analogy: 'You just go on your nerve. If someone's chasing you down the street with a knife you just run, you don't turn around and shout, "Give it up! I was a track star for Mineola Prep."' It's a defining analogy, but even so I'm aware of contrivance, aware of seeming too easily to bring an argument about O'Hara's thinking round to light-footedness; which is to say that just as one is in danger of over-burdening his thought so one runs the risk of pushing his metaphor too hard; which is to say that in thinking about O'Hara's thinking one puts one's own thinking on trial. Even so, and for all the caveats, as one thinks about O'Hara's style and performance, his way of conducting himself on and off the page, one quite readily finds oneself thinking about the way he places his feet.

One thinks about it because he thinks about it, and though of course one can always find evidence of a preoccupation, it is clear that in O'Hara's poetry he allows his thought to settle around the gesture of the step. One thinks of him – because he thinks of himself this way – as stepping out into the New York street. The photograph on the back of Brad Gooch's biography, taken on 20 January 1960 by Fred W. McDarrah, shows him, one foot on the ground, one foot raised, exiting the swing doors at the Museum of Modern Art.[2] He frequently pictures himself walking in his poetry, of course, and in walking arrives at some of his most memorable poems – though I will want to make a distinction later between the walk and the step. In one of his love poems, 'Steps' (written for the dancer Vincent Warren), he presents himself in a New York pictured 'like Ginger Rogers in *Swingtime*'. Others present him this way too. James Schuyler remembered him as 'the most elegant person I ever met' and how he 'moved lightly on the balls of this feet, like a dancer or somebody about to dive into waves'.[3] For Charles Olson, making the step a matter of poetics, 'He was the other poet for all of us to have lived out the rest of the century by [...] he was so capable of footing the measure once his feet were on the way'.[4] Then, in the poet's portrait at the hand of Larry Rivers, it was O'Hara's feet above all that got the attention, Rivers having O'Hara pose nude but for a pair of boxing boots.

And so one could set about tracking the trope, because there is no question that the footstep is a trope in O'Hara. One would have fun doing so and in having the fun one would be appreciating an aspect of O'Hara's thought. But the fun isn't equal to the thought, and the play of the metaphor isn't equal to the achievement of the poetry. Because in O'Hara, as Olson suggests, the step is a measure: is the way, in his thinking, he gets a measure of the world.

The argument here, then, is this: that the step, in O'Hara's poetry, is integral to his thinking, that in thinking he steps, that in stepping he thinks; that the term, in its recurrence in the poetry, works as metaphor but also as the trace of gesture, and

2 Brad Gooch, *City Poet: The Life and Times of Frank O'Hara* (New York: Alfred A. Knopf, 1993).
3 Bill Berkson and Joe LeSueur (eds.), *Homage to Frank O'Hara* (Berkeley: Big Sky, 1978), p. 82.
4 Berkson and LeSueur (eds.), *Homage*, p. 178.

that in the combination of metaphor and gesture is the order of O'Hara's thought. Or as I put it just now, following Olson, 'the measure'. The step, I want to argue, is the measure of O'Hara's thinking, which is as much as to say that it is the prosody of his cognition. Of all poets it can be said of Frank O'Hara that there is something, in his poetry, he gets to know. What he gets to know is his relation to his world, New York. And the way he gets to know it – in the fullest possible sense of the term – is by stepping it out. All of which will be to advance a point about O'Hara in particular, but will also be to make a point more generally about contemporary critical practice; that these days, in British universities not least, it is good to give thought to the matter of measure.

Prosody and Cognition

'Prosody as Cognition' is Simon Jarvis's phrase.[5] In addressing the network of issues – call it a can of worms – the phrase indicates, Jarvis's overarching objective is to move towards a language for the discussion of literature which is not borrowed from another practice; a language that speaks to the character and impulse of literature, but which is also, nonetheless, legitimate. As Jarvis thinks of literature it is poetry he has in mind, and so it is natural enough that his thinking turns towards prosody. Except that on arriving at prosody he finds that the damage has already been done. Hephaestion's *Handbooklet*, he observes,

> already represents an advanced stage of oblivion of the bodily experience which lies, desiccated, inside its own terminology: its feet not only no longer dance but cannot remember why they bear their name or why they might need to ask about it.[6]

The problem, animated by the image of the dancing feet, is that on arriving at the language of prosody one doesn't find, as one might hope, a language instinct with the movement of poetry. This is to make a general point, no doubt, about metrics, about how the language of metre seems not best cultivated to tell us what we want to know when we consult it. The real point, though, for Jarvis, is that it was always thus. Which is to say that you go to prosody, the language of the music of poetry, and what you find is number. The impulse in prosody is to enumerate the points of stress, and so the 'bodily experience' which one might want to think informs poetry, 'lies, desiccated, inside its own terminology'. This criticism seems broadly true to the practice of scanning, even as it points in passing to a thought in Derrida which has to give one pause. As Derrida reads Rousseau on melody, Rousseau seeks to deny the imported character of harmony, which is to say the supplementary complication by number: which observation, on the one hand, should warn us against naivety, but which might also seem, on the other, to permit any manner of measure (trouble).

---

5 Simon Jarvis, 'Prosody as Cognition', *Critical Quarterly* 40.4 (1998), pp. 3–15.
6 Jarvis, 'Prosody as Cognition', p. 5.

The question is, how troubled should we be? Conventional prosody, as Jarvis sees it, misrepresents, or at least mechanizes, the aesthetic experience it is meant to help understand. More than this, the language of prosody matters because what it claims to register is emphasis, where emphasis, understood in the context of poetry, is the attribution of meaning to the passage of time. Hence the call, as Jarvis articulates it, for a new method of prosody. More than this still, emphasis, being the ground of poetry, is the attribution or discovery or creation of meaning, and cognition, the way we get to know things, is not thinkable without emphasis. Somewhere, then, in prosody, is the possibility of knowledge. Which means that the search is on for an appropriate measure.

Broadly speaking Jarvis's objective is to rescue the body of poetry from its mechanical foot, from analysis and composition by, as Pound put it, the metronome; and since it is regularity and routine that are at issue it is no surprise that what Jarvis's argument should eventually point towards is not another universally applicable measure, but an approach which 'place[s] the individual poetic authorship at its centre'.[7] Which is to say that what we should think about are cases – about how in any given body of work its prosody informs and is informed by its material – and it is in this spirit that in a moment I will return, via William Carlos Williams, to O'Hara. For a moment, though, I want to stick with prosody and cognition as an abstract relation, and in doing so I want to think for a moment about Heidegger, Heidegger providing a background (and counter) to O'Hara's step.

Heidegger addresses the question of prosody and cognition in, among other settings, the lectures entitled *Was heisst Denken?* – where as he examines both what is called thinking but also what calls for thinking, he asks whether it is possible, in thinking about thinking, to think about poetry. Heidegger doesn't mention prosody as such in *Was heisst Denken?* but there is unmistakably a prosody to his thought there (especially if we want to insist on the rejuvenated body of poetry), the prosody of Heidegger's lecture being the *leap*. Which is to say that in thinking about poetry and thought Heidegger repeatedly returns to the metaphor of the leap. The leap is the measure he alights on for the way poetry and thinking work. It is in the leap, so he wants to persuade us, that his discourse finds its natural pace.

The 'leap' is a most appealing metaphor. It implies adventure and radical disjunction. As it claims to catch the movement of poetry it surely promises to free it from the regularity of number. What it claims, as metaphor, to show, is that however one might account for the process of poetry's sound, what one also has to appreciate is its uncontainability, its unpredictability as act of thought. We need for a while, Heidegger says, to 'keep the distance needed for a running start by which one or the other of us may succeed in leaping into thinking'.[8] 'There is no bridge here,' he

7   Jarvis, 'Prosody as Cognition', p. 12.
8   Martin Heidegger, 'What Calls for Thinking?', in *Basic Writings*, ed. David Farrell Krell (London: Routledge, 1993), p. 373.

asserts a little later '– only the leap.'[9]

As earlier with O'Hara, I want to try to resist the sway of Heidegger's metaphor. It is, after all, a compelling image. One only has to say ' – only the leap' and one gets all 'leapy', as if in saying *leap* one had actually *leapt* into thought. What I want to distinguish, rather, is the way the gesture works in to Heidegger's thinking about thinking, the way the leap doesn't so much describe as inform and shape his sense of cognition. Which leads one to notice that the leap, for all that it would seem to imply adventure and advance, is, in fact, a movement back. It takes a little while for this to come through. What Heidegger tells us at first is that 'the leap takes us to a place where everything is strange'. The truer statement of the leap's trajectory, however, implies not simply a strange place but a place that, strangely, we should recognize as home. 'They can never again,' he says of the sciences, 'by their own power [...] make the leap back into the source from whence they have sprung.'[10] It is important to hear the play of the German in this, the fact that in source, or origin, *Ursprung*, one locates the act of leaping, *springen*; which is to say that for Heidegger the leap and the source are on the closest possible terms.

Heidegger's 'leap' is very much his own. The way he helps us here is in the relation he constructs between prosody and cognition. The leap, as he presents it in the lectures, is the fundamental movement and pace of thought. He can't think about thinking without the leap. Prosody, from this point of view, is not brought in to organize the poetry of Heideggerian thought but is, rather, integral to it. What the Heideggerian leap tells us is that underpinning his thought is an act of faith. You can only leap, after all, if you are confident you will be held, that at some level or other in leaping you will be caught.

O'Hara, it will be recalled, doesn't share Heidegger's confidence.

> As for measure and other technical apparatus, that's just common sense [...]. There's nothing metaphysical about it. Unless, of course, you flatter yourself into thinking that what you're experiencing is 'yearning'.

O'Hara doesn't yearn and he doesn't look back. He is, though, for all his insouciance no less serious about the relation between prosody and cognition. The difference is that he thinks that relation in the tradition of American poetics, a tradition that thinks of poetry not primarily, as Jarvis and Heidegger do, in terms of temporality, but, as Olson insisted, primarily in terms of space.

Williams' Step

The American poetic tradition is distinguished not least by the thought it has given to the matter of measure. In O'Hara's time the poet most conspicuously engaged in this enquiry was Olson – Olson, in the early 1950s, like Heidegger, addressing

9   Heidegger, 'What Calls for Thinking?', p. 373.
10   Heidegger, 'What Calls for Thinking?', p. 382.

the question of prosody as a response, in part, to the preferred metrics of the contemporary university. For Heidegger the issue is the prevalence of methodologies governed by a technical sense of scientific inquiry. 'Is there any place compelling us more forcibly to rack our brains than the research and training institutions pursuing scientific work?'[11] He says 'research and training institutions' but the phrase is a substitute for 'universities'. We should not pass over, in this Anglo-American context, the use of the word 'rack'.[12] We should not pass over, equally, the distinction Heidegger prepares in this sentence between 'research', 'training' and 'thinking'. For Heidegger, then, the cognitive prosody obscured by the practices of the university is that of the 'leap'. For Olson, at Black Mountain College, the objective, as stated in his earliest manifesto 'Projective Verse', was to found a version of the academy on the issue of the breath. 'Verse now,' he asserts – in one of those magisterial poetic statements O'Hara was so keen ('dripping') to avoid – 'if it is to go ahead, if it is to be of *essential* use, must, I take it, catch up and put into itself certain laws and possibilities of the breath, of the breathing of the man who writes as well as of his listening.' Olson would thus seem to satisfy the need to recover the 'desiccated body of poetry' from the machinery of prosody, but, as it turns out, only at the cost of a sentimental division. He notes in poetry two halves, 'the HEAD, by way of the EAR, to the SYLLABLE/ the HEART, by way of the BREATH, to the LINE'. [13] This is not an opposition it is easy to maintain now, and Olson's investment in breath as a unit of measure has suffered as a consequence. But then it sat somewhat oddly in his open field poetics anyway, a method of composition informed by Olson's stronger observation of the emphasis in American poetics on space. Thinking this through in *Call Me Ishmael*, he identified in Melville a foundational gesture, 'a way of reaching back through time until he got history pushed back so far he turned time into space'.[14]

Thoreau stood behind Olson on this question also. Witness the opening of *Walden*: 'When I wrote the following pages, or rather the bulk of them, I lived alone, in the woods, a mile from any neighbor'.[15] Just far enough that he could do things differently, but not so far, as Stanley Cavell notes, that he could be ignored, and where what Thoreau's neighbours couldn't ignore him doing was measuring things contrariwise.[16] As Emerson recalled:

11 Heidegger, 'What Calls for Thinking?', p. 378.
12 Heidegger's 'dass wir uns den Kopf zerbrechen' plays on the German for 'to break one's head', which can be taken both metaphorically (Heidegger's primary meaning) and, being only slightly mischievous, literally. It is not therefore, perhaps, too great a leap to catch the sound of the rack in 'to rack our brains'.
13 Charles Olson 'Projective Verse', in Robert Creeley (ed.), *Selected Writings of Charles Olson* (New York: New Directions, 1966), pp. 15, 19.
14 Charles Olson, *Call Me Ishmael* (Baltimore and London: The Johns Hopkins University Press, 1997), p. 14.
15 Henry David Thoreau, *Walden* (Oxford: Oxford University Press, 1999), p. 6.
16 Stanley Cavell, *The Senses of Walden: An Expanded Edition* (Chicago and London: University of Chicago Press, 1992), p. 27.

He could pace sixteen rods more accurately than any other man could measure them with a rod and chain. [...] From a box containing a bushel or more of loose pencils, he could take up with his hands fast enough just a dozen pencils at every grasp.[17]

It's the 'pace' not the pencils I want to pick out here, the image of Thoreau measuring a distance by pacing it out, and where a pace, as Thoreau the Latinist would have known, means the stretch of a leg. William Carlos Williams would have known that also, and in the American tradition it was Williams – 'better than the movies'– who gave the fullest thought to the question of the poet's measure. As he says, in his utterly ground-breaking volume *Spring and All*, his intention there is

the annihilation of strained associations, complicated ritualistic form designed to separate the work from 'reality' – such as rhyme, meter as meter and not the essential of the work, one of its words.[18]

There is a reading of this kind of statement in Williams which would find in it an unstudied sense of priority, as if the object of his experimentalism was to clean poetry's act up, make it more receptive to what is given. This reading would understand Williams as writing a found poetry, as taking his terms and his forms from what happened, in New Jersey, to be lying around him. This seems to me a wrong way to present Williams; and wrong in ways that can affect one's reading of O'Hara. What Williams criticizes in his statement is not the failure of art to match up to reality, but the failure to recognize that the presumed separation is false in the first place. And consonant with this resistance to the imagery of separation is the desire for a continuity of prosody with the body of the work. What Williams seeks is an idea of prosody where metre (as metre) is not something imported, but where, as he puts it, metre is 'the essential of the work', or as he puts it better, 'one of its words'.

The word is 'step'. The word throughout *Spring and All* is 'step'. Thus as Williams writes, in the marvellously knowing, Whitmanesque prose overture with which the volume begins:

Every step once taken in the first advance of the human race, from the amoeba to the highest type of intelligence, has been duplicated, every step exactly paralleling the one that preceded in the dead ages, gone by. [...]

At this point the entire complicated and laborious process begins to near a new day. But for the moment everything is fresh, perfect, recreated.

In fact now, for the first time, everything IS new.[19]

17 Ralph Waldo Emerson, 'Biographical Sketch', in Henry David Thoreau, *Excursions* (New York: Corinth Books, 1962), p. 15.
18 William Carlos Williams, *Collected Poems I 1909–1939* (New York: New Directions, 1986), p. 189.
19 Williams, *Collected Poems I*, p. 181.

This, it needs to be kept in mind, is prologue. The poem that is being heralded hasn't arrived yet. Much, though, inevitably, is now expected of it. A great deal for Williams, in other words, rests on the step, on the step he is about to take: 'now, for the first time, everything IS new'. The reason Williams can make this claim – and the reason the claim comes in fact not to seem unfounded – is that in the idea of the step he is persuaded that he has established the prosody of cognition. As he reflects later in the volume, regarding his failure previously to achieve what he has achieved in *Spring and All*:

> though I have felt 'free' only in the presence of works of the imagination, knowing the quickening of the sense which came of it […] yet being of a slow but accurate understanding, I have not always been able to complete the intellectual steps which would make me firm in the position.[20]

Or as he says of aesthetic experience:

> The reason people marvel at works of art and say: How in Christ's name did he do it? – is that they know nothing of the physiology of the nervous system and have never in their experience witnessed the larger processes of the imagination.
>
> It is a step over from the profitless engagements of the arithmetical.[21]

Here, then, we are back to number, to the arithmetical measure against which Williams wishes to pose the intellectual 'step'. The impression he wants to give is that he can't do without the term. Just as to understand Heidegger we have to grasp the leap, so with Williams we have to appreciate that the 'step' is cognate with his understanding, that it is integral to his thinking about thinking. That thinking (like the step) is, as he conceives it, incremental; that it is tentative and wary; that it is inquiring and uncertain, that as such it is properly exploratory. And then, above all, what we have to appreciate is that in the step, what Williams considers himself to have identified is the measure of the passage of a body through time into space.

Here, then, is the opening of the poem Williams identifies as number 1:

By the road to the contagious hospital
under the surge of the blue
mottled clouds driven from the
northeast – a cold wind. Beyond, the
waste of broad, muddy fields
brown with dried weeds, standing and fallen

patches of standing water
the scattering of tall trees

All along the road the reddish
purplish, forked, upstanding twiggy

20 Williams, *Collected Poems I*, p. 210.
21 Williams, *Collected Poems I*, p. 210.

stuff of bushes and small trees
with dead, brown leaves under them
leafless vine –

Lifeless in appearance, sluggish
Dazed spring, approaches – [22]

This is a quiet poem that makes an extraordinary claim. The extraordinary claim is that here, for the first time, spring has finally arrived. The claim, manifestly, is unsustainable – with the qualification that just possibly what Williams establishes here is a measure for transition. What I want to draw attention to in the poem are the parts of speech: the arrangement of prepositions that shape the opening stanza – the 'By', 'to', 'under', 'from', and 'beyond'; the noun phrases of the second strophe; the fact that it is not until the fourth strophe (and the third, as it were, sentence) that we get a main verb ('approaches'). What Williams presents, in other words, is a poetry of things and relations between things, a poem whose basic measure has to be thought of not as time but as space. All of which is decidedly spring-like. The subject of Williams' fundamentally traditional poem is the emergence of new life, where what new life establishes first and foremost is room, where the objective, in a physical sense, is definition; and where the measure of this activity is the incremental step: 'One by one objects are defined'. 'Now,' as the poem puts it, 'the stark dignity of/ entrance'.

Melville, as Olson put it, had a 'a way of reaching back through time until he got history pushed so far he turned time into space'. Williams shows present time becoming present space: one by one; all along; the stark dignity of entrance. He has arrived, in 'Spring and All', at a prosody for his cognition: what he was happy to term the 'intellectual step'.

A Step Away From Them

Like Williams, O'Hara is suspicious of a prosody that construes 'meter as meter and not the essential of the work, one of its words'. Which is, of course, to overstate the matter:

> if you're going to buy a pair of pants you want them to be tight enough so everyone will want to go to bed with you.

From which it can sound as if discussion of O'Hara and technique is redundant, as if in some casual, commonsense way he had got beyond such concerns. And in one sense this is what one is to conclude: if, that is, talk of technique reverts too readily to a borrowed or an imported idiom. But we should not mistake insouciance for indifference. O'Hara, that is, can say what he does about apparatus because he has thought so intelligently about technique. As a consequence of which thought

22 Williams, *Collected Poems I*, p. 183.

the achievement and drama of his poetry can well be understood as a matter of measure.

That O'Hara thought hard about technique is apparent in his art criticism. A deeply committed art critic, almost all of whose criticism was devoted to artists for whom he had an enthusiasm, O'Hara's discussions – as is more the way with art criticism than with literary criticism – lingered lovingly over the question of the artist's technique. From which it follows that sometimes the criticism is an act of pure description. In 'Porter Paints a Picture', for example, O'Hara dwells at length on Fairfield Porter's selection of materials: 'For the first oil sketch he used sized canvas but did not spread it with medium first, as is often done, because it makes colors blend more than he wanted them to' (*SS*, 54). What matters as O'Hara presents a painting is not so much what it means as that, and how, it was made – to understand how it was made, the thought goes, being to understand its significance. It is an idea forwarded by Williams. 'Only,' he proposes in *Spring and All*, 'as the work was produced, in that way alone can it be understood.' Not that O'Hara's criticism is purely description. Elsewhere, more speculatively, technique is more closely aligned with what one could call content but which is perhaps better understood in this context as 'insight'. Thus, as he puts it in his account of Pollock: 'In the state of spiritual clarity there are no secrets. […] This is not a mystical state, but the accumulation of decisions along the way and the eradication of conflicting beliefs toward the total engagement of the spirit in the expression of meaning' (*AC*, 25). The decisions in question are technical and they represent, in Pollock in particular, a process of elimination through which he arrives at a technique equal to the significance he desires to present.

The continuity in O'Hara's art criticism is the integrity to it of his discussion of technique: integrity in that the discussion is central to the criticism itself, but integrity also in that the sense and language of technique varies substantively from work to work. This is measure as essence, not measure as measure, measure as one of the creation's words. Likewise, I want to suggest, in O'Hara's own creations the drama and inquiry invariably turns on the question of what constitutes the appropriate measure. This, I take it, is the point of his marvellously mischievous poem 'Khrushchev is coming on the right day' (*CP*, 340), where the poem, rather than acceding to an account of the day in question which reduces it to its headline event, offers instead a poet's report. Similarly, 'The Day Lady Died', where O'Hara's elegiac question is how to get the measure of the death of Billie Holiday, and where the decision, as it turns out, is to recall the fact that on hearing the news O'Hara was shopping for gifts. Both poems find O'Hara characteristically in motion. In both poems, as he tries to get the measure of the situation, he generates a sense of space. This, as he understood it, was the poet's task – at least as that task is articulated in 'A True Account of Talking to the Sun at Fire Island', where the sun tells O'Hara:

always embrace things, people earth
sky stars, as I do, freely and with
the appropriate sense of space. (*CP*, 307)

Metaphorically speaking, in so far as what is at issue is appropriateness – fitness, to take a word from Whitman – what these various gestures might be said to amount to is 'buying a pair of pants': except that as one moves away from 'Personism' what becomes apparent is that O'Hara's self-presentation there is not sufficient. What's at issue in O'Hara is the prosody of cognition, where prosody (as with technique in painting) is integral to insight. For O'Hara, as for Williams, it is an issue that goes to the heart of his work, and is nowhere more consciously explored than in his reflective masterpiece, 'In Memory of My Feelings'.

'In Memory of My Feelings' has a special status in O'Hara's career. For an otherwise frighteningly prolific poet, the period prior to the composition of 'In Memory of My Feelings' had, as Joe LeSueur tells us, been relatively unproductive.[23] The previous three months he had been out of New York, at the Poets' Theatre in Cambridge, and during that time he had written almost no poetry. A special significance of 'In Memory of My Feelings', then, is that the poem finds O'Hara remembering what it is that he does. In a lifetime of being, poetically speaking, in the action, this poem finds him reflecting on the act. 'In Memory of My Feelings', in other words, unusually for O'Hara, is an *ars poetica*.[24]

One way of reading the poem is as a drama of the self, poetic or otherwise, as a presentation of a self seeking to protect itself in a life of scrutiny and high exposure. Such a reading of the poem is hardly wrong – 'In Memory of My Feelings' is hardly *not* about the self – the drama of the poetic self being apparent from the poem's opening lines:

My quietness has a man in it, he is transparent
and he carries me quietly, like a gondola, through the streets.
He has several likenesses, like stars and years, like numerals. (*CP*, 252)

Quite clearly there's a self at issue here, in the man and in his transparency, in the quietness, and the likenesses, in the general sense of vulnerability. But there is an issue, also, of what one might term conduct – an issue raised by the word 'carries'; an issue of conduct which passes into a question of measure as it alights on the term 'numerals'. To spell this out, one way of reading this poem of the vulnerable self is as a poem, also, and centrally, of measure, where the question throughout is whether one thing, a self, can be rendered in terms of – can be likened to – another. Or to put it another way, the question the poem asks is how can it, as

---

23 Joe LeSueur, *Digressions on Some Poems by Frank O'Hara* (New York: Farrar, Straus and Giroux, 2004), p. 100.

24 Unusually but not exceptionally; 'Memorial Day 1950', with its comparable gesture of recollection, being another work which consciously reflects on O'Hara's thought.

poem, be most like itself? What language best articulates what *it* is? How, really, is *it* carried?

One language which is tried, and which comically fails, is the language of what one might call epoch. At various moments in the poem O'Hara tries on – quite uncharacteristically – a sort of mythic-historical mode. The Chinese are here, imagined at some putative high point of their cultural trajectory; we glimpse the French Revolution, we hear news of the Greeks. This is a poem that, as one of its procedures, is making leaps. And in another poet, Ezra Pound say, the leaps would arrive at something, at a sense of the accumulated achievements, perhaps, of human culture. Here, though, the achievements don't stack up, rendered cumbersome in their abstraction:

> For we have advanced, France,
> together into a new land, like the Greeks, where one feels nostalgic
> for mere ideas, where truth lies on its deathbed like an uncle
> and one of me has a sentimental longing for number (*CP*, 254–55)

What is at issue here is the question of measure, of how one gets the measure of, as O'Hara indicates, 'truth', and where truth, as the poem suggests later on, might be thought of as something like lived history. A history of ideas won't do, though one can feel nostalgic for it. Nor will 'number' suffice. In fact number, the numbering of truth and experience, is what the poem is most keen to declare itself against. 'Numerals', it will be recalled from the beginning of the poem, are one of the 'likenesses', one of the forms of measure the poem means to address, and at various points throughout its five sections it flirts with the sense-making quality of number. But the numbers are always unequal, witness the scrambled sense of the poet's own biography:

> My 10 my 19,
> my 9, and the several years. My
> 12 years since they all died, philosophically speaking. (*CP*, 254)

'In Memory of My Feelings', then, finds O'Hara coming back to poetry, and in so doing recollecting the nature of the act, reflecting on the questions of what poetry is and does. In that process the poem acts out, at the level of aesthetics, the variousness that is its advertised sense of self. Which is not to say that all aesthetic modes are here. But it is to say that in this poem of July–August 1956, as he reacquaints himself with the quality and nature of his art, O'Hara casts widely among procedures and idioms for an idea of measure equal to his contemporary understanding of the poem. Which is, with Marjorie Perloff, to hear in the poem's five sections and its recurring quest imagery a trying out of *The Waste Land*. Which is to notice the poem's name-checking of Romanticism, its Whitmanesque 'globe of spit'. Which is to hear the poem shuttling between the surreal (without which it couldn't exist linguistically speaking) and the historic, between Poundian Kulchurpronouncements and fragments of autobiographical fact. And perhaps because this poem is a recollection, a reflection *on* the act of writing, this trying out (and casting off) of others' modes and measures is quite largely the fabric of the poem. Which is to say that this brilliant poem of self and measure can be thought also to fail, finally, in its attempt to get the measure of itself, in its attempt fully to name a measure by which an O'Hara poem itself might be carried. Except perhaps in fragments. Except, perhaps, in the definition of 'humanism' as 'the mere existence of emphasis'. Except, perhaps, in the final section where, as opposed to the numerous 'sordid identifications' it is the serpent's turn, and where the serpent says what it's like to be him:

> When you turn your head
> can you feel your heels, undulating? that's what it is
> to be a serpent. (*CP*, 256)

The serpent's question tells us something very important and also not quite enough. 'In Memory of My Feelings' was a major summation, as he turned 30, of O'Hara's aesthetic inheritance and understanding. In its variousness it defines – and declares the obsolescence of – the modes of measure that have come to inform its own. It is perhaps in the nature of the poem's retrospective task, though, that this last, the poem's own measure, is less than fully articulated. Except that we glimpse it there, in the serpent's 'undulating' 'heels'. And except that we find it expressed fully and beautifully in the poem O'Hara wrote next, the poem 'In Memory of My Feelings' can be thought to have prepared for: 'A Step Away From Them'.

One way of reading 'A Step Away From Them' is as a poem of and about time, as a poem caught in and looking to deny time, a poem striving to keep pace with the event. The poem was composed the day after Jackson Pollock's funeral. Time *is* very much on O'Hara's mind. He hasn't much of it. He seeks to register time's effects. But in the history of a culture and a consciousness whose primary fact, as Olson argued, is space, it is necessary also to appreciate 'A Step Away From Them' as a spatial event.

'A Step Away From Them' is spatial in the sense that 'Spring and All' is spatial, in the sense of its parts of speech: in its 'among', 'down', 'from', 'onto', 'over', 'above' and 'up'. In 'Spring and All' what gave rise to this prepositional sense of space was the emergence of new life, of new things establishing a space for themselves upon the dignity of their entrance. In 'A Step Away From Them' what initiates the sense of space is death, a sense that with the deaths of Bunny Lang, John Latouche and Jackson Pollock, the space of the living has been drastically diminished. 'But is the/ earth as full,' the poem asks, yearningly, as 'life was full, of them'. To which question the poem's response is to fill life, to create a space in which the fullness of life can be registered: 'among', 'down', 'from', 'onto', 'over', 'above' and 'up'. The sun's injunction to the poet on 'Fire Island' was to 'embrace things [...]/ freely and with/ the appropriate sense of space'. 'A Step Away From Them', not least in the advertised warmth of its racial politics, is a freely created space.

Where 'A Step Away From Them' differs from 'Spring and All' is in its sense of movement. At which point it is necessary to return to O'Hara himself, to the way he conducted himself and to the way others pictured him. Many of these pictures were offered in response to Bill Berkson and Joe LeSueur's call for a book-length *Homage to Frank O'Hara*, and what a number of friends were keen to bring attention to was the way O'Hara carried himself in his environment. Schuyler's elegy, 'To Frank O'Hara', like his prose tribute, pictures O'Hara 'poised on the balls/ of your feet ready/ to dive'. Peter Schjeldahl recalls how '[his] every movement bespoke will and self assurance, a kind of unmannered courtliness'.[25] For Laurence Osgood, 'When he walked down the street, Frank held his head tipped up as if he had perfect confidence'.[26] Joe Brainard remembered

> Frank O'Hara's walk. Light and sassy. With a slight twist and a slight bounce. With the top half of his body slightly thrust forward. Head back. It was a beautiful walk. Casual. Confident.[27]

It was a thing, in other words, that people noticed about O'Hara, the way he carried himself. He had a way of walking that people noticed, a characteristic step. O'Hara noticed it in himself also, of course, hence the closing lines of 'In Memory of My Feelings', where the serpent feels his heels. But it is there, also, in the grace of the poem's opening statement: 'My quietness has a man in it, he is transparent/ and he carries me quietly, like a gondola, through the streets'. Here, then, O'Hara pictures himself carrying himself, pictures himself as others came to see him. He is looking to catch himself in the act here, trying to get the manner of his composition. The name he gives to that state is 'quietness', the concentration necessary for poems.[28] What he wants to present, at the beginning and the end of 'In Memory of My Feelings', is the measure of his thought. And he almost does, but doesn't quite. Almost has the word, but stops just short. Actually to catch O'Hara catching himself, the poem to consider is 'A Step Away From Them'. It is there that he's in the act, there that metre, as Williams put it, becomes one of the words, in that poem that O'Hara settles on the prosody of his cognition.

If O'Hara is not actually writing as he walks, in 'A Step Away From Them', he is thinking, as he walks, of what he will write very shortly. He is composing as he steps; the step, throughout, is the measure of his composition. And then as he steps he becomes acquainted with the environment that forms the fabric of his poem. Like Thoreau, then, what O'Hara establishes is a human measure, a

25 Berkson and LeSueur (eds.), *Homage*, p. 141.
26 Berkson and LeSueur (eds.), *Homage*, p. 24.
27 Berkson and LeSueur (eds.), *Homage*, p. 168.
28 I consider the issue of O'Hara's 'quietness' at greater length in *Enthusiast! Essays on Modern American Literature* (Manchester: Manchester University Press, 2007).

prosody of cognition which finds its metric in (his own) human form. Where he differs from Thoreau is in the sense of distance at which he operates; and one can say in Thoreau's favour that the 'mile' he put between himself and his neighbours permitted a degree of critique that O'Hara's writing lacked. But by the same token what O'Hara discerned in that distance was a Romantic illusion, as if it were possible to stand somewhere where one could imagine oneself not involved with, not complicit in, events. As he put it with reference to *Doctor Zhivago*:

> What, then, after rejecting the concept of the Romantic 'pose' in relation to his own life and art, does Pasternak's position become? [...] In a later volume he chooses the title from a poem, 'My Sister Life'. This expresses very clearly his position: the poet and life walk hand in hand. Life is not a landscape before which the poet postures, but the very condition of his inspiration in a deeply personal way: 'My sister, life, is in flood today...' (*CP*, 503)

What I want to say here is that the condition of O'Hara's inspiration became 'the step', that 'the step' became the prosody of his cognition. By which I don't want to try to insist that the step was the governing (which is to say limiting) principle throughout O'Hara's work; rather that at least from the mid-1950s onwards his thinking settled happily around the gesture of the step. Which in one way is to consolidate a not unfamiliar point. Poets, at least since Romanticism, have been thought of as walkers. City poets since Baudelaire, and including O'Hara, have, as Geoff Ward has articulated eloquently, been comprehended in terms of the *flâneur*.[29] O'Hara was both a walker, and in walking a *flâneur*, but he was as well, in a very full sense, in a sense that I think the idea of the 'step' helps catch, a thinker *in* poems.

To spell this out: Heidegger developed his sense of 'leap' through his articulation of philosophy in relation to poetry, where the poem, in the special sense Heidegger accords it, is that which almost uniquely among the productions of human thought has access to being. The leap is thus the prosody of Heideggerian cognition, which is to say the measure of his ontology; a movement of thought out from and towards its origin which the numerals of technology and the technocratic institution are always threatening to obscure. When O'Hara steps, I want to suggest, he steps away from poetic ontology. He steps rather than leaps because, for O'Hara, there is nothing ready made, no spring to spring back to, no originary space. Rather there is the space that the poem, as it steps, has to open up, the space of the poem; the space the poem creates and in which it becomes itself. It is in the act of *stepping*, I want to suggest, that such space is generated.

As with 'In Memory of My Feelings', there are, in 'A Step Away From Them', competing measures at work. The whole poem is framed, from one point of view, by the constraints of the working day. It is the poet's lunch hour. He has to get

---

29 Geoff Ward, *Statutes of Liberty: The New York School of Poets* (London: Macmillan, 1993), pp. 137–39.

back. The clock is ticking. He looks at 'bargains in wristwatches'. It is '12:40 of/ a Thursday' (*CP*, 257). Against these temporal, and inevitably capitalistic, drivers O'Hara places the step: light and graceful, poised and human; incremental, which means that nothing is taken for granted; 'undulating', which means that in the step's conduct there is a relatedness to perception; creative, in that, in the step away, just sufficient distance for imaginative reconstruction opens up.

> A step.
> There is a step.
> O'Hara takes a step.

All of which said, I am aware of sounding cumbersome, of not catching the full achievement of O'Hara's step. But that's okay because that's what the poems do. Or to put it another way, what O'Hara does as he steps things out is insist, always, on poetry's own measure. He steps back to work but:

<blockquote>
My heart is in my
pocket, it is Poems by Pierre Reverdy. (*CP*, 258)
</blockquote>

'A Certain Kneeness':
The Boring and the New
in Frank O'Hara's Poetry

Tadeusz Pióro

'The avant-garde has been made up, I think, completely, and all through history, with people who are *bored* by other people's ideas' (*SS*, 9), Frank O'Hara told Edward Lucie-Smith in 1965, narrowing down to vanguard art Larry Rivers' earlier claim, in a 1959 interview with O'Hara, that 'the history of art and the history of each artist's development are the response to the discomforts of *boredom*'. O'Hara's observation pertains to individuals and their subjective appraisals of the 'ideas' in question, rather than to the avant-garde as a historicized and ideologically determinable construct. Emphasis on the individual seems inevitable here, for boredom is always – and merely – whatever you or I say it is. Neither Rivers nor O'Hara was trying to define the avant-garde in theoretical terms, and it is not surprising that production, reception and historical context blend into one another in these remarks. Their insights, however, refer only to the initial impulse to experiment, or 'make it new', and not to what enables an already vanguard artist to stay vanguard. If this were to be, above all else, boredom, Frank O'Hara during the last ten or twelve years of his life would hardly have qualified as an avant-garde poet. Whenever he mentions boredom explicitly in his poems, there is nothing inspiring about it, and even a suspicion that he might get bored in any kind of circumstances makes him act in self-defence: 'I drink to kill the fear of boredom, the mounting panic of it' (*CP*, 330). Commenting on these lines from 'Joe's Jacket', Patsy Southgate said that 'the reason he drank so much was out of boredom. I think that his mind and body worked at a far faster rate than most people's. Part of the effect of the alcohol was to slow him down to a more normal metabolism.'[1] Clearly, this is a different kind of boredom to the one O'Hara invokes in his remarks about the avant-garde. It brings no productive impulse and is rather similar, as I will later argue, to Baudelairean spleen. Still, boredom and the vanguard enter into an uneasy and vague alliance in at least one major poem by O'Hara, 'Poem Read at Joan Mitchell's', written in 1957.

In this poem, O'Hara plays on the notion of the 'vanguard', using it along with a string of other adjectives to describe Jane Freilicher's decision to marry Joe Hazan.

---

1 Brad Gooch, *City Poet: The Life and Times of Frank O'Hara* (New York: HarperPerennial, 1994), p. 333.

If marriage itself is scarcely 'vanguard', the term, as John Lowney points out, does not apply merely to the nuptial occasion. Thanks to pronominal ambiguity, the ironically celebratory poem itself becomes 'vanguard':

> It's so
> original, hydrogenic, anthropomorphic, fiscal, post-anti-aesthetic,
>   bland, unpicturesque and WilliamCarlosWilliamsian!
> it's definitely not 19th Century, it's not even Partisan Review, it's
>   new, it must be vanguard! (*CP*, 265)

Lowney quotes these lines to show that 'like so much of [O'Hara's] poetry, this "occasional poem" self-consciously reflects on its own place in the "tradition of the new"'.[2] This is certainly so, yet 'the new' in this poem cuts both ways: its second line – 'the effort to be new does not upset you nor the effort to be other' – initiates a narrative in which a reciprocal relation will eventually be established between Freilicher's and O'Hara's efforts 'to be new'. In his case, being new means writing a playful and unconventional epithalamium, in hers (and, presumably, Joe Hazan's) – just following conventions. Since getting married can mean being 'new' and 'other' only in a devastatingly ironic sense, a poem celebrating this newness and otherness necessarily stages its own newness and otherness at the expense of the soon-to-be newlyweds. Could this be why O'Hara claims: 'Only you in New York are not boring tonight', confidently adding a few lines later: 'no one will be bored tonight by me because you're here'? (*CP*, 265). At Joan Mitchell's party, reading a poem, even this poem by Frank O'Hara, most likely would have been an 'entertainment' – whether cute or sublime or just rude, each listener could decide. If the assertion that 'no one will be bored tonight by me because you're here' refers specifically to the anticipated public reading of the poem, might we take it to mean that 'no one will be bored by *you* tonight' because *I* will be there, entertaining the crowd with my vanguard epithalamium? And for the same reason: 'only you in New York are not boring tonight?' Freilicher's marriage was not an unambiguously joyful occasion for O'Hara, who feared it might cause his close friendship with her to erode, and his anxiety shows through the catalogue of nuptial attributes, in which the 'bland' and 'unpicturesque' stand beside the 'original' and 'new', as well as the mysteriously 'hydrogenic'.[3] Its concluding exclamation – 'it must be vanguard!' – comes after a dozen heterogeneous assertions and negations which may or may not fall into a causal sequence. Does 'it' have to be 'vanguard' because of what precedes this claim, or could the pronominal ambiguity Lowney points to abate at the end of an apparently metonymic chain and allow the poem to take precedence over the marriage? In other words, are the two really interchangeable? If we take 'must' to have the same grammatical function as in Wallace Stevens' 'it must change, it must

---

2 John Lowney, 'The Post-Anti-Esthetic Poetics of Frank O'Hara', *Contemporary Literature* 32.2 (1991), pp. 244–64, at p. 244.
3 See Gooch, *City Poet*, p. 293.

be abstract, it must give pleasure', then the last in O'Hara's whimsical series of adjectives might signal a turn from whimsy to necessity, from forced cheerfulness to a more generally meaningful aesthetic imperative that he mocks mercilessly, if only by juxtaposing it with a staid custom, legally restricted to heterosexuals.

But be that as it may, the question of what makes a poem vanguard, if only in O'Hara's opinion, remains unanswered. When Lucie-Smith interviewed him in October 1965, the 'make it new' mantra seemed to have lost its overriding and compelling meaning, or at least acquired a more nuanced character. When asked whether he thinks it is 'important to be new', O'Hara answers: 'No, I think it's very important not to be bored, though' (*SS* 9). Similarly, in 'Another Word on Kenneth Koch', published ten years earlier, he first claims that 'Mr. Koch intends to 'make it new', then sums up with the accolade: 'most important of all, he is not *dull*' (*SS*, 59, 60). In his statement for the Paterson Society, written in 1961, he refuses to give an account of the formal workings of his poetry because, 'if I went into that thoroughly enough nobody would ever want to read the poems I've already written [...] and I would have to do everything the opposite in the future to avoid my own boredom' (*CP*, 510). And in 'Ode to Michael Goldberg ('s Birth and Other Births)' (*CP*, 290), written in 1958, a passage in quotation marks suggests that there is something dully repetitive about the avant-gardist imperative:

"the exquisite prayer
to be new each day
brings to the artist
only a certain kneeness" (*CP*, 297)

These lines are probably meant to flesh out the abstract assertion which directly precedes them: 'too much endlessness/ stored up, and in store', yet even if we consider them in isolation, a clear image of ritualistic futility emerges, in which the prayer 'to be new each day' implicitly becomes the opium of the avant-garde. The new cannot stave off boredom merely by virtue of being new. The extent to which the new is also vanguard becomes irrelevant if O'Hara finds the aesthetic object in question boring. This switch from the sphere of production to that of reception suggests that boredom need not be caused by the aesthetic object itself, but may be a result of the context in which it functions, and specifically the fetishistic qualities with which it is endowed by modern metropolitan culture. Walter Benjamin's remarks on Baudelaire's Paris lose nothing of their force when applied to O'Hara's New York:

Novelty is a quality independent of the intrinsic value of the commodity. It is the origin of the illusion inseverable from the images produced by the collective unconscious. It is the quintessence of false consciousness, whose indefatigable agent is fashion. The illusion of novelty is reflected, like one mirror in another, in the illusion of perpetual sameness. The product of this reflection is the phantasmagoria of 'cultural history', in which the bourgeoisie savours its false consciousness to the last. The art that begins to doubt its task and ceases to be 'inseparable from utility' (Baudelaire) must make novelty its highest value. The snob becomes its *arbiter novarum rerum*. He is to art what the dandy is to fashion. As in the seventeenth century the canon of dialectical imagery came to be allegory, in the nineteenth it is novelty. The *magasins de nouveauté* are joined by the newspapers.[4]

Crucially, Benjamin historicizes the category of 'novelty', rendering it as a 'perpetual sameness' that is integral to the 'false consciousness' of modernity. With this in mind, Pound's slogan 'make it new' can be approached from a different perspective. It would be interesting to know just how many of his early followers were aware of the source of this quotation, namely Tseng's commentary on Confucius:

In letters of gold on T'ang's bathtub:
>   AS THE SUN MAKES IT NEW
>   DAY BY DAY MAKE IT NEW
>   YET AGAIN MAKE IT NEW.[5]

The referent of 'it' is not limited to art or literature, although it subsumes them, as well as everything else under the sun. 'Although Chou was an ancient kingdom/ The celestial destiny/ Came again down on it NEW'.[6] 'It' is the 'ancient kingdom of Chou', as well as the Chinese empire in later times, and, in Pound's view, also the modern state, no matter whether Mussolini's, Roosevelt's or Stalin's, to which the obligations of the poet are just as great as the statesman's. The Confucian backbone of Pound's political theories is one of their most retrograde and anti-historical aspects, yet given the impact he made on American poetry, the bona fide reception of his decontextualized slogan in O'Hara's time should not come as a surprise. Another famous dictum of Pound's, 'Literature is news that STAYS news', conveniently narrows down the scope of the new in question, but far from being a definition of the vanguard, it puts forth a model of canonization, or at least a sure way of spotting a classic.[7] The question of who decides what makes the 'news' news troubles the egalitarian part of Pound's political and aesthetic sensibility, but ultimately no doubts remain that this decision must be made for the projected readers of his *ABC of Reading* by the author himself. By no means does this make him the *arbiter novarum rerum* Benjamin identifies with dandyism and snobbery, for the authority to which he lays claim effectively transcends historical determinants: the new will be new always and unmistakably. Still, both Pound and Benjamin emphasize the *process* of making 'it' new, even though the criteria they rely on are

---

4 Walter Benjamin, *Reflections* (New York: Schocken Books, 1986), p. 158.
5 Ezra Pound's translation of the Chinese formulation is published in his *Confucius* (New York: New Directions, 1951), p. 36.
6 Pound, *Confucius*, p. 37.
7 Ezra Pound, *ABC of Reading* (New York: New Directions, 1960), p. 29.

hard to reconcile: on the one hand, a Confucian sense of duty and the obedience that comes from an unreserved identification of the subject with the state, and on the other an aesthetic anarchy which only insufficient credit might fetter. In each case, 'a certain kneeness' is likely to afflict the subject that fails to realize just how much 'endlessness' is 'stored up and in store'.

One of the more quizzical lines of 'Early on Sunday' (*CP*, 404), written in 1961, seems to raise the question of the new on to a more socially relevant and less idiosyncratic level than that apparent in 'Poem Read at Joan Mitchell's'. O'Hara is reading an article about the Masai and the Kikuyu: 'one keeps and identifies/ the other keeps and learns/ "newfangledness" in Wyatt's time was not a virtue was it' (*CP*, 405). Wyatt and, by implication, the English Renaissance appear abruptly and for no apparent reason in this poem.[8] Wyatt's presence here might be explained as a result of O'Hara's reflection on the cultural dynamism of New York and on whether what was happening then in literature and the arts could be compared to the prodigiousness of the Renaissance. And yet, at the same time, Wyatt and 'newfangledness' are juxtaposed with ethnographic observations about two East African tribes, one of which 'identifies', while the other 'learns'. In other words, only one makes epistemological progress by recognizing the new for what it is. In Wyatt's time the genuinely new was certainly recognizable, while in O'Hara's the capacity for such recognition and the discrimination it entails seem lacking. It is not just a question of the difference in knowledge that separates their historical epochs, but of the metropolitan space which encloses O'Hara's reflections on all of the issues I have mentioned. Wyatt and 'newfangledness' cross his mind as he reads the Sunday edition of the *New York Times*, which had been 'put to bed' earlier in the week. O'Hara feels behind the times by three, maybe even four days. Instead of panicking, getting up (he's still in bed) and going to Washington Square, where Joan Baez will be singing folk songs, to witness the counterculture in action, he thinks of Wyatt, decides to linger and is rewarded by the return of the familiar in the shape of his intoxicated flatmate making loud noises in the kitchen: 'everyone is happy again'.[9] The compound irony of this little narrative relies in part on O'Hara's refusal to go out in search of the new. Staying put also gives him the opportunity to take a leisurely look around, if only through the window at his unglamorous neighbourhood:

---

8 The younger O'Hara had a keen interest in Wyatt and the Renaissance sonnet, as is evidenced by several poems of the early 1950s.

9 Joe LeSueur's not having spent the night at home may have more to do with Wyatt's presence in the poem than my reading of it allows for. In the lines 'And I have leave to go, of her goodness,/ And she also to use newfangleness' from Wyatt's 'The Lover Showeth how He is Forsaken of Such as He Sometime Enjoyed', 'newfangleness' means infidelity. However, at that stage of O'Hara's relationship with LeSueur the question of infidelity probably did not take precedence over the other issues raised in the poem, even though the sense of loss comes through quite strongly in this allusion.

they have their hats on across the street in the dirty window
leaning on elbows
without any pillows
how sad the lower East Side is on Sunday morning in May
eating yellow eggs
eating St. Bridget's benediction
washing the world down with rye and Coca-Cola and the news (*CP*, 405)

'Washing the world down with rye and Coca-Cola and the news' presumably refers to the way he washes down a breakfast of eggs benedict, but also synecdochally to the daily fare of the underprivileged people he sees in the surrounding buildings and streets, who experience the meaninglessness of 'the news' as acutely as the uncomfortably static and stagnant positions of their bodies suggest.

Images of not-merely-personal sadness, inertia or decrepitude are relatively rare in the poems referencing Manhattan. In the exuberant narrative of O'Hara's city life, they appear as brief interludes, moments of sobriety, or rather the kind of sobering up that tends to involve melancholy and dejection, and are all the more important for that. Of course, he expressed his enthusiasms in poems much more powerful than those in which he holds back, doubts, and complains, so the relative neglect of the latter by critics should not be surprising. But even readings of the former tend to take the 'enthusiasm-prone' poet at his word and focus on what he says he did rather than on what made him do it. For instance, when Marjorie Perloff compares Allen Ginsberg's and O'Hara's representations of New York, she finds that for Ginsberg 'New York is a kind of urban hell, the city of cops and drug raids, of crime and ugliness and injustice; it is the opposite of O'Hara's companionable, exciting and eternally entertaining Manhattan'.[10] The comparison occludes O'Hara's own position within this 'eternally entertaining' city, or at least one vital aspect of it, which Perloff discusses earlier in her book, in the chapter devoted to 'the aesthetic of attention'. In the epigraph to this chapter, she quotes a comment O'Hara made in a television programme about David Smith: 'Don't be bored, don't be lazy, don't be trivial and don't be proud. The slightest loss of attention leads to death.'[11] These injunctions resonate in the lines from 'Meditations in an Emergency' – 'I am bored but it's my duty to be attentive, I am needed by things' (*CP*, 197) – Perloff quotes later in her argument. She takes them to mean that 'it is the artist's "duty to be attentive" to the world of process in which he finds himself. And such attention requires a peculiar self-discipline, the ability to look at something and, paraphrasing Ezra Pound, to "See It New!"'[12] She also makes a connection between this adumbration of an artistic ethos and a similar formulation in Rilke's *Duino Elegies*:

10 Marjorie Perloff, *Frank O'Hara: Poet Among Painters* (Chicago and London: University of Chicago Press, 1998 [1977]), p. 186.
11 Perloff, *Poet Among Painters*, p. 1.
12 Perloff, *Poet Among Painters*, p. 20.

Yes, the seasons of spring needed you. Some of the stars
made claims on you, so that you would feel them. In the past
a wave rose up to reach you, or
as you walked by an open window
a violin gave itself to you. All this was your task.[13]

Yet, in my view, the more influential predecessor here is Baudelaire, whom Perloff
mentions time and again in other contexts. The reason for the claim that 'the slightest
loss of attention leads to death' can be traced directly to Baudelaire's dramatiza-
tions of spleen. When he suffered from spleen, Baudelaire was unable to take an
interest in anything at all; his spleen meant more than just apathy, for it involved a
constant fear of some unspecified calamity, as well as an acute sensation of being
crushed by the burden of the present. Loss of attention as an index of indifference
is both a symptom and a cause of spleen. O'Hara's frenetic activity could have been
precisely a method of combating spleen. The metropolis provides the weapons for
this eternal struggle, a struggle Baudelaire associated with the devil, who lures the
flâneur into a network of perilous games that presage the technologies of entertainment Walter Benjamin identified with 'the modern':[14]

I think that it would be nice to go away
but that's reserved for TV and who wants to end up in Paradise
it's not our milieu
we would be lost as a fish is lost when it has to swim (*CP*, 385)

'Fond Sonore', from which I quote these lines, does not have a happy ending like
'Early on Sunday'. It was written three days before Christmas 1960, which may
partly account for its desolate mood. Abandoning New York, presumably as a
means of fighting spleen, belongs to the realm of the physically impossible, jointly
created by television and religion. 'Our milieu', addicted to the 'eternally entertaining', would find Paradise uninhabitable primarily because living there appears
to rule out the vanguard artist's daily toil, so no matter what we take Paradise to
mean here, its attractions would be inimical to the avant-garde ethos. The prospec-
tive displacement leads to a curious formulation in which the feeling of being lost
is compared to a fish's impulse to swim. On one hand, a fish out of water must
indeed be lost when it 'has to swim'. On the other, it is implied that the felt necessity
of staying put in New York is somehow unnatural. '[A]nd yet and yet', the poem
continues, 'this place is terrible to see and worse to feel'. This disillusioned assertion
is the culmination of a series of complaints that begins with a play on a cliché about
the natural world and ends with an image of stale habit and boredom:

13 Perloff, *Poet Among Painters*, pp. 19–20. Perloff's translation.
14 This splenetic undercurrent in O'Hara's writing complicates the expressions of enthusiasm – albeit
inflected with camp irony – for the commodified entertainment of television and cinema that can
be found in his poetry.

you would think that the best things in life were free
but they're the worst even the air is dirty
and it's this 'filth of life' that coats us against pain
so where are we back at the same old stand buying bagels (*CP*, 385)

To use Beckett's formulation from his essay on Proust, 'the boredom of living' has become a defence against 'the suffering of being'. Boredom is implicit in 'the same old stand', while the 'the filth of life' (suggesting a 'filthy habit', as in Beckett's 'Breathing is habit. Life is habit') suggests a physicality that O'Hara sets against emotional pain.[15] Bagels are not incidental here: usually eaten for breakfast, they imply the sameness of each day's beginning, a repetitiousness that might be blamed on habit as well as on the lack of real choice, a mechanically performed ritual that neither satisfies nor inspires. In the first stanza, O'Hara admits: 'I wish that I might be different but I am / that I am is all I love so what can I do' (*CP*, 384), mockingly juxtaposing the absolute self-identity of God with his – or His – inability to change this.[16] For all of the 'many selves' celebrated in earlier poems, especially 'In Memory of My Feelings', when it comes to 'going away', there remains but one, complete and immutable self. The ecstatic, Nietzschean becoming of 'In Memory of My Feelings' gives way to figures of necessity, to a determinacy the poet takes great pains to resist even as he is forced to acknowledge its fated victory.

Significantly, when he gives reasons for not 'going away', O'Hara uses the pronominal plural: 'it's not our milieu / we would be lost'. This implies an identification with at least one other person in the same predicament, or with a larger collectivity, perhaps a 'coterie', as Geoff Ward calls metropolitan artistic communities.[17] The coterie, he claims,

> might be read as a symbol that attempts to cheat temporality by ingesting and acknowledging certain of its powers. The artists' circle, be it in Second Empire Paris or New York in the 1960s is therefore, leaving aside its vanguardist claims, a microcosm of urban life which has itself replaced Nature by the City [...] The lack of resemblance between the subject and Nature is conceded by the twentieth-century city-dweller who in places like New York has made a cult of living against the 'natural' grain, *à rebours*.[18]

The opposition between urban and rural space is certainly relevant to 'Fond Sonore', since 'Paradise' need not be restricted to its religious meaning – advertisements for holiday destinations make use of this noun so frequently that its once-unimaginable plural form should fit comfortably into the discourse of commodity fetishism. Yet in either case the question of leaving the metropolis involves not just

---

15 Samuel Beckett, *Proust; Three Dialogues with Georges Duthuit* (London: John Calder, 1965), p. 19.

16 The mockery is perhaps intensified by an allusion to Popeye's 'I yam what I yam!'

17 The term is explored at length in Lytle Shaw's *Frank O'Hara: The Poetics of Coterie* (Iowa City: University of Iowa Press, 2006).

18 Geoff Ward, *Statutes of Liberty: The New York School of Poets* (New York: Palgrave, 2001), pp. 60–61.

the disappearance of a life-line of friends and rivals, but the exchange of a constant threat of boredom for its dead certainty.

Religious concepts such as 'the soul' or 'Paradise' are alien to O'Hara's rhetoric, but very much at home in Baudelaire's, and this is why I bring them up. 'Fond Sonore' pulls in several directions simultaneously, but its main concern remains clear: 'going away', if only for aesthetic reasons, and just for the Christmas holidays, would mean indulging in the false comforts of an artificial paradise. We might find here ironic echoes of a prose poem from *Le Spleen de Paris*, the only one bearing an English title: 'Anywhere out of the world'. In this poem, the poet addresses his soul, suggesting they go away together. Possible destinations include Lisbon, Rotterdam and Batavia, the charms of each eloquently put forth, but to no avail – the soul does not respond. Finally, after he advertises the Arctic as a site of perfect monotony, where the *aurora borealis* glitters like fireworks from Hell, the soul exclaims 'in its wisdom': 'n'importe où! pourvu que ce soit hors de ce monde!'[19] Liberation from 'this world' might be exactly what lies behind the erratic movements of O'Hara's poem, the title of which means 'background noise' – something always there, but rarely, if ever, welcome; persistent, but hard to grasp semantically, and yet, thanks to its difference from the music we try to hear in 'this world', enabling the difference necessary for meaning. Again, this is not a religious or metaphysical figure. 'Going away' would not be a real or effective liberation from the boredom or dissatisfaction the poem's opening lines invoke: 'In placing this particular thought/ I am taking up the cudgel against indifference'. The desire implied here and throughout is to overcome indifference without resorting to travel or any radical change of external circumstances. The bitterness of the poem's ending – 'it is Christmas and the children are growing up' – might be to some extent explained biographically: in August 1960, with Vincent Warren's definitive move to Montreal, O'Hara's relationship with him had come to an end. Yet the dejection of 'Fond Sonore' is better understood when we set it against another poem, 'You Are Gorgeous and I'm Coming', a love poem to Warren.[20] Written a year earlier, in August 1959, it celebrates just the kind of liberation 'Fond Sonore' posits as infinitely desirable and quite probably unattainable, or at least unrepeatable.

The poem opens with a synaesthetic image of the 'purple roar of the torn-down 3rd Avenue El' (*CP*, 331), which O'Hara hears 'vaguely', as we might suppose the non-existent sounds of no-longer-running trains are usually heard. This 'fond sonore' is echoed in the poem's second section, in which the Paris Metro becomes part of an extended simile, joining forces with 'an acceleration of nerves' to 'rend' 'the sound of adventure' and become 'ultimately local and intimate'. Neither

---

19 Charles Baudelaire, *Le Spleen de Paris* XLVIII; 'Anywhere! Anywhere! as long as it's out of this world!', in the translation by Rosemary Lloyd: *The Prose Poems and La Fanfarlo* (Oxford: Oxford University Press, 1991), pp. 102–103, at p. 103.
20 The poem contains an acrostic, the first letter of each line cumulatively producing 'Vincent Warren'.

the '3rd Avenue El' nor the Metro is physically present: as synecdoches of urban travel and more generally of life in a metropolis, they serve as mere props for the exuberant coupling the poem celebrates. The specific identity of the city in which this sexual act takes place does not matter nearly as much as the liberation making love to Vincent Warren brings from metropolitan din and dirt – and, hopefully, from boredom, whose death is 'nearing', extending a promise of exposure to 'pure air' and 'light' coextensive with a transformation that begins with destruction and leads to a radical renewal:

> [...] the death of boredom
> nearing the heights themselves may destroy you in the pure air
> to be further complicated, confused, empty but refilling, exposed to light (*CP*, 331)

Although many of the images in this poem can be associated with the mechanics or hydraulics of sexual intercourse, identifying the proximate 'death of boredom' with the titular 'coming' would be too reductive. The 'dark and purifying wave' which precedes boredom's nearing death is in turn preceded by an emotional realization: to put it plainly, O'Hara feels he is falling, or has already fallen, in love with Warren. The emotion is 'simple and very definite/ even lasting, yes it may be that dark and purifying wave', and it gives rise to anxieties the rest of the poem will do its best to assuage.

Nowhere are the stakes involved in this effort higher than in the attempts to distinguish renewal from repetition. Explicitly, this happens only once, when 'an acceleration of nerves' and/ or 'a realm of encircling travel' repeat(s) 'the phrases of an old romance which is constantly renewed by the / endless originality of human loss'. Yet an underlying fear that this putative renewal might be nothing but a restaging of earlier losses persists and finds its expression in the games the poem plays with temporality. The title sets permanence, or at least stability ('you are gorgeous') against a fleeting moment of ecstasy ('I'm coming'), though we should keep in mind the spatially progressive, and not just sexually climactic, meaning of this verb. The poem ends with an image of stasis – 'the captured time of our being'. The word 'captured' here implies both a removal from historical progression, as if we were dealing with a photograph or portrait, and a deliberate effort to do just that: capture time and our 'being' in it, as one captures a wild beast or an escaped convict, in order to intervene in its procedures. In other words, the poem's ending annuls the temporal differences implied by its title, or at least tries to do so: 'we are all for the captured time of our being' indicates support or desire, not necessarily success. But only time 'captured' can guard against 'human loss' and its 'endless originality': the closure allows O'Hara *not* to say 'I'll keep coming as long as you stay gorgeous', and it also keeps out of the poem explicit considerations of the iterability of his ecstatic and transformative experience. There is no escaping them, however, since the notion of the endless renewal of the past depends on repetition for its meaning. The splenetic cast of 'Fond Sonore' may be seen as a realization of the illusory character of the victory over time the earlier poem celebrates.

O'Hara's 'urban hell' is quite different from Ginsberg's, of course, but nevertheless real and tangible. Neither his ecstasies nor his attacks of spleen can be taken out of their urban context: when 'eternally entertaining Manhattan' ceases to entertain, the poet finds himself in a predicament suggestively described by Walter Benjamin in *The Arcades Project*:

> The 'modern', the time of hell. The punishments of hell are always the newest thing going in this domain. What is at issue is not that 'the same thing happens over and over', and even less would it be a question here of eternal return. It is rather that precisely in that which is newest the face of the world never alters, that this newest remains, in every respect, the same. – This constitutes the eternity of hell. To determine the totality of traits by which the 'modern' is defined would be to represent hell.[21]

This may sound like a self-referential comment, for *The Arcades Project* is nothing if not an attempt to 'determine the totality of traits by which the "modern" is defined', and therefore 'to represent hell', if only as the hell of a totalizing representation. Still, the 'modern' as Benjamin understands it is not limited to his time, nor to Baudelaire's: O'Hara's New York would certainly fall under this rubric. 'The modern' is essentially a technology of entertainment, unlimited in its scope and bearing a false promise of providing the means to overcome temporality.

If we now return to O'Hara's comments about vanguard art and literature, the stakes involved in the distinction between the new and the not-boring should come more sharply into relief. Newness as a cognitive and aesthetic category is always suspect on account of the pressure brought to bear on the producers of artworks, as well as their critics, to value it above anything else. 'It must be vanguard' – otherwise, why should we bother with it? Yet 'the exquisite prayer / to be new each day' is a figure of sameness, repetition and boredom – precisely what O'Hara tries to elude or overcome. Love makes this overcoming possible, despite all the reservations that lurk in 'You Are Gorgeous and I'm Coming'. So does intoxication, as recommended by Baudelaire: 'Pour ne pas sentir l'horrible fardeau du Temps qui brise vos epaules et vous penche vers la terre, il faut vous enivrer sans trève'.[22] Since the meaning of newness is bound to temporality, its constant presence might suggest a breaking out of temporality, not into the realm of freedom, however, but the eternity of hell, as Benjamin figuratively suggests. In 'A True Account of Talking to the Sun at Fire Island' (*CP*, 306), the poet is told to

---

21 Walter Benjamin, *The Arcades Project* (Cambridge, MA, and London: Harvard University Press, 1999), p. 544.

22 Baudelaire, *Le Spleen de Paris* XXXIII. In Lloyd's version, 'In order not to feel the horrible burden of Time which breaks your back and bends you down to earth, you must be unremittingly intoxicated'.

always embrace things, people earth
sky stars, as I do, freely and with
the appropriate sense of space. That
is your inclination, known in the heavens
and you should follow it to hell, if
necessary, which I doubt. (*CP*, 307)

The Sun's encouragement and advice are strangely skewed by this reference to hell. Rhetorically, it's just a hyperbole, part of the Sun's assurances that the poet has the courage to carry out his vanguard project. But then why does the Sun doubt that following 'it to hell' will be necessary? The doubt problematizes or even disables the hyperbolic function of hell, unless we assume that the Sun's speech means merely that O'Hara will be critically acclaimed before he has a chance to grow disillusioned or bitter, which is of course a legitimate reading. But we might also take the Sun's words as a warning that the inclination to embrace 'things' and 'people' as an implicit way of escaping boredom may have just the opposite effect, that there is an infernal aspect to the eternal pursuit of the new: 'I know you love Manhattan, but/ you ought to look up more often'.

According to Joe LeSueur, O'Hara almost certainly did not show this poem to anyone. It was found among his papers and first publicly read by Kenneth Koch at New York University's Loeb Center: 'Less than two months had passed since Frank's death, so the reading was like a memorial.'[23] Could this memorial reading be 'the event' John Ashbery alludes to nebulously in a poem from *Houseboat Days*, entitled 'The Other Tradition?'[24] Before I explain why I think this might be the case, I'd like to bring up two of the claims Ashbery makes in his lecture, 'The Invisible Avant-Garde'. He gave this talk at the Yale Art School in 1968, and it's possible that his status as a non-academic art critic and avant-garde poet who had spent ten years in Paris – in other words, as an insider, but not necessarily as a close friend of the late Frank O'Hara – was one of the reasons for which Jack Tworkov invited him to speak. At the outset, in a splendidly mock-Eliotic sentence, Ashbery insinuates that 'this force in art which would be the very antithesis of tradition if it were to allow itself even so much of a relationship with tradition as an antithesis implies, is, on the contrary, a tradition of sorts'.[25] From a European perspective, this was perfectly obvious by 1968, but Ashbery clearly wished to address the question of American

---

23 Joe LeSueur, *Digressions on Some Poems by Frank O'Hara* (New York: Farrar, Straus and Giroux, 2003), p. 180.

24 John Shoptaw makes a similar observation in his book on Ashbery, calling 'The Other Tradition' a 'gently versified memorial service' that 'seems to recall the scattered New York school, its unnamed leader, Frank O'Hara, in particular, who had died ten years earlier [...] Ashbery refers to this other tradition periodically through his career, but nowhere more compellingly than here.' *On the Outside Looking Out* (Cambridge, MA, and London: Harvard University Press, 1994), p. 149.

25 John Ashbery, 'The Invisible Avant-Garde', in *Reported Sightings* (New York: Alfred A. Knopf, 1989), p. 389.

vanguardism, and went on to give a thumbnail sketch of the generally hostile reception of avant-garde art, music and literature in post-war America, passing to the appropriation of the 'make it new' slogan by the media – 'turning the avant-garde from a small contingent of foolhardy warriors into a vast and well-equipped regiment' – before eventually arriving at the second claim I wish to highlight: 'that the avant-garde artist is a kind of hero, and that a hero is, of course, what everybody wants to be'. The artist's heroism is partly, or perhaps even overwhelmingly, due to his recklessness: 'Most reckless things are beautiful in some way, and recklessness is what makes experimental art beautiful, just as religions are beautiful because of the strong possibility that they are founded on nothing'.[26]

Ashbery's theses simultaneously aestheticize and historicize avant-gardism, while ignoring the demands of academic theoreticians that the avant-garde present to them a coherent political identity. Heroes must be dealt with on a case-by-case basis, for otherwise their heroism becomes merely generic and highly ironized, as in Ashbery's 1950 play *The Heroes*. The existence of 'the other tradition', however, implies both a community and a commonality of aims, if not always means, which bestows at least a provisional identity on our 'heroes' and situates them within a historical continuum. Something similar seems to unfold in the 'narrative' of 'The Other Tradition', even though the referential aporias of this poem make the possibility that interpretations of it 'are founded on nothing' very strong indeed. In the first section, the sense of an ending is the most consistently recognizable motif. The lateness of the hour, the setting sun, 'the end of something', are nevertheless parts of an account of a meeting, or rather the preliminary stages of a meeting, which is finally 'called to order', that is, officially begun. In the second section, the meeting is already over and the 'Troubadours' are 'dispersing', so we don't really know what happened or what the meeting's purpose was, unless we take the section's opening lines as a synecdochal hint: 'I still remember/ How they found you, after a dream, in your thimble hat,/ Studious as a butterfly in a parking lot'.[27] The words 'I remember' bring to mind a memorial service and suggest an elegiac mood, and even if the rest of the sentence remains referentially indeterminate, three lines further on the dispersing troubadours' comments 'about how charity/ Had run its race and won, leaving you the ex-president/ Of the event' reinforce the finality that rings throughout the first section. If an event can have a president, an ex-president might be so called only if an ex-event is in question. We could take this to mean that at least one of the poem's 'yous' has played the starring role in a memorial reading in his honour, as well as that the 'event' denotes not just a specific reading, but O'Hara's already fabled life among the New York avant-gardists, over whom he effectively 'presided'. The reading was well attended:

26 Ashbery, 'The Invisible Avant-Garde', p. 391.

27 Ashbery, 'The Other Tradition', from *Houseboat Days* (1977), collected in *Three Books* (New York: Penguin Books, 1993), p. 4, and in *Collected Poems 1956–1987* (Manchester: Carcanet, forthcoming).

> They all came, some wore sentiments
> Emblazoned on T-shirts, proclaiming the lateness
> of the hour […]

Yet before it actually begins, 'something' must come to an end:

> The endless games of Scrabble, the boosters,
> The celebrated omelette au Cantal, and through it
> The roar of time plunging unchecked through the sluices
> Of the days, dragging every sexual moment of it
> Past the lenses: the end of something.

The roar of the '3rd Avenue El' is audible here, thanks to the sexual dimension of time, but it is the end of someone's time, not just the end of the sexual act, that comes through most forcefully in the final words of this passage, which bring to mind 'the captured time of our being' and bitterly ironize the implied illusion in O'Hara's image of permanence. The referential uncertainty of the poem's final sentence suggests that a strong emotion has been concealed or disguised, yet the opposition between 'you' and 'them' is sufficiently stable to allow a guess at what Ashbery is hiding, if not a foolproof identification:

> […] You found this
> Charming, but turned your face fully toward night,
> Speaking into it like a megaphone, not hearing
> Or caring, although these still live and are generous
> And all ways contained, allowed to come and go
> Indefinitely in and out of the stockade
> They have so much trouble remembering, when your forgetting
> Rescues them at last, as a star absorbs the night.

The initial figures of death and oblivion give way to a stronger image of leadership, with suggestions of a heroic – and possibly self-sacrificial – coming to the rescue of all those 'others' who have to struggle against the 'night' of Tradition. On the one hand, these are the 'Troubadours' trying to 'make it new' in the manner of the Provençal poets popularized by Ezra Pound, whose enthusiasm for them was so infectious partly because of the belatedness and insularity of American culture Ashbery points to in his lecture. On the other, they are also those who wear 'senti-ments/ Emblazoned on T-shirts' – mass-produced and, by implication, as banal as Pop-art seemed to be to the proponents of Abstract Expressionism. In each case the vanguard impulse is ambiguously caught up in the contradictions and paradoxes of newness and sameness or boredom. Rescue in Ashbery's poem means setting an example or showing the way: the 'star that absorbs the night' is also a guiding light, a signpost pointing towards the future, an image of the avant-garde in its most relevant and moving incarnation, making 'The Other Tradition' the elegy for Frank O'Hara John Ashbery never wrote.

2
Selves

'Where Air is Flesh':
The *Odes* of Frank O'Hara

John Wilkinson

The inaugural anti-monumentalism of Frank O'Hara's great long poem 'In Memory of My Feelings' (*CP*, 252–57) responds not only to T. S. Eliot's solicitude for Western civilization but to Ezra Pound; the Venice which figures as the transcendent site of art wholly integrated with natural materials and location in the *Cantos* is here reduced to a façade sinking slowly into the Grand Canal. The time-defeating Venetian light sputters out as the rocket-trails of a Chinese technology, while navigation and mathematics are tracked back to the Arabs. The civilized European façade is also that of 'my incognito', a mythic singularity harried by sheer numbers – both human mass and spatial distance. But O'Hara's anti-monumentalism is not satisfied with overthrowing, vandalizing or discrediting art objects; he does not submit to the fleeting moment, nor seek to belittle any artist or author the *Odes* turn to. Rather, both 'In Memory of My Feelings' and the *Odes* verge on the rapturous; to be given birth, the work of art requires of its creator a profound sacrifice of personal history, of self-knowledge and of conscious obligation, and an expense in real pain, eulogized in Willem de Kooning and leading to the *Odes*' delirious sexual and social transformations:

> And yet
> I have forgotten my loves, and chiefly that one, the cancerous
> statue which my body could no longer contain,
>
> against my will
> against my love
> become art,
> I could not change it into history
> and so remember it,
> and I have lost what is always and everywhere
> present, the scene of my selves, the occasion of these ruses,
> which I myself and singly must now kill
> and save the serpent in their midst. (*CP*, 257)

In the wake of this grotesque birth, Frank O'Hara's *Odes* reanimate the dead by shattering their monuments and breaking their statues, disdaining to shore fragments, and they wrestle with their own marmorializing tendency. Artistic monuments are restored in the instant of encounter with their undeniable greatness; restoration provokes their further collapse. Through reconciling instantaneity with eternity, aesthetic encounter promises life in an impossible fulness. But the encounter itself depends on life's sexual, painful, transient (and joyful) acceptance and sacrifice, or else it is sterile and the work of art a funerary monument. In Frank O'Hara's *Odes* works of art are presented and become present as at once marmoreal and pulsing, exact, mobile and sexual – and this is true of the *Odes* themselves. The life of any artist's line is specified precisely, Jackson Pollock's lines 'thin as ice, then swell[ing] like pythons' (*CP*, 302) and Willem de Kooning's 'line that's beautifully keen,/ precarious and doesn't sag/ beneath our variable weight' (*CP*, 284). The *Odes* arrogate the authority of the dead and the finished, as well as the undead and suffering Promethean, to the lyric voice emerging and made flesh through the poems' radically expansive but also highly particular prosody. But how to read these poems without turning them into monuments?

Prometheus appears in the *Odes* variously as Manfred (derived from Lord Byron's verse play), as a youthfully phallic O'Hara, as a painter, as 'a spatial representation of emptiness', as 'Aurora when she first brought fire' and, bathetically, as 'Bath' in 'Ode on Lust'. The *Odes* worry at how to reconcile the multiple and provisional individual in all his or her living energy, with that heroic reserve which may seem demanded by a lyricism 'where reticence is paid for by a poet in his blood' ('Ode: Salute to the French Negro Poets' [*CP*, 305]). Reticence is not however a quality attributable to O'Hara's poetic models in the *Odes*, nor to the *Odes*' frequently vatic voices. No slave of respectability, O'Hara feared neither self-dissipation and multiplication nor the individual performance he unhesitatingly named 'genius'. What allows the democratic union of multiplicity and individuality in the *Odes* is prefigured in European Romanticism, where Prometheus and his creative work instantiate an ambivalence between the Promethean rejection of patriarchal authority (as in the Titanic figure of Aeschylus' *Prometheus Bound*), and the deaf, mute and blind statues Ovid's Prometheus models from clay – figures of art freed of the eternal pain he endures, but which the winds inspire, bless and curse with mortal life. The theft of fire links these Promethean stories, and the fire of dawn recurs time and again in O'Hara's *Odes*; breathing flesh constitutes a continuing challenge to authoritarianism, continuously reproducing and decaying. Art may restore immortality to clay, but it is a senseless immortality, embodying the death drive. Art may be wrested from 'the scene of my selves' but in an instant reverts to a statue. Rock must be shattered or defaced, or, as the 'Ode on Causality' bluntly proposes, fucked, then to be encountered again as art, then to calcify once more. Such marmorealizing can never be defeated permanently; even Shelley's *Prometheus Unbound*, an anti-marmoreal tract obsessed with transforming marble into breathing flesh, re-establishes

The image of a temple, built above,
Distinct with column, arch, and architrave,
And palm-like capital, and over-wrought,
And populous most with living imagery –
Praxitelean shapes, whose marble smiles
Fill the hushed air with everlasting love. (III, iii, 161-66)[1]

Indeed in *Prometheus Unbound* it is an 'amphisbænic snake' that yokes the statues of 'wingèd steeds' to both instantaneity and eternity (III, iv, 119-21), frozen while the snake of history (and of an unfertile phallicism) still writhes and consumes itself. Eros is the only agency capable of reanimating the dead statue, powerful enough to confront death in art, although destined to fail in the mortal; this conviction is Shelley's as much as O'Hara's, who must 'save the serpent in their midst'. In the *Odes* 'what goes up must/ come down' ('Ode on Causality'), from marble erection into erotic variety, and from textual plaque to vocal tonguing.

O'Hara's *Odes* work within a Romantic project, and a secular one: the confusion of unborn, living, dead and undead, and the unbinding of tenses. Where O'Hara departs from Romanticism is marked in the evacuated statue of 'In Memory of My Feelings' being termed 'cancerous'; the work of art grows in the human flesh, at once dead and hectic. Lacking functioning organs and able only to turn away from patriarchal authority, not to see it off, the statue, painting or poem resists any attempt to 'change it into history'. The artwork lives and dies only in encounter. In the Ode addressed to him De Kooning's paintings are described as 'stunning collapsible savages' (*CP*, 285), ahistorical, immediate constructions liable to revert (to collapse) to dead canvas, before being raised as flags again in the Whitmanesque dawn ending this ode in another beginning. But de Kooning achieves this through the Promethean pain his body suffers, as do the bodies of all who face the day 'not forward or backward', enduring 'the red drops on the shoulders of men' (*CP*, 284) in their trivial vexations and deep agonies ('the blames/ and desperate conclusions of the dark'). 'Our lives' unite darkness and light. Conjunctions of black and white, light and darkness, heat and iciness, are contrived time and again in the *Odes*. O'Hara departs from Romanticism also in his urbanity (in both senses). City life, not the Wordsworthian influence of rivers and mountains, inculcates the moral influence expressed in human generosity and gentleness. The Romantic sublime is deadly and phallic; the urban sublime is erotic and polymorphic.

As a group, Frank O'Hara's *Odes* has received piecemeal attention, although a reading of 'Ode to Willem de Kooning' is central to Lytle Shaw's fine book *Frank*

1 Percy Bysshe Shelley, *The Poems of Shelley. Volume Two: 1817–1819*, ed. Kelvin Everest and Geoffrey Matthews (London: Longman, 2000). I am grateful to the National Humanities Center for a Carl & Lily Pforzheimer Fellowship in 2007–8, allowing me the time and facilities to write this essay and much else; and to Maud Ellmann for her careful and constructive scrutiny of a draft.

O'Hara: The Poetics of Coterie.[2] One reason for such relative neglect is that *Odes* was published in 1960 as a *livre d'artiste* collaboration with the painter Michael Goldberg, to whom the most extensive of the *Odes* is addressed. This was a book of very limited circulation, unlike *Second Avenue*, written five years earlier than the *Odes* but first published in full in the same year and far more accessibly. Although *Odes* was reprinted as a chapbook in 1969, after O'Hara's death, this was a fugitive edition, and in the meantime the mass-market edition of *Lunch Poems* had come to signify Frank O'Hara to the wider poetry readership. The chronological presentation of O'Hara's *Collected Poems* (1972) then subsumed the *Odes* amongst contemporary poems, and effectively suppressed O'Hara's ordering of them – which was not chronological. Within O'Hara's oeuvre the *Odes* follow hard after 'In Memory of My Feelings' and precede the most celebrated of the so-called 'I do this, I do that' poems collected in *Lunch Poems*; that is, they separate O'Hara's best-recognised poetic achievements. The high Romantic tenor of the *Odes* is both amplified and undermined through the influence of Walt Whitman, his 'great predecessor' in urban Romanticism, and through the poems of Vladimir Mayakovsky, Aimé Césaire and Blaise Cendrars, all of whom shared with Whitman a conflicted relationship with European poetic tradition. Lytle Shaw has provided a substantial account of O'Hara's adoption and adaptation of the Mayakovskian voice, and the influence of Cendrars has been discussed by Marjorie Perloff in an extended essay.[3] Hence the present focus on the Romantic Prometheus.

This interpretation of the *Odes* as working through and revising a Romantic aesthetics proposes that Frank O'Hara developed not one but two unorthodox modes of lyric address, so challenging profoundly both the cult of authentic selfhood in lyric, and the historically reactive extirpation of subjectivity through the linguistic turn. For text must become physical voice even as voice must consort with social and cultural text. The unorthodoxy of the *Odes* is not superseded by the unorthodoxy of the 'I do this, I do that' poems; the two addresses play off each other in a switching that accelerates towards the alternating current of 'Biotherm (for Bill Berkson)', a kind of frantically decentred version of 'Ode to Michael Goldberg ('s Birth and Other Births)'. The earlier poem's self-portrait apparently cleaves to personal childhood experience, but although written in 1950s' New York stays resolutely unpsychological – Freudianism features as just one narrative genre amidst the Westerns, the anthropological expeditions, the American panoramas, the *Catcher in the Rye* parodies and the template of *The Prelude* through which the

---

2 Lytle Shaw, *Frank O'Hara: The Poetics of Coterie* (Iowa City: University of Iowa Press, 2006), especially pp. 179–87.
3 Marjorie Perloff, '"Alterable Noons": The "poèmes élastiques" of Blaise Cendrars and Frank O'Hara', *Yearbook of English Studies* 15 (1985), pp. 160–78. This includes a discussion of 'Ode to Michael Goldberg ('s Birth and Other Births)' largely as a set of freewheeling and 'amusing connections'. Chapter 4 of Shaw, *Frank O'Hara: The Poetics of Coterie*, discusses the poetical and political importance of Mayakovsky and Pasternak for O'Hara.

poem part-filters and part-constructs individual identity. Such pastiche opportunistically deploys a dazzling range of versification, styles picked up and tossed aside with the nonchalance of a great jazz improviser toying with Tin Pan Alley motifs. By the time of 'Biotherm' the organizing centre of O'Hara's version of the Wordsworthian coming-of-age Ode has dispersed. The social voice subsequently developed in the 'I do this, I do that' poems struggles to assert itself amidst teasing and maddening seizures of genre (advertising slogans, pulp magazines, recipes etc.), virally rampant whenever the mouth is opened or the typewriter key struck. Now the poetic object is reliant on such cosmetics as Biotherm (a preparation still available), and both instantaneity and eternity are referred to an unapprehensible totality composed only through distraction. 'Biotherm' anticipates the postmodern *text* but threaded by vocalese, a vocal line that like de Kooning's is 'precarious but doesn't sag'. Of course the word 'Biotherm' (from the Greek for 'life' and 'heat') also signifies the Pygmalion effect on text of sexual activity, voice screwed into and out of it.

Before exploring the *Odes* in more detail it will be useful to set out O'Hara's ordering for their original publication. The collection begins with two odes to painters, 'Ode on Causality' (to Jackson Pollock) and 'Ode to Willem de Kooning'. These are followed by 'Ode to Joy', 'Ode on Lust' and 'Ode (to Joseph LeSueur) on the Arrow That Flieth By Day', where love, lust and *timor mortis* contend – but this might be said of all the *Odes*. Then follow the two odes to poets: 'Ode: Salute to the French Negro Poets' and 'Two Russian Exiles: An Ode'. The collection ends with another ode to a painter, the collaborator in the original *livre d'artiste*, 'Ode to Michael Goldberg ('s Birth and Other Births)'. The trajectory of the book therefore leads from death (at Jackson Pollock's graveside) back towards birth, a reversal enacted in the transfiguring of negation into 'joyous night' in every one of these poems. To attain this *verklärte Nacht* necessitates, more specifically, the negation of a succession of temptations each poem offers, perhaps the most insistent being Romantic sublimity, guyed already in 'In Memory of My Feelings':

> At times, withdrawn,
> I rise into the cool skies
> and gaze on at the imponderable world with the simple identification
> of my colleagues, the mountains. Manfred climbs to my nape,
> speaks, but I do not hear him,
>> I'm too blue. (*CP*, 253)

Here Manfred stands atop the Jungfrau surveying the world as in Byron's play, envying the eagle the freedom projected on to the swooping bird, and erect in the loneliness of his Godless and Faustian aspiration (but rejecting the Faustian ministry of spirits). Manfred is apotheosized over mass humanity and at the same time casts himself as fallen abjectly below the moral status of any 'free-born peasant' upright in his certainties. He speaks, but his is a soliloquy he does not expect to be heard; neither can he hear human discourse, for although alert to the shepherd's pipe and yearning to become 'the viewless spirit of a lovely sound' – that is, a lyric poet like his creator – Manfred fails to perceive the approach of the Chamois Hunter or to hear him when he addresses him as 'friend' and expresses both human care and God's love. Prometheanism has turned him into a statue. 'I'm so blue' then is O'Hara's pithy deflation of this scene, at once laying claim to the blue empyrean's ultimate overview, and reducing Manfred's wordy angst to a vernacular shrug. O'Hara follows this repudiation of the heroic pose with a flickering montage of part-identifications. The deposition of the inflated self supplies a moment of bathos opening the way not to a chosen 'personality', but to a flood of historically enjoined identifications and responsibilities, at once personally intimate and common property in popular and high culture – for one of O'Hara's governing intuitions was that the inner world is populated with screen idols as much as screen memories.

This bathos is sexual too, and 'Ode on Lust' opens with some crossbreed between Tarzan and Manfred bounding on to stage:

> Asking little more than
> a squeal of satisfaction
> from a piece of shrapnel,
> the hero of a demi-force
> pounces cheerfully upon
> an exalted height which shall
> hereafter be called Bath (*CP*, 282)

– Bath, which is to say, bathos. As in the earlier poem, bathos serves for overture to 'an over-prodigal need of dispersal' where 'of' is carefully ambiguous, for the dispersed 'fragments of love' feel as needy for dispersal as the promiscuous do in putting them – and themselves – about. This poem issues in a passage seeming to exalt gay debauchery. The most delirious become almost ascetic in their dedication to being 'stripped of their seeds', since the rewards of the erections on which they stand and which they embody are few and transient:

> Poor Bath! and poorer still
> are his pursuers, seeking only
> the momentary smile of clouds
> and underneath, a small
> irresponsible glory that fits (*CP*, 282)

Looking down becomes a wearisome posture, whatever variety of persons it sexually does over. In both this ode and 'In Memory of My Feelings' the Romantic statuesque of Manfred is subject to bathetic reduction, assuming that position figures as a necessary prelude to its sacrifice for the unselfing multiplicity which in turn must be negated to 'save the serpent in their midst'. Erection and fragmentation precede a depressive reintegration in a humanly inhabited world, which the *Odes* insist must be urban, so that 'one alone will speak of being/ born in pain/ and he will be the wings of an extraordinary liberty' (*CP*, 298). The self that survives is chastened and reduced from its primitive authority to a mortal, social humanity. This is how Manfred's pastoral yearning gets fulfilled; the bawling, suffering infant born to die, not the sublime hero but the non-transcendent hero fully accepting of his suffering physicality, inherits the pinions on which lyric rides. Such a concatenation of bathos and heroism is marked equally in the dawn of part three of the 'Ode to Willem de Kooning', 'reaching for its/ morning cigarette in Promethean inflection', where the Promethean act amounts to little more than striking a match, but serves as prelude to a flurry of disconnected street activity before returning in 'the individual dawn of genius' (*CP*, 285). When de Kooning is addressed, bathos may seem to have been made nugatory by the painter's achievement; but this achievement is represented as democratic and social, requiring the 'fluttering newspapers' of Gotham to bring down to earth the individual Prometheus before he can rise again from his bed. In their encounter with great art people become, like de Kooning's paintings themselves, 'stunning collapsible savages' who might fall back to the mattress or rise to the heights (*CP*, 285). The pinions on which one rides are both private and common to everybody. But so as to sustain this Whitmanesque conviction, there are other temptations O'Hara has to dispatch.

In the *Odes* especially, Frank O'Hara openly displays and revels in his sense of working within a poetic tradition or several simultaneously; and typically, rather than adopting a stance vis-à-vis tradition, he lights on the materials available, both parodically and affectionately. To succumb to any fixed form would set in stone. But the two opening *Odes* addressed to painters, one of them dead and the other raised in O'Hara's eyes beyond any sense of adequacy to address on equal terms, do follow broadly the same pattern. They open with fragmented, hesitant and personally vulnerable movements; a central portion then calls on historical antecedents, and a final section rises to a grand affirmation rooted in the ordinary life of a city and of the body. This pattern parallels the Pindaric ode through seeking the aid of the gods or muses in tackling the theme of celebrating a great hero, before turning to a disquisition on the history and present pertinence of the model of heroism. Then it celebrates a revisionist heroism framed in democratic, vernacular terms, reaching a pitch of unabashed joyousness equalled only by Whitman. The attribution of heroism to the making of art is not repudiated by this gay poet, despite its connection with *machismo* and especially the contrived but persistent mythology surrounding Jackson Pollock. O'Hara's poems fall into line with a conception of the artist at the far limit of spiritual risk, while linking this to the contradictions, the rudeness, of democracy. What O'Hara admires is the kind of democratic sublime which endures bathos so as to reassert itself, to deserve 'the title *Bird in Flight*' (*CP*, 303). It is noteworthy however that O'Hara would not describe his poetic vocation in these terms – this rhetoric is reserved for painters rather than great poets, whom

O'Hara commends (and embraces ecstatically in 'Ode: Salute to the French Negro Poets') for talking to the heart rather than rising to the sublime.

The posture of mastery is a deathly one, and its works form its own epitaphs. 'Ode on Causality', which starts in an uncharacteristic mood of introspection, its opening seven lines first drafted under the more sardonic title 'Ode on Causality (in the Five Spot Cafe)',[4] chafes at the memory of the 'cancerous statue' evacuated from the body as art. It chafes too at its own inscriptions, and chafes at the bronze and stone of Jackson Pollock's grave. The marmoreal becomes associated with poetry (or any art) conceived as 'important' and 'Suddenly everyone's supposed to be veined, like marble' – marble whose veins then run into the main body of the poem along the parallel lines of 'fucked' and 'your grave', veined like an erect penis and at the same time signifying the grave, and yet 'it isn't pathetic and it's lasting' (*CP*, 302). But for that to be true, for 'your grave' to be fucked as living art, a deathly priapism must be *sent up* in both senses, mortality and orgasm alike treated vulgarly.

This sending-up is managed by O'Hara in an uninhibitedly carnivalesque style, and begins by relocating Baudelaire on to a 20th Century Fox film set where he morphs into a mortician presiding over melodramatic rewrites of *King Lear*. In such a solipsistic genre death merely satisfies the beholder's desire for 'ugliness' and indulgence in the ham-tragic. Now the ode switches target to mock historical and social delusion and mendacity, parodying 'Old Romance' in a send-up of Oirish-ness iconoclastic indeed for an Irish American, inventing the preposterous title '*The Orange Ballad of Cromwell's Charm Upon the Height "So Green"*'. Not that O'Hara discounts the uncomfortable possibility that great art can be made out of propa-ganda; Andrew Marvell's 'Horatian Ode upon Cromwell's Return from Ireland' might exemplify the ideological grooming described in the line 'sweet scripts to obfuscate the tender subjects of their future lays'. O'Hara cannot suffer the sexual possibilities of 'lays' to pass under-exploited, and the next spin of this verbal whirl-igig exclaims 'to be layed at all!' before charging at various Aunt Sallies and other enemies of eroticism.

A further temptation to be dismissed, and a thoroughly unsexy one, is the call to a detachment and quietism evading the pains and pleasures of physical reality. Reference to a 'Buddhist type' and the insistence, after sketching an amusing tableau of Japanesery, that the moon is 'not our moon', seem to comprise O'Hara's earliest response to the Buddhism which increasingly claimed some Beat poets, including his friend Allen Ginsberg (not that it quashed Ginsberg's libido). While O'Hara was impatient with all religion impartially, the poem 'Image of the Buddha Preaching', written a year after 'Ode on Causality', achieves an asperity perhaps unequalled in his work, hailing the work of Aryan Indologists as 'hopeful of a new delay in terror/ I don't think' (*CP*, 323). The dismissal of Buddhism, including this unfair smirching with Nazism, is important to O'Hara in measure with the importance

---

4 See Donald Allen's note to the poem (*CP*, 542).

accorded pain in the *Odes*. The contingency of liberty on the human condition of being 'born in pain' (*CP*, 298), meaning born *into* pain as well as through pain, is the assertion on which the *Odes* as a book conclude, and it also forms the central claim of 'Ode to Willem de Kooning'. This may approach Buddhist doctrine, but its implications are quite other. The Buddhist moon is 'not our moon'

> unless the tea exude a little gas and poisonous fact
> to reach the spleen and give it a dreamless twinge that love's love's near
>
> (*CP*, 303)

The 'twinge' here is 'dreamless' not only because it is a real twinge that hinders sleep or awakens from dreamy 'spirituality', but because the sexual response will not allow love to be thought transcendent and unmediated. Similarly 'poisonous fact' generates a bit of Baudelairean spleen to counter a romanticized Irish history, any 'Old Romance' or repetitive melodrama. Love has a bearing only when named as love, splitting into 'love's love's near' – named because it cannot be wholly entertained or realized (and by naming the split is consolidated). As it happens, the *coup de foudre* and the sexual act unite when 'love's love's near' in a satisfying 'bang', 'the bang of alertness, loneliness, position that prehends experience' (*CP*, 303).[5] The sexual bang and the bang of love collapse emotional duration into an 'alertness, loneliness, position' analogous to aesthetic experience; art whose impact is total, a bang, a whole thing, a statue even, which 'prehends experience' but is dependent on its carcinogenic growth in flesh. The combination of distance and immediacy is registered by the compaction of 'poisonous fact', the physical and emotional synthesis of 'spleen' and the linguistic fault of 'love's love's near'. Meanwhile the 'Buddhist type' has been caught 'with his sickle banging on the Monk's lead window', frustrated by a deathly chastity; religion enjoins a leaden retreat while the world of facts seethes erotically.

Here 'Ode on Causality' makes explicit the complication of life and death informing the entire book of *Odes*, 'each in asserting beginning to be more of the opposite' (*CP*, 303) – so what is alive is also 'sick' and what is dead is 'dying', not sealed in the past participle. This heroically ambitious poem finds life in death, resolving its introspective hesitations through narrating a visit to Pollock's grave, and 'seizing a grave by throat/ which is the look of earth' (*CP*, 302). The look of earth is what paint discloses; paint has the look of earth because pigment is mineral (or vegetable and therefore earthy) – and through paint's brilliance, earth also looks back. The 'bronze JACKSON POLLOCK' refers to the plaque affixed to the rock marking Pollock's grave at Springs. When O'Hara conjures himself to 'read and read through copper earth' (*CP*, 302) the reading-through is as reciprocal as earth's manifestation in paint, seeing through the name to the life of earth and of Pollock's art, then reading back from the dead the words inscribed in verse. The words on

---

5 *OED* records 'bang' for sexual intercourse as current from 1937.

the plaque have prepared for the 'energy I burn for art' to 'read and read through copper earth', and transmuting earth into language provides a crucial transition to language as spoken, for the grave is seized 'by throat': therefore 'the look of earth' proclaims:

> its ambiguity of light and sound
> the thickness in a look of lust, the air within the eye
> the gasp of a moving hand as maps change and faces become vacant (*CP*, 302)

Sexuality gets down to the look of earth from the solitary and deathly erection, and language fluently sexualized makes air move as poetry consorts with the sexual ground of Pollock's painting; the *air* within the eye connotes a song, along with the *lay*. At the end of the poem, the 'sexual bliss' O'Hara has asked to be inscribed 'upon the page of whatever energy I burn for art' is brought to a preposterous orgasm:

> over the pillar of our deaths a cloud
> heaves
> pushed, steaming and blasted
>   love-propelled and tangled glitteringly
>   has earned himself the title *Bird in Flight* (*CP*, 303)

After overcoming the terrible prediction of 'the pillar of our deaths', for the prematurely killed Frank O'Hara was to be buried in the same graveyard eight years after this poem, it is hard not to gasp at the audacity of this image, or rather this machinery, where death explodes seminally and launches 'himself' (whether Pollock or O'Hara or another) into flight as art, as immediate and thoroughly mediated as love itself. The *name* JACKSON POLLOCK has now transformed into the *title* 'Bird in Flight', the title of a work in marble by Constantin Brancusi – who died between Jackson Pollock's death and the writing of this poem and therefore combines into 'the pillar of our deaths', 'tangled glitteringly' in the same heaving cloud, a heaving not only of ejaculation but of giving birth. The cycle this poem describes is repeated on a larger scale in the reverse biography of the *Odes* as a group, from the elegy of 'Ode on Causality' to the nativity of 'Ode to Michael Goldberg ('s Birth and Other Births)'.

Ejaculation blasts off a sculpture of a bird in motion as instantaneous and eternal as Shelley's 'wingèd steeds' and similarly announced by an 'amphisbænic snake' in the line 'each in asserting beginning to be more of the opposite' (*CP*, 303). The earlier prayer to 'make my lines thin as ice, then swell like pythons' conflates O'Hara's prose description of Pollock's paint-lines: 'that amazing ability to quicken a line by thinning it, to slow it by flooding, to elaborate that simplest of elements, the line – to change, to reinvigorate, to extend, to build up an embarrassment of riches in the mass by drawing alone' (*AC*, 32). Here ice and snake again combine as do death and the penis in marble; O'Hara's description applies precisely to his own lines in the *Odes*, and their quickening across enjambment, slowing through staggering, then a vertiginous and unpunctuated opening-out keeping them as restlessly alive as a high-wire walker's pole. What has O'Hara done here with the dead? It is the obverse of what, according to Paul de Man,

> we have done with the dead Shelley, and with all the other dead bodies that appear in romantic literature – [...] to bury them in their own texts made into epitaphs and monumental graves. They have been made into statues for the benefit of future archeologists 'digging in the grounds for the new foundations' of their own monuments. They have been transformed into historical and aesthetic objects.[6]

Instead 'what dooms must do' and death's seals and memorials become art's medium; O'Hara disfigures brass and marble, makes earth a living pigment, like Pygmalion breathes on it, and sets the incised line snaking across the page in its variable speed and length.

The reversal of death into birth at the end of 'Ode on Causality' anticipates the astonishing reversals enacted by 'Ode to Willem de Kooning', from its first couplet: 'Beyond the sunrise / where the black begins' (*CP*, 283). Night can follow sunrise on canvas, as where dark structures underlie a sluice of brilliance, but here blackness is properly heralded by dawn because, as the ending of the poem asseverates, 'only darkness lights our lives' (*CP*, 285). The poem's opening section strongly echoes Guillaume Apollinaire's 'Les Fenêtres', especially its central passage:

Le pauvre jeune homme se mouchait dans sa cravate blanche
Tu soulèveras le rideau
Et maintenant voilà que s'ouvre la fenêtre
Araignées quand les mains tissaient la lumière
Beauté pâleur insondables violets
Nous tenterons en vain de prendre du repos
On commencera à minuit
Quand on a le temps on a la liberté
Bigorneaux Lotte multiples Soleils et l'Oursin du couchant
Une vieille paire de chaussures jaunes devant la fenêtre
Tours
Les Tours ce sont les rues
Puits
Puits ce sont les places
Puits
Arbres creux qui abritent les Câpresses vagabondes[7]

---

6 Paul de Man, 'Shelley Disfigured', in *The Rhetoric of Romanticism* (New York: Columbia University Press, 1984), pp. 93–123, at p. 121.

7 Guillaume Apollinaire, *Caligrammes*, trans. Anne Hyde Greet (Los Angeles and London: University of California Press, 1991), pp. 27–29 [parallel text]. This section of the poem is translated as: 'The poor young man blew his nose with his white tie / You'll raise the curtain / And now see the

Here too curtains rise in the city, a window opens and ('On commencera à minuit') 'we'll begin at midnight'. At the end of 'Les Fenêtres', 'Le fenêtre s'ouvre comme une orange/ Le beau fruit de la lumière' ['The window opens like an orange/ The lovely fruit of light'], while O'Hara seeks through de Kooning's art 'but to be standing clearly/ alone in the orange wind' (*CP*, 284), orange being the colour O'Hara associates especially with de Kooning because it dominates the small de Kooning he possesses – 'I think it has an orange/ bed in it, more than the ear can hold' ('Radio' [*CP*, 234]).

Darkness and light oscillate in the 'Ode to Willem de Kooning', between a separation as categorical as Genesis or St John's Gospel, a merged identity, and a dialectic which leaves the poem poised in its final lines both painfully and gloriously. O'Hara is found at dawn after a 'white night' among artists – central to the poem is the idea of the 'white night' celebrated in Russian literature. This recalls Ben Jonson's line 'Thou that mak'st a day of night' ('Hymn to Diana'), perhaps supplying a faint audible echo to the poem's second part ('Stars of all passing sights,/ language, thought and reality' [*CP*, 284]). At a high latitude the sun does not go down deep enough for the sky to get dark; dusk meets dawn and in summer in St Petersburg, for instance, there is no need to turn on street lighting. In the night is both inspiration ('the face/ of future senses may appear/ in a white night that opens') and delirium ('an eye inflamed' and 'messages were intercepted/ by an ignorant horde of thoughts' [*CP*, 285]). While an urge is felt towards a light which is 'broad and pure' and towards a clearly tensed demarcation like a line by de Kooning, that line is held to be 'precarious'; and when dawn 'leads us up the rocky path' to a place where white night lasts to eternity, it also might be leading us up the garden path. As in 'Ode on Causality', the moment of transcendence abuts on suffering physicality – 'white night' transmogrifies into the violent 'prehistoric light' generating 'the terrible systems/ of belief' in the third section (*CP*, 285).

Is the dawn of this second section entirely delusory? It certainly seems radically different from the dawn breaking at the poem's close, celebrating the 'Athenian contradictions' of American democracy. Art lives only in contradictions, and the contradictions the poem spirals about cannot be recognized by the 'blinded heroes' next to the 'pink seas' (eerily reminiscent of Picasso's shoreline figural groups of the early 1920s). Either heroes of faith ('where death/ can disappear') or of reason (they 'were not/ mad enough'), they are overwhelmed by the physical world and its violence 'when the blood began to pour down/ the rocky slopes into pink seas' (*CP*, 285). By contrast, the dawn of the third section is wholly unironical:

---

window opening/ Spiders when hands wove the light/ Beauty paleness fathomless violets/ Vainly we'll try to take some rest/ We'll begin at midnight/ When you have time you have liberty/ Winkles Codfish multiple Suns and the Sea Urchin of sunset/ An old pair of yellow boots in front of the window/ Towers/ Towers are the streets/ Well/ Wells are the squares/ Wells'.

A bus crashes into a milk truck
>   and the girl goes skating up the avenue
with streaming hair
>   roaring through fluttering newspapers
and their Athenian contradictions
>   for democracy is joined
with stunning collapsible savages, all natural and relaxed and free

as the day zooms into space and only darkness lights our lives,
with few flags flaming, imperishable courage and the gentle will
which is the individual dawn of genius rising from its bed

'maybe they're wounds, but maybe they are rubies'
>   each painful as a sun (*CP*, 285)

Here democracy is joined in personal liberty, contradictions and dailiness ('a bus crashes into a milk truck' is a prosaic accident after the mock grandeur of the Promethean cigarette). For all that dawn 'blot[s] out stars', de Kooning's art ensures that still 'darkness lights our lives'; when 'the day zooms into space', neither the white night nor the winking stars sustain, but de Kooning's art draws on both the light of democracy and the darkness and pain of human existence. The pain of birth, the inevitability of death and what any mortal is fated to endure, comprise the 'musts' which end the first section of the poem:

>   [...] always the musts
like banderillas dangling

and jingling jewellike amidst the red drops on the shoulders of men
who lead us not forward or backward, but on as we must go on (*CP*, 284)

– and eventually are redeemed though art, its transforming of wounds (including love's darts, no doubt) into rubies, as de Kooning's own words have it. The need to go on is stated here as strongly as it would be in 'Adieu to Norman, Bon Jour to Joan and Jean-Paul', 'the only thing to do is simply continue' (*CP*, 329). In the *Odes* the basis of this modest daily heroism characteristic of the *Lunch Poems* is worked out against many temptations – the Romantic heroism of a Manfred, sustained by blindness and insensitivity; the primitive light sustained by bloody sacrifice up to Abraham; the Buddhist quietism denying the body; and a rigid and inhumane commitment to faith or reason:

yes! for always, for it is our way, to pass the teahouse and the ceremony
>   by and rather fall sobbing to the floor with joy and freezing
>   than to spill the kid upon the table and then thank the blood (*CP*, 298)

Against such temptations the urbane O'Hara uses the word 'gentle' in the de Kooning and Michael Goldberg odes, with full attention to its intimations of nobility and modesty. 'Gentleness' is rooted in an acknowledgement of commonality and exchange. It is because 'democracy is joined' that 'the gentle will/ which is the individual dawn of genius' can rise – and it rises in its works, the flags generously visible in de Kooning's eyes in the first part of the ode, and 'flaming' at the end once realized in the warmth and terror of the human darkness as magnificent works of art (*CP*, 285). 'Ode on Causality' accepts that 'what goes up must/ come down', the fate of the phallus as it is the fate of the Romantic artist 'to be inimitably weak/ and picturesque, my self'. But the 'Ode to Willem de Kooning' celebrates the civic, gentle and democratic artist, moving past the Romantic posture in both its erect and declining forms.

At the end of the *Odes*, the 'Ode to Michael Goldberg' shifts out of the autobio-graphical modes which have governed it (even if its first person remains always under construction), to recognize 'the gentler animals like our-/ selves' (*CP*, 297). The 'I' is allowed to fall away in the last twenty lines, first for the first person plural, then for the displaced first person 'one' and finally, and disconcertingly, for a bold 'he' in a transfer of the particulars of one autobiography – O'Hara's – to another self – Michael Goldberg. This radical move conforms the seriousness of the parodic coming-of-age gallimaufry leading up to it. The most intimate personal experiences are so far mediated through the products of a culture that they must be presumed deeply shared (with the odd pronominal tweak). The democratic 'I' starts in 'we', and echoes of Whitman's 'Song of Myself' – 'We also ascend dazzling and tremendous as the sun' (l. 562) – are attendant. Such gentleness is particular to the shared civic life; the pastoralism and primitivism spoofed throughout the poem can subserve true gentleness only because in the poem's closing passage, slaves 'found a city' *we* inhabit. Similarly, the audacious 'we' standing at the head of the first two grand strophes of the 'Ode to Joy' does not comprise an easy claim of kinship with the reader. It follows the civic achievement of 'we' that

> We shall have everything we want and there'll be no more dying
>   on the pretty plains or in the supper clubs (*CP*, 281)

It was the envious resentment of nomads that destroyed Sodom and Gomorrah, a bunch of shepherds inaugurating a death cult because they hated urban life and its gentleness. Therefore this Ode reiterates that a city must be founded in order for *us* 'to go on as we must go':

> [...] or as the legends ride their heroes through the dark to found
> great cities where all life is possible to maintain as long as time
>   which wants us to remain for cocktails in a bar and after dinner
>   lets us live with it
> > No more dying (*CP*, 281)

To be oneself is a great temptation for the post-Romantic artist. It may be true, as de Man puts it, that 'any reading is a monumentalization of sorts', but O'Hara was as determined a disfigurer as Shelley, and resists with ceaseless perspicacity the ingenious ploys that contrive erection of the self as phallic monument; he dismembers, corrupts, covers with graffiti.[8] Reading O'Hara must honour the ceaselessly active intelligence of a poetry always alert to its own temptations. At one extreme, the 'we' of the 'Ode to Joy' issues a full-on challenge to the blatant self-marmorealization of a Manfred declaring that

> Thou hast no power upon me, *that* I feel;
> Thou never shalt possess me, *that* I know (III, iv, 125-26)

Feeling and knowing here are the blinders, the deafeners and the physically numbing; they secure the perimeters of the statuesque self. But there are more present and subtle temptations, and O'Hara's courage, perspicacity and impishness are fully engaged in the most challengingly 'incorrect' of the *Odes*, 'Ode: Salute to the French Negro Poets' (*CP*, 305).

This poem's opening invocation echoes from the same city 'near the sea' where Whitman delivered the international invocations of 'Salut au Monde!': 'What cities the light or warmth penetrates I penetrate those cities myself'.[9] O'Hara calls all people who willingly or fatedly inhabit 'the terrible western world' to an imagined America of 'our total mankind', a potential vitiated by the shame or reticence underpinned by the 'shibboleths' and rationalizations of cowards. Neither Whitman nor Aimé Césaire, the second spirit presiding over O'Hara's lines, was much afflicted by these inadequacies. In everything but name 'Ode: Salute to the French Negro Poets' is an Ode to Love, based on an anti-essentialist construal of 'our nature' as defined by the ability to love across categories, allegiances and racial and sexual differences. This urban civilization represents an achievement greater than Pound's Venetian light, incorporating contradiction and 'the most difficult relationship'. It is inclusively democratic where Pound was elitist and racist. At the start 'one who no longer remembers dancing in the heat of the moon may call/ across the shifting sands', for this city acknowledges in its people no origin or certain foundation. Cultural attributes and retrieved history as a basis for what now would be termed identity politics are dismissed because they are insufficient to assuage 'a barren and heart-sore life'. Addressing Césaire's negritude and his black American contemporaries' cultural assertiveness, O'Hara insists: 'neither cool jazz nor devoured Egyptian heroes'. This phrase recalls the cool/hot temptations of 'the teahouse' and 'the kid upon the table' in the 'Ode to Michael Goldberg', but here a cross-racial and 'queered' physical love and its contests have become the proving ground for a love so inclusive it can restore those 'who once shot at us in doorways'. *They* and *we* become capacious entities, 'we' including the black victims of colonialist brutality as well as 'our hearts in adolescent closets' and 'they' being absolved because 'too young then to know' – so 'they' includes 'we' and 'we' includes 'they'. By brazenly

---

8 De Man, 'Shelley Disfigured', p. 123.

9 Walt Whitman, 'Salut au Monde!', in *The Complete Poems*, ed. Francis Murphy (London and New York: Penguin, 2004), p. 178.

asserting such kinships O'Hara claims equity through 'the love we bear each other's differences/ in race' without a trace of liberal compunction. Sociology counts for nothing next to the living 'I's who matter 'in the midst of sterile millions': those 'I's come to matter and bring each other to matter because 'the only truth is face to face'. The poem culminates in a final line compacting flesh, spoken words and print in one magnificent proclamation:

> the beauty of America, neither cool jazz nor devoured Egyptian heroes, lies in
> lives in the darkness I inhabit in the midst of sterile millions

> the only truth is face to face, the poem whose words become your mouth
> and dying in black and white we fight for what we love, not are

This 'poetic ground' of race and of sexual relations transgresses what we *are*, mobilizing 'the heat of the moon', 'the shifting sands' and 'the sun of marshes', and working through poetic language like 'the love we want upon the frozen face of earth'. The sequence recapitulates the reproductive cycle tracked in 'Ode on Causality'. In that poem 'Aurora when she first brought fire' provokes the resolve, 'a sexual bliss inscribe upon the page of whatever energy I burn for art'. A sexual bliss reanimates Jackson Pollock's physical remains, both his body and his oeuvre, producing through Frank O'Hara the text 'read and read through copper earth'. Language seizes 'grave by throat'. In 'Ode: Salute to the French Negro Poets' the text emerges out of a fervent and vocal coupling, 'the poem whose words become your mouth'. This rejigs the vocal-textual temporal priority whereby earth or rock can be transformed into a painting or a plaque labelled JACKSON POLLOCK, and where sexual desire must succeed the 'Promethean inflection' to animate the work of art. The air is made flesh in this Pygmalionism. Look again and it has turned into a pillar. But temporal order is of small account in the white nights and illuminating darkness of these poems. The last of the *Odes* recasts the creative dawn in its coming-of-age repertoire. A 'falling dream' characteristic of male pubescence leads to the physical and sexual confidence whose incipient Prometheanism must be disavowed. Physical pain and imperfection are the precondition for gentleness:

> the wind soars, keening overhead
> and the vestments of unnatural safety
> part to reveal a foreign land
> toward whom I have been selected to bear
> the gift of fire
> the temporary place of light, the land of air

> down where a flame illumines gravity and means warmth and insight,
> where air is flesh, where speed is darkness
> and
> things can suddenly be reached, held, dropped and known

> where a not totally imaginary ascent can begin all over again in tears (*CP*, 293)

Here the sequence changes again, for sound and air reveal a 'foreign land'; the childish dreams and ambitions of the fire-bearer are visible briefly in 'the temporary place of light, the land of air'. But it is the word 'whom' applied to that 'foreign land' which is both jarring and absolutely right, predicting the transition to a shared and gentle world of 'warmth and insight', of acquisition, fallibility and pain. This world where 'things can suddenly be reached, held, dropped and known' corresponds to O'Hara's infinitely flexible prosody, neither marmoreal form nor hot-air effusion, – or better, *both* marmoreal form and hot air effusion, 'to be more/ alive, sick; and dead, dying/ like the kiss of love', a very Galatea, deaf, dumb and blind no longer. How like the paintings of the artists O'Hara admired, able to return the viewer's gaze on account of

> the artist assuming responsibility for being, however accidentally, alive here and now. Their gift was for a somber and joyful art: somber because it does not merely reflect but sees what is about it, and joyful because it is able to exist. It is just as possible for art to look out at the world as it is for the world to look at art. (*AC*, 67)

Close Writing

Keston Sutherland

Incompleteness has to do above all with a fiction of closeness…

– T. J. Clark

Rêve: La plus aimée est toujours la plus loin…

– Corbière

For Grace, After a Party

>   You do not always know what I am feeling.
> Last night in the warm spring air while I was
> blazing my tirade against someone who doesn't
> interest
>   me, it was love for you that set me
> afire,
>   and isn't it odd? for in rooms full of
> strangers my most tender feelings
>   writhe and
> bear the fruit of screaming. Put out your hand,
> isn't there
>   an ashtray, suddenly, there? beside
> the bed? And someone you love enters the room
> and says wouldn't
>   you like the eggs a little
> different today?
>   And when they arrive they are
> just plain scrambled eggs and the warm weather
> is holding. (*CP*, 214)

This must, I imagine, be among the best known of Frank O'Hara's poems, though I confess I imagine that it must only because my friends have so often read and talked about it, and because I have myself loved it since I first discovered O'Hara's poetry around thirteen years ago. There is as yet, to my knowledge, little mention of it in printed criticism. Marjorie Perloff, in *Poet Among Painters*, calls it a 'bittersweet love poem' and says that its images bleed into one another as do the images in Grace Hartigan's painting.[1] Neither of the recent books by Lytle Shaw and Andrew Epstein makes any comment on it.[2] Ira Sadoff's recent essay, 'Frank O'Hara's Intimate Fictions', about which I'll say a few things later on, is, I think, the only one yet published to do anything more than glance in passing at 'For Grace, After a Party'.[3] The poem exists, I continue to imagine, much as O'Hara claimed to hope that all his poetry might, between persons and comparatively untouched by the fixatives of critical industrial promotioneering, not to mention by criticism. So now here it is, between O'Hara and you, if you like, or now instead between you and me, in print on this page, if either of these descriptions makes sense for you, in this room, if you are in one – and what should be done with it? What I hope this essay will do is move us a little closer to it.

What do I mean when I say that we could move closer to this poem? The trope of reading as microscopy too often proposes as its end and limit that, in effect, the poem simply be shifted from one category into another, say from spontaneity into factitiousness, from impact into contrivance, from improvisation into composition, or from presumptively straight, as an uninquiring reader might assume, into masqueradingly or openly queer. *If we look closer we see that*, really, what we took for an expression of despair on impulse is a remanufacturing of the history of Surrealism, etc. There is something to be said even for this practice of close reading, but I think that, fortunately, Frank O'Hara has said a great deal about it already in his poems; more than enough, indeed, to pre-empt the next century's discussions of his relative artifice and candour, if not yet to prevent them. The poem I just read has a lot to say about closeness as the shift from impact to stasis, like an imaginary car crash in rewind, particularly in its climb down into a disimpacted prosody which is, I will go on to argue, both the most Reverdian thing in all O'Hara's work and also not at all like anything Pierre Reverdy would ever have written. But the poem is not just about transitions and shifts of perspective and category. There is another closeness in it.

O'Hara, we know, was close to lots of people. In Merle Brown's hilarious view, he was much too close to them. O'Hara, Brown writes in 1978, 'valued certain persons more than most people think any person should be valued. To be as serious about individuals as O'Hara is, is not psychically safe.'[4] These derangedly

1 Marjorie Perloff, *Frank O'Hara: Poet Among Painters* (Chicago and London: University of Chicago Press, 1998 [1977]), p. 79. Thanks to Sara Crangle and Pam Thurschwell for organising the symposium on O'Hara at the University of Sussex, April 2008, for which a first version of this essay was written. Thanks also to Geoff Gilbert, Ian Patterson, Neil Pattison and John David Rhodes for their helpful, critical comments.

2 Lytle Shaw, *Frank O'Hara: The Poetics of Coterie* (Iowa City: University of Iowa Press, 2006); Andrew Epstein, *Beautiful Enemies: Friendship and Postwar American Poetry* (New York: Oxford University Press), 2006.

3 Ira Sadoff, 'Frank O'Hara's Intimate Fictions', *American Poetry Review* 35.6 (November/December 2006), pp. 49–52.

4 Merle Brown, 'Poetic Listening', *New Literary History* 10.1 (Autumn 1978), pp. 125–39, at p. 135.

overvalued individuals are everywhere in O'Hara's poems, as has been much noticed, or I might say, too much noticed, or rather, noticed too exclusively, since the important but also rather serviceably breathtaking set of preoccupations with whom O'Hara knew, whose names he dropped or clung on to, and how enviable his social life was, has played a good part in distracting attention and interest away from another fact about O'Hara's poems, namely, that they are full of anonymity. There are anonymous individuals everywhere. Often, in fact, in the majority of cases, it is not a named person but an anonymous person who is addressed most tenderly by O'Hara or with the greatest passion or consternation. He is close, and his poems try often to move him closer, to you who are someone. Someone who doesn't interest me, someone you love – even you, simply, whoever you are, who do not always know what I am feeling. Not only are these people anonymous, but what matters most about them is their anonymity. Even when we know of course, in one way, that you is Grace Hartigan, yet in another way we do not know in this poem who you are, for the good reason that instinctively we don't yet want to know, as we read that first line; indeed, I push the knowledge of who you are away from me, for a moment, to keep alive its suspense in generality, and the line itself urges me to do exactly that. You do not always know what I am feeling.[5] Not merely an utterance, this, but demonstratively an utterance, an utterance that has been prepared for, even if only in the space of a conscious brief inhalation, or in the space of a typographic inset reminiscing about how easy it is to begin paragraphs in prose and how much easier paragraphs make things. The prepared utterance meets its nearly prepared echo in a sudden congeries of memories and sensations of our own intimacies, real or imagined and both at once. I will myself have said this, I say to myself, though of course I do not say it, and then I say too, it has been, it must be said to me, about me, whether or not I am present to hear it. I do not always know what you are feeling. Well, of course, obviously not, how could you – and yet, how could you. But who are you? Anonymity is the element of this first line and the precondition of its remaining, as it precariously but fixedly does, half in prose. Here, at its first line, we know already that the poem, as we will better know it later, will not keep up pointing utterances so directly at anyone, not at least after its direct utterance of love in the still close and nearly still warm past tense, where versification begins almost calmly apportioning itself limb from limb, but that what begins as a direct address to you will soon drift into a spread of indefinite pronouns; and that instead of continuing in its early preparation to defy enjambment, the

---

5 This first experience of anonymity isn't one that features in Ira Sadoff's account of the poem. Sadoff's answer to what he implicitly takes to be the question posed by the first line is that 'Grace doesn't know what he's feeling because his feelings are confused, surprising and uncontrollable, and are not always available to him when she's present' ('Frank O'Hara's Intimate Fictions', p. 52). To my mind, insofar as the line may be asking me something, what it is asking me is not the single question 'why not?', but a complex series of half questions, as much simply identified as asked, earliest among which are, as I go on to suggest, 'who are you?' and 'why almost prose?'.

verse line will step away from prose and into its practised dilatoriness, resembling O'Hara's practised dilatoriness, at once passionate and very normal, reaching beyond its own syntax to make new starts on new lines not because the last line has ever been met on its own terms and fulfilled, as Whitman's great lines are met on their own terms and fulfilled, but because, after all, how inaccurate, how lying would be the perseverance that would carry out these verses to some end fixed on by counting on it? '[W]ouldn't/ you like the eggs a little/ different today?' You can count on it. Those not detestable, merely impossible trochees.

But here we are at the first line looking forward, and though we can't help but do that it nonetheless has something contrary about it, because this is a poem in which O'Hara is saying how difficult and impossible it is to look forward, how impossible it is that there should be anything to look forward to. Elsewhere and in another poem he says, with equal impossibility, and this time neither close nor distant but 'a block away', that 'love is love nothing can ever go wrong' ('Poem [Light   clarity avocado salad in the morning]' [*CP*, 350]) and elsewhere, again impossibly, that 'everything continues to be possible' ('Adieu to Norman, Bon Jour to Joan and Jean-Paul' [*CP*, 329]) and even that, in yet another poem and this time in outright homage to the impossible, 'We shall have everything we want and there'll be no more dying' ('Ode to Joy' [*CP*, 281]). But in this poem it is not clear that nothing ever going wrong, or everything continuing to be possible, or even our having everything we want and never dying can really be anything worth looking forward to. This poem wants to tell us that if nothing will ever go wrong it is because compulsorily it will not: the bed, the room, the eggs cannot go wrong, because the definite article is the epithet of their sure and certain continuity. The bed, the room, the eggs. The shift from indefinite pronouns to definite articles, from someone to the room that someone merely enters, is a gain neither in specificity nor closeness, or is a gain in both specificity and closeness but only as I know them in their anonymity, as anonymous specificity and anonymous closeness. Their anonymity will not be broken down or analysed into meaningful familiarity by any trick of Cubism, any disposable shift of disposition, or other mental outdistancing of objects. There they simply are, and here you are who love in them and next to them, you who are no closer to the anonymous room just because you are in it.

The poem then looks forward from its first line but cannot. Does it instead look back, as though looking back were an alternative to looking forward? Its second line begins telling us and telling Frank O'Hara that yes, we will look back. It begins telling a story, and the direct utterance of the first line passes and shades half into half-utterance, half into the factitious privacy of memoir. Last night in the warm spring air, the warm confessional syllables of *langage poétique*.[6] Compare,

---

6 I take the phrase from Jules Laforgue's 'Une Étude sur Corbière', in *Mélanges posthumes*, ed. Philippe Bonnefis (Paris: Ressources, 1979), p. 121: *il n'y a pas un autre artiste en vers, plus dégagé que lui du langage poétique* ['there is no other artist in verse freer than he is from poetic language' (my translation)]. O'Hara must have known Corbière's 1873 collection of poems *Les Amours jaunes*, from

for another moment, another poem about having left a party or some scene of conviviality, the sonnet written by John Keats in March 1819 and sent to George and Georgiana Keats in a long letter, where he reassures his distant siblings that 'it was written with no Agony but that of ignorance; with no thirst of any thing but knowledge when pushed to the point though the first steps to it were throug [sic] my human passions'.[7]

> Why did I laugh tonight? No voice will tell:
>   No God, no Demon of severe response
> Deigns to reply from heaven or from Hell. –
>   Then to my human heart I turn at once –
> Heart! thou and I are here sad and alone;
>   Say, wherefore did I laugh? O mortal pain!
> O Darkness! Darkness! ever must I moan
>   To question Heaven and Hell and Heart in vain!
> Why did I laugh? I know this being's lease
>   My fancy to its utmost blisses spreads:
> Yet could I on this very midnight cease,
>   And the world's gaudy ensigns see in shreds.
> Verse, fame and Beauty are intense indeed
> But Death intenser – Death is Life's high meed.

Keats's poem is funnier than O'Hara's. Never, perhaps, has any poem made the experience of trying not to laugh into such an intense torture, by going to the great length of trying not to have laughed. Keats's poem is also a great deal more passionate, Shakespearean in its overwhelming of the corrections and pettiness of the sonnet form, incapable of discharging its versification into dilatoriness and anonymity. This being's lease is very much of this being, definitely named. But the two poems share more than their drama of exit, reminiscence and essential solitude. 'I know this being's lease/ My fancy to its utmost blisses spreads'. Fancy here is passive and manipulated by an economizing mortality, but the lease extends

---

which I take one of my epigraphs, at least by its title, since the title of his own 1950 poem 'Les Étiquettes jaunes' is obviously a pun on it. I wonder, though, how literally to take Kenneth Koch's remark, cited by Perloff, that O'Hara was immersed in and influenced by the entire history of French poetry from Baudelaire to Reverdy. If O'Hara was indeed much influenced by Corbière and Laforgue, it must have been in a manner quite different from Ezra Pound's, whose *Hugh Selwyn Mauberley* shows off the study of their versification, and different too from T. S. Eliot's, whose early poetry is famously indebted to Laforgue in particular, for the relish it takes in the ironies of monologue. I add this thought because, although as Perloff says, 'O'Hara's heart was, from the very beginning, French', its beat was never Anglo-Gallic modernist; and it may be that a study of O'Hara's uninterest in the accomplishments of Corbière and Laforgue – those two in particular – represented selectively to English-speaking readers by Pound and Eliot would be a good way to begin an account of his difference from that moment of modernism. Perloff, *Poet Among Painters*, p. 33.

7 *The Letters of John Keats*, ed. Hyder Edward Rollins (Cambridge: Cambridge University Press, 1958), vol. 2, p. 159.

at least to the utmost blisses, and Keats's fancy is his own because, or most of all when, it is spread to them, to its utmost blisses. That passivity really matters to Keats, as he says elsewhere in talking about negative capability.

In O'Hara's poem it's not clear that there is finally much to choose between passivity and activity. The difference between blazing my tirade and being set afire is plain enough, but this is early on in the poem, not after a party but during one. After a party there is nothing but activity, and in this sense there is nothing much to choose. Look at the grammar. Activity is not action, here, and when the eggs arrive they are not a painting. To prove this, though after a party it no longer needs to be proved, since there is no longer any someone to blaze at, the poem requests an act. Put out your hand, – and then the comma, and then the end of the line, – put it out toward what? What will it knock into, at its utmost? Toward some utmost bliss? Its utmost bliss? But again we are looking forward, for the bad and good reason that we can't help it. To stay then for the moment with this line and at the end of it, it might be that this act requested of you, put out your hand, is prelude to a gift, or a shock to the flesh, or a close reading of your destiny in the lines of your palm that darken when you close your fingers and make as though to grip something. Whatever comes next, what you do know is that you have been asked to expect something. The line ending, too, is telling you that, and saying also, to you, if you like, that suspense is of course automatically poetic, and so this prelude to whatever comes next is the poem continuing to be possible as a poem, however much its versification may already have dallied in prose and stepped away into practised dilatoriness. When the line turns and it turns out that an ashtray is there, isn't it, beside the bed, suddenly and slowly, there is, if we want it, a moment of quite abrupt looking and revising backward. If I put out my hand and suddenly there is an ashtray, was my hand on fire? Have I been asked, calmly, slowly, in proof of the indifference of activity and passivity, to extinguish my burning hand? In any case what I will not do now is shift this moment into the category of Surrealism, priding myself on the yield of my microscopic interest in idiom; and I won't do that despite the fact that this is possibly the most surreal moment in all O'Hara's poems. Because I have been asked to expect something, I have been asked not to know what this something will be, but instead to guess at it and to be wrong. What is so fantastic and normal about this ashtray, an ashtray, is that when I put out my hand and touch it, there, as I later know, beside the bed, it is both what I genuinely did not expect and what I of course must expect; and the sensation of compulsorily expecting this named but anonymous object is pathetic because I have just been asked not to expect it by someone who is now using the possessive pronoun 'your' as though suddenly it were indefinite, when just a few lines back this same person has used the very definite pronoun 'you' in a passionate utterance of love. It was love for you that set me afire: put out your hand.

I want finally, though of course I am not close to the end of knowing this poem, to do what I said I would do earlier on and say something about Reverdy and why I think both that this is O'Hara's most Reverdian poem and that Reverdy would never have written it. O'Hara was, famously, a great admirer of the French poet. Marjorie Perloff, Geoff Ward and other critics have quoted as evidence of Reverdy's influence the end of the poem 'A Step Away From Them', where O'Hara says that his heart is in his pocket and that it, his heart, is 'Poems by Pierre Reverdy' (*CP*, 258); but I don't think anyone has yet said in print that no such book existed in 1956 when O'Hara wrote that poem.[8] The author's heart, which is not possibly in his pocket, is also not possibly a commodity called 'Poems by Pierre Reverdy'. His heart then is the phantasm – imagine! – of that book, yet to be translated and put in print.

Reverdy published in *Mercure de France*, on 1 August 1950, an essay called 'Cette émotion appelée poésie', this emotion called poetry, which is I think where Reverdy says yes to the possibility of being happy and not unhappy, which O'Hara of course loves him for at the end of 'Adieu to Norman, Bon Jour to Joan and Jean-Paul'. Everything, writes O'Hara, well knowing how anonymous this everything must be in the delight of his rush to invoke it and his rush not to explain why, 'everything continues to be possible' –

> René Char, Pierre Reverdy, Samuel Beckett it is possible isn't it
> I love Reverdy for saying yes, though I don't believe it (*CP*, 329)

'Cette émotion appelée poésie' is where Reverdy dismisses Baudelaire's splenetic account of beauty bound forever to misfortune, and confesses that he, on the contrary, finds the whole point of art to be its hoisting of the artist out of a dreary reality and up into the abruptly more breathable atmosphere of aesthetics.[9] The

---

8 Perloff, *Poet Among Painters*, p. 30; Geoff Ward, *Statutes of Liberty: The New York School of Poets* (Basingstoke: Palgrave, 2nd edn, 2001 [1993]), p. 58. Neither does *Poems by Pierre Reverdy*, or *Poems by Pierre Reverdy*, yet exist, incidentally. Ward's chapter on O'Hara is excellent and perhaps still the best general account there is, but his reading of this last moment of 'A Step Away From Them' misses the gist of it, I think. O'Hara never said that 'one's heart is in one's pocket and [...] it is the poems of Reverdy' (Ward, p. 61), nor even that this is what his own heart is. He said that his heart is Poems by Pierre Reverdy.

9 This moment is, at least, a strong candidate for the job of 'saying yes' to the question 'it is possible isn't it': 'Baudelaire has said, in better terms that I don't now have before my eyes, something like, that he cannot conceive of Beauty in art without the idea of misfortune, of morbidity, of suffering. This is not at all what I think myself. Quite to the contrary, I believe that the point of art, the role of art, is not to sink man still deeper into his misery, into his suffering or his sadness – but to deliver him from it, to give him a key to the exit by lifting him up from the weightily quotidian plane of reality [*le soulevant du plan réel, lourdement quotidien*] to the free plane of aesthetics on to which the artist hoists himself to live and breathe'. Pierre Reverdy, 'Cette émotion appelée poésie', in *Au soleil du plafond* [and other texts], ed. Étienne-Alain Hubert (Paris: Gallimard, 2003), pp. 101–102. My translation. Compare O'Hara, 'Leafing Through Florida': 'not to be morbid to be beautiful at everything/ you do' (*CP*, 344); 'Adieu to Norman, Bon Jour to Joan and Jean-Paul': 'surely we shall not continue to be unhappy/ we shall be happy' (*CP*, 329); 'Poem' ['A la Recherche de Gertrude Stein']: 'into the infinite air where since once we are/ together we always will be' (*CP*, 349). The most interesting and compelling comparison, because it may show to us O'Hara answering Reverdy back and uncertainly mocking his own love for Reverdy, is with 'Sleeping on the Wing': 'to travel

essay also includes the following statement:

> Because the constant drama of the poet is his aspiring more than anyone else to stick
> to the real [*adherer au réel*] – as in the Absolute – the excess of his sensibility itself
> forbids him to adapt himself to it, to accommodate himself to it, – in the Relative –
> like everyone else – and forbids him to take from it, for the sake of enjoyment, even
> the least of whatever benefits it can offer. For sure, it is not lust for life [*le goût de
> vivre*] which he lacks. On the contrary, what constrains him is his having this lust in
> excess. So that, whatever might be the social circumstances of his life, he can never
> avoid knocking into limits and wounding himself on them. And these limits, which
> make even the widest world suffocating, he discovers again in his work, which the
> demands of his nature and his character forbid him ever to find satisfying.[10]

O'Hara's lyric is everywhere both the confession of excessive sensibility and the
theatrical attempt to claim an impossible new possession of it, both the 'most
tender feelings' locked into the expense of purpose of a perfectly marvellous life,
and at the same time, always, the excess of lust for that life, voiced in both love and
defiance of the most anonymous person in the hundred anonymous rooms full of
strangers, where the excess of voice in screaming is compelled by anonymity to
mature into mere mellow fruitfulness and so become compulsorily bearable. But
if my most tender feelings in rooms full of strangers bear the fruit of screaming,
why do I not walk out on them? Could my simple act of leaving not become that
complex *action* of fidelity to excess, can I not be as spontaneous as a cord of paint
flung across a nameable canvas and out across its edge on to the never anonymous
because never named floor? For Reverdy, 'excess of […] sensibility' is a kind of
honorific and distinguishing case of Hegel's restless 'consciousness' moving toward
its own essence, consciousness putting out its ungloved hand in the dialectical
element of the Absolute to grasp at the Science of Spirit. This is what Reverdy hints
at and possibly defers to with his passing but for him decisive reference to *l'absolu*,
the Absolute. The poet is Hegel's restless consciousness at its most impossibly
restless. But 'excess of sensibility' is also, and still, *le drame constant du poète*, of him
very specifically, his irritable reaching after fact and reason in rooms, like theatres,
full of strangers. The poet with his excess of sensibility and his excess of lust for life
and for the real will never be Hegel's consciousness 'being-for-itself', no matter how
much he may frequent the circles of the Absolute, since it is the poet's own specific
falseness and his own pathogenic 'justesse dans l'absurde', in Reverdy's phrase, that

---

always over some impersonal vastness,/ to be out of, forever, neither in nor for!' (*CP*, 235–36).
Geoff Ward quotes the same lines from 'Adieu to Norman, Bon Jour to Joan and Jean-Paul', again
in evidence of the importance of Reverdy to O'Hara, and adds that each 'proper name is chanted
like a talisman against restriction and in favour of possibility', but that this time, in contrast with 'A
Step Away From Them', the 'reference to Reverdy is more melancholy' (Ward, *Statutes of Liberty*,
pp. 61–62). Ward doesn't ask, though, when or where, or in answer to what question, O'Hara might
have thought that Reverdy said 'yes'.

10 Reverdy, 'Cette émotion appelée poésie', p. 103.

he will never be a poet for-himself.[11] As Reverdy puts it, 'On n'écrit pas pour soi', one doesn't write for oneself; and O'Hara's 'Personism' is, besides other things, a kind of deadly frivolous confession of exactly that. The solitude suffered by the poet in his incommensurable excessive aspiration and lust is thus never absolute solitude, not even in the numberless 'places vides'[12] or empty places of Reverdy's most analytically empty prose poems, but only the solitude of reaching always for the other person, 'l'autre', who is his own fit audience though few, or less than few, or compulsorily anonymous, or even professionally unreal. But how can the other person whom I write for and reach for be any of these things interchangably? Is 'you', are you, ever conceivably, not to mention ever really, so easy to reduce to nothing but a case of the indefinite pronouns, or to nothing? Are you nothing more, fundamentally, than the forensic evidence, always and again given back to me, that I do not write for myself? No, you are both more and less than that. Less, because you do not prove anything: 'On n'écrit pas pour soi' is a pronouncement just as justly absurd and impossible when I am in your presence feeling life is strong as when you are a block away, feeling distant (*CP*, 350). Nothing, not even you, will ever prove that I don't write for myself. But you are more too, because even when the you I move toward is my most garish confabulation, absolutely kitsch and faceless, the almost pure narcissistic projectile I toss around while windowshopping and mostly not real-shopping,[13] you are nonetheless forever the limit of my own solitude. As 'Cornkind' would have it, in a phrase that casually lacks a central noun and that, by that lack, lets its most tender stress fall on the fragile and indefinitely not broken genitive preposition 'of', – 'you are of me' (*CP*, 387).[14] The eternal circle of your arms and legs is eternally the circumference of my reaching through the infinite air toward the limit of my singleness; I hold you in a circle around me.[15] The social circle whose circumference is my utmost bliss is made of this necessary anonymity, when I am its poet. This is, strangely, just what O'Hara makes his poems tell him, not only in rooms full of strangers but also in anyone's arms.[16] The closeness of the

11 Reverdy, 'Circonstances de la Poésie', in *Au soleil du plafond*, p. 117.
12 Reverdy, 'Contre le mur des places vides', 'Figure', in *Au soleil du plafond*, p. 20.
13 From O'Hara's description of Belgrade at dusk in his letter to Joe LeSueur, published as *Belgrade, November, 1963* (New York: Adventures in Poetry, 1972 or 1973) [undated, unpaginated]: 'all the places (or Trgs, as they're called here) fill with people and many of the streets too, all of them looking dark and sort of ominous in the light, strolling and windowshopping and real-shopping and talking'.
14 What 'of' lacks is the limit to its reference that any anterior noun would infix for it; the noun that it lacks is *limit*.
15 'Poem' ['A la Recherche de Gertrude Stein'] (*CP*, 349); and see Maurice Merleau-Ponty, *L'Œil et l'Esprit* (Paris: Gallimard, 1964), p. 19: *il tient les choses en cercle autour de soi*.
16 By 'anyone' I of course do not mean anyone: who ever did? I mean anyone (within limits). If we take a step away from O'Hara's poem and into his letter to Joe LeSueur from Belgrade, published since O'Hara's death, the anonymity of erotic and sentimental encounters described is of a quite different order. Not the indefinite pronoun at once summarizing and distancing a person who might be anyone because he or she is just someone, but 'two [male] Ghanaians' on the plane and 'a soldier'

poem to you who do not always know what I am feeling is known by putting out your hand, when I ask you to, as though to touch me, that is, in Reverdy's phrase, to discover the limit, since I am the real limit of your solitude and you are the limit of mine, but to discover the limit only after knocking into it and being wounded by it. 'For Grace, After a Party' knocks into you in love, discovers that you are the limit of its excessive longing, and wounds itself by wounding you into anonymity, not even into someone I love but, in fixated indefiniteness, into someone you love. Reverdy wouldn't have written it because there is much too much of a person at the centre of it doing everything and wanting everything and loving everything,[17] some

---

in the Octobuarski Salon, a Belgrade queer bar, are the object of O'Hara's 'real-shopping' *goût de vivre*. Unfortunately, as he reports to LeSueur, 'it is very difficult to make out in Serbo-Croatian' (O'Hara, *Belgrade, November, 1963* [unpaginated]). O'Hara's sexuality is of course not altogether kept out of his poems but is directly celebrated in some of them, as a number of critics, including Shaw, Russell Ferguson and others have discussed; and the anonymous stranger in an O'Hara poem can just as well be a hate-filled 'someone' as someone you love, as in 'Biotherm (for Bill Berkson)', when O'Hara reports having the other day, on a train, 'overheard someone say "speaking of faggots"' (*CP*, 441); but while this essay has not the least intention to generalize O'Hara's sexual feelings out of their queer specificity in the name of anything more straightspokenly 'universal', I have thought it interesting to focus attention, in this essay deliberately as in my own reading experiences without prior deliberation, on the experience of reading O'Hara's poem and not yet knowing, or deciding to know, how to situate and flesh out its pronouns or how to specify the social meaning and detail of the desires that are summoned up in lyric to surround them. I've done that because many of O'Hara's poems demand it, often of course playfully and as a way of masking the identity of their author, though I don't think it's done playfully or as a masquerade in 'For Grace, After a Party'; and I've done it, too, because 'For Grace, After a Party' in particular, from its first line, emphatically demands to be read in that suspense, rather than because I've wanted in any way to reposition the poem by muting any instruction it may give to read it first of all, emphatically, or always as the queer text that it of course must be. It's not, in my view, simply that 'there's no evidence of the speaker's being gay, but the emotional landscape of this poem would make an excellent "cover"', as Ira Sadoff puts it ('Frank O'Hara's Intimate Fictions', p. 52), since, surely, the evidence lacked by one reader may from the perspective of another reader just have been missed, and since, too, the suggestion that the poem would make an excellent cover insinuates that it couldn't possibly be read as a candid and undisguised queer love poem, which in my view it could (insistence that the first 'you' is anonymous and not simply or only Grace Hartigan keeps open exactly that possibility). I think instead that what makes this such a beautiful love poem is its at once delicate and emphatic assertion, only failingly confessional, that evidence itself is at root somehow irresistibly pathetic; and that the closer I am to self-evidence, sexual or otherwise, the stranger I am; or that, if I can get the verse close enough, this is how it will seem, albeit perhaps only after a party, to the stranger I am. On O'Hara as queer poet see Shaw, *Frank O'Hara: The Poetics of Coterie*, p. 86, p. 94ff.; Russell Ferguson, *In Memory of My Feelings: Frank O'Hara and American Art* (Los Angeles: The Museum of Contemporary Art, 1999), pp. 92–99; and Joe LeSueur, *Digressions on Some Poems by Frank O'Hara* (New York: Farrar, Straus and Giroux, 2003), *passim*. See also Terrell Scott Herring, 'Frank O'Hara's Open Closet', *PMLA* 117.3 (May 2002), pp. 414–27, from which, however, the present essay early on fundamentally departs in disagreeing with Herring's unqualified statement (in a brief account of 'Personism') that 'for O'Hara there is no distinction between the language found in the poem [but which?] and the language of everyday life [but whose?]' (p. 417).

17 As David I. Grossvogel put it at the time when O'Hara was writing these poems, 'Reverdy's devotion to the primacy of the object excludes the human dominant'. 'Pierre Reverdy: The Fabric of Reality', *Yale French Studies* 21, 'Poetry Since the Liberation' (1958), pp. 95–105, at p. 99.

poet who will have all the world to satisfy his *goût de vivre* but who never learned, not from reading Hegel nor from overlistening on any train full of ugly strangers, to forbid himself the enjoyment of his queenly *drame constant*; and worse still, that person is Frank. And that is exactly why Frank would have written it and did.

Naming the Seam:
On Frank O'Hara's 'Hatred'

Richard Deming

Given that, at some level, lyric poetry is always dealing with the warp and woof of language – its register and measure – the most important poetry affects how we think of language and the work it does in making a world available, or in making a self available to a world beyond the self. Charles Altieri writes: '[The lyric poem] comes very close to serving as our finest philosophical instrument for dealing with agency because its abiding question is what is involved in making those [social] investments.'[1] In giving a view, however implicit, of language, of representation, of ethics, poetry becomes a moment of real philosophic complexity. Frank O'Hara, who has become one of the major figures of the pluralist situation of post-war American poetry, is a poet who provides the means for considering such an investment.

As many will insist, the social is a crucial element of O'Hara's poetics.[2] However, I want to discuss a specific poem that takes the title – and, we might say, takes on the question – of 'Hatred'. This is a poem that in many respects – in particular its emotional intensity and its representation of a destructive tendency – is anomalous in O'Hara's oeuvre. In discussing it, I will suggest that the 'social' in O'Hara's poetics goes beyond considerations of the historical milieu of the poet's immediate circle of friends and interlocutors. The idea of the social is of real importance in a poem such as 'Hatred', which might be perceived as *anti*-social. Ultimately this thinking about being a being among other beings orients my discussion towards a consideration of ethics. Because the poem is explicitly about a specific affective state, we can consider the claims O'Hara's poems make about affect in general, about affect's role in art, and about art's role in providing experiences of ourselves and our internal modes of experiencing. Thus, despite its violent and negative valences, 'Hatred' may not be so far from O'Hara's explorations of feelings in countless other poems. He is the author of 'In Memory of My Feelings', after all,

---

1 Charles Altieri, *Postmodernisms Now* (University Park, PA: Pennsylvania State University, 1998), p. 123.
2 On this question, the two studies one should begin with are Andrew Epstein's *Beautiful Enemies: Friendship and Postwar American Poetry* (Cambridge: Cambridge University Press, 2006) and Lytle Shaw's *Frank O'Hara: The Poetics of Coterie* (Iowa City: University of Iowa Press, 2006).

131

wherein he writes, 'My quietness has a number of naked selves' (*CP*, 253). The poems, then, are a means of articulating these selves in their nakedness. In a later poem, O'Hara writes:

> Hate is only one of many responses
> true, hurt and hate go hand in hand
> but why be afraid of hate, it is only there
> think of filth, is it really awesome
> neither is hate
> don't be shy of unkindness, either
> it's cleansing and allows you to be direct
> like an arrow that feels something (*CP*, 333–34)

As this suggests, acknowledging hatred – our own – allows us to be direct and to be aware of our feeling something, transformed from an inanimate, unfeeling object into an emotional, emoting being. 'Hatred' maintains, uncharacteristically for O'Hara, its violent tone and brutal language, never muting the emotional intensity it both expresses and explores. The poem and its negative emotions become the ground from which we can assess affect and its stakes in O'Hara's poetics and from which we can ask philosophically important questions about the ideas and ideals that arise from O'Hara's work.

'Hatred', a poem too often overlooked in O'Hara's oeuvre, was composed in the summer of 1952. It is a long piece – 27 stanzas of five lines each – and has a grander ambition than is usually evident in an O'Hara poem. The first line alone is enough to demonstrate the difference between 'Hatred' and most other poems by this poet: 'I have a terrible age', he writes (*CP*, 117). Only 'Easter', another long poem from this period, has a similar dark intensity from the very beginning: 'The razzle dazzle maggots are summary/ tattooing my simplicity on the pitiable' (*CP*, 96). Yet 'Easter', a poem in which O'Hara's interest in French Surrealism is strongly evident, is an undisciplined cascade of language that undercuts and even ironizes any epic tendencies by its fifth line, 'O the glassy towns are fucked by yaks'. 'Easter' may have an intensity that comes from its violent images and uncharacteristically brutal language, but it also undercuts that violence as it manifests an irony open to the possibilities of camp and the polyvalence of the ideas and language of the poem.

'Hatred' is another matter, however. Even the title serves as a kind of challenge to the reader, raising as it does a series of questions about what it refers to, and how. Does the title announce the topic of 'Hatred' in a dramatic sense, preparing us for an ode or meditation, perhaps? Or does the poem explore the state of hatred? Is the poem an attempt at definition – or expression? Since hatred needs an object – indeed it marks a relationship between the hating subject and that which is hated – what is it that is being hated? Is the poem *about* hatred or does it *speak* hatred? Is it about *being* hated? And does this poem (want to) create the conditions of hatred in the reader? The title suggests that the poem must either represent that particular emotion or that it must take on some larger consideration of emotional systems – as the lyric mode, in its insistence on address and addressee, so often does. In leading up to the question of 'Hatred', then, we might see the 'social' as a space of contesting and complementary values and meanings. Read this way, the social involves more than the designation of the terms of specific relationships: it is the very way in which subjectivity becomes an experience of itself. Discussing this particular poem, then, leads to a consideration of the larger implications for O'Hara's poetry of ethics and affect, categories that are inextricably connected to one another.

In his book *City Poet*, Brad Gooch notes that O'Hara composed 'Hatred' on an extended roll of office paper, which provided a large canvas suited to the kind of epic concentration O'Hara was striving to create.[3] The dimensions of the paper offered a material field of negotiations that allowed for new compositional and aesthetic possibilities. That these conditions provided the 'landscape' for the poet reveals O'Hara's desire to achieve a form that was appropriate to the large network of intensities he was attempting to set in play.

The first line ('I have a terrible age') lets us know that O'Hara will be stalking big game in his indictment of an entire age. In many ways, O'Hara's poem suggests that hatred is not a solitary condition, though it is an alienating one. The third stanza tells us:

> But if I'd broken you one of my wings,
> shaft darkening over the prairie of your soul,
> for the sea's split resistance I'd never snout.
> I'd retch up all men. (*CP*, 117)

The poem clearly is an address to someone, someone who is not the target of the hatred – and in the absence of any clear indications otherwise, the 'you' is the reader – a witness, perhaps, or someone who receives the confession of hatred. However, the fractured syntax of that first sentence, extending over four lines (try to parse that conditional), does a kind of violence to the language that is supposed to carry the freight of the emotion, the hatred. The intensity overwhelms the ability to communicate, though the lines do express the depth of the emotions.

'Hatred' is as different from the rest of O'Hara's work as 'The Sleepers' is from the rest of Walt Whitman's poetry. The comparison, however brief, between 'Hatred' and 'Sleepers' is apt in that both employ Surrealist (or, in Whitman's case, proto-Surrealist) images as well as an epic sense of descending into amorphous states of intense emotion. By and large, Whitman's poem may not be as rage-filled as 'Hatred', and yet 'The Sleepers', Whitman's darkest poem, certainly complicates any reading of Whitman as an unwaveringly celebratory poet. Beginning with 'I

---

3 Brad Gooch, *City Poet: The Life and Times of Frank O'Hara* (New York: HarperCollins, 1994), p. 225.

wandered all night in my vision', the speaker, in Surrealist fashion, metamorphoses continually, identifying with murderers, 'ennuyes', and even a swimmer whose body is dashed upon the rocks. Perhaps the darkest connection is the suture that occurs between 'the gashed bodies on battlefields' and 'the newborn emerging from gates'. It is in the following section that we see the closest connection between the two poems:

> Now Lucifer was not dead .... or if he was I am his sorrowful terrible heir;
> I have been wronged .... I am oppressed .... I hate him that oppresses me,
> I will either destroy him, or he shall release me.
>
> Damn him! how he does defile me,
> How he informs against my brother and sister and takes pay for their blood,
> How he laughs when I look down the bend after the steamboat that carries away
>   my woman.[4]

Rather than finding a way to recognize the oppressor in the hope of creating the means of mutual identification (elsewhere in the poem, Whitman writes, 'The call of the slave is one with the master's call,/ and the master salutes the slave'),[5] Whitman damns 'him', ironically turning an action born of righteous anger and directed towards the slave trader against himself as the terrible heir of Lucifer. While these days this condemnation seems a decidedly appropriate stance, in Whitman's own historical context the damnation, let alone the inversion of moral polarities by identifying positively with Lucifer *and* the oppressed, would have been more controversial. In any event, Whitman becomes the terrible heir and takes on the debts owed him. Whitman's earlier identification with the master sets himself against himself, and the damnation is a performative speech act born of hatred for an entire class, the oppressors. What creates the link to 'Hatred' is the presence of complicity within hatred. This form of hatred is thus always also a form of self-loathing.

In 'Personism', O'Hara mentions Whitman as one of only three American poets who are better than the movies (the other two are Crane and Williams [*CP*, 498]). In 'Hatred', O'Hara, however unconsciously, draws not upon his predecessor's emphasis on praise and celebration, but on the dark vision that must accompany that praise in order to justify it.[6] Whitman in 'The Sleepers' and O'Hara in 'Hatred'

---

4 Walt Whitman, 'The Sleepers', in *Poetry and Prose*, ed. Justin Kaplan (New York: Library of America Press, 1996), p. 113. This section of the poem was omitted by Whitman from the 1871 and subsequent editions.

5 Whitman, 'The Sleepers', p. 116.

6 Michael Davidson draws a link between Whitman's poem and O'Hara's poem 'Easter', in *Guys Like Us* (Chicago: University of Chicago Press, 2003), p. 117. Davidson observes Whitman's poetics of homoerotic longing informing O'Hara's representation of the cross-dressing fluidity of identities. While there is reason to believe that 'Hatred' is his response to the oppression of homoerotic desire and homosexuality, that too easily locates O'Hara's subject position. The poem is a more fraught space than that reading would suggest.

critique America and American ideology more explicitly than in any other poem either poet wrote. 'I'd retch up all men', the third stanza of 'Hatred' continues, 'I would give / up America and her twenty twistings of my years' (*CP*, 117). Influence is not the issue; rather, both poems enact extreme states of emotion and passion in nearly epic terms, and the negative modality of these two poems counterbalances the more celebratory and even ecstatic stances the two writers take in the rest of their work. Thus, what O'Hara's attention to hatred means in terms of available kinds of experience is essential to understanding the range and depth of what Marjorie Perloff describes as O'Hara's 'aesthetic of attention'.[7]

'Hatred' can be seen to provide a complicating context for the ease and apparent nonchalance of the 'lunch poems'. In Whitman's case, his praise or – more rightly – his *acknowledgment* of the low and the despised can only be meaningful if he also courts the opposite within him: violence and hate. Praise only matters if one has the capacity to condemn or destroy. O'Hara's acknowledgment of love, friendship, and feeling in his later work – another Whitmanian inheritance of sorts – is the more persuasive because he also harbours the capacity to destroy, dismantle and tear apart. Thus, the poems of O'Hara's that come after 'Hatred' can be read as choosing to engage one mode of experiencing and relating to the world over another – 'Hate is only one of many responses'. This choice has ethical ramifications.

As I indicated earlier, the poem levels a critique – or a condemnation, actually – at America and what the speaker describes as a violence that is intrinsic to the nation's identity. The poem's concluding lines are: 'I shall forget forever America, / which was like a memory of an island massacre / in the black robes of my youthful fear of shadows' (*CP*, 120). The allusion to genocide and conquest that dates back to Cortez is evident, just as 'In Memory of My Feelings' will also suggest the lingering ghost of Western imperialism in its references to the *Niña*, the *Pinta*, and the *Santa Maria* and the splintering of the contemporary self. More complex is this sentence's construction, which makes America *always already* (to use the vernacular) 'like a memory' to be forgotten. As a memory, it is at a distance temporally; as a simile, it is at a distance materially. There is a further temporal dislocation as well – the 'shall' expresses a futurity which is the erasing of a memory, the eradication of a past. At the same time as expressing a cognitive distancing (itself a split), the speaker is caught up in the 'massacre'. If we see 'shadows' as a racially charged trope, then the speaker implies that he himself was guilty of racial hatred as a youth. A shadow, moreover, is often a trope for one's own doppelganger, the self's most intimate Other. These readings are a cleaving, and this splintering of the self is present throughout the poem, notably in the following passage:

---

7 The phrase provides the title for the first chapter of Perloff's book *Frank O'Hara: Poet Among Painters* (Chicago and London: University of Chicago Press, 1998 [1977]).

I have hounded myself out of the coral mountains
when my flesh quivered controllably upwards
into the chimneys of a black horde
which were the liberty to work beautifully.

I hounded and hounded into being born
my own death and the death of my country
at the stick, aloft and articulate,
so that the wry words of prophetic ravens
recognized themselves in clutching my wounds

and instantly died as I have wished to be dead
lately. (*CP*, 118)

The speaker is split apart by the violence while also a participant in it in ways that
go beyond a measure of complicity because that violence which attends hatred is
an inescapable element of the speaker's identity. But is this an identification with
the victims, or does that quivering flesh signal an erotic response to the violence, a
response that could either be from the victimizer (a familiar enough perversity) or
the victimized (a perhaps even more disturbing possibility)? The linking of violence
with eroticism creates the shifting position of the speaker, and thus although the
language so obviously does display anger, sometimes a self-righteous anger, the
cause of that response is not clear. Moreover, the eroticism yokes together desire
and hatred in ways that not only complicate either response, but that complicate a
reader's response as well.

One immediate reading of the poem might suggest that nationalism is O'Hara's
target: in the poem, America's hatred seems to be have been always and everywhere,
from its very inception: 'America/ watches at the feet of my ramparting brow/ and
in a three thousand of years of brutes/ will violate the wistful sphinx of myself'
(*CP*, 118). Hatred is part of America's discourse, its culture, part of its *Lebensform*.
The Wittgensteinian concept of a 'form of life' does not mean biological life but
instead refers to historical groups of individuals who are bound together into a
community by a shared set of complex, language-involving practices. The community is formed not by agreement but by a pattern of activity and mores, and these
include the demonstration and interpretation of affect. The *Lebensform* Wittgenstein describes is the frame of reference we learn to work within when initiated into
the language of a given community.[8] Learning that language is thus learning the
outlook, assumptions, and practices with which that language is inseparably bound
and through which its expressions come to their meaning.

Affect in O'Hara's poems is determined by means of its response to a familiar,
intimate Other, as I noted in the address to the 'you' in 'Hatred', and community and

8 See Ludwig Wittgenstein, *Philosophical Investigations*, trans. G. E. M. Anscombe (Englewood Cliffs,
NJ: Prentice-Hall, 3rd edn, 1958). This frame is especially useful in thinking of the presence of
camp, for instance, in O'Hara's work.

Lebensform are the necessary corollaries of that address. Wittgenstein writes, 'What belongs to a language game is a whole culture'.[9] Thus, a *Lebensform* comprises every part of the language use that marks its field of action. How the self is designated within that field is what is at stake in the point of contact that forms between the public and the private (that conception necessary for there even to be a self). To enquire into one aspect of language, in other words, is to begin to think about the broader chiastic relationship between language use and one's being in a world of possible worlds. To think about O'Hara's poem gives insight into what hatred does in forming and informing experiences. Thus, the speaker of 'Hatred' arises out of American violence; as the voice of hatred it only exists because of that hatred. Thus, when the poem says in its first and second lines, 'I part/ my name at the seams of the beast', this bifurcation of identity (the name parting, the *I* itself coming apart) will be a continuing crisis of the poem. If lyric poems express subjectivity, then here the subject's sense of coherence is torn asunder – a problem that unites the poem's tropes, even as it disrupts the poem's syntax. As the passages I have cited indicate, this is one of O'Hara's most disjunctive poems. The disjunctiveness of the poem works against the utilitarian or the more narrowly communicative possibilities of language, with the fractured syntax holding at bay the possibility of resolving the poem's various affective tensions through logic.

'Hatred' is something more than an angry poem. Indeed, it offers the possibility of considering the difference between anger and hatred. Hatred, according to Aristotle, is an ongoing condition and is directed toward a class or group of people, or a type, and, unlike personal anger, is incurable.[10] So, while anger wishes to inflict pain, hatred, widespread and encompassing, wishes to inflict harm. Hatred, again in Aristotle's terms, can only be brought to an end when the hated type or group ceases to exist, when the hatred no longer has an object. Hatred is a trajectory of a self that is formed out of a resistance to the Other, a resistance that wishes, much like sexual desire, to consume the Other. Powerful, destructive, and relentless, hatred perpetuates its own conditions of coming to be.

In O'Hara's poem, paradoxically, the intensity of emotion will always (and necessarily) travel inwards, even if directed outwards toward 'the terrible age' or America. As the poem states, 'I hounded and hounded into being born/ my own death and the death of my country' (*CP*, 118). The hatred feeds on itself, and only by bringing an end to the hated can the hatred be brought to an end. To hate America (in O'Hara's poem) is to hate oneself because the one doing the hating is produced by and therefore produces America, and here 'America' names a condition of hatred. While it is very easy to read this as indictment of American domestic history and the record of its foreign policies, that would limit the referent to its political constitution (for lack of a better term), and would preclude a more

---

9 Ludwig Wittgenstein, *Lectures and Conversations on Aesthetics, Psychology and Religious Belief*, ed. Cyril Barrett (Berkeley: University of California Press, 2007 [1966]), p. 8.
10 Aristotle, *Rhetoric: Book II*, trans. J. E. C. Welldon (New York: Macmillan, 1886), pp. 132–34.

phenomenological reading of the term 'America' as that which names a collective *Lebensform*. If the hatred is brought to an end, the hating subject is also ended. If this is the case, then the unclear 'I' may be hatred itself speaking – the poem being an elaborate prosopopoeia, a mechanism that makes the directness of this voice possible. The 'I' that is born in and of hatred is indistinguishable from the intensity of that emotion. Recognizing that hatred – and the subjectivity that is forged in its kiln – means recognizing it within ourselves and, what is more, acknowledging ourselves by way of its intensity.

What has O'Hara created in this disjunctive, violent, Surrealistic epic poem? The last line of the poem is effectively a fragment: 'So easily conquered by the black torrent of this knife' (*CP*, 120). The fragment gives no clear idea of what is 'so easily conquered'. Moreover, it isn't evident what the knife is. Given the intensity and pace of the poem, the black torrent may be the words themselves as black marks on the page – in that case the knife is the poem. Yet, that seems too easy, too clean, too *symbolic*. With such a reading, the poem would be made to suggest that there is a logic to hatred, and that it is something to be understood. The poem works against just such a proposition. To reassemble the poem in such a way would be a process undertaken *outside* hatred. Literally, with this poem we are brought to read the actions and conditions of hatred, to make sense of that which evades sense. We come now to what it is that the poem might be doing: it presents a constellation of irresolvable intensity.

If, for O'Hara, poetry is either that which finds the poet or that which the poet finds (a formulation to which I will return below), hatred is a passion in excess of choice that comes upon the hating subject. To actively invest in realities at hand, O'Hara seems to offer, is a way of staving off the negative transcendence of hatred by means of an absorption in concrete events and things. This is not to suggest that hatred is simply personal choice or can be responded to merely by changing one's mind the way one changes a television channel. However, it does suggest that poems convey more than just ideas, and that they are more than simply engagements with form. They are also emotional responses that call for the reader to negotiate these responses as affective experiences.

What I have sought to describe are the ways in which O'Hara's poetics is based on a perception of an interpretive dilemma in terms of one's stance toward the world. 'Hatred' is a poem that simultaneously challenges investments and reinforces them. The social, in these terms, is not represented or thematized. Nor is it (merely) the historical milieu – that is, his friends and associates – in which he produced the work. It is the necessary context for subjectivity and experience. In his 'Statement for *The New American Poetry*', O'Hara writes: 'It may be that poetry makes life's nebulous events tangible to me and restores their detail; or conversely, that poetry brings forth the intangible quality of incidents which are all too concrete and circumstantial' (*CP*, 500). Thus, O'Hara's poems can be seen as presenting themselves as enactments and investigations of a self experiencing its own emotions and then making meaning from them. This suggests that seeing O'Hara's poems as mapping the events of the quotidian in urban life does not take O'Hara's claims seriously enough, no matter how useful such an approach might be, in that it would not entail the attempt to discern (or be discerned by) either nebulousness or essence. Poems acknowledge emotional states – either positive or negative – that are too amorphous and complex to put easily into words. At the same time, O'Hara does not offer a solipsistic model of selfhood. Subjectivity is revealed in its negotiations with others, thereby making the poem an ethical encounter of selves that, as literature, remains open and negotiable.

At the heart of O'Hara's statement is the idea that something needs to be expressed (even to oneself), but what that may be is not yet itself expressed: it remains 'nebulous'. In fact, O'Hara's proposition is formed out of one claim and then an opposite claim – the 'or' makes all the difference. In 'Personism', O'Hara emphasizes that negotiation is not just a matter of composition, it is part of the very poetics: '[abstraction in poetry] appears mostly in the minute particulars where decision is necessary' (*CP*, 498). With this in mind, I turn back to O'Hara's two-headed statement. Two very different understandings of poetry are described: one sees poetry as that which restores life and its particularities, the tethering of abstraction to particularities; the other posits the opposite motion, that the world is too leaden in its particularities, and that poetry makes its immanence into a kind of luminescence. These claims are, literally, an ambivalence. The tension is similar to the tension through which one discerns subjectivity out of the push and pull of identification with and resistance to Others and to the Real. Does one resolve that ambivalence, that tension, however, or does it become a generative tension that needs to be sustained lest one come to the inertia of closure and conclusion? O'Hara's poetry shuttles between these two worldviews, these two propositions of poetry's relationship to the world and to the world in which a given reader lives. This is what causes O'Hara's exploration of feeling to be ethical – through it we see how affect guides one's decisions in the world and toward others. That these explorations are undertaken in his poetry suggests that his texts are offered as a means of reading the tension between what one feels and how one externalizes those internal states. We might even say that O'Hara's writing is a two-way listening for this productive tension. In point of fact, when it comes to such dichotomies, one inevitably makes decisions and resolves such tensions. Yet, with O'Hara's comments in mind, such decisions will always be *apparently* contingent and will reveal the ways that one brings one's values to bear on any choice. The scepticism here makes one's choices earned or arrived at, rather than simply performed. How one works to resolve a dilemma (which by its nature resists resolution) reveals subjectivity and produces it. Therein lies the impetus to think about certain philosophical implications of this work, even if O'Hara rarely positioned himself in such a way.

To get to a wider consideration of the ethical dimensions of the social in his poetry and how we might conceive of O'Hara's poems as ethical, affective engagements, I want to include here what might be an overlooked passage from his introduction to a catalogue published in 1966 by the Museum of Modern Art and featuring the work of Robert Motherwell. The ideas within these sentences are central to an understanding of O'Hara's poetics. He writes,

> A symbolic tale of our times, comparable to the legend of Apelles' leaving his sign on the wall, is that of the modern artist who, given the wrappings from issues of a foreign review by a friend, transforms them into two collage masterpieces; and who, given a stack of Japan paper, makes six drawings and on seeing them the next day is so excited by the black ink having bled into orange at its edges that he decides to make six hundred more drawings.[11]

The description of the modern artist refers, of course, to Motherwell, an identification to which O'Hara appends the question, 'Does art choose the artist, or does the man choose art?' To put this in the terms of the current discussion, does the feeling choose the artist, or does the artist choose the feeling? To choose hatred would mean to acknowledge what is otherwise repressed, sublimated, or somehow rationalized, but is no less destructive. We are back to O'Hara's two-part paradox – poetry conceived as either something that happens to things and events, or some essence arising from them. Again, this tension, and not its quick resolution, is the engine of O'Hara's aesthetics, for the dilemma necessitates – provides an occasion for – acts of attention. To ignore or repress are acts of negative attention.

This passage from O'Hara's discussion of Motherwell distils many of the poet's aesthetic values and indicates how the social bears on them. The reference to Apelles fashions a genealogy stretching from antiquity to O'Hara's contemporaries, a genealogy that provides the foundation for the poet's own values and strategies. Each painter (Apelles and Motherwell) creates work that forges a dialogue of materials between artists. Apelles, the finest painter in Ancient Greece, arrives one day at the studio of his fellow artist, Protogenes, in order to strike up an acquaintance. Since the reputation of both artists travelled very far, it was time, or so Apelles believed, that the two met. Finding Protogenes away, Apelles paints a line on an available easel and leaves it as the sole means of identifying himself to the other painter. Upon being shown the line by one of the servants, Protogenes recognizes the mark immediately and then, in response, makes his own.

It is obvious why this would be a crucial moment for O'Hara in terms of his curatorial, art-historical perspective. Apelles's line becomes a gestural rendering of a self, a kind of proto-expressionism. Extending that genealogy, in the more contemporary case of the 'modern artist', Motherwell transforms the gifts of friends into works of Abstract Expressionism: work – that is, *art* – that expressed deep interiority, the very stuff of consciousness, in purely formal terms. O'Hara's comments emphasize the importance of both immediate materiality and one's

---

11 Frank O'Hara, *Motherwell* (New York: Museum of Modern Art, 1965), p. 8.

relationships to the Other as the domain of art. Motherwell's transformation of the materials into art provides for the aesthetic transformation of everyday materials to be sure, but at least as important is the process of relocating his friends' gifts as gestures that can be represented – returned, in a sense – as works of expressivist art. The gifts, as exchanges, are the sign of friendship and Motherwell's transfer of those objects and materials from the ordinary world of discrete, inert objects into art becomes his own gift to his friends in ways that are not sentimental but aesthetic. In short, it is a manifestation of experience as experience, which keeps the poem or work of art open as an unfolding present tense. In this way, the experience continues to begin again, to be ever new and thus is modernist in its foundations. Moreover, Motherwell's activity allows for an example of affect in art as an imaginative response to the world that transforms one experience (sensory *and* emotional) into another legible experience. This begins to sound a great deal like O'Hara's poetry.[12]

O'Hara offers a response to the dilemma he proposes in the question, 'Does art choose the artist, or does the man choose art?' in his 'Statement for *The New American Poetry*', in which he writes, 'What is happening to me, allowing for lies and exaggerations which I try to avoid, goes into my poems. I don't think my experiences are clarified or made beautiful for myself or anyone else; they are just there in whatever form I can find them' (*CP*, 500). This includes the feeling of hatred and the experience of hating. How one finds them, that is, how one undertakes this finding, is the question posed as art. Again we see that the poem enacts a process of negotiation for O'Hara, of getting how things are *as* language *into* language. As with Motherwell – and perhaps now we are free to think of Abstract Expressionism as 'marks that mean' – the material of one's situation (literally and figuratively) becomes art in that it asks for a response, and art, as it was with Apelles, is a conversation with others. That such a conversation perhaps happens often or especially with one's friends and peers does so for the clear reason that these others are those with whom the artist has an existing exchange. But the conversation extends beyond these immediacies to those who have the ability to 'hear' the work – a social constellation of affinities whose economy of shared values and under-

---

12 See also O'Hara, 'The Grand Style of Robert Motherwell', in *SS*, 174–79. In this essay O'Hara indicates that he and Motherwell were friends and that their friendship grew out of conversations about poetry, not art. The poetic resonance of Motherwell's transformation of gifts from friends would thus not be lost on O'Hara. Moreover, the reference is even more instructive in that Protogenes painted a line next to the one made by Apelles and left instruction that it be shown to Apelles if he returned. Apelles made a finer stroke between the two lines. Thus, O'Hara's essays could be seen as his transforming Motherwell's work into something else, language, for instance, or an occasion for experience. O'Hara mentions Apelles in connection with Motherwell again at the end of 'The Grand Style of Robert Motherwell', which appeared first in the pages of *Vogue* in 1965. 'With each line, mass, and torn edge, he is, like Apelles, erecting for us the noble wall of his aspiration against the darkness without' (*SS*, 179). Clearly, these two figures remain closely linked in O'Hara's mind.

standings provides a framework within which the poetry and the art will exist. These relationships are the stuff of elective affinities, a shared sense of ethics and aesthetics that make the exchange even possible. The art or poetry becomes the means by which one's subjectivity can be rendered as a legible object to oneself and for others. This is a far cry from a Wordsworthian overflow of emotion 'recollected in tranquillity' in that the poem is itself the experience of experience made into a public site of negotiation, the poem thus becoming an equivalent incident – at once nebulous, detailed, essential – in the world. Any reader (or viewer) who engages with the work is part of that field of others.

O'Hara's emphasis on feelings is the place at which these things meet – comparable, one might say, to the screen on which a film is projected. The screen shapes those projected images and is what allows an audience to see them. Taking O'Hara's poems seriously entails discovering the work that they do in setting the parameters of affect. The poems are notes of one's subjectivity meant for others that remain other and intimate at the same time. Motherwell transforms his friend's gift – itself an expression of feeling – into another gesture, that of his paintings and collages. One feeling begets another, and yet each feeling is an affective text to be read. In a sense, these aesthetic responses objectify the expressed feeling. O'Hara then reads that gesture and performs another one, the writing of his essay, and within this essay one scries the values and beliefs and modes of experience that also guide O'Hara's poems. The poem is the gestural act of the self, the interior that is read only by its activity in the world. 'The wistful Sphinx' that O'Hara mentions in 'Hatred' (borrowing the trope Nietzsche uses at the beginning of *Beyond Good and Evil*) is how we seem not only to the world, but to ourselves as well. Emotional conditions are thus connected with ethical considerations, since emotions are responses to the world as well as a means of discovering one's stance towards others – and, by discovering that stance, revealing oneself in those emotions. As O'Hara writes in the last stanza of an early poem, 'And the landscape will do/ us some strange favor when/ we look back at each other/ anxiously' (*CP*, 42). In O'Hara's self-conscious poetics, the landscape's 'favour' becomes the occasion for a glance between two subjects to become a meaningful text to be read by each (and by a reader). Just as the glance back to the other reminds us that verse is always involved in the action of turning – by, in other words, negotiating another's experiences – we reveal our own subjective investments through how, when, and at whom we look.

Earlier, I cited O'Hara's ideas about abstraction in poetry, which 'appears mostly in the minute particulars where decision is necessary'. Rather than creating a poem that symbolizes emotion, O'Hara has created a space that enacts hatred in all its complex rage and undecidability. In doing so, the poem forms an encounter with hatred that one can learn to identify, and that entails acts of decision and judgment. If, in his work, O'Hara transforms experience into experience, one that the reader then participates in and can come to invest in, then the relentless intensity of the poem gives one the possibility either to meet or to turn away from hatred *by* meeting it, through revealing its tendencies to oneself.[13] Yet to turn away from it means that the voice of the poem remains unacknowledged. To leave it unacknowledged means that hatred, in all its permutations, is literally unrecognizable. If it is part of that which is called 'America' as an ontological reality, to deny that hatred is to deny oneself, to split oneself, and thereby 'split [one's] name'. Thus, O'Hara's poem makes central the process of making decisions within an undecidable condition. We cannot be made to understand hatred, since there is no perspective from which that would be possible. It is enough to recognize that hatred is recognizable. That way, at least, we cannot deny that it has been denied. Only that way can we come to see poetry's singular means of facilitating acknowledgment. And so, in this case, does the hatred find us or do we find it, and once found what, literally, are we to make of it? O'Hara makes a poem of it; a reader makes an experience out of that poem. There are worse things to do with hatred, and, as O'Hara's poem shows us, worse things to become.

---

13 I am borrowing here from an expressivist model developed from Hegel's ideas of art. As Hegel writes in his lectures on aesthetics, 'the universal need for expression in art lies, therefore, in man's rational impulse to exalt the inner and outer world into a spiritual consciousness for himself, as an object in which he recognizes his own self. He satisfies the need of this spiritual freedom when he makes all that exists explicit for himself *within*, and in a corresponding way realizes this his explicit self *without*, evoking thereby, in his reduplication of himself, what is in him into vision and into knowledge for his own mind and for that of others.' See G. W. F. Hegel, *Introductory Lectures on Aesthetics*, ed. Michael Inwood, trans. Bernard Bosanquet (New York: Penguin, 1993 [1886]), p. 36.

'A Gasp of Laughter at Desire': Frank O'Hara's Poetics of Breath

Josh Robinson

for Jason Wirth

The physical body is prominent in Frank O'Hara's poetry. His own writings on poetics emphasize the role of the body in the process of artistic creation:

> It seemed to me that the metrical, that the measure, let us say, if you want to talk about it in Olson's poems or Ezra Pound's, comes from the breath of the person just as a stroke of paint comes from the wrist and hand and arm and shoulder and all that of the painter. So therefore the point is really more to establish one's own measure and breath in poetry [...] rather than fitting your ideas into an established order, syllabically and phonetically and so on. (*SS*, 17)

As part of this emphasis on the body, he explicitly draws parallels between writing and production within other artistic media, whether the tongue-in-cheek comparison in 'Why I Am Not a Painter' (*CP*, 261–62) of the writing of 'Oranges: 12 Pastorals' (*CP*, 5–9) with Mike Goldberg's *Sardines*, or the lines in 'Far from the Porte des Lilas and the Rue Pergolèse' that suggest techniques of poetic production derived from the gestural abstraction of the New York School painters: 'a dream of immense sadness peers through me/ as if I were an action poem that couldn't write' (*CP*, 311). My intention in this essay is neither to elide nor to investigate the differences between painterly and poetic modes of production.[1] Indeed, O'Hara himself emphasizes the difficulty of carrying out such a comparative study and warns against the dangers of ignoring the singularity of distinct forms of aesthetic activity:

> Well, you can't have a statement saying 'My poetry is the Sistine chapel of verse,' or 'My poetry is just like Pollock, de Kooning and Guston rolled into one great verb,' or 'My poetry is like a windy day on a hill overlooking the stormy ocean' – first of all it

---

1 Unsatisfactory generalizations such as Marjorie Perloff's claim that O'Hara 'wrote primarily for the eye rather than the ear' warn against the dangers of the former; *Frank O'Hara: Poet Among Painters* (New York: Braziller, 1977), p. 117. 'The Visual Poetic of Frank O'Hara', *QUID* 16 (2006), pp. 7–15, is my attempt to carry out the latter. I would like to express my thanks to Ian Noonan; to Isaac Gewirtz, Stephen G. Crook, Nina Schneider and Philip Milito at the Berg Collection in the New York Public Library; and to Beci Carver, Elizabeth Pender and Ian Patterson for their comments on an earlier version of this paper at a workshop at the University of Cambridge.

isn't so far as I can tell, and secondly even if it were something like all of these that wouldn't be because I managed to make it that way. I couldn't, it must have been an accident, and I would probably not recognize it myself. Further, what would poetry like that be? It would have to be the Sistine Chapel itself, the paintings themselves, the day and time specifically. Impossible. (*CP*, 510)

In the argument that follows I hope to do justice to the singularity of poetry – and of O'Hara's poetry in particular – as an incorporation of bodily activity. This essay's concern is to investigate one aspect of the different ways in which the body might be thought of as 'producing' a poem, and some of the points at which the body intrudes into the poem, leaving a perceptible trace. My focus is the manifestation of breath and laughter within his poems.

When I describe O'Hara's poetry as singular there are two things in particular that I mean, and several that I do not mean. I am obviously not seeking to advance the claim that laughter is unique to poetic or literary works, less still that O'Hara's are uniquely funny. Rather, I want to claim that there is a particular way in which his poetic texts relate to breath and voicing, and that laughter is an important aspect of this. I will examine how breath is configured and performed, both in the poetic voice and in the readerly response. My hope is that what follows can contribute to a phenomenological account of reading, developed from close consideration of particular aspects of the experience of one form of artwork. That is, when I refer to O'Hara's poems I am talking not only about the particular arrangement of ink on paper, but also about my experience of them, how they feel both within and beyond my voice. It is an attempt to discuss his poetry as I experience it, and, indeed, as I might expect or hope others to experience it.

As I read O'Hara's poems, I would like to advance two hypotheses, not in order to subject them to scientific investigation, but to consider what they might tell us about the experience of reading. The first and weaker of the two is that there is a connection between the physical activity that constitutes laughter – particularly the muscular contractions as one breathes in a particular way – and the affective state with which we associate it. Indeed, it seems uncontroversial to claim that there is a link between laughter and mirth.[2] What is not so clear is the precise nature of the relationship between these two phenomena. My second and stronger – and perhaps therefore more tendentious – hypothesis is that breathing in particular ways can induce particular affective states. This is not to rest my case on the claim that such states are necessarily always caused by breathing, but rather to suggest that particular observable phenomena in the ways in which we breathe – such as laughter – are not mere manifestations of or responses to our affective state. That

---

2 Anyone who has been tickled will be able to confirm that laughter can be induced by external physical stimuli. Researchers at UCLA have managed to isolate an area of the brain where an electrical stimulus can elicit a similar response: Itzhak Fried and others, 'Electric Current Stimulates Laughter', *Nature* 391 (1998), p. 650.

laughter and the particular ways of breathing that characterize it often go hand-in-hand with mirth is not in doubt. I would like to suggest not that these ways of breathing directly control our emotional and affective state, but rather that they affect it – that mirth, for example, can to an extent be reinforced, if not induced, by breath.[3] I do not wish simply to claim that laughter and mirth constitute a particular example of breath and emotion in general – for laughter can of course be associated with feelings other than mirth – but rather, that breath plays a part in the complex bodily systems that influence emotion.

Equally important are more social aspects of breath and laughter, which have been debated at least since Aristotle's assertion that humans alone have the capacity to laugh.[4] Both phenomena have the potential for social effects, although given that their influence on others is likely to be manifested at least partly physiologically, the separation between the physiological and social spheres should not be treated as absolute. Listening to others' laughter has been shown to induce 'positive affect', a trend that is more pronounced when listening to voiced rather than unvoiced laughter.[5] It is not only the acknowledgement of someone else's mirth that has an effect on the observer, but also the particular way in which the breath and vocal cords combine to express this mirth, in this case in laughter. This is not to claim that an individual's reactions to laughter can be satisfactorily explained by means solely of physiological or psychological investigation. These reactions are also, of course, historically, culturally and socially mediated, as are the ways in which both breath and laughter can be used as a conscious means of visibly responding to others' actions, even when it is unclear exactly what reaction is intended. And in the particular society in which we live, the signification of laughter is not necessarily positive:

> In wrong society laughter has infected happiness like a sickness, and draws it into society's worthless totality. Laughing about something is always laughter at its expense, and the life that according to Bergson breaks through rigidity in laughter is in truth a barbarity that breaks in, the self-assertion that dares to celebrate its liberation from scruple at the first opportunity. The collective of those who laugh parodies humanity.[6]

3 For example, I know that if I breathe in quick, shallow breaths, I begin to feel panic, whereas if I breathe slowly and deeply from my diaphragm, I feel more relaxed. Scientific study has observed increased muscular relaxation after 'simulated laughter' and even some respiratory exercises, as well as after 'true laughter': Mary Payne Bennett and Cecile Lengacher, 'Humor and Laughter May Influence Health: III. Laughter and Health Outcomes', *Evidence-based Complimentary Medicine* 5.1 (2008), pp. 37–40, at p. 38.

4 *Parts of Animals*, translated by W. Ogle, in *The Complete Works of Aristotle*, ed. Jonathan Barnes (Princeton: Princeton University Press, 1985), 2 vols., vol. I, pp. 994–1086, at p. 1049.

5 Jo-Ann Bachorowski and Michael J. Owren, 'Not All Laughs Are Alike: Voiced But Not Unvoiced Laughter Readily Elicits Positive Affect', *Psychological Science* 12.3 (May 2001), pp. 252–57, at pp. 253–56.

6 Theodor W. Adorno and Max Horkheimer, *Dialektik der Aufklärung*, vol. 3 of Theodor W. Adorno,

Laughter is no longer, if it ever was, simply a means of expressing and sharing mirth. Its social function has become debased, along with society, permeated by what Adorno and Horkheimer term the 'triumph over beauty executed by humour', the domination of everyday life by the culture industry to the extent that aesthetic experience worthy of the name is no longer possible.[7] This state of affairs is of course closely tied up with political trends, inextricably linked to the growth of authoritarian influences in society: 'Reconciled laughter resounds as the echo of having escaped from power; bad laughter copes with fear by defecting to the authorities that are to be feared.'[8] In the form that it is prescribed by the entertainment industry, laughter becomes deferential in the face of illegitimately and dangerously wielded power. Adorno insists that we have reached a point at which laughter has become thoroughly distorted: 'Laughter, in which for Bergson life restores itself from its hardening into convention, has in fact long since become convention's weapon of convention against uncomprehended life, against the mere traces of something natural that has not been completely domesticated.'[9] Indeed, the complaint is not only against laughter as an expression of unease, but also against the emotions that sometimes accompany it, as Adorno, claiming that communication has become impossible, asserts that 'the smallest step towards joy is one towards the hardening of pain'.[10]

But while this disaffection, seen in the light not only of the events of the mid-twentieth century but also of some trends in mass and popular culture since then, seems perhaps not unreasonable, it would be dangerous to think that it represented the full story. Indeed, as Adorno and Horkheimer recognize, not all imaginable laughter is the bad kind. This is perhaps unsurprising, given the ambiguous status of their rejections of culture and society under late capitalism. Adorno does indeed proclaim that there is no possibility of finding right life within wrong life,[11] but this has to be understood in the context of the claim that 'consciousness wouldn't be able to despair over the colour grey at all if it didn't harbour the idea of a different colour whose dispersed trace is not absent from the negative whole'.[12] The decree, then, that there is no right life to be found within the wrong one that we are compelled to live, is not so much a claim that nothing remains that allows us to imagine the possibility of redemption, as an injunction not to attempt to become satisfied with the traces we can find of life lived as it should be.

Gesammelte Schriften (Frankfurt am Main: Suhrkamp, 1981), p. 163. All translations from the German are my own.

7   Adorno and Horkheimer, *Dialektik der Aufklärung*, p. 162.

8   Adorno and Horkheimer, *Dialektik der Aufklärung*, p. 162.

9   Theodor W. Adorno, *Negative Dialektik*, in *Gesammelte Schriften*, vol. 6 (Frankfurt am Main: Suhrkamp, 1973), pp. 7–408, pp. 327–28.

10 Theodor W. Adorno, *Minima Moralia*, in *Gesammelte Schriften*, vol. 4 (Frankfurt am Main: Suhrkamp, 1980), p. 27.

11 Adorno, *Minima Moralia*, p. 43.

12 Adorno, *Minima Moralia*, p. 370.

And despite the invective Adorno deploys against both laughter and some of the emotions with which it is associated, there remains within his theory a significant role for pleasure, sensory and otherwise: 'The happiness that rises in the eye of the person who thinks is the happiness of humanity. [...] Thought is happiness, even where it determines unhappiness: by expressing it.'[13] Happiness, 'the only aspect of metaphysical experience that is more than impotent longing', refuses to allow us to forget that things might be otherwise.[14] But the price for this knowledge is that we must not treat moments of happiness as ends in themselves, as substitutes for utopian thinking: 'All happiness up until today promises what has not yet been, and the belief in its immediacy stands in the way of its becoming.'[15] We must not allow ourselves to think that the happiness we can experience today is anything more than a fragment of reconciled happiness in its entirety[16] – but nor is it something we can afford to ignore.

That is, although we undeniably live in a late capitalist society with all its wrongness, there are still traces within it of something better. Not traces that allow us to reconcile ourselves to wrong life as we live it, but traces that sustain the thought that things might one day be different, that suggest how right life might be lived. Such traces allow us not only to despair, but also to hope. Artworks and our experience of them are one such trace. I do not wish to imply that we might be able to base an idea of some sort of non-parodic human collective on our understanding of how we respond to a work, less still that talking about poems might be a vehicle for re-establishing a lost mode of human communication. Rather, it is an attempt to recognize the glimpse within aesthetic experience not of a reconciled state of being, but of its possibility. And I would like to claim that there is something in particular about aesthetic experience – not necessarily something about the experience of his poems – that we can learn from O'Hara's poetics.

My discussion of his poetry begins, therefore, with the examination of some manifestations of breath and laughter within a few of his earliest published poems, some in which laughter and mirth seem coextensive, others in which the relationship is more problematic. I consider situations in which laughter can be understood to signal feelings other than mirth, and the influence of breath on some other emotional states. I then look at instances within O'Hara's oeuvre in which both breath and laughter appear as a means, not always intentional, of communicating emotion. Finally, I address aspects of the role of breath and laughter within what might broadly be called aesthetic experience, focusing on four later poems, all from 1959 or 1960. I attempt to address the question of how these four poems might be thought of as inducing a particular bodily response in their readers, through, for

---

13 Theodor W. Adorno, 'Kritik', in *Kulturkritik und Gesellschaft II*, *Gesammelte Schriften*, vol. 10.2 (Frankfurt am Main: Suhrkamp, 1977), pp. 794–99, at pp. 798–99.
14 Adorno, *Negative Dialektik*, p. 367.
15 Adorno, *Negative Dialektik*, p. 346.
16 Adorno, *Negative Dialektik*, p. 396.

example, the stimulation of laughter or even the manipulation of the speaker's breath.

Perhaps the most striking juxtaposition of emotion and laughter within O'Hara's poetry appears in 'Night Thoughts in Greenwich Village' (*CP*, 38). The poem opens with a succession of vocatives, punctuated with exclamation marks: 'O my coevals! embarrassing/ memories! pastiches! jokes!' The thoughts referred to in the poem's title are the speaker's recollections of his contemporaries, to whom the poem is addressed, along with some of the diverse thoughts that they inspire, and that bring their thinker to laughter. Written in 1950 or 1951, the poem is among O'Hara's earliest. The speaker's youth is prominent in the text, but in such a way as to highlight its transience:

All your pleasaunces and
the vividness of your ills
are only fertilizer for
the kids. Who knows what
will be funny next year? (*CP*, 38)

A few lines further on, the phrase 'The too young' provides an explicit point of contrast to the speaker – 'at twenty four' this speaker and his 'coevals' appear not to have much time left. This sense of transience is expressed through rhythmical irregularity, the stark pauses that occur within the opening lines accentuated by the difficulty of constructing any sort of syntactical relation between the nominal phrases. As the poem continues, many of the line-breaks seem positioned in order to avoid the possibility that they might coincide with or emphasize a syntactical pause. Indeed, in ten of the poem's 25 lines a pronounced pause falls before the line's final monosyllable, as if to displace that word into the next breath-unit. The effect is a voice that feels slightly rushed, not so much because it is difficult to find a point at which to breathe, as because these points occur irregularly, almost unexpectedly. Indeed, when the speaker asks 'Who knows what/ will be funny next year?', it seems that what brings laughter is a surprise.

This poem's laughter is by no means co-existent with mirth.[17] Rather, it is something to be coaxed out or hoped for, then refused. 'The days will not laugh'. At times it is even something to be scared of, as the speaker seems to fear 'the harrowing laugh/ of children at my heels – directed at me!' The final three words of this quotation, almost semantically unnecessary, suggest further discomfort, a sense emphasized by the hesitancy of the pause at the end of the previous line, one of the few that coincides with a line-break. Indeed, the fact that this pause is followed by a reiteration of the perception that the poem's speaker is the target of

---

17 In contrast, the lyric I in 'Just for Now', O'Hara's unpublished translation from Reverdy, subsumes his entire 'joy' into 'A single peal of laughter' that resounds through the house. The translation held at the Koch Archive, Berg Collection, New York Public Library. Box 182, Folder 23 (see Appendix, below).

the laughter serves to strengthen the impression of unease. The laughter 'becomes defensive!' Others' laughter no longer produces an ambience of pleasure, but is associated with a very different effect. Laughter is a constant presence throughout the poem – the words 'laugh' and 'laughter' appear three times within the short text – but its significance varies. And yet, despite this registering of discomfort, the poem remains apparently light-hearted, as if its speaker, 'the Dada / baby', should not be taken too seriously.

Similarly, in a later poem such as 'The Afternoon' (*CP*, 173–75), for example, 'They laugh when I describe the ghosts', but we cannot know whether the laughter is appreciative, nervous or derisory. And again, in the unpublished poem 'Love', there is the injunction to 'Look across the brook / To where the man is / Laughing'.[18] Despite the man's definite article, we are told nothing more about him, left unaware of the cause of his laughter. It is a situation in which one might somehow expect there to be something to notice, something to which our attention is being drawn, signified by the laughing man (indeed, we are told not to look at him, but to look 'to where' he is). But instead, he is simply there, to be noticed. Laughing without cause, and without a discernible object of amusement. His laughter is reduced to – if it were ever more than – a means of facilitating others' conversation.

'A Quiet Poem' (*CP*, 20), in contrast, breathes more easily. Laughter is absent from the poem, but breath is foregrounded. It is mentioned only twice, in the second and the last of the poem's seven non-rhymed couplets, but it is through the poem's management of the breath that it enacts its title. It dates from the same period as 'Night Thoughts', probably slightly earlier, but the two poems have a very different rhythmical feel – as is perhaps to be expected given that whereas 'Night Thoughts' displays the almost restless anxiety of a speaker concerned with the passing of time, 'A Quiet Poem' concerns itself with repose. In contrast to the systematic enjambment of 'Night Thoughts', the ends of 12 of the poem's 14 lines coincide with a syntactical pause, although only three of these are marked by punctuation (this, though, in a poem that contains only six punctuation marks). The lines are slightly longer than those of 'Night Thoughts' – to use an arbitrary measure, median line-length is seven syllables in 'Night Thoughts', nine in 'A Quiet Poem'. 'A Quiet Poem' feels much slower, partly, I suspect, because of the white space between each of the couplets, but partly because of this coincidence of pauses, with the result that when attempting to voice the poem I begin to expect to pause at the end of each line. My experience of the enjambment in the third couplet thus differs considerably from those in 'Night Thoughts': 'The cloud is then so subtly dragged / away by the silver flying machine'.

Whereas while reading 'Night Thoughts' I feel compelled to pause before the line reaches its end, as if preparing myself to race across the line-break to avoid having to acknowledge it, in this couplet I find myself lingering over the word 'dragged', as

18 Koch Archive, Berg Collection, New York Public Library. Box 182, Folder 21 (see Appendix, below).

if the line-break delays the adverbial 'away' that modifies the verb which it follows. This impression is accentuated when I attempt to read the lines aloud, something I find myself unable to do without lengthening the vowel in 'dragged', delaying the consonants, often adding a pause before the start of the following line. It is as if the objects 'without breath' are not breathless in the sense of needing more air, but simply calm and in no need of breath. This calmness remains till the poem's close: 'Now,/ slowly, the heart breathes to music'. It is as if the beating of the heart has become a much slower process, almost as if voluntarily slowed. My impression, however, is not of an external force that in some way compels the heart to breathe at a certain speed, but rather of two factors that establish themselves in harmony, as if the music is at least in part the heart's own creation. Like the secrecy of the breath in 'How Roses Get Black' (*CP*, 3) – according to Donald Allen, the earliest of all the poems that O'Hara 'conceivably would have wanted to see in print' (*CP*, v) – breath here, even without laughter, seems to be a deeply personal, perhaps even clandestine, form of emotional cognition, at least at the moment at which it is experienced. Breath is presented as a sort of deeply personal reflection that is fundamental not only to recognizing the breather's affective state, but also to allowing this state to come into existence.

Breath, of course, can equally function as a means of conveying emotions and recognizing those of others. Those who stand and watch in 'The Clown' (*CP*, 26–27), for example, express their reaction in audible sighs, while without breath the responses of the eponymous figure are more ambivalently presented as 'He smiled at their solicitude'. Similarly, the speaker of 'October 26 1952 10:30 O'Clock' (*CP*, 105–106) acknowledges the addressee's 'sigh/ of boredom'. By the time of 'Poem' ['I am not sure if there is a cure'] (*CP*, 165), written a year later, the relationship between breath and emotion seems to have become more uncertain. The slowness enacted and induced by the breath of the speaking voice resembles that of 'A Quiet Poem', but to a different end. Instead of objects 'without breath', we witness a speaker who 'can barely draw breath any more'. But this is hardly a cry for help from someone unable to inhale enough oxygen. Rather, breath seems to be used metaphorically to suggest something like indifference. Perhaps the acknowledgement that 'I am in a quarry' is somehow a lazy, vandalized or misheard expression of quandariness – or perhaps more accurately, of resignation in the face of impotence, as if whatever emotion is felt cannot have an effect on anything. Resignation then gives way to anger:

> Clouds! do you see this fist?
> I have just put it through you!
> Sun! you do well to crouch
> and snarl, I have willed you away. (*CP*, 165)

This verse-paragraph interrupts the calmness as the emphatic stresses combine with the marked pauses that occur within three of the lines to generate what I can best describe as a form of tension. I feel myself wanting hurriedly to spit out the words between the stress-maxima, in stark contrast to the resigned slowness of the 'sighing, sighing' that precedes this section. But the interruption is temporary, the poem ending, after a gentle exhalation, with a return to poise and resignation. The understatedness of breath here is almost coeval with the ambivalent non-expression of emotion: 'if she falls, she falls'.

Meanwhile, in 'Poem' ['There I could never be a boy'] (*CP*, 216–17), the connection between breath and emotion is played out rather differently, as a mother 'wishes upon herself/ the random fears of a scarlet soul, as it breathes in and out/ and nothing chokes'. Here breathing is at once something perfectly normal and to be expected, as if synonymous with the soul's being, and something strangely incongruous. It seems that the soul's breathing induces its 'random fears', which another person then hopes to assume. Similarly incongruous are Daphnis' lines to Chloe in 'Very Rainy Light, an Eclogue' (*CP*, 135–36): 'You must come when my throaty heart/ traces the wiry meteors to breathe/ in your ear its invitation to the beach'. This time it is not the soul but the heart that breathes, as three organs combine to make an invitation. Both the desire to invite and the execution of that desire seem to come from the heart, while 'breathe' is used to refer to the entire act of expression, a metonymic reduction that makes the act of breathing identical not only with living and feeling, but also with sharing what is felt.

Breath and laughter are prominent in a very different way in O'Hara's unpublished 'Variations on a Theme of Kenneth Koch after his Variations on a Theme by William Carlos Williams'.[19] Each of the four stanzas consists of two sentences, the second always a question referring to one or both of the 'two poets', who are introduced in the poem's first line. The third stanza ends 'Are all the/ Poets out of wind?' and the fourth 'Why/ Is our Poet giggling?' This is not the place to discuss the relative inferiority of this poem to Koch's 'Variations on a Theme by William Carlos Williams' or indeed to Williams' 'This Is Just to Say'. What is at stake here is the way laughter takes on an almost conspiratorial role, as one of the two 'out of wind' poets (devoid of inspiration or energy, perhaps) is observed giggling, a form of laughter that depends on interaction with others. The rhetorical question as to the inspiration for laughter seems posed almost in faux-innocence, emphasizing the fact that the giggling is what Adorno and Horkheimer might have condemned as a parody of human communication. This laughter seems to be social in a particular way: two characters, one of whom is the poem's speaker (in this case, one presumes, identical with its writer) colluding to amuse themselves and each other. If it is indeed the case, as the sirens claim in the poem, that 'poetry is dead' – or in Adornian terms, that it is barbaric to write a poem after Auschwitz[20] – then the only response is to giggle inanely. However, as Adorno himself conceded, poetry

19 Koch Archive, Berg Collection, New York Public Library. Box 182, Folder 21 (see Appendix, below).
20 Theodor W. Adorno, 'Kulturkritik und Gesellschaft', in *Kulturkritik und Gesellschaft I*, *Gesammelte Schriften*, vol. 10.1 (Frankfurt am Main: Suhrkamp, 1973), pp. 11–30, at p. 30.

is not dead.[21] My claim is not that bad laughter does not exist, but that it is not all that exists; not that Adorno and Horkheimer are wrong, but that their critique of laughter in response to the culture industry is not the full story. I wish to advance this claim in relation to four late poems, all dating from 1959 and 1960.

The importance of breath not only to the expression of emotion but also to its very existence is perhaps most strikingly realized in 'Poem [light   clarity   avocado salad in the morning]' (*CP*, 350), dated December 1959. Here, breath is presented as essential to cognition, which is itself something almost immediate, a bodily state of being. The presence of the poem's 'you' is implied throughout: although the second-person pronoun appears only once, towards the end of the poem, the repeated nouns 'forgiveness' and 'love' (the former used three times, the latter five, within an eleven-line poem) both suggest that another person is at least present in the speaker's thoughts. But the status of this presence is problematic, almost denied by the acknowledgement that 'you feel distant', although only 'a block away'. Instead, the speaker presents an intense degree of familiarity not with the absent addressee but rather with his own body: 'and all thoughts disappear in a strange quiet excitement/ I am sure of nothing but this, intensified by breathing'.

I find myself unsure as to whether the certainty that is intensified is that of the love, or that of the singularity of its experience, the feeling that in comparison with it everything else fades into insignificance. Either way, this clarity takes place against the backdrop of an almost tumbling breathlessness, in which the relatively long lines fall into one another, hardly punctuated (the poem contains only two commas). The lines are not entirely paratactic, but as there is no clear indication where each clause ends, the limits to the scope of the conjunctions are also unclear. In the fifth line the tautology 'love is love' combines with the apparent self-contradiction of 'how amazing it is/ to find forgiveness and love, not even forgiveness' to establish a voice expressing anything but certainty, as if the speaker were trying to convince himself of the truth of the claim that 'nothing can ever go wrong'. After this the calmness of the final two lines, slowed by the juxtaposition of heavily stressed monosyllables and a strong syntactic pause in the final line, provides a clear resolution. The emotional content of 'Poem [light   clarity   avocado salad in the morning]' depends explicitly on the breath of its speaker and implicitly on the control of the breathing of its reader.

And yet breath and emotion are not identical: the final certainty is merely 'intensified by breathing'. There is nothing like the immediacy implied in the 1953 poem 'River' (*CP*, 123), in which the speaker explicitly identifies existence with thoughts and emotions through the medium of breath: 'My very life/ became the inhalation of its weedy ponderings'. Indeed, it is only with the final words of 'Poem [light   clarity   avocado salad in the morning]' that the breath is able to intensify certainty, after the sparsely punctuated and often syntactically ambiguous clauses

---

21 Adorno, *Negative Dialektik*, p. 355.

have come to an end. The first-person pronoun with which the final line begins signals the beginning of a new clause to coincide with the line-break, slowing the tempo at which the poem's words can be read, an effect that is emphasized by the pause forced by the mid-line comma. It is as if the certainty can only be achieved through the act of relaxation after the almost breathless hesitancy played out in the earlier part of the poem. Attuned situatedness within the physical body enables emotional self-recognition

'Having a Coke with You' (*CP*, 360) does not foreground breath in the same way. The single explicit reference to it takes place within a simile, as the speaker describes his being with his lover as 'drifting back and forth/ between each other like a tree breathing through its spectacles'. The scene seems relaxed: still, but by no means lifeless. Yet the scope of breath's influence extends well beyond this clause. As I attempt to read the poem aloud, I feel myself almost compelled to breathe in a particular way. None of its long lines is end-stopped, and while most of the lines coincide with the ends of clauses, the points at which there is no such coincidence feel much less poised:

> it is hard to believe when I'm with you that there can be anything as still
> as solemn as unpleasantly definitive as statuary when right in front of it
> in the warm New York 4 o'clock light we are drifting back and forth
> between each other like a tree breathing through its spectacles (*CP*, 360)

I am unable to perform these lines in any way that does not induce in me a sense of breathlessness and physical difficulty as the unpunctuated clauses follow one another, combining dense and difficult imagery with an uncertainty as to the precise syntactical relationship between the clauses. Each time I read these lines I find myself unable to construe them as anything other than a single compound sentence, with no period construed either before or during the third line. The effect is an almost breathless sequence of clauses, followed by the substantial pause required to regain enough breath to continue, perhaps triggering, or at least allowing, the transition to a more reflective topic that follows. This is not to claim that they necessarily induce the same effect in a silent encounter with the text, but it seems unlikely that a silent reading would not at some level notice the fact that this sequence of words is longer than can be comfortably voiced in one breath, as if thoughts are flowing unchecked into one another more quickly than they can comfortably be enunciated.

While laughter is not mentioned within the poem, it is nonetheless present. Indeed, it is a text that brings me to mirth (and usually laughter of some sort) every time I read it. The grammatical and apparent causal equivalence drawn between 'my love for you' and 'your love for yoghurt' raises a smile partly because of the two so widely differing senses in which 'love' is used, partly because of the apparent absurdity that spending time with someone is fun because he enjoys eating yoghurt. And then the paintings, apparently of diminished significance in comparison to the speaker's lover, only seem able to break into the poem as a point of comparison:

> [...] I look
> at you and I would rather look at you than all the portraits in the world
> except possibly for the *Polish Rider* occasionally and anyway it's in the Frick
> which thank heavens you haven't gone to yet so we can go together the first time
>
> (*CP*, 360)

The almost flippant concessive clause in the third cited line first disrupts the almost formulaic praise for the interlocutor's beauty with an honesty that rather than softening the compliment makes it seem all the more genuine, after which the thought is developed, almost rescued, into an endearing suggestion for a shared plan to look at paintings together. It is almost as if the words flow out one after another, as if the thoughts they express are unpremeditated and spontaneous, such that they need to be corrected, refined. The effect is without doubt mirthful, but I do not see in this poem a trace of the sort of laughter that might reasonably be denounced as a sickness infecting happiness. I would like to suggest that this is because the poem's laughter does not take place at the expense of other affective responses, but rather within the context of other emotions which are also experienced within the body. It is part of a range of sensations, a range of ways of communicating those sensation. Its purpose is not to reveal that the person laughing is somehow more aware than those who watch. Rather, its mirthfulness is one aspect of the breath that is essential in the act of recognizing a 'marvellous experience' and 'telling you about it'.

In 'On Rachmaninoff's Birthday #158' (*CP*, 418–19), although the emotion is sadness rather than mirth, there is a similar immediacy to the experience of listening, the need to:

> [...] finish this
> before your 3rd goes off the radio
> or I won't know what I'm feeling
> tonight
> tonight
> anytime
> or
> ever

The affective experience must be described – described is perhaps an inadequate concept; it would perhaps be more accurate to think of it as a capturing, a recreating or even a performing – while it happens. The response to the music, then, is initially almost one of bewilderment. The account that follows is almost paraliptic: the description is more of the difficulty of describing the experience than of some notional experience itself. The speaker is not so much breathless as lost for words. Indeed, the speaker is explicitly not breathless as he implores 'kiss me again / I'm still breathing'. There is something erotic about it, as if the best description is through the analogy with sexual desire – indeed, as if the particular sensation is best conveyed by an analogy to the desire to be kissed, as long as one is alive. It is not simply the case that poetry is not dead, that the experience of artworks is still possible, but rather that it is necessary, that such experience is a means of responding to a burning imperative felt in the body.

'The Day Lady Died' (*CP*, 325) performs a different reaction to the experience of listening to music. It is not so much an account of aesthetic experience as of the way in which the news of someone's death recreates such an experience – or, to put it the other way round, the ability of such aesthetic events to reside in the memory and to make themselves present. At the start of the poem, life is anonymous, surrounded by people 'I don't know', measured in terms of what can be bought, whether for oneself or for someone else. Although hardly punctuated (the poem contains only five commas) and not at all end-stopped, the short lines leave plenty of space to breathe, as if the poem is following an unmeasured and meandering course through New York. But the course is insistent. While the poem does not seem to rush, it does not give an opportunity to do anything other than be carried along. Its course cannot be broken off. Until the sight of the cover of the *New York Post* breaks this temporal order:

> and I am sweating a lot by now and thinking of
> leaning on the john door in the 5 spot
> while she whispered a song along the keyboard
> to Mal Waldron and everyone and I stopped breathing

'I am sweating' is the poem's first use of the continuous present: up until this point, every action has been something either that has happened or that will happen. The sudden shift of tense interrupts the flow of events, suspending the poem, and with it the day, within the memory triggered by the fact that Holiday is now literally out of breath. There is also the implicit suggestion of a link between the breathlessness of the aesthetic event and the breathlessness of death: by the end of the poem aesthetic appreciation takes place in the context of the awareness of mortality. It is unclear whether the poem's closing words describe people holding their breath in order to hear Holiday's whispering voice or in response to it. Indeed, the distinction is perhaps irrelevant, since my aim throughout this essay has been to suggest that holding one's breath is not simply a response to an emotional state, but also something that affects that very state. This response, moreover, is not that of one person alone. Nor is it merely a generalized response from a universalizing 'everyone'. It is a collective that does not seek to erase the individual's response, but rather is based on it. And as the poem ends, its controlled breathlessness remains, shared. Like the relaxation at the end of 'Poem [light   clarity   avocado salad in the morning]', the breathlessness with which this poem ends results from the fact that further speech is at this point not necessary.

My claim, then, is that breath is at once a fundamental part of the generation of an affective response to a poem and a means of sharing that response through its use in communication, verbal and non-verbal. At the interface between these two functions lies the capacity of an encounter with a poem to induce readers and listeners to breathe in particular ways in performing or responding to the text. And contra Adorno and Horkheimer's more pessimistic assertions, there is a role in such encounters for a laughter that is neither the bad laughter that parodies human inter-action as it might be, nor the reconciled laughter for which we must wait. Laughter need not be the sole preserve of convention. Indeed, its capacity to work against the hardening of life into convention – or, put differently, its role in art's seduction – requires closer examination, something which must take place in connection with that which we might think of, to use the closing words of the second section of 'Second Avenue', 'as a gasp of laughter at desire, and disorder, and dying' (*CP*, 141).

★ ★ ★

Appendix: Three Unpublished Poems from the Koch Archive

Just for Now

Life it's simple it's great
The clear sun rings a sweet noise
The song of the bells has died away
The morning passes the light all through
My head is a re-flooded shell
And the chamber I inhabit is finally cleared

A lone ray suffices
A single peal of laughter
My joy which shakes the house
Restrains those who wish to die
With the very notes of its song

I sing false
Ah but isn't it dross
My mouth wide to all the winds
Launches everywhere its mad notes
Which depart I don't know how
To fly towards the ears of others

Listen I'm not crazy
I'm laughing at the foot of the stairway
Before the great wide open door
In the squandered sunshine
At the wall midst the wines the greens

Selves

And my arms are stretched towards you

It's today that I love you

Pierre Reverdy,
translated by Frank O'Hara
NYPL, Berg Collection, Koch Archive. Box 182, Folder 23

Love

Watch the winter sky, dear.
It's about to rain, the
Bushes will be so icy tomorrow.
And you are carving our names
On your apple.

Look across the brook
To where the man is
Laughing.

Behind us is the statue
Of Romeo, there is a live dove
On his nose. The trees
And the sky are his
Balcony, and we his audience.

There's a monkey swinging
Beyond the brook.

All about are cushions of green,
The great pines above the soft
Foliage. In our house we will
Have green cushions, our home
Will be concretely loving.

Across the brook there are
Little smiling animals always dancing.
And there is cartoon music.

[Handwritten note, arrowed to fourth chunk: 'might be better to close with the monkey? the "smiling animals" seem far less relevant.']

NYPL, Berg Collection, Koch Archive. Box 182, Folder 21

Variations on a Theme of Kenneth Koch

after his Variations on a Theme by William Carlos Williams

I

There are two poets sitting
On a doorstep, staring
At the sky. Are they thinking
Only of Nature's grace?

II

There is a beautiful garden
Here. Behind which bush is
Our Poet urinating?

III

The poetry of Nature is a
Subtle breeze. Are all the
Poets out of wind?

IV

The sirens of the sea moan
That poetry is dead. Why
Is our Poet giggling?

NYPL, Berg Collection, Koch Archive. Box 182, Folder 23

3
The Work of Others

Frank O'Hara, Alfred Leslie and the Making of *The Last Clean Shirt*

Daniel Kane

Alfred Leslie Plus Ezra Pound Equals King Kong

Born in New York in 1927, by the late 1940s Alfred Leslie was grouped among the younger members of an emerging generation of artists, taking his place alongside painters including Joan Mitchell and Larry Rivers. His relationship to the New York School poets began in 1952 when he had his first solo show at the Tibor de Nagy gallery. Tibor de Nagy was a home base for O'Hara, Ashbery, and their painter friends. The gallery's director, John Bernard Myers, first published the poets and bestowed the name 'New York School' upon them. In 1960 Tiber Press published a set of four volumes of poetry by Kenneth Koch, John Ashbery, Frank O'Hara and James Schuyler illustrated with original silkscreen prints by Alfred Leslie, Joan Mitchell, Michael Goldberg and Grace Hartigan. Leslie would be affiliated with the New York School poets throughout his career.

As with so many of the film-makers affiliated with the New American cinema, Leslie found a trace of a filmic aesthetic in modernist poetry that resonated with his developing practice:[1]

> Pound connected to my sensibility. I was brought up in a literary sense in the movies. To me one of the greatest juxtapositions was one of Pound's unintelligible Chinese ideograms followed by a reference to the nobility of a certain class of Chinese emperors [...] and then all of a sudden he quotes from a letter of Thomas Jefferson and says 'what I require is a light-skinned slave who is clean and who is a good cabinet maker and who can live in the house and play the oboe.' And I thought, 'this is unbelievable.' Why should this touch me? I think it touched me because I crawled under the seat when *King Kong* was released. Cinema brought all that into my head at a time when I was just part of that generation – the touch of modernism when it

---

1 The work of non-mainstream and formally experimental film-makers of the 1950s and 1960s including Ken Jacobs, Stan Brakhage, Marie Menken, Jonas Mekas, Shirley Clarke, Robert Frank and many others was variously classified as 'underground', 'avant-garde', 'personal', 'poetic', 'independent' and 'New American' film or cinema. Leslie's connection to the New American film scene was further established in 1961, when Jonas Mekas invited him to be part of the cinéaste collective known as 'The Group'. See David E. James, *To Free the Cinema: Jonas Mekas and the New York Underground* (Princeton: Princeton University Press, 1992), p. 9.

came into public life perhaps. We had Irwin Piscator, Brecht's associate in Germany, he was brought over to the New School in the 40s. That sense of cinematic *layering*, it was given by that transformative generation at the cusp of the 20th century, it was given over, and I got it![2]

Leslie's reference to Pound's montage practice as 'cinematic layering' certainly corresponds to recent critical work that explores the connections between Pound's imagist theory and Eisenstein's notion of montage as informed by the ideogram and hieroglyph. Bruce E. Fleming, for example, notes:

> The interest in the ideogram of [Eisenstein and Pound] clearly has to do with what both conceived to be a certain manner of signifying, a more direct connection between signifier and signified than they thought existed in the art of the previous century, or even in language itself [...] In the Kabuki theater [Eisenstein] saw example after example of 'pure cinematographic method'; in Japanese painting it was the possibility of picking out the detail that intrigued him. And the ideogram was offered as an example of the infinite number of cinematographic traits present in all of the Japanese culture – save, he thought, in its cinema.[3]

Susan McCabe historicizes the emergence of the modernist lyric by aligning it with the development of avant-garde cinema. In her view, 'the 'renovation of the lyric coincided with the beginnings of experimental montage. Imagism with its ideographic roots anticipated Eisenstein's theory of montage as "copulation (perhaps we had better say, combination) of two hieroglyphs."[4] Eisenstein, like Pound, turned to the lyric forms of haiku and tanka as "montage phrases" or as "shot forms".' McCabe goes on to provide us with an elegant reading of Pound's 'In a Station of the Metro' that illustrates her theory of an image-based poetic as fundamentally cinematic: 'Pound's poem approximates a long shot to clear a visual pathway for the sake of a brief close-up and then withdraws'.[5]

The crucial difference between Leslie's appreciation of Pound and Leslie's own practice in his film *The Last Clean Shirt* (1964) is that Leslie scampers away from Pound's reputedly grander project, one that aimed to employ 'layering' in a scheme that would result in imagistic and thematic synthesis achieved through juxtaposition of conventionally disparate objects. While Leslie appreciates Pound's disjunctive formalism, he nevertheless wilfully misreads *The Cantos* by highlighting the pleasure of 'layering' as primarily surface-oriented. Leslie does not pay particular attention to Pound's attempts to create a transnational model of social order

---

2 Interview with the author.
3 Bruce E. Fleming, 'The Ideogram in Pound and Eisenstein: Sketch for a Theory of Modernism', *Southwest Review* 74.1 (Winter 1989), pp. 87–98, at p. 88.
4 Susan McCabe, *Cinematic Modernism: Modernist Poetry and Film* (Cambridge: Cambridge University Press, 2005), p. 32. McCabe cites Eisenstein from an essay entitled 'The Cinematographic Principle and the Ideogram'.
5 McCabe, *Cinematic Modernism*, p. 33.

through his juxtaposition of Chinese potentates and practically deified Founding Fathers. Rather, Leslie is interested primarily in the *pleasures* of the juxtapositions, the ways in which they intimate that the artist is free to use whatever strikes him to create new sensations and ideas that are not necessarily tied into some overarching vision. We sense this when Leslie links his appreciation for Pound's montage work to that moment when he 'crawled under the seat when *King Kong* was released'. Joy here is not centred on creating juxtaposition that leads to insight, to (in Pound's own oft-quoted words) present an 'emotional and intellectual complex *caught* in an instant of time' (my italics). Leslie's joy is one that revels in experiencing new sensations created out of unexpected and funny combinations and juxtapositions, producing a thrilling disorder that does not, however, preclude intellectual delight and wonder.

Pound's radical montage practice offered artists including Leslie and Frank O'Hara new models for art making, even as both Leslie and O'Hara rejected Pound's cultural and economic programme and the attendant vision of the artist as Manichean seer. Kenneth Koch's comments on Pound define why he and other New York School affiliated writers took only so much from *il miglior fabbro*: 'Pound has this very quirky way of talking, very conversational. He gives you all these pleasures – a very flat, spoken style mixed in with unexpected quotes and other languages. I think I, and John [Ashbery] and Frank [O'Hara] were all influenced by Pound's way of referring to all kinds of things all at once. But Pound did it to make some kind of point, whereas I think we did it because we just liked the splash of it, having everything in.'[6] O'Hara's field of reference, which is arguably as encyclopaedic as Pound's, is, in Lytle Shaw's words, 'far more quotidian than most other famous attempts by modern poets to synthesize or monumentalize cultural knowledge within poetic discourse [...] Though O'Hara was unquestionably affected by reading *The Pisan Cantos* [...] his response is anything but admiring.'[7] Ultimately, the philosophy behind Pound's montage practice was just too unnecessarily *serious* as far as O'Hara and his cohorts were concerned, even if his poetics were positively adaptable.

As Alfred Leslie suggests, it is exciting to leap from subject to subject, particularly if those leaps are represented visually. Instead of using Pound's montage poetics to extend a transcendent model for being and thinking in the world, however, Leslie adapted Pound's work to produce his own affirmative, unanchored aesthetic, one that delighted in creating practically random juxtapositions and connections between, say, *King Kong* and Thomas Jefferson. Pound's modernism, as Leslie states, 'was given over, and I got it!'

---

6 Cited in Daniel Kane (ed.), *What is Poetry? Conversations with the American Avant-Garde* (New York: Teachers & Writers, 2003), p. 96.
7 Lytle Shaw, *Frank O'Hara: The Poetics of Coterie* (Iowa City: University of Iowa Press, 2006), p. 64.

Put On Your Last Clean Shirt

What 'happens' in *The Last Clean Shirt* is perhaps as far as one can get from Poundian monumentalism – a black male driver and white female passenger drive a car up Third Avenue, make a couple of turns, and park uptown around 34th Street and Park Avenue. This scene is then repeated three times, and the film ends. Olivier Brossard usefully describes the three parts of the film as a 'triptych', and demonstrates how the subtitles for section two represent the woman's speech and, in section three, the driver's thoughts.

Leslie has described the fascinating process of making the film: 'O'Hara would write whatever he wanted. I would adapt the transfer, the timing, and the word and letter spacing of the subtitles on the screen. I could also repeat any line or lines as frequently as I wanted, as long as they remained in the original sequence.' Unfortunately, the reception of the finished product among Leslie's own contemporaries was unfavourable, to say the least:

> A complete version of the film was screened at the Museum of Modern Art in San Francisco in the summer of 1964. The showing there was the only sympathetic viewing of the film I have ever known of. More usual was the hissing, booing, slow clapping, and foot-stamping that greeted the film at the New York and London Film Festivals. A description of the London screening appears in a very complete and sympathetic review by Philip French in an issue of *Encounter* magazine, 1964. A piece about the film in *The Catholic Film Review* saw the film as a search for truth, and eventually the film won an award in Bergamo, Italy. It then was ignored.[8]

As Leslie indicates, *The Last Clean Shirt* was not well received in the one environment in which we would expect it to have been adored – the underground film scene in New York. Soon afterwards, a fire in Leslie's loft destroyed much of the art he had produced up to that point. The film has since followed a familiar narrative – that of the avant-garde film so ahead of its time that it would take decades for critics to recognize its importance.[9]

Admittedly, watching *The Last Clean Shirt* for the first time can be hard going. The film begins with a two-minute static shot of a Polish film logo – 'Zléyiuz EDU Filméei' – as the sound of a howling wind plays in the background. Seconds into the shot, however, the viewer receives a crucial clue about the function of the film we are about to see – a non-diegetic female voice is heard singing an adaptation of James Russell Lowell's poem 'The Present Crisis' to the tune of Thomas John Williams' 'Ton y Botel':[10]

8 Alfred Leslie, 'Letter to Peter', in *Moving Picture Poetics: Sampling 50 Years of Poets and Cinema* (San Francisco: Hugo Ball Room Press, 2004), p. 8.

9 See Blaine Allen's *The New American Cinema, 1956–1960* (Toronto: Funnel Experimental Film Theatre, 1984), n.p., for a survey of the ways in which *The Last Clean Shirt* anticipated the work of later structural film-makers.

10 The Lowell poem, however, is not credited as such at the end of the film. Rather, the only attribution

Once to every man and nation, comes a moment to decide,
In the strife of truth with falsehood, for the good or evil side;
Then it is the brave man chooses while the coward stands aside,
And the choice goes by forever, 'twixt that darkness and that light.[11]

It is important to focus on the role 'The Present Crisis' played in America in 1964 – the poem was, after all, written by Lowell in 1845 as a protest against America's imperialist war with Mexico; Lowell was an abolitionist and editor of the progressive magazine *The Atlantic Monthly*; and the poem inspired the nascent National Association for the Advancement of Colored People to call its institutional magazine *The Crisis*.[12] That Leslie chose to open his film with this song was sure to resonate with the fact that the only two people in *The Last Clean Shirt* are a mixed-race couple. For those politically aware members of the audience seeing the film in 1964, Lowell's poem might very well have been considered more generally in the context of the Civil Rights movement and increasing American participation in the Vietnam War. The period around the production and distribution of Leslie's film was one of great political upheaval, witnessing the assassination of civil rights activist Medgar Evers and President John F. Kennedy; the March on Washington; the bombing of the Sixteenth Street Baptist Church; Freedom Summer; the passage of the Civil Rights Act; the murder in Mississippi of civil rights workers James Chaney, Michael Schwerner and Andrew Goodman; and the Gulf of Tonkin incident, followed by US bombing raids in North Vietnam; and so on. Certainly any film that uncritically presented a laughing, affectionate mixed-race couple prefaced by a poem affiliated with the Civil Rights movement would have been viewed against the incendiary background of its times.

Leslie himself, in R. C. Baker's account, has read the film retrospectively as participating in debates characteristic of the 1960s: "'As the Vietnam War escalated," Leslie says, people saw "an American soldier [on TV] firing an M-16 into a man's

---

we have is for the hymn music, which was written by nineteenth-century Welsh composer Thomas John Williams. The credits read '"Ton-y-Botel" sung by Blair Resika at Splash Productions'.

11 James Russell Lowell, 'The Present Crisis', in *The Poetical Works of James Russell Lowell* (Boston: Houghton Mifflin, 1978), p. 67.

12 See Mary White Ovington, 'How the National Association for the Advancement of Colored People Began', *The Crisis Online*, http://www.thecrisismagazine.com/excerpt1914.htm: 'Our history, after 1910, may be read in our annual reports, and in the numbers of THE CRISIS. We opened two offices in the Evening Post Building. With Dr. Du Bois came Frank M. Turner, a Wilberforce graduate, who has shown great efficiency in handling our books. In November 1910 appeared the first number of THE CRISIS, with Dr. Du Bois as editor, and Mary Dunlop MacLean, whose death has been the greatest loss the Association has known, as managing editor. Our propaganda work was put on a national footing, our legal work was well under way and we were in truth, a National Association, pledged to a nation-wide work for justice to the Negro race. I remember the afternoon that THE CRISIS received its name. We were sitting around the conventional table that seems a necessary adjunct to every Board, and were having an informal talk regarding the new magazine. We touched the subject of poetry. "There is a poem of Lowell's," I said, "that means more to me today than any other poem in the world – 'The Present Crisis'." Mr. Walling looked up. *"The Crisis,"* he said. "There is the name for your magazine, *The Crisis.*"'

head" while voice-overs told viewers "something entirely different, and the people believed it". Leslie wanted [*The Last Clean*] *Shirt* to force the question "What the fuck is going on?" because "to most people, reality is nothing more than a confirmation of their expectations".'[13] Lowell's poem, designed as it was to provoke the individual to ask 'what the fuck is going on?' and then choose to join the 'good' side, was a fitting introduction to *The Last Clean Shirt*.

The political connotations implicit in Lowell's stanza are further established in the opening scene, which features a shot of a stationary convertible parked on Astor Place. The passenger door opens, and an animated young white woman gets in speaking in gibberish. A young black man enters, tapes an alarm clock to the dashboard while generally ignoring the laughter and babble of the woman, and adjusts the clock's time from 11:10 to 12:00. (The way this draws our attention to a specific time certainly evokes O'Hara's poems that situate the reader within a given moment – 'it is 12:40 of a Thursday' ('A Step Away From Them' [*CP*, 257]); 'It is 12:20 in New York' ('The Day Lady Died' [*CP*, 325]); 'It is 12:10 in New York' ('Adieu to Norman, Bon Jour to Joan and Jean-Paul' [*CP*, 328]). He then begins the drive to Macy's. Within the first two minutes or so of the drive, as the man makes a U-turn on Third Avenue and heads north towards Cooper Square (while the white woman smiles and laughs at the black man, at times leaning in closely to him) an aural collage of car horns is heard that is artificially manipulated by Leslie to sound more cacophonous and chaotic than usual.[14] We might argue that this moment resonates, if elliptically so, with the evocation of the Civil Rights movement suggested by the Lowell poem and the inherent cosmopolitanism of the mixed-race couple: the appearance of a benign and safe interracial relationship is implicitly threatened by the welter of car klaxons overwhelming the woman's own babble.

As the road trip continues north, the viewer is struck by the fact that Leslie's New York is barely recognizable in terms of conventional ideas about what constitutes the city's landmarks. There is no Brooklyn Bridge or Empire State Building, no bird's-eye views of teeming masses. Instead, we join an anonymous, mixed-race couple in which the only speaking subject emits gibberish, nursery-type songs, affectionate gestures and laughter as she and her friend make their way through some of Manhattan's more anonymous and visually unremarkable avenues.

That said, the apparent dullness of this particular stretch of Third Avenue is not quite so dull when we consider the fact that this film is designed in part as a conversation with Frank O'Hara's poetry. While O'Hara's lines have not yet appeared in the film, we can nevertheless detect his presence in the very beginning, where we find the interracial couple driving north on Third Avenue between Fifth and Sixth Streets. This juncture was a crucial spot for the developing countercultural scene

---

13 R. C. Baker, 'The Octopussarian Drugstore Cowboy: Alfred Leslie Has Not Left the Building', *Village Voice* [New York], 24–30 November 2004, p. 30.

14 Sound technician Tony Schwartz electronically manipulated and inserted non-diegetic sounds including layered honking, rumbling thunder, gunshot-like sounds, and so on.

in and around the Lower East Side. The first incarnation of the legendary Five Spot bar, after all, was located precisely on Third Avenue between Fifth and Sixth Streets.[15] 'In the late 1950s,' remarks Michael Magee, 'O'Hara was introduced to the Five Spot, a downtown club that featured the live music of the new jazz avant-garde […] He would come to associate this music and the social milieu in which it was performed with other forms of egalitarian desire, including his own poetry and the Civil Rights movement'.[16] At The Five Spot in the late 1950s and early 1960s, one could find a mixed-race crowd enjoying the new sounds of Ornette Coleman, Thelonious Monk, and others. Kenneth Koch and Larry Rivers held their jazz poetry nights at the Five Spot, and O'Hara himself referred to the club in poems such as 'The Day Lady Died' and 'Poem Read at Joan Mitchell's'. We should note that in the third section of *The Last Clean Shirt*, O'Hara goes so far as to include the exclamation 'Ornette!', serving to further identify the location of the film with the Lower East Side jazz and poetry scene he was a part of. (Coleman and his band performed at the Five Spot for a legendary ten-week stint in 1959, and released an album entitled *Ornette!* in 1961.) In the 1950s and 1960s, then, Third Avenue between Fifth and St Mark's streets was an increasingly important if temporary site for a multi-racial avant-garde. In Leslie's film, the apparently barren stretch of Manhattan territory, framed through the bodies of Leslie's interracial couple, becomes particularly numinous when contextualized through O'Hara's references to this jazz-soaked location.

As O'Hara went uptown to work from his home in the East Village, so the couple in the film continue their drive by heading north. The woman becomes more animated, singing 'la la la la lah lah lah laaaa' and so forth, as the man variously ignores her, smokes his cigarettes, or smiles with a mixture of affection and conde-scension. At points, the sound of police sirens and fire engines is heard, again inserting somewhat anxious notes into the otherwise light-hearted scene. The couple smoke together as they continue their way up the avenue. What sounds like thunder is heard repeatedly, despite there being no sign of rain. Then, suddenly, a voiceover is heard over the tolling of bells: 'From dust thou was taken, and unto dust thou shalt return. Ashes to ashes, dust to dust.' Directly after this intona-tion, Lieber and Stoller's song 'Brother Bill (the Last Clean Shirt)', as performed by Charles 'Honeyman' Otis, is played while the car remains stationary. A close-up of a WALK sign serves as a kind of cue for us finally to transfer our focus from the couple to the street itself. The camera cuts away from our subjects and is pointed backwards towards the street. The car begins to move again, but this time we see the street as if we were facing backwards – the lens of the camera is then closed to evoke a human eye.

---

15 In its final years the Five Spot was located just a couple of blocks north, on St Mark's just off Cooper Square.

16 Michael Magee, *Emancipating Pragmatism: Emerson, Jazz, and Experimental Writing* (Tuscaloosa: The University of Alabama Press, 2004), p. 130.

The car backs up into a parking space, and the camera once again focuses on the couple. The black man removes the clock from the dashboard, opens the door for the woman who then steps out, and both subjects disappear from the frame. The section ends with 'Brother Bill (the Last Clean Shirt)' playing over a static shot of the car, looking exactly as it did at the opening of the film. The end of this first part of the film is comically emphasized when Leslie presents us with more Polish film stock, reintroduces the sound of howling wind, and superimposes the sound of a crowd applauding and cheering wildly over the wind. Exactly the same scene will be repeated twice before the film is fully over, though it will take on different meanings predicated very loosely on point of view.

Importantly, these fluid points of view are generated by a series of subtitles that begin during what could be described as an intermission between sections one and two, where the lines are superimposed over film leader and stock. These initial 'intermission' lines work to extend the political undertones of the film overall. Though the tone of the film has so far been generally comic, the political issues inherent in the Lowell song (and developed via the presence of the mixed-race couple, the combination of the woman's laughter and singing with abrupt and aggressive street sounds, and the funerary invocation juxtaposed with Lieber and Stoller's song) suggest that Leslie and O'Hara were committed to displaying and celebrating a progressive – if light-hearted – politics.

The first subtitle we see in the film reads 'Of course I resent/ Bernice saying I have…'. The notion of the 'personal' is here neatly contained in what sounds like the fragment of an overheard conversation referring to the problems one person has with his intimate other, Bernice. O'Hara's aesthetic is in full force even in this little fragment. The comically petulant tone we associate with many of O'Hara poems – for example, 'a lady asks us for a nickel for a terrible/ disease but we don't give her one we/ don't like terrible diseases' ('Personal Poem' [*CP*, 335]) – is contained in the phrase 'Of course I resent', with its implicitly stressed 'course' adding a humorous patina to the lines. The funny nostalgia of the archaic proper name 'Bernice', evocative as it is of the 1920s and glitzy nightlife, certainly resonates with O'Hara's general inclination to celebrate flapper-era icons. (We can refer back to F. Scott Fitzgerald's short story 'Bernice Bobs her Hair' for an idea of where O'Hara plucked this name from.)

However, the whimsical is almost immediately complicated by the serious – a turn typical of O'Hara's poetry, where, to cite the most famous example, one can list the quotidian and even banal details of the day only to end in elegy with 'everyone and I stopped breathing' ('The Day Lady Died' [*CP*, 325]). Read as a single sentence, the two subtitles following the 'Bernice' line practically shock the viewer by their violence of contrast: 'You don't say that the victim is responsible'/ 'for a concentration camp or a Mack truck'.[17] Certainly, the presence of the 'Mack truck' maintains

17 While O'Hara chose the order in which the subtitles appeared, Leslie decided how the subtitles would be broken up on the screen.

the light-hearted tone of the 'Bernice' subtitle, but nevertheless the personal is here categorically linked to the political. One's wholly self-involved concern with one's own Bernice is here put into perspective by a statement that invites reflection on one of the major sources of existential trauma for the post-war generation. The fact that humour is maintained even when referencing the Holocaust invites us not to diminish the horror of the event, but to examine our own complicity in pushing harrowing historical narratives outside the boundaries of our own experience. If 'the victim' is not responsible for the concentration camp, then who is? And why are we still moved to smile, even invited to do so, by the appearance of the Mack truck? Does that somehow make the 'concentration camp' less serious? And, if so, what does that say about us and the ways in which we allow comedy to alleviate suffering?

O'Hara wants us to ask these kinds of questions – during the second repetition of the car ride uptown, the 'concentration camp' lines are repeated and followed up with a particularly trenchant assertion: 'You don't say / that the victim is responsible for a concentration camp / or a Mack truck. / You know what I mean. / Breathing is not all about breath. / Peace not just the absence of war.' By recycling Spinoza's oft-quoted maxim 'Peace is not an absence of war, it is a virtue, a state of mind, a disposition for benevolence, confidence, justice', O'Hara plays off the basic content of the film by tacitly suggesting we work towards something approaching social equity. Once again, O'Hara uses the subtitle to gently encourage us to read political significance into *The Last Clean Shirt* generally and the presence of the mixed-race couple driving together in 1964 in particular.

While we can laugh and wonder at – and even get bored by – the apparently meaningless series of images so far experienced in this odd little road movie, O'Hara and Leslie nevertheless prod us into questioning *why* we are doing precisely that – why do we choose to consume a film, a poem, a ballet, and how do those choices reverberate with our other choices to ignore or merely report on the fact of the horrors outside our apartment doors? Such an imperative to question our political responsibility as readers in the face of a profoundly violent society is found in a number of O'Hara poems – we can return to 'Personal Poem' for example, where, in the midst of 'lunchtime', the 'House of Seagram', and sexy construction workers we learn that 'Miles Davis was clubbed 12/ times last night outside BIRDLAND by a cop' (*CP*, 335). This is not to suggest O'Hara did not believe in joy – rather, I want to suggest that O'Hara's poetics connected the development of a political awareness to joy, much as Emma Goldman insisted on her right to dance as she staged revolution.

Alfred Leslie's comments in an interview with Brossard militate against any reading of the film – and, by extension, O'Hara's poetry – as somehow 'non-political':

> This is a gun that's being put to your head like the Dada poets and threatening you and saying: 'you gotta pay attention to what's going on at the beginning of the

turmoil in the country culturally and politically [...] You gotta pay attention,' I mean it means something, you read those newspapers and maybe you need to understand that what's being printed in those newspapers is not true and that you have to hold back a little bit.[18]

Out of the disorientation that results from watching and reading the film – its insistent repetition coupled with discontinuous intertitles and subtitles – the viewer must decide to be 'the brave man' who 'chooses while the coward stands aside,/ And the choice goes by forever, 'twixt that darkness and that light'. Choose the light, O'Hara and Leslie quirkily implore us. As if to emphasize the 'ethical' nature of the film, the final intertitle we read before the second repetition of the car journey reads 'It's the nature of us all to want to be unconnected.' Yes, we want to be unconnected – free – but the film has already begun to suggest, however lightly and humorously, that perhaps we resist that part of our nature in an effort to be connected members of a community, one which delights in the possibilities of urbane love, laughter, and a casual interracial accord.[19]

'Go to India and Get Lost, as Allen Ginsberg Says': *The Last Clean Shirt* in the Lower East Side Arts Community

Prior to the second repetition of the trip uptown, we hear the Lowell poem/song one more time. After a short pause, we are back where we started from – the parked car on the street, followed by the entry of the couple into the car, followed by the identical 10-minute drive uptown. Olivier Brossard has already done us the favour of tracking many of the quotations and allusions to the corpus of O'Hara's work, from 1950 to the early 1960s, found within the subtitles that follow in the second and third parts of *The Last Clean Shirt*.[20] I would add to Brossard's list the

18 Cited in Olivier Brossard, 'The Last Clean Shirt', *Jacket* 23 (August 2003), http://jacketmagazine.com/23/bross-ohara.html.

19 Concluding lines in the 'intermission' extend the theme of responsibility, community, and personal freedom: 'I have the other/ idea about guilt', 'It's not in us, it's/ in the situation', 'It's a rotten life', and, finally, 'It's just that things get too much', a line which is repeated a number of times using a kind of flicker effect.

20 As Brossard points out, the word 'zoo', mentioned in the subtitles, can be found several times in the poem 'Second Avenue' (*CP*, 139). The numerous references to a 'kangaroo' featured near the end of the film echo O'Hara's 'Today', where he writes 'Oh! kangaroos, sequins, chocolate sodas!' (*CP*, 15). Repeated references to India, Allen and Peter surely point readers to similar references in the poem 'Vincent and I Inaugurate a Movie Theater' (*CP*, 399). Entire lines from poems that are used as subtitles include 'is that me who accepts betrayal/ in the abstract as if it were insight?' ('Death', *CP*, 187); 'I know so much/ about things, I accept/ so much, it's like/ vomiting' ('Spleen', *CP*, 187); 'I am assuming that everything is all right and difficult' ('Ode to Michael Goldberg ['s Birth and Other Births]' [*CP*, 297]); 'the rock is least living of the forms man has fucked' ('Ode on Causality' [*CP*, 302]); 'I am ashamed of my century / for being so entertaining/ but I have to smile' ('Naphtha' [*CP*, 338]); 'NEVERTHELESS (thank you, Aristotle)' ('Biotherm [for Bill Berkson]' [*CP*, 437]); '1. If only more people looked like Jerry Lieber we would all be a lot happier, I think.'; '3. There is a

Figure 1 Still from Alfred Leslie, *The Last Clean Shirt*, 1964

subtitle 'We shall have everything we want and there will be no more dying', which is the first line of O'Hara's poem 'Ode to Joy' (*CP*, 281); a reference to the poems 'Oranges' and 'Why I Am Not a Painter', evident in the subtitle 'And Not of Grace and her Oranges' (Figure 1); a rephrasing of the lines 'I don't know as I get what D. H. Lawrence is driving at/ when he writes of lust springing from the bowels' from 'Poem' (*CP*, 334);[21] the subtitle 'A lady in foxes on such a day puts her poodle in a cab' from the poem 'A Step Away From Them' (*CP*, 258); the subtitle 'My friends are roaming or listening to La Bohème', cut from O'Hara's poem 'Thinking of James Dean' (*CP*, 231); and multiple references to one of O'Hara's best poems, 'In Memory of My Feelings' (*CP*, 252).[22]

---

man going by with his arm in a sling. I wish men could take care of themselves better.'; '7. There are certainly enough finks in the world without going to a German restaurant.' (all from O'Hara's poem 'The Sentimental Units' [*CP*, 467]).

21 The subtitle adaptation reads 'You get what D. H. Lawrence is driving at' followed by 'when he writes of lust springing from the bowels?'

22 Subtitles in the film that O'Hara adapted from his poem 'In Memory of My Feelings' include 'I am a girl walking downstairs in a red pleated dress with heels', 'I am a jockey with a sprained ass-hole', 'I am the light mist in which a face appears', 'I am a dictator looking at his wife', and 'The hero trying to unhook his parachute stumbles over me'.

Through such poetic cannibalization, Leslie and O'Hara manipulate the very notions of stable genre associated with film and subtitle to enact formal disruption. In Brossard's view, O'Hara's subtitle text 'opens up the space of the subtitles, a well defined format, to poetry. This opening up of the subtitle format to poetry is going to alter the nature of the film: the subtitles are not here to be mere appendixes to dialogues, they are not dependent on a preexisting meaning, they create a self-sufficient space which interacts with images on an equal footing.'[23] Film becomes poetry – or film interacts with poetry. Or poetry extends film. Or poetry becomes subtitle, thus yoking high culture to a kind of base functionality not ordinarily associated with the lyric. Such moves invite the spectator/reader experiencing the no-longer-autonomous work of art to 'pay attention', to participate in making meaning in response to a form that no longer adheres to conventional definitions of genre as she negotiates the political themes introduced by the film.

We might also suggest that film's material ability to perform presence invites O'Hara to reimagine the function his poems could play in the space of *The Last Clean Shirt*. Given the opportunity to attach his text to a form that could only exist in the moment, predicated as it was on what McCabe calls 'the continuous supplanting or erasing of one image by another', O'Hara restructures and collages lines from a number of his poems, some of them written many years before the collaboration with Leslie.[24] By chopping, cutting, and revising specific lines, attaching them to brand new phrases developed specifically for the film, and allowing his text to be absorbed by and inform an entirely new genre, O'Hara brought his work into a new kind of life that was mechanically predicated on the immediacy and instantaneity he so desired.

We should not, moreover, overlook the *social* function of O'Hara's revisions. A series of subtitles in the second part of the film offer the informed reader a rich social and literary world paradoxically playing against the dullness of the road journey:

I was thinking about India just now …
Big bags of sand…
… birds swooping down and gulping …
… helpful creatures everywhere …
We could be alone together at last.
Who needs an Ark? a Captains table?
Anyway India should think about China.
And the Chinese could build another wall.
Maybe even bigger if they're feeling so ambitious.
It would keep everybody busy.
And the Africans can go on building dams.
What I really would like to do is go to Havana…
for a weekend –

23 Brossard, 'The Last Clean Shirt', n.p.
24 McCabe, *Cinematic Modernism*, p. 57.

Why might O'Hara be thinking about India – and, subsequently, China, Africa, and Cuba – 'just now', circa 1963 and early 1964 when *The Last Clean Shirt* was being produced? It is probable that O'Hara was referring to his friend Allen Ginsberg's recent return from a well-publicized trip to India with his lover Peter Orlovsky, a trip that was discussed widely in the Lower East Side poetry community thanks to Ginsberg's indefatigable ability to maintain a steady stream of correspondence.[25]

Such a reading is all the more likely when we consider that Ginsberg was considering going to Cuba around the time *The Last Clean Shirt* was produced.[26] Cuba was a *cause célèbre* for many in the downtown poetry scene. In his essay 'Cuba Libre', written after his return from Havana and first published in *The Evergreen Review* in 1961, Amiri Baraka (then Leroi Jones) made much out of what he believed to be an ideal socialist paradise. Alfred Leslie himself published Castro's 1960 Address to the General Assembly of the United Nations in his one-shot literary review *The Hasty Papers*, a journal that also featured work by O'Hara, Ashbery, Orlovsky, Kerouac, and others.

Of course, O'Hara's love for movies from the 1930s and 1940s surely played a part in these lines as well. As Brossard points out, 'there was a movie [...] called *Weekend in Havana* (1941) directed by Walter Lang which starred Carmen Miranda and Alice Faye'. Given that O'Hara had addressed Faye in his poem 'To the Film Industry in Crisis', we see that a rich and deliberately outrageous link is being made between a markedly progressive, even radical politics and the kind of queer, urbane subjectivity that delights in watching 'Alice Faye reclining / and wiggling and singing, Myrna Loy being calm and wise, William Powell / in his stunning urbanity, Elizabeth Taylor blossoming' ('To the Film Industry in Crisis' [*CP*, 232]). Unlike Ginsberg's and Baraka's highly politicized analyses of and responses to the Castro government, O'Hara provides us with a typically light-hearted assertion that *his* – or rather, *her*[27] – trip to Cuba would be limited to a weekend jaunt that takes place in the imaginative and resolutely lavender world we associate with Miranda, Faye, and other glamourpusses of the 1940s.

As usual, O'Hara likes his revolution taken with a dash of bourgeois ease and comfort. This is not to say that O'Hara is attacking dissenting voices like Ginsberg's or Baraka's, which, after all, offered alternative ways of thinking about socialist governments, ways more complex than American consensus culture was capable of providing at the time.[28] Rather, by aligning his queer sensibility to socialism,

25 See Ginsberg's *Indian Journals* (San Francisco: City Lights Books, 1970).

26 Ginsberg would ultimately go to Cuba and Czechoslovakia in the early months of 1965, though he was deported from Cuba for speaking out against the Castro regime's persecution of homosexuals. He was crowned 'King of May' in Czechoslovakia, where he also encountered trouble from the authorities and was subsequently deported.

27 The subtitles are, after all, apparently representing the gibberish of the female protagonist in the film.

28 Brad Gooch's *City Poet: The Life and Times of Frank O'Hara* (New York: Knopf, 1993) helpfully documents a number of instances that show O'Hara's commitment to progressive politics. See, e.g., p. 425.

Figure 2 Still from Alfred Leslie, *The Last Clean Shirt*, 1964

O'Hara opens up the discursive field of revolutionary politics by suggesting that the queer dandy can participate as well, on his or her own terms. We *can* have our revolutionary cake, and eat it too. The tacit suggestion in these subtitles is for more socialism, albeit a champagne socialism that is in no way hostile to a bit of camp.[29] Such campness is established further in the third section of the film through the subtitles 'When does the camp close?' and 'The close never camps'.

The subtitles discussed above, when read in combination with succeeding titles, also lead readers to specific poems in O'Hara's corpus that highlight his participation in the Lower East Side poetry community and his acknowledgment that underground cinema was part of the overall landscape. The third section of *The Last Clean Shirt* finds O'Hara calling upon the ringmaster of underground film himself to show up to the party when the subtitle 'Jonas Mekas where are you I'm worried' appears on the screen (Figure 2).

The phrase allows O'Hara to acknowledge lightly that a social and aesthetic link between New York School poet and underground film entrepreneur is potentially

---

29 Before those of us who resist reading O'Hara as in any way politicized begin spluttering, let us remember, as Bill Berkson states, that 'O'Hara thought of himself as a Communist in his youth'. Email to the author, 17 April 2003. See also Gooch, *City Poet*, p. 28.

surprising but certainly welcome. The interplay between these various subtitles works to position O'Hara in active relationship with the Beat cinema world, particularly when we consider that Allen Ginsberg wrote and narrated the text for Mekas's film *The Guns of the Trees*, and that O'Hara addresses Ginsberg directly in the third part of the film via the subtitle 'Allen I wish we were uptown doing the "Bronx Tambourine"'. O'Hara in part uses the opportunity afforded to him by Leslie's film to yoke the urbane New York School dandy to the bearded downtown bohemians he lived among. In *The Last Clean Shirt*, such sociability is often performed through a cut-up of O'Hara's earlier poems.

The subtitle 'India! India! India!', for example, is succeeded by 'I really am kind of worried Orange New Jersey…', and then, 'My friends are roaming or listening to La Boheme' [sic]. Consider that 'India!' alludes to O'Hara's poem 'Vincent and I Inaugurate a Movie Theater', where O'Hara writes 'Allen and Peter, why are you going away / our country's black and white past spread out / before us is no time to spread over India' (*CP*, 399); that 'I really am kind of worried Orange New Jersey…' points to O'Hara's poems 'Oranges: 12 Pastorals' (*CP*, 5–9) and 'Why I Am Not a Painter' (*CP*, 261–62) and that the line 'My friends are roaming or listening to La Boheme', lifted from O'Hara's poem 'Thinking of James Dean' (*CP*, 230–31) can be interpreted as referring to Ginsberg's and Orlovsky's 'roaming'. The reference to *La Bohème* further underscores the invocation of the downtown scene – Puccini's opera, detailing the charmingly dissolute lives of artists and poets living in the kind of garret-type abodes that Lower East Side denizens would find familiar, would surely resonate with O'Hara's peers.

In these three charged subtitles, O'Hara creates connections between New York School sophistication, predicated in part on the kind of urbanity inherent in the gallery and loft scene depicted in O'Hara's poem 'Why I Am Not a Painter', and the somewhat wilder Beat aesthetic championed by Mekas, Ginsberg and others. From the mid-1950s, O'Hara had supported the work of poets including Gregory Corso and John Wieners, and Allen Ginsberg has said of O'Hara, 'I was amazed he was so open and wasn't just caught in a narrow New York Manhattan Museum of Modern Art artworld cocktail ballet scene'.[30] O'Hara uses *The Last Clean Shirt* to continue yoking bohemia to his 'artworld cocktail ballet scene' in a film that, significantly, begins in the Lower East Side and heads uptown. What results is a further blurring of the lines between uptown and downtown, New York School and Beat, disengaged aesthete and nascent revolutionary, film and poem.

30 Quoted in Gooch, *City Poet*, p. 280.

Kites and Poses: Attitudinal Interfaces in Frank O'Hara and Grace Hartigan

Redell Olsen

Do you hear them say painting is action? We say painting is the timid appraisal of yourself by lions[1]

In 1952 Grace Hartigan threw a kite-flying party, documented in photographs by her friend Walter Silver (Figure 1) and subsequently described by John Bernard Myers:

> Grace invited about twenty people, all the gallery artists and her friends, to a kite-making party. The kites were constructed in her Essex Street loft, but the following day they were carried up to Sheep Meadow in Central Park to be sent aloft. The kites, some big and lengthy, others small, were colourful, goofy and beautiful. But as we got to the park the wind began to blow at what seemed a hurricane speed. Simply hanging onto the kites became difficult. Still determined to get them into the air, we did our best, only to have them dashed to the ground or blown to bits. All of the kites were ruined. 'A real fiasco is what we've got!' yelled Grace. 'Let's get out of here.' How I wish someone had taken pictures of the mess![2]

I have not been able to find any record of paintings Hartigan made from the images that Silver took, or any reference to this event in Frank O'Hara's poems. This occasion nevertheless prefigures what became known as 'happenings', and is suggestive for the ways in which both Hartigan and O'Hara used the event to stage interfaces between art and life. This essay explores how their respective construction of performances, paintings and poems was mutually informing. It also explores ways in which their work differentiates itself from Abstract Expressionism. Harold Rosenberg famously described the canvas of the Abstract Expressionist painter

---

1 Frank O'Hara with Larry Rivers, 'How to Proceed in the Arts' (*AC*, 92), from *Evergreen Review* (August 1961), pp. 97–101.
2 John Bernard Myers, *Tracking the Marvellous: A Life in the New York Art World* (London: Thames and Hudson, 1983), pp. 139–40. For images of the party, including an image of people (one of whom might be Frank O'Hara) gathered in Hartigan's studio making kites, see Special Collections Research Center at Syracuse University Library, http://library.syr.edu/digital/exhibits/i/imagine/section3a.htm.

Figure 1 Grace Hartigan at her kite-flying party, 1952

as 'an arena in which to act',[3] but the sense of artistic and social performance in the work of Hartigan and O'Hara suggests a different kind of art action. While they both have much in common with Abstract Expressionism, they also share a distinct interest in performance and the staging of events. In Hartigan's work, performance-related gestures are linked to her use of photography in the process of making her paintings, especially in *Grand Street Brides* and *Masquerade* (1954). Her use of photography anticipates artists such as Cindy Sherman, Eleanor Antin and, more recently, Sam Taylor-Wood. O'Hara's poems use paintings, often Hartigan's

3 David Shapiro and Cecile Shapiro, *Abstract Expressionism: A Critical Record* (Cambridge: Cambridge University Press, 1990), p. 76.

paintings, as a comparable device, mediating between experience and the poem. Such mediations offer a different model of the relationships between performance, painting and photography to the myth-making of Hans Namuth's celebrated pictures of Jackson Pollock at work in his studio.[4]

Grace Hartigan, along with Larry Rivers, Joe Brainard and Norman Bluhm, was one of the painters with whom O'Hara enjoyed a relationship of 'strong mutual influence'.[5] O'Hara features in a number of Hartigan's paintings, including *Frank O'Hara and The Demons* (1952), *Ocean Bathers* (1953), *Masker* (1954) and *Masquerade* (1954). Evocations of Hartigan's paintings appear in O'Hara's poems, notably 'Second Avenue' (*CP*, 139) and 'In Memory of My Feelings' (*CP*, 252). He dedicated numerous poems to Hartigan, including 'In Memory of My Feelings', 'Christmas Card to Grace Hartigan' (*CP*, 212) and 'For Grace, After a Party' (*CP*, 214). She is also the subject of 'Portrait of Grace' (*CP*, 87) and 'Poem For a Painter' (*CP*, 80), and the play *Grace and George* (*AN*, 87). In addition, in 1953, Hartigan exhibited a series of 12 paintings at the Tibor Nagy Gallery in New York which she described in the gallery flyer as 'paintings for "oranges" 12 pastoral poems by Frank O'Hara'.[6] O'Hara's own role as subject or object in relation to poems and paintings shifts as he successively inhabits the roles of model, critic, curator, poet, lover, friend, but never detached bystander. What Norman Bryson calls 'The Natural Attitude' of monocular single point perspective is never an option for O'Hara, variously embedded as he is in both the paintings of Abstract Expressionism and the social context in which they were painted.[7]

In 1950, aged 28, Hartigan first exhibited in New York. Three years later the second sale she ever made of a painting was to the Museum of Modern Art in New York.[8] She was the only woman represented in the 1958–59 exhibition *The New American Painting*, an exhibition responsible for introducing Abstract Expressionist painters to Europe, and which O'Hara in his role as assistant curator at the Museum of Modern Art helped organize. *Life* magazine called her 'the most celebrated of the young American women painters', Cecil Beaton photographed her and she was discussed by *Newsweek* in columns alongside those about Judy Garland.[9] The subjects and methods of Hartigan's paintings overlap with the subjects and methods of O'Hara's poems. In an early review the critic Emily Dennis described her canvases as 'deliberate catchalls' which 'seized and probed' the exterior world:

4 Brian O'Doherty, *The Voice and the Myth: American Masters* (London: Thames and Hudson, 1988), pp. 92–96.

5 Lytle Shaw, *Frank O' Hara: The Poetics of Coterie* (Iowa City: University of Iowa Press, 2006), p. 105.

6 For further discussion of Hartigan's paintings made in response to O'Hara's poem 'Oranges' see Terence Diggory, 'Questions of Identity in Oranges by Frank O'Hara and Grace Hartigan', *Art Journal* (Winter 1993), pp. 41–50.

7 Norman Bryson, *Vision and Painting: The Logic of the Gaze* (London: Macmillan, 1983), p. 6.

8 Vicki Goldberg, 'Grace Hartigan Still Hates Pop', *The New York Times*, 15 August 1993, www.nytimes.com/1993/08/15/arts/art-grace-hartigan-still-hates-pop.html?pagewanted=1.

9 Goldberg, 'Grace Hartigan Still Hates Pop'.

'her painting was one of street markets, store windows, billboards, public parks, and mannequin brides [...] nothing seen or felt escaped them'.[10]

In 1958, Allan Kaprow, who had trained as a painter, coined the term 'happening' to refer to artworks which blurred the boundary between art and life, events involving multiple participants, often with no formal outcome or product:

> A Happening, unlike a stage play, may occur at a supermarket, driving along a highway, under a pile of rags, and in a friend's kitchen, either at once or sequentially. If sequentially, time may extend to more than a year. The Happening is performed according to plan but without rehearsal, audience, or repetition. It is art but seems closer to life.[11]

Happenings anticipated Fluxus performances of the early 1960s, which in turn anticipate and coincide with what Lucy Lippard termed the dematerialization of the art object.[12] Hartigan may simply have thought of her 1952 kite-flying event as a party, but, as a gathering of artists assembled to make and stage an event, it could be understood as an early happening. For both Hartigan and O'Hara 'art' often does seem 'closer to life' and Silver's photographs have the same status of documentation as the photographs of the later happenings.

In 1954, Hartigan deliberately involved photography in the making of her painting. *Grand Street Brides* is based on a photograph that she commissioned from Walter Silver:

> My studio in New York was on the Lower East Side. It was two blocks away from Grand Street where there is one bridal shop after another. I am very interested in masks and charades. It can be women or it can be something else – the face the world puts on to sell itself to the world. I have always been interested in empty ritual. I thought of the bridal thing as a court scene like Goya or Velásquez and I posed the bridal party in the same way. I had a photographer friend take the pictures and I bought a bridal gown at a thrift shop and hung it in the studio. Every morning I would go out and stare at the windows and then come in and paint.[13]

Hartigan explicitly connects the charades and masks of dressing up with capitalism, 'the face the world puts on to sell itself to the world'. She also recognizes but refuses to be constrained by the implicit connection this metaphor has to the masks and charades of femininity.[14] Her paintings and art practice were the 'masks and

---

10 Emily Dennis, 'Grace Hartigan: The Ordered Creation of Chaos', in B. H. Friedman (ed.), *School of New York: Some Younger Artists* (New York: Grove Press, 1959), p. 24.

11 Allan Kaprow, *Some Recent Happenings* (a Great Bear pamphlet) (New York: Something Else Press, 1966), p. 5.

12 See Lucy Lippard, *Six Years: The Dematerialization of the Art Object from 1966 to 1972* (Berkeley: University of California Press, 1997).

13 Cindy Nemser, *Art Talk: Conversations with 15 Women Artists* (New York: Icon Editions, 1995), p. 135.

14 This is clearly an important metaphor in feminist theories from critics as diverse as Joan Rivière ('Womanliness as a Masquerade', *The International Journal of Psychoanalysis* 10 (1929)) and Judith

charades' with which she herself faced off the market. However, her re-examination of the court paintings of Goya and Velásquez is clearly at odds with much of Abstract Expressionism, and Hartigan notes that it 'cost' her a 'great deal' in terms of her friendships with Pollock, de Kooning and Kline to work in this way.[15]

In her description of the painting of *Grand Street Brides*, Hartigan stresses the artificial set-up of her mannequins, how she 'posed the bridal party'. The history of the word 'pose' intersects painting, life-drawing and photography. The *OED* glosses it as 'To place in a certain attitude or position, esp. to be painted or photographed; to cause to adopt a certain pose'. The first example of its use is given from 1826 in which a tutor 'posed the figure' for the benefit, presumably, of a drawing class. The next two examples given are concurrent with the invention of photography.[16] Roland Barthes suggests that 'what founds the nature of Photography is the pose'.[17] The possibilities of the pose are also foundational in the work of both Hartigan and O'Hara and this sets them apart from their contemporaries. The pose of the artist in the work of Hartigan and O'Hara distinguishes itself from the mythic genius and macho posturing associated with Abstract Expressionism. This in part reflects their respective marginality within or in relation to Abstract Expressionism. Terence Diggory, for example, suggests that '[as] a woman artist confronting "the misogyny of the New York School" –the phrase used by her "first generation" colleague Lee Krasner – Hartigan played at switching gender roles with an attitude similar to that adopted by O'Hara as a gay man in a heterosexual society'.[18]

Beyond the threat of macho violence, O'Hara's critical writing was also at odds with those around him in other ways.[19] As Lytle Shaw points out, both Clement Greenberg and Michael Fried 'single out poetic criticism as the primary threat to the legibility of a modernist art-critical vocabulary'.[20] Shaw argues that O'Hara's poems and critical writings suggest 'a new way to picture abstraction within a more socially informed framework than was available to 1950s critics'.[21] This socially

---

Butler (*Bodies That Matter: On the Discursive Limits of Sex* (London: Routledge, 1993)).

15 Nemser, *Art Talk*, p. 135.

16 '1868 H. T. Tuckerman *Collector* 70 In studied attitude, like one poséd for a daguerreotype. 1878: W. De W. Abney *Treat. Photogr.* (1881) 240 In posing a group, let it be remembered that each figure is animate, and should not be made to look as lifeless as a statue' (*OED*).

17 Roland Barthes, *Camera Lucida: Reflections on Photography*, trans. Richard Howard (London: Jonathan Cape, 1982).

18 Diggory, 'Questions of Identity', p. 49. Brad Gooch, in *City Poet: The Life and Times of Frank O'Hara* (New York: Harper Perennial, 1994), notes that on at least one occasion Jackson Pollock 'called O'Hara a "fag" to his face and was enough of a menace that O'Hara fled the Cedar one night when he heard that Pollock was on a drunken rampage' (p. 204).

19 See Shaw, *Frank O'Hara: The Poetics of Coterie*, ch. 5; for further critical contexts see Clement Greenberg, *The Collected Essays and Criticism*, vol. 4, *Modernism with a Vengeance, 1957–1969*, ed. John O'Brian (Chicago: University of Chicago Press, 1993), p. 85; Michael Fried, *Art and Objecthood: Essays and Reviews* (Chicago: University of Chicago Press, 1998), p. 3.

20 Shaw, *Frank O'Hara: The Poetics of Coterie*, p. 154.

21 Shaw, *Frank O'Hara: The Poetics of Coterie*, p. 158.

informed framework obviously includes the need to consider contemporary attitudes to gender and sexuality.[22] This, in turn, led to writing strategies involving irony, parody and posing. The anti-manifesto manifesto pastiche of 'How to Proceed in the Arts', jointly authored by O'Hara and Larry Rivers, is so far removed in tone from the writing of Greenberg and Rosenberg that it is easy to miss its important critical staging of tensions in Abstract Expressionism. The aphoristic statements of 'How to Proceed in the Arts' read as a series of poses struck against the critical strictures and myths of Abstract Expressionism.

6. Do you hear them say painting is action? We say painting is the timid appraisal of yourself by lions.

8. They say painting is action. We say remember your enemies and nurse the smallest insult. Introduce yourself as Delacroix. When you leave, give them your wet crayons. Be ready to admit that jealousy moves you more than art. They say action is painting. Well, it isn't, and we all know Expressionism has moved to the suburbs.

14. [...] Try something that pricks the air out of a few popular semantic balloons; groping, essence, pure painting, flat, catalyst, crumb, and how do you feel about titles like 'Innscape,' 'Norway Nights and Suburbs,' 'Nos. 188, 1959,' 'Hey Mama Baby,' 'Mondula,' or 'Still Life with Nose'? Even if it is a small painting, say six feet by nine feet, it is a start. If it is only as big as a postage stamp, call it collage – but begin.[23]

The heroics of painting as 'action' are mocked, as are the sensibilities of the puffed-up 'introduce yourself as Delacroix' artist for whom size ('You do have a loft, don't you, man?') is everything.[24] Amid direct and witty observations of what Abstract Expressionism had become, the artificiality of the poses struck by those involved in the movement is countered by a rhetorical posturing that acknowledges its own inauthenticity. Other aphorisms, however, betray the troubled difficulty of too neatly inverting the binary and laying claim to a position of critique for all modes of rhetorical posturing, as if this might somehow let you off the responsibility of qualifying lines like 'All we painters hate women; unless we hate men', which seems to allude both to the general sexism of Abstract Expressionist artists and to attacks levelled at de Kooning's *Women* paintings. This entry, like the unsettling 'the Nigerians are terrible Negro haters', treads a fine line between capitulation and distance which only just survives scrutiny of the contextual mimicry in this performance of critique.[25]

Nevertheless the artificiality, and the use of the critical pose as a distancing device, is heightened by the knowledge that this piece of writing, despite reading

22 Although Lee Krasner, Pollock's widow, liked O'Hara's monograph *Jackson Pollock* (1960), it was not so well received by the established art critics of Abstract Expressionism. See Gooch, *City Poet*, p. 342.
23 O'Hara and Rivers, 'How to Proceed in the Arts', pp. 92, 93, 95.
24 O'Hara and Rivers, 'How to Proceed in the Arts', p. 94.
25 O'Hara and Rivers, 'How to Proceed in the Arts', p. 95.

like one person talking to another on a telephone, is a collaborative outcome of dialogue between two people. The strength and force of the 'I' is simply illusory and not to be traced back to one authentic source, but understood rather as a refraction across diverse selves saturated with found material. The entry 'Don't just paint. Be a successful all-round man like Baudelaire' is more true than not of O'Hara and cannot easily be dismissed as a put-down of artistic pretension.[26] This highlights the unstable seriousness underlying the rhetorical pose: beyond pastiche and critical coherence, the postures work through varying levels of intimacy and distance. 'How to Proceed in the Arts' is, in effect, a durational event of performance: writing as action that risks its own messy failure. No one is excluded from the charges against Abstract Expressionism, not artists, not critics, not teachers, not the writers of the article: 'we are a complete waste of time'.[27]

Hartigan's relationship to Abstract Expressionism is similarly fraught. As noted above, Hartigan was the only woman included in the *New American Painting* exhibition and her marginal position is implicit in Alfred H. Barr's introduction, which notes that the 'artists in the exhibition compromise the central core as well as the major marginal talent in the movement now called "Abstract Expressionism"'.[28] In a 1993 interview with Vicki Goldberg for an article for the *New York Times*, Goldberg records how the 71-year-old Hartigan described meeting Pollock and de Kooning:

> Ms. Hartigan called up Pollock cold to say she admired his work; he invited her out to his Long Island studio. Overcome by what she saw, she asked who else was making important art. Only de Kooning and me, Pollock said, so she called de Kooning, who befriended her but told her she completely misunderstood modern art. She wept uncontrollably but soon began a deepening dialogue with Abstract Expressionism.[29]

This account of male self-confidence is matched by the lack of self-confidence shown by Hartigan herself in her 1974 interview with Irving Sandler.

> I began to get guilty for walking in and freely taking their [Pollock and de Kooning's] form [...] [without] having gone through their struggle for content, or having any context except an understanding of formal qualities [...] I decided I had no right to the form – I hadn't found it myself – and that I would have to paint my way through art history [...][30]

Goldberg, Sandler, and Hartigan do not point out the obvious ironies and complex power relations at work. The cultural space associated with Abstract Expressionism appeared to offer women the equally unpromising roles of muse or child who must

---

26 O'Hara and Rivers, 'How to Proceed in the Arts', p. 93.

27 O'Hara and Rivers, 'How to Proceed in the Arts', p. 93.

28 Françoise S. Puniello, *Abstract Expressionist Women Painters: An Annotated Bibliography* (London: Scarecrow Press, 1996), p. 219.

29 Goldberg, 'Grace Hartigan Still Hates Pop'.

30 Irving Sandler, *The New York School: The Painters and Sculptors of the Fifties* (London: Harper and Row, 1978), p. 113.

learn from her masters.[31] Hartigan also needed to work against the equally essentialist discourses of feminism from this period:

C.N. But you had this very sensuous touch – a love of paint and the stroke.

G.H. If you are insinuating that it is because I am a woman…

C.N. No not at all.

G.H. I don't know if there is any more sensuous touch than a Rothko's for instance.

C.N. Also de Kooning.

G.H. Excuse me for being defensive.

C.N. You have every right. It has become a stereotype to associate women with the sensuous.

G.H. Exactly. That is what I am absolutely against. I would like to see the point were we can use words without these prejudiced sexual connotations.[32]

In an early article on Hartigan's work, Emily Dennis struggles to articulate the connection and distance between Hartigan and her Abstract Expressionist contemporaries. She does so in terms which reveal gendered tensions:

She makes her achievement not by a cool removal into abstract invention, but by articulating a raw, wild world of perceptions with the deft sensibility of a woman, not with a frenzied and sensational revel in paint, but with the ease and control of a powerful artist.[33]

Dennis falls into the obvious traps of essentialism but her description articulates an important attempt to wrest Hartigan's work from the gendered constraints of its cultural surrounds. Although Hartigan has denied that her decision to exhibit under the name George Hartigan for her first four exhibitions in New York had anything to do with potential discrimination against women artists,[34] the context was clearly difficult. In her exhaustive bibliography, Puniello frequently highlights the way in which the three female painters most closely associated with Abstract Expressionism – Elaine de Kooning, Helen Frankenthaler, Grace Hartigan– are often excluded from discussion by reviewers or mentioned only in passing.[35] In addition, the play between figuration and abstraction in her work sets Hartigan's

---

31 Her tone in retrospective interviews with Sandler and Goldberg is not matched by her fiery statement for the *12 Americans* exhibition catalogue (Dorothy C. Miller, *12 Americans* [New York: Museum of Modern Art, 1956]): 'I have found my "subject", it concerns that which is vulgar and vital in American modern life [...] [The] rawness must be resolved into form and unity; without the "rage for order" how can there be art?' (quoted in Sandler, *The New York School*, p. 115).

32 Nemser, *Art Talk*, p. 134.

33 Dennis, 'Grace Hartigan: The Ordered Creation of Chaos', p. 29.

34 See Goldberg who, without irony, reports her conversation with Hartigan: 'She [Hartigan] insists this was not a response to discrimination against women, which did not exist in the art world then, but a homage to two great Georges, Eliot and Sand. "Men really Love women as comrades and fellow creators," she [Hartigan] says. "What they don't want is to share any of the goodies with them. I was friends in a period when there weren't any goodies. There wasn't any fame, there wasn't any money, there wasn't any power"'; 'Grace Hartigan Still Hates Pop'.

35 Thomas B. Hess, 'New York's Avant-Garde', *Art News* 50.4 (June–August 1951), pp. 46–47. For further context, see Puniello, *Abstract Expressionist Women Painters*.

painting apart from that of many of her contemporaries in ways which led to her being effectively written out of many critical histories. Goldberg notes that after 1960 'she sank from view faster than the Titanic'.[36] In the light of this, her answer in 1961 to a question about her influences, to which she replied by saying, 'In a sense I had to make my own art history', is neither surprising nor unexpected.[37]

Hartigan and O'Hara negotiate the difficult social and political tensions involved in their associations with Abstract Expressionism through the use of poses. They also use poses as ways of articulating interfaces between art and life. Unlike many around them, they were not using a pose to draw attention to their authenticity as serious artists but rather foregrounding their seriousness as artists by the rejection of such a pose of authenticity. Hartigan's *The Masker* (1954), for example, looks very much like a portrait of O'Hara posed in harlequin costume. His own poem 'Homosexuality' (*CP*, 181) is inspired by James Ensor's *Self-Portrait With Masks* (1937).[38] O'Hara's poem begins 'So we are taking off our masks, are we, and keeping / our mouths shut? as if we'd been pierced by a glance!' (*CP*, 81). Ensor's turn-of-the-century paintings featuring macabre images of people in costumes and disguises may also have inspired Hartigan's painting featuring O'Hara: O'Hara in turn may have been thinking through Hartigan's image of himself posed as one of Ensor's and Hartigan's masquers. The possibilities of the pose become circuitous and muti-valent rather than directly singular in their points of reference.

Later in 1954 Hartigan staged another series of photographs as the basis for a painting that involved real people rather than mannequins. In her journal she noted:

> In the market Thursday I came upon piles of old clothes and costumes and bought some that excite me – a long black hooded cape, a red hunter's coat and beaded twenties dress. Since then I can think of nothing but making a large painting called 'Masquerade' for which I shall use the *Folder* people.[39]

In these photographs, Hartigan poses herself as bride and Frank O'Hara as groom. As with the kite-flying party, the posing of these photographs is an event in its own terms. Sam Taylor-Wood provides a precise point of comparison. She has also made pictures featuring artists and performers drawn from the art scene in ways that trouble the boundaries between performance and reality, and between still photography and film.[40] Hartigan was already exploring such questions in her

---

36 'Grace Hartigan Still Hates Pop'.
37 Puniello, *Abstract Expressionist Women Painters*, p. 215.
38 Russell Ferguson, *In Memory of My Feelings: Frank O'Hara and American Art* (Berkeley, Los Angeles, London: California University Press, 1999), p. 93.
39 Robert Mattison, *Grace Hartigan: A Painter's World* (New York: Hudson Hills, 1990), p. 36. *Folder* was a journal issued by Tiber Press that featured work by both O'Hara and Hartigan, among other poets and painters of their immediate circle.
40 This aspect of Taylor-Wood's work has much in common with the photographs taken for *Life* magazine during the 1950s which show Pollock's murals in the interior of Clement Greenberg's apartment.

Figure 2 Contact sheet for *Masquerade*, 1954

paintings of the 1950s. Like Taylor-Wood's *Five Revolutionary Seconds XI*, Hartigan's *Masquerade* captures multiple time-frames. The difference in Hartigan's case is the way the resulting painting offers a synthesis of multiple photographs of the same event, as is made clear by the use she makes of photographic contact sheets to paint *Masquerade* (Figure 2). The final painting is not copied from one chosen image but gathers its poses from multiple frames; reference is dispersed across and through the staged event, which itself *mimics* a carnival but is in fact only a pose. The images are not the record of an actual bridal party or an actual carnival.

This staging of event and the self in performance is also central to O'Hara's poetry and the myths that have grown up around O'Hara's writing process. O'Hara is reputed to have written poetry in public spaces away from his desk; out on his lunch break 'he would go out, often writing poetry on the sample typewriters at the nearby Olivetti showroom',[41] on the Staten Island ferry on the way to a poetry reading at which he would read the poem ('Poem [Lana Turner has collapsed]' [*CP*, 449]), or even at parties. Gooch notes how he often 'scribbled poems at Cronin's', 'jotting down overheard phrases he liked the sound of while squeezed into a noisy booth'.[42] This might document O'Hara the writer at work, but it is also O'Hara staging himself as a writer in a public way which might have masked his actual writing process.

O'Hara is similarly noted for his collaborative self-staging through both photography and art. The artists Jane Freilicher, Nell Blane, Larry Rivers, Grace Hartigan, Phillip Guston, Alex Katz and Fairfield Porter all painted portraits of O'Hara. In the 1940s while at Harvard he was photographed as Ronald Firbank with multiple scarves tied around his head, and he later posed for a series of photographs depicting him 'as all the animals in a medieval bestiary'.[43] These apparent turns as artist's model emphasize O'Hara's status in the art world and the control he had of his own representation. These images not only reflect but also inform and construct his own self, a fact that is evident in his use of many of the portraits of himself in his own poetry. Paintings of O'Hara offered him alternative poses, attitudinal interfaces with which he could be in dialogue in his poetry. The contact sheets for *Masquerade* seem to offer Hartigan a similar resource in the process of painting.

Roland Barthes describes photography as 'literally an emanation of the referent' which 'radiates like the delayed rays of a star'.[44] In 'A Pleasant Thought from Whitehead' (*CP*, 23), O'Hara imagines similar emanations from his poems:

> Ah!
> reader! you open the page
> my poems stare at you you
> stare back, do you not? my
> poems speak on the silver
> of your eyes your eyes repeat
> them to your love's this
> very night. Over your naked
> shoulder the improving stars
> read my poems and flash
> them onward to a friend.

41 Ferguson, *In Memory of My Feelings*, p. 118.
42 Gooch, *City Poet*, pp. 149, 202.
43 Gooch, *City Poet*, plate after p. 142; p. 161.
44 Barthes, *Camera Lucida*, pp. 80–81.

The eyes the poems of the

world are changed! [...] (*CP*, 23)

The poem puns on stares and stars and fuses the metaphors of a mirror and a photographic print (the 'silver/ of your eyes'). Looks or 'stares' between reader and poem, reader and lover become stars that physically radiate the poems outwards into the world. As in 'Personism: A Manifesto' O'Hara is interested in the properties of a poem that might be 'at last between two persons instead of two pages' (*CP*, 499). His tongue-in-cheek observation that he 'could use the telephone instead of writing the poem' (*CP*, 499) highlights O'Hara's interest in a poetics of ephemerality that might blur the distinctions between art and life. The ironic tone of the manifesto suggests that he was well aware that this could only come into being at the expense of the work of art itself, through a kind of self-cancelling gesture: 'Poetry being quicker and surer than prose, it is only just that poetry finish literature off' (*CP*, 499).

O'Hara's eclogue *Grace and George*, written in 1952, features a conversation between the two eponymous characters who appear to be the same split-self ('I fainted near the door, knowing I was you' [*AN*, 89]) in a meandering and surreal exchange. The play ends with the phrase 'Adieu, my twins'. What or who these twins represent seems successively and simultaneously to include Hartigan and O'Hara, Hartigan the artist and Hartigan the woman, the public and private selves of O'Hara, Romanticism and anti-Romanticism. Joe LeSueur suggests that it was not 'written for the stage' (*AN*, xix). Certainly the stage directions are hyperbolic, directions for the reader to imagine rather than for a director to interpret. An unwieldy wooden sail 'creaks out the message of perfunctory freedom and commerce, drawing unerringly with its wavering wake across the faces of George and Grace the frightful distinction of line between freedom which is tartar and slavery which is self' (*AN*, 88). In lines which echo Shakespeare's *Julius Caesar* O'Hara uses the image of newly planted gardens to suggest that it is the commercial and social pressures which dictate the split between the two selves of George and Grace who, like Hartigan and O'Hara, must leave 'our private walks and arborways, common pleasures, to walk abroad and recreate yourselves' (*AN*, 89). The shifting pronouns, splitting and fluctuating selves reflect the pressures on the self of the artist and the selves ('yourselves') which are created in the work. This is at once the Romantic impulse behind being an artist – its absolute connection to the natural – and also a spotlight on its absolute artificiality, its constructed nature which comes into being in public performance as a series of poses. There is nothing natural about the 'message of perfunctory freedom and commerce', but it is the naturalized landscape in which the poet and artist find themselves *posed* and within which they are consequently caused to 'adopt a certain pose' of their own. In this case, it is also a pose which can never actually be adopted if the eclogue remains in its form as a deliberately unperformable play.

Hartigan is one of three prominent female muses in O'Hara's poems, the others being Bunny Lang and Jane Freilicher. Hartigan often functions in the traditional role of an idealized muse, despite the way that in 'Poem for a Painter' the speaker announces he has 'no Muse but the whore' (*CP*, 80). In the same poem 'Grace' appears as a 'flowergirl on the candled plain / with fingers smelled of turpentine', an image which emphasizes O'Hara's staging of her as artist. By contrast, 'Portrait of Grace' (*CP*, 87) appears to be a highly romanticized depiction of her with conventional resort to images of pre-Raphaelite beauty ('Her spinning hair webbed lengthening through/ amber silk'). However, it is O'Hara's play with artifice and the self-staging of Hartigan's paintings that ultimately links the strategies of the two most closely. In 'Christmas Card to Grace Hartigan' (*CP*, 212), her enigmatic smile makes her a kind of Mona Lisa which 'must be/ protected from spilling into/ generality by secret meanings, / the lipstick of life hidden / in a handbag against violations' (*CP*, 212). As in *Grace and George*, O'Hara is investigating the drag of self as much as the self in drag.

In a later poem, 'Far from the Porte des Lilas and the Rue Pergolese', which is addressed to the painter Joan Mitchell, this image of lipstick is used again:

Ah Joan! there
you are
surrounded by paintings
as in another century you would be wearing lipstick
(which you wear at night to be old-fashioned, of it!
      with it!   out! (*CP*, 311)

As Shaw notes, the poem 'puns back to, and genders, Rosenberg's description of the abstract expressionist painter for whom the "act is inseparable from the biography of the artist"'.[45] Lipstick is a means to make up a new face, to adopt a necessary pose for life and for the camera. The paintings are lipstick; to be worn out as part of the stance that *makes up* the self. 'To reinvent a face, to reinvent any part of the figure, is a formidable problem' remarked Hartigan in discussion of her painting.[46] For O'Hara, the lipstick – this reinvention of the face through the pose of self in artificiality – is the metaphorical equivalent of the brush of the Abstract Expressionist painter who 'acts' out her performance/action in painting as she would previously have done in lipstick.

In his discussion of Hartigan's work in his essay 'Nature and New Painting' O'Hara describes her as a 'painter of heterogeneous pictures which bring together wildly discordant images through insight into their functional relationship (their "being together in the world")' and speaks of 'the progress of inclusion, a continual effort to put more into the picture without sacrificing the clarity that she loves in Matisse nor subduing the noise of the desperate changes she perceives in the world

---

45 Shaw, *Frank O'Hara: The Poetics of Coterie*, p. 163.
46 Nemser, *Art Talk*, p. 137.

around her' (*SS*, 45). These observations might equally apply to the Frank O'Hara who wrote 'Second Avenue', 'In Memory of My Feelings' and 'Biotherm'. These poems 'bring together wildly discordant images', such as 'a guitar of toothpaste tubes and fingernails, trembling spear' (*CP*, 149), 'a flaking moon drifting across the muddied teeth' (*CP*, 253) or 'the works carbonateddrugstorewater hiccups' (*CP*, 437), as juxtapositions which foreground the 'noise' of the world around him. 'Biotherm', like the lipsticks in 'Far from the Porte des Lilas and the Rue Pergolese', becomes associated with the making up, the putting on and the wiping out of a new face ('when we meet we smile in another language' [*CP*, 444]) or self-acknowledging pose ('I want swimmingpool mudpacks the works' [*CP*, 437]). These three poems, like Hartigan's paintings, gain their strength from their layers of inclusive imagery at the same time as each nearly buckles under the weight of maintaining the singular 'clarity' of particular elements, the quality that both Hartigan and O'Hara admired in Matisse.

Like O'Hara, Hartigan early on incorporated found objects into her work. *Rough Ain't It!* (1949–50) is a collage of packaging and paint, the slogan on the papers clearly showing through. Irving Sandler characterizes Hartigan, along with other painters such as Larry Rivers, as a gestural realist: 'In their preoccupation with nature, art history, and self-conscious conceptions of style, gestural realists rejected the dogmatic demands of some of their contemporaries who held that gesture painting to be genuine had to be based exclusively on what Kandinsky called "inner necessity," and thus had to exclude stimuli from sources external to self'.[47] O'Hara and Hartigan both construct selves from 'sources external' which are successively tried on both literally and metaphorically. Indeed, in some of O'Hara's poems, these costumes in which to pose as new and multiple selves seem to be fabricated from considerations of paintings and in particular those of Hartigan. Significantly, O'Hara referred to Hartigan's painting as 'the tragic Masquerade [1954] where the individual identities are being destroyed by costumes which imprison them' (*SS*, 45).

In 'Second Avenue', O'Hara uses an image of Hartigan's painting as well as his knowledge of her painting process in order to find a metaphor for his emotions:

> and when the pressure asphyxiates and inflames, Grace destroys
> the whirling faces in their dissonant gaiety where it's anxious,
> lifted nasally to the heavens which is a carrousel grinning
> and spasmodically obliterated with loaves of greasy white paint
> and this becomes like love to her, is what I desire (*CP*, 149)

To O'Hara, the figures in Hartigan's painting exist in tension between the potential qualities of the 'loaves of greasy white paint' and the figurative representation of the 'whirling faces' which are 'spasmodically obliterated' in the act of painting. A similar process occurs in the syntax and grammar of O'Hara's poem which 'spasmodically' obliterates clear connections between subject and object, between

---

47 Sandler, *The New York School*, p. 50.

word and referent. Thus, in the passage just quoted, it is unclear who or what is 'anxious'; the painter as she paints or the figures in the painting. This sense of anxiety extends the earlier descriptions of 'racing towards nervousness' into the 'puree of the crime' (*CP*, 140), a crime that seems to involve the murderous intentions of the speaker towards his own 'I' which appears periodically detached and under threat of dissolution:

> I suffer accelerations that are vicarious and serene,
> just as the lances of an army advance above the heat of the soldiery,
> so does my *I* tremble before the getting-out-of-bedness (*CP*, 140)

The way sense and subjectivity are detached and operate along different temporal coordinates is echoed in the lines which describe the speaker as 'a nun trembling before the microphone/ at a movie premiere while a tidal wave has seized the theatre/ and borne it to Siam, decorated it and wrecked its projector' (*CP*, 140). The hilarious image of a nun about to host a movie premiere that is suddenly transported to the comparatively sordid context of Siam stands for the sudden recontextualization of the speaker. This speaker is surprisingly engulfed by sexual desires but must still overcome nervousness about speaking into a microphone and introducing a film whose projector has been ruined. The wrecked projector is both a version of the lyric self and an 'I' attempting to make use of technological interfaces, here the microphone and the projector. This poem is presented as a mediated performance of levels of artifice corrupted and overlaid with each other in a conflicting mesh of systems which are all attempts to cope with the 'paralysis' that 'becomes jaundice' (*CP*, 144) or 'the paralyzin rush / of emotion' whose 'fists' are 'caught in the Venetian blinds' (*CP*, 148). Indeed, the poem is itself the 'rush of emotion' whose lines are caught in 'blinds' of O'Hara's lines (*CP*, 148). Rather than develop a recuperable response to one event, the poem documents a self involved in a theatricalized process of destruction. The 'you' this poem is addressing is a prosthetic extension of the self:

> [...] When the chips are in,
> yours will spell out in a wealth of dominoes, YOU, and you'll
> be stuck with it, hell to anybody else, drowning in lead (*CP*, 148)

The poem thus has affinities with Hartigan's contact sheets: rather than resolve each moment of event into one whole, O'Hara presents his fluctuating images in an unfolding sequence. 'Second Avenue' is an action poem that cannot write itself out of its paralysis: 'a dream of immense sadness peers through me/ as if I were an action poem that couldn't write' (*CP*, 311).

Amid this 'drowning' or 'endurance of water', Hartigan's painting surfaces in the poem (*CP*, 148). Who or what is being lifted 'nasally to the heavens' is unclear. There is a tension here between the reading of the image as one of extreme bodily pain, even torture, and the possibility of it as an image of the artist high on inspiration in the act of transcendence. Similarly, the phrase 'this becomes like love to her' is ambiguous as to whether it is the act of painting – an act here specifically connected with the continuous negotiation of the fluctuating dividing line between abstraction and figuration – or the final painting which 'becomes like love to her'. It is this ambiguous 'this' which is what the 'I' of 'Second Avenue' 'desire[s]', and 'this' is at once a metaphor for his feelings as well as a statement of intent for his own poetic process. He has approached the representation of his tempestuous love-affair by placing the grammar and syntax of the poem under a 'pressure' which 'asphyxiates and enflames' the networks of reference invoked. At the same time, writing for O'Hara, like painting for Hartigan, becomes a way of displacing what might otherwise potentially annihilate the artist if they could not express it through art. For both of them the attempt to explore the process of making art is a way 'to destroy something but not us' (*CP*, 149).

'In Memory of My Feelings', addressed to Grace Hartigan, engages with similar concerns. The 'naked selves' that the speaker must protect are threatened by 'creatures' who 'have murder in their heart' (*CP*, 253). These many selves are also represented as being 'transparent' (*CP*, 252) and as 'my transparencies' (*CP*, 253). They are projected slides from the faulty projector of 'Second Avenue' or like the multiple selves that Hartigan stages in the contact sheets of the photographic versions of her events: 'One of me rushes/ to window #13 and one of me raises his whip and one of me/ flutters up from the center of the track amidst the pink flamingoes' (*CP*, 253). Indeed, O'Hara specifically considers himself through Hartigan's painting *The Bathers* (which he had posed for):

> One of me is standing in the waves, an ocean bather,
> or I am naked with a plate of devils at my hip.
>
> Grace
> to be born and live as variously as possible. The conception
> of the masque barely suggests the sordid identifications. (*CP*, 256)

In *Masquerade*, Hartigan considers herself through the photographs of an event which she directed. Her paintings (and those in which he appeared in the work of other painters) become O'Hara's contact sheet of selves. He is a model for her painting, but he then uses her painting as a stage, an interface, for his poem in a way which implies a mutuality of exchange both personally and artistically.

In the processes of making of both Hartigan and O'Hara there is an interpenetration of art and life, imagination and fantasy. O'Hara describes his thought processes as a kind of projector and screen:

> I watch
> the sea at the back of my eyes, near the spot where I think
> in solitude as pine trees groan and support the enormous winds,
> they are humming *L'Oiseau de feu!*
> They look like gods, these whitemen,
> and they are bringing me the horse I fell in love with on the frieze. (*CP*, 256)

The power of the imagination is so great that it can turn art into life and vice versa, hence, 'they are bringing me the horse I fell in love with on the frieze'. There is a dynamic translation of conceptual thought across media, across fantasy and the imagination. The body is only 'naked host to my many selves': it is the projector – or the screen onto which these selves are projected (*CP*, 256). While Hartigan's paintings are used by O'Hara in his poems as representations which generate metaphors for subjective states, they also function as dynamic instances of processes which find overlaps in O'Hara's own writing activities.

This staging of events is not completely dissimilar to Harold Rosenberg's description of the Abstract Expressionist painter. For Rosenberg the canvas is 'an arena in which to act – rather than [...] a space in which to reproduce, re-design, analyze, or "express" an object, actual or imagined. What was to go on the canvas was not a picture but an event'.[48] However, Rosenberg also calls Abstract Expressionism 'a movement to leave behind the self'. As we have seen, O'Hara and Hartigan detach, re-stage and reinhabit a variety of selves but do not leave the self behind. In 'The Romantics Were Prompted' Mark Rothko writes that he thinks of his 'pictures as dramas: the shapes in the pictures are the performers'.[49] For O'Hara and Hartigan the process of making the work is also part of this performance and might involve the striking of a pose or series of poses in which the self is both subject and object. For Hartigan, photography usefully facilitates this possibility. O'Hara approaches Hartigan's paintings as Hartigan would the multiple and successive images on her contact sheets; each finds an interface through which to mediate painting or writing.

In O'Hara and Hartigan, the work articulates itself through the negotiation of events and selves posed in attitudinal interface between art and life, between different systems of representation. Each investigates the processes and possibilities, obstacles and objects that get in the way of making art but which are also a type of art-making. The interruption of figuration through abstraction and vice versa is one way of considering this, as is the refraction of self through successive forms of mediatization; disrupted images cast in the light of a faulty projector. This method of working carries with it the risk that the staging of an event, its kite-flying, might eclipse the work of art altogether. This is precisely the function and dangerous possibility of the pose, an attitude struck which necessitates the redefinition of the cultural, social and artistic boundaries around it.

48 Shapiro and Shapiro, *Abstract Expressionism*, p. 76.
49 Shapiro and Shapiro, *Abstract Expressionism*, p. 397.

'In Fatal Winds':
Frank O'Hara and Morton Feldman

Will Montgomery

O n new Year's Day 1952 something changed for John Ashbery. He had been unable to write for some time, inhibited by low spirits that he attributed, in part, to the political situation.[1] But the clouds began to lift when he attended a musical event with his friend Frank O'Hara. The event was a recital by the pianist David Tudor that included John Cage's *Music of Changes*, a piece composed through randomizing use of the I-Ching.[2] 'It went on for over an hour and seemed infinitely extendable,' said Ashbery. 'I felt profoundly refreshed after listening to that. I started to write again shortly afterwards. I felt that I could be as singular in my art as Cage was in his.'[3] In his introduction to O'Hara's *Collected Poems* Ashbery stresses that his companion had also been greatly impressed by Cage's composition, going on to describe the general importance of music to O'Hara:

> what mattered was that chance elements could combine to produce so beautiful and cogent a work. It was a further, perhaps for us ultimate proof not so much that 'Anything goes' but 'Anything can come out'.
>
> This climate – Picasso and French poetry, de Kooning and Guston, Cage and Feldman, Rachmaninoff, Schubert, Sibelius and Krenek – just about any music, in fact – encouraged Frank's poetry and provided him with a sort of reservoir of inspiration: words and colors that could be borrowed freely from everywhere to build up big, airy structures unlike anything else in American poetry and indeed unlike poetry, more like the inspired ramblings of a mind open to the point of distraction. The result has been a truly viable freedom of poetic expression, which, together with other attempts at technical (Charles Olson) and psychological (Allen Ginsberg) liberation has opened up poetry for today's generation of young poets. (*CP*, ix)

1 He later recalled: 'It [coincided] with the beginnings of the Korean War, the Rosenberg case and McCarthyism. Though I was not an intensely political person, it was impossible to be happy in that kind of climate. It was a nadir.' Interview with Richard Kostelanetz, cited in Marjorie Perloff, '"Transparent Selves": The Poetry of John Ashbery and Frank O'Hara', *The Yearbook of English Studies* 8, American Literature Special Number (1978), pp. 171–96, at p. 172. My thanks to Chris Villars and Brian Marley for commenting on an earlier draft of this essay.

2 The performance was held at the Cherry Lane Theatre, home of Judith Malina and Julian Beck's Living Theatre.

3 Perloff, '"Transparent Selves"', p. 172.

Leaving aside the unfortunate phrase 'inspired ramblings', it is significant that what is at stake here, in Ashbery's eyes, is a kind of freedom. For Ashbery, some sort of refuge from the unpleasantness of the American political climate of the early 1950s can be found in these liberatory aesthetic rhetorics. As has been widely observed, such a vocabulary was also at work in the manner in which Abstract Expressionism was discussed and promulgated in the 1950s. This often involved a translation of the theatricalized subjectivism of existentialism into a quasi-ideological commitment to individual autonomy.[4]

Despite O'Hara's close involvement with Abstract Expressionism, it would be a mistake to assign to his poetry a close investment in expressivist paradigms. However, it is certainly the case that a range of freedoms are envisaged in the writing, most important of which is perhaps the dark and delirious democracy of poems such as 'In Memory of My Feelings' (*CP*, 252) and 'Ode to Michael Goldberg ('s Birth and Other Births)' (*CP*, 290), which assign a kind of beneficent polyphony to both individual and collective being. Such visions of freedom in O'Hara's writing are always self-subverting, however: the multiple and the singular, each a staging of a liberatory moment, qualify and deny one another's claims.[5] Thus, for example, it is certainly possible to argue that O'Hara's freedom was, in Brian Kim Stefans' words, 'the liberty of the French poets, of Apollinaire and Breton, which bore on its shoulders a philosophy that argued against the possibility of personal agency'.[6] Yet this aspiration to cede control to the unconscious needs qualifying. Although important in greater or lesser degree to many of O'Hara's poems, it does not obviate the potential of personal agency, at work both in the poems' considered construction and in the sheer wilfulness and ironic self-direction of the voices that speak in O'Hara's poems.

The year that began with David Tudor's recital, 1952, was the year in which O'Hara consolidated his presence in New York, making many friendships with artists, writers and composers.[7] His first book of poems, *A City Winter and Other*

---

4 For discussion of O'Hara, Abstract Expressionism and Cold War constructions of 'freedom', see Lytle Shaw, *Frank O'Hara: The Poetics of Coterie* (Iowa City: University of Iowa Press, 2006), especially chapters 4 and 5. See also Serge Guilbaut, *How New York Stole the Idea of Modern Art* (Chicago and London: University of Chicago Press, 1983), particularly the conclusion's remarks on alienation and 'liberal ideology'.

5 See T. J. Clark's essay 'In Defense of Abstract Expressionism', which concludes that modernist art in general and Abstract Expressionism in particular cannot escape from the 'singular voice or viewpoint' of lyric. 'Lyric cannot be expunged by modernism, only repressed. [...] lyric in our time is deeply ludicrous. The deep ludicrousness of lyric is Abstract Expressionism's subject, to which it returns like a tongue to a loosening tooth.' In *Farewell to an Idea: Episodes from a History of Modernism* (New Haven and London: Yale UP, 1999), pp. 371–401, at p. 401.

6 Brian Kim Stefans, 'Frank O'Hara', in *Before Starting Over* (Cambridge: Salt, 2006), pp. 169–71, at p. 169.

7 O'Hara settled in New York in late August 1951. See Brad Gooch, *City Poet: The Life and Times of Frank O'Hara* (New York: Alfred A Knopf, 1993), p. 189. The 'Short Chronology' in *Art Chronicles* notes that in 1952 O'Hara met, among others, 'Helen Frankenthaler, Barbara Guest, Grace

Poems, was published, and he began appearing on discussion panels at the Club, an influential forum for debate among the downtown artists. Its members included Robert Motherwell, Willem de Kooning, Franz Kline, Robert Rauschenberg, Helen Frankenthaler and, joining in 1952, Philip Guston, Mike Goldberg, Larry Rivers, Grace Hartigan and Alfred Leslie.[8] In summer 1952, he wrote 'Easter' and 'Hatred', two long and violent poems that captured the growing vigour and singularity of his voice. 1952, in other words, was the year in which O'Hara became the O'Hara that we know.

In Ashbery's view, he and O'Hara were involved in a form of poetic self-realization that was closely informed, although not directly influenced, by developments in both painting and music:

> the artists liked us and bought us drinks and we, on the other hand, felt that they
> – and I am speaking of artists like de Kooning, Franz Kline, Motherwell, Pollock –
> were free to be free in their painting in a way that most people felt was impossible for
> poetry. So I think we learned a lot from them at that time, and also from composers
> like John Cage and Morton Feldman, but the lessons were merely an abstract truth
> – something like Be Yourself – rather than a practical one – in other words nobody
> ever thought he would scatter words over a page the way Pollock scattered his drips,
> but the reason for doing so might have been the same in both cases'.[9]

While this provides further evidence of the liberating effect of other art forms on the young poets, 'Be Yourself' gives us (designedly) little purchase on the complicated versions of selfhood in either Ashbery's or O'Hara's poetry. In this essay I want to develop some of the questions opened up by Ashbery's references to 'freedom' in his reminiscences of the early 1950s. O'Hara's engagement with avant-garde music provides a particularly useful lens for examining this impulse. However, it is with Cage's friend Morton Feldman, rather than Cage himself, that O'Hara had a particular affinity. Ashbery doesn't mention in his recollections that *Intersections II*, a strikingly original Feldman piece for solo piano, was also performed at that New Year's Day concert.[10] This was a realization of one of Feldman's early graphic

---

Hartigan, Joan Mitchell, Edwin Denby, Alfred Leslie, Michael Goldberg, Franz Kline, Elaine and Willem de Kooning, Philip Guston, Jackson Pollock, [and] Ned Rorem' (*AC*, 158).

8 Gooch, *City Poet*, pp. 211–31. See also Irving Sandler, 'The Club', *Artforum* 4.1 (September 1965), pp. 27–31.

9 John Ashbery, 'The New York School of Poets', in *Selected Prose* (Manchester: Carcanet, 2004), p. 115. See also Morton Feldman's remark, 'It is not freedom of choice that is the meaning of the fifties, but the freedom of people to be themselves.' 'Give My Regards to Eighth Street', in *Give My Regards to Eighth Street: Collected Writings of Morton Feldman*, ed. B. H. Friedman (Boston, MA: Exact Change, 2000), pp. 93–101, at p. 99.

10 As were Pierre Boulez's second piano sonata and Christian Wolff's *For Prepared Piano*. See John Holzaepfel, 'Painting by Numbers: The Intersections of Morton Feldman and David Tudor', in Steven Johnson (ed.), *The New York Schools of Music and Visual Arts* (New York, London: Routledge, 2002), pp. 159–72, at p. 161.

scores, in which register is relatively indeterminate, as only high, middle and low are indicated – the choice of precise pitch is left to the performer. Indeed it was Feldman, not Cage, who had led the way in the rejection of conventional scores in 1950: 'Feldman left the room one evening, in the midst of a long conversation, and returned with a composition on graph paper', is Cage's account, as cited by David Nicholls. Nicholls continues: 'The work in question was *Projection 1*; remarkably, it was completed in 1950, before Cage had even commenced – let alone finished – the precisely notated and therefore "photographically still" *Music of Changes*'.[11] Feldman himself was ambivalent about his innovation, returning to conventional notation for most of 1952, using graphic scores in 1953 and then abandoning them until 1957. Nicholls suggests that these oscillations, and the increasing 'specificity' of the graph pieces, indicate Feldman's 'wish that both freedom and control operate together'.[12]

There are many dimensions to the relationship between O'Hara and Feldman. O'Hara studied music at the New England Conservatory and still planned to become a composer when he entered Harvard as a Navy veteran in 1946.[13] When he first met Ashbery towards the end of his final year at Harvard in 1949, it was twentieth-century music that they discussed.[14] O'Hara and Feldman were part of the social group that drank at the Cedar Bar in the 1950s – the meeting point of the three New York 'schools', poetry, painting and music.[15] Both also took an active part in the proceedings of the Club. In 1957, O'Hara dedicated a poem to Feldman, 'Wind'. Feldman would set this twice, first in his *O'Hara Songs* (1962) and second in his *Three Voices* (1982), a piece for solo soprano and tape that, he wrote, he intended as a dual elegy for O'Hara and Philip Guston.[16] Feldman also composed 'For Frank O'Hara' (1973), a brooding homage to his late friend scored for an unconventional eight-piece ensemble.[17] In addition to these reciprocal dedications, the two might have collaborated – in a 1959 letter O'Hara wrote of his intention to write an opera libretto, with Feldman suggested as a collaborator.[18] O'Hara contributed a

11 See David Nicholls, 'Getting Rid of the Glue: The Music of the New York School', in Johnson (ed.), *The New York Schools*, pp. 17–56, at p. 26.
12 Nicholls, 'Getting Rid of the Glue', p. 30.
13 Gooch, *City Poet*, pp. 55–58, pp. 92ff.
14 Gooch, *City Poet*, p. 136. Gooch goes on to narrate the development of friendship fired by shared passions for both 'high' and 'low' culture, Schoenberg *and* Looney Tunes cartoons.
15 Feldman writes 'without exaggeration' of going to the Cedar Bar with Cage every night from 6pm to 3am for five years. See 'Liner Notes', in *Give My Regards*, pp. 3–7, at p. 5.
16 Beckett and O'Hara were the only authors whose words Feldman set to music in work he published as a mature composer. However, he wrote music for texts by Rilke, cummings and Céline very early in his career, in 1947, before he had even met John Cage. In 1960, he also set music to another poem entitled 'Wind', by Boris Pasternak (whose writing O'Hara, coincidentally or not, greatly admired). The MS for this unpublished setting is in the Paul Sacher archive in Basel.
17 The piece is scored for flutes, clarinet, percussionists, piano, violin and cello.
18 See Michael Magee, *Emancipating Pragmatism: Emerson, Jazz, and Experimental Writing* (Tuscaloosa: University of Alabama Press, 2004), p. 230, n. 67.

perceptive essay as a sleevenote to Feldman's first long-player, *New Directions in Music 2* (1959). [19] And, in 1961, the two even performed a piano duet at a benefit for Leroi Jones's *Floating Bear* magazine held at the Living Theater.[20] In 1972, Feldman published an essay on O'Hara that describes the sheer range of the poet's cultural enthusiasms and notes that the chatty surface of the poems by no means exhausts them: 'these poems, so colloquial, so conversational, nevertheless seem to be reaching us from some other, infinitely distant place'.[21]

In what follows, I will discuss O'Hara's description of Feldman's music in the light of some of Feldman's own positions. I will examine O'Hara's 'Wind' and Feldman's various settings of the words. Finally I will explore the relationship between 'Wind' and a much more famous poem, 'Ode to Michael Goldberg ('s Birth and Other Births)', in the context of the issues of freedom, art and selfhood raised in earlier parts of the essay.

O'Hara's Feldman

There is at times a curiously religious register to O'Hara's sleevenote discussion of Feldman. In response to Feldman's suggestion that Guston's paintings had helped the composer locate a 'metaphysical place' in his music, O'Hara writes:

> I interpret this 'metaphysical place', this land where Feldman's pieces live, as the area where spiritual growth in the work can occur, where the form of a work may develop its inherent originality and the personal meaning of the composer may become explicit. In a more literal way it is the space which must be cleared if the sensibility is to be free to express its individual preference for sound and to explore the meaning of this preference. That the process of finding this metaphysical place of unpredictability and possibility can be a drastic one is witnessed by the necessity Feldman felt a few years ago to avoid the academic ramifications of serial technique. Like the artists involved in the new American painting, he was pursuing a personal search for expression which could not be limited by any system.[22]

---

19 The recordings, first released as *New Directions in Music 2: Morton Feldman* (Columbia Records ML5403/MS6090, 1959), were recently reissued on a double CD entitled *John Cage: Music for Keyboard 1935–1948/Morton Feldman: The Early Years* (New World Records 80664, 2007).

20 See Bill Berkson's 'A New York Beginner', *Modern Painters* (Autumn 1998), pp. 49–53, at p. 52. Berkson comments: 'Frank complained afterward of the difficulty of matching the lightness of touch that Feldman's pieces required and that Feldman's own large fingers could muster.' Touch, as the 'New Directions in Music' sleevenote makes clear, was crucial to O'Hara's understanding of Feldman.

21 'Frank O'Hara: Lost Times and Future Hopes', in Feldman, *Give My Regards*, pp. 103–108, at p. 107. The essay, originally published in *Art in America*, is also reprinted in Bill Berkson and Joe LeSueur (eds.), *Homage to Frank O'Hara* (Bolinas, CA: Big Sky, 1988).

22 Frank O'Hara, 'New Directions in Music', in Feldman, *Give My Regards*, pp. 211–17, at p. 212. The essay also appears in Frank O'Hara, *Standing Still and Walking in New York*, ed. Donald Allen (Bolinas, CA: Grey Fox Press).

O'Hara advances a position that favours the exercise of 'individual preference' over 'system'. 'Expression' is an ungovernable and unpredictable field of energy that cannot – or should not – be brooked. What is praised might be described as an art of immediacy, dependent on principles of 'unpredictability and possibility' and highly sceptical of theories of art and formal systems. O'Hara admiringly describes Feldman's *Structures for String Quartet* as 'without sonata development, without serial development, in general without benefit of clergy', and writes of his identification of 'a personal and profound revelation of the inner quality of sound' in Feldman's music.[23]

O'Hara's somewhat coy religiosity in this essay, while disclaiming priesthood, finds echoes in similar passages in Feldman's own writings, notably in the conclusion to 'A Life without Bach and Beethoven': 'If I want my music to demonstrate anything, it is that "nature and human nature are one". Unlike Stockhausen, I don't feel called upon to forcefully "mediate" between the two. Stockhausen believes in Hegel, I believe in God.'[24] Elsewhere Feldman contrasts the 'Messianic' art of 'religion' (i.e. an art derived from some 'organizing principle' – analogous, perhaps, to O'Hara's 'clergy') with that of the 'religious', which he understands as a transcendent space of unrepresentability, 'not involved with ideas'.[25]

What are the formal consequences of this set of nebulous, quasi-mystical propositions advanced by Feldman and O'Hara? O'Hara, in reaching some point of aesthetic sympathy with Feldman in his essay, is arguing that a work of art must develop according to its own immanent formal laws, rather than to a set of extrinsic principles. This motivates his rather surprising comparison of Feldman's conventionally scored *Structures for String Quartet* (1951) to the poetry of Emily Dickinson:

> Like Emily Dickinson's best poems, it does not seem to be what it is until all questions of 'seeming' have disappeared in its own projection. Its form reveals itself *after* its meaning is revealed, as Dickinson's passion ignores her dazzling technique.[26]

O'Hara seeks to draw a distinction between passion and immediacy on the one hand, and technique and 'seeming' on the other. He is writing against the kind of formal law that might make itself the salient aspect of a work of art – serial or chance methods, for example. The uninhibited self-expression of the artist, he seems

23 O'Hara, 'New Directions in Music', p. 21, p. 217.
24 Morton Feldman, 'A Life without Bach or Beethoven', in *Give My Regards*, pp. 15–18, at p. 17.
25 Feldman, 'Give my Regards to Eighth Street', pp. 93–101, at p. 99; and 'After Modernism', in *Give My Regards*, pp. 67–79, at p. 74. For Feldman, in other words, the non-cognitive aspects of artistic experience had a religious character. See also the praise of Abstract Expressionism in 'After Modernism': 'Here, in reaction to modernity, there is an insistence that one can no longer take refuge in ideas, that thought is one thing and its realisation another, that real humility does not lie in all this superrationality, but again, in trying to paint like a god' (p. 70). And: 'Guston, neither close nor distant, like a fleeting constellation projected on the canvas and then removed, suggests an ancient Hebrew metaphor: God exists but is turned away from us'.
26 O'Hara, 'New Directions in Music', p. 215.

to be saying, overrides the demands on our attention of artifice, however 'dazzling' the latter might be. We might compare this to his refusal to supply a statement on poetics for the Paterson Society – O'Hara declined to comment on 'form, measure, sound, yardage, placement and ear', his chief reason being that 'I can't think of any more than one poem at a time, so I would end up with a "poetics" based on one of my poems which any other poem of mine would completely contradict except for certain affections or habits of speech they might include' (*CP*, 510).

Although O'Hara rejects an all-encompassing 'poetics', I think it is possible to identify an important attraction to instability in his thinking in his praise of a quasi-metaphysical 'unpredictability' in Feldman. Feldman sought to let 'sounds exist in themselves – not as symbols, or memories which were memories of other music to begin with'.[27] His aim in this early work to 'unfix' the formal relationships between 'rhythm, pitch, dynamics'[28] is broadly comparable to O'Hara's rejection of a 'poetics' of 'form, measure, sound, yardage, placement and ear'. Feldman too scorns metre, seeking to recover a more complex and subjective experience of temporality: 'I am not a clockmaker. I am interested in getting to time in its unstructured existence. That is, I am interested in how this wild beast lives in the jungle – not in the zoo.'[29] In this last statement, Feldman is close, I think, to the formal and conceptual negations of some of O'Hara's poems – the nihilism of 'Hatred', for example, the darkness that fringes some of the Odes, or the dizzying temporal and referential leaps of 'Second Avenue' or 'Biotherm'.

It is with the category of 'design', discussed in notes apparently prepared for a talk at the Club in 1952 but given no full elaboration in his writings, that O'Hara reaches a precarious accommodation with the structuring and destructuring energies in his poetry.[30] In his notes on this, in ways that complicate the distinction he makes between form and passion in his discussion of Feldman and Dickinson, he stresses that the poet must avoid the dead weight of prior formal associations on one hand, and the uncontainable emotion of the 'poet's passion for poetry and his own ideas' on the other (*SS*, 35). If he succumbs to this passion, indeed, the poet will come to feel that the emotions, not words, '*are* the poem' (*SS*, 35). O'Hara's cautionary remark returns the poet to the specificity of his or her medium, urging a commitment to language itself that is mediated by the operations of 'design', the 'clear-headed, poetry-respecting objectivity' that can stand between the twin threats that 'formal smothering and emotional spilling over' pose to the compositional process (*SS*, 35).

Like Feldman in his remarks on 'sounds [...] in themselves', O'Hara shows a radical commitment to the material he works with, language. This is more important than either poetic form or feeling. While he may exalt the 'individual

27 Morton Feldman, 'Predeterminate/Indeterminate', in *Give My Regards*, pp. 33–36, at p. 35.
28 Feldman, 'Predeterminate/Indeterminate', p. 35.
29 Morton Feldman, 'Between Categories', in *Give My Regards*, pp. 83–89, at p. 87.
30 Frank O'Hara, 'Design etc', in *SS*, 33–36.

preference' of the artist in his writing on Feldman, the real force of his essay lies in its recommendation of 'unpredictability', a category that can be decoupled from conscious operations, as an aesthetic principle. O'Hara's invocation of unpredictability implies an openness to all the things that language can do while the poet isn't looking. This is not the liberty of the realized autonomy of the self nor of the somehow unfettered energies of the unconscious. It is a liberty that realizes the limits of the self in directing language but does not relinquish the commitment to the lightly ordering touch of 'design' in the poem's composition.

At the end of his invaluable book on O'Hara, Lytle Shaw carefully questions the applicability of the term 'immediacy' to O'Hara's work, citing the ways in which proper names, gestural painting, and collage all show themselves to be in some way mediated:

> [O'Hara] is famously attracted to immediacy. But what links all of the writings we have been considering is a process of denaturalising the field of attributes one associates with seemingly immediate markers or marks: the meaning of a proper name, painterly gesture, or collage configuration. The phantom immanence of the proper name might thus be considered along a continuum with the seeming immediacy of gestural painting and supposedly autobiographical collage: would-be markers or designators in language behave instead as wild signs; seemingly emphatic and particular marks by painters that would index private psychic states instead escaping into more public fantasies and nightmares of popular culture (especially Hollywood) and the Cold War; or, what appears to be the visual proof of a self and its history in collage keeps turning in on the syntactical codes by which such a self has been educed, mingling with other selves and with culture more broadly. It is the gradually destabilised rhetoric of immediacy that guides each of these processes – the vanishing of secured immanence.[31]

For Shaw, then, while immediacy is a key term, it is greatly complicated by the public nature and the relative indeterminacy of 'markers' such as proper names. O'Hara's poetry, in this view, mobilizes energies proper to both private and collective experience. What happens, though, when it is not popular culture that is engaged by O'Hara, but the smaller world of contemporary composition? And how might the individuality that O'Hara celebrates in his essay on Feldman translate into a reflexive questioning of selfhood? Can the 'personal and profound revelation of the inner quality of sound' be understood both in terms of Feldman's temporal 'jungle' and Shaw's linguistic equivalent, 'wild signs'? All of these issues are engaged by 'Wind', the poem O'Hara dedicated to Feldman and which Feldman twice set to music.

---

31 Lytle Shaw, *Frank O'Hara: The Poetics of Coterie* (Iowa: University of Iowa Press, 2006), p. 233.

'Wind'

Wind

Who'd have thought
             that snow falls
it always circled whirling
like a thought
             in the glass ball
around me and my bear

Then it seemed beautiful
                  containment
snow whirled
             nothing ever fell
nor my little bear
             bad thoughts
imprisoned in crystal

beauty has replaced itself with evil

And the snow whirls only
                in fatal winds
briefly
             then falls
it always loathed containment
                  beasts
I love evil (*CP*, 269)

'Wind' was written on 31 March 1957.[32] The poem's 21 short lines are either ranged left or indented to varying degrees. The spacing on the page has an antiphonal structure; the sometimes precarious lines on the right hand side of the poem tend to reinforce the idea of falling. However, if the indented lines are read as continuations of the lines above them, the poem begins to resemble a sonnet, with 13 lines and a fairly clear division between mock 'octave' and (foreshortened) mock 'sestet'.[33] The poem begins with the image of whirling snow in a child's snow ornament. The speaker is perplexed by the thought that snow might actually fall, rather than whirling endlessly 'around me and my bear', an image of the loneliness and apparent temporal arrestedness of childhood.

The poem divides between this recollected 'then' and a fruitfully disillusioned 'now'. It appears to describe an aesthetic coming-of-age that is fraught with pain and ambivalence. In the past of which the speaker speaks, the snow indicates a 'containment' that, although 'beautiful', is equated to 'bad thoughts/ imprisoned

32 It was first published in *Locus Solus* 3–4, five years later.
33 O'Hara had investigated the sonnet form in the early 1950s with such poems as 'A Sonnet for Jane Freilicher', 'After Wyatt', 'The Tomb of Arnold Schoenberg', and the short sequence 'A City Winter'.

in crystal'. (The suggestion of 'impure thoughts' seems inescapable given O'Hara's Catholic upbringing.) In the implied 'now' that frames these thoughts, beauty has 'replaced itself with evil'. Now the snow only whirls in 'fatal winds' and 'then falls', free of a 'containment' that it had always 'loathed'. The poem concludes with the near-palindrome 'I love evil', a repetition that, given the dedication, may invoke Feldman's use of near-repetition particularly in his later music (this is certainly a feature of Feldman's various settings of the poem).

It is perfectly plausible to suggest, as Epstein does, that 'the free, wind-driven snow outside (like both "good" thinking and the mobile self) "always loathed containment". O'Hara explicitly pits liberating motion against "containment"'.[34] The poem is complicated, however, by the strong suggestion of risk in the second half of the poem. This is no straightforward narrative of liberation, leading towards a joyously multiple experience of selfhood. Liberation itself is hedged about with death – the snow that falls to the ground melts and vanishes. Wind, that conventional image of spirit and of poetic inspiration, is now 'fatal'. Beauty has not become somehow evil, it has *replaced itself* with evil. Beauty thus becomes in the mouth of the speaker a contemptible 'beauty', a merely ornamental quality that has nothing in common with the hazardous experiences that the poet now encounters.

What is meant by this slide towards evil? On one level, the poem may describe the movement from sexual repression to the fulfilment of desires that a Catholic upbringing had anathematized. In this sense, 'falling' has a metaphysical resonance that is reinforced by the 'fatal' quality of the evil winds. The falling snow may be ejaculatory and the oddly isolated word 'beasts', echoing the isolation of child and bear, might refer to the 'natural brute beasts' (2 Peter 2:13) of Sodom, which O'Hara, of course, celebrates. At another level, the poem might move from the contemplation of a static, display-cabinet form of beauty to an involvement in a Faustian vision of artistic production. The poem can thus be also read as a kind of hymn to contamination, a knowing *poète maudit*'s self-celebration that sullies and wilfully perverts the spirit-wind.[35] This was also the period in which O'Hara wrote the playful 'Ode on Necrophilia', and 'Ode to Joy' and 'Ode to Michael Goldberg ('s Birth and Other Births)', each of which applauds the 'sculptural necessities of lust' in an atmosphere that is all too aware of the attendant risks in an America dominated by the 'heat-hating Puritan' (*CP*, 281).[36]

34 Andrew Epstein, *Beautiful Enemies: Friendship and Postwar American Poetry* (New York and Oxford: Oxford University Press, 2006), p. 97. Epstein's suggestion that 'containment' is a resonant Cold War term is strong, and may be reinforced by the presence of the poem's 'little bear'. See also Michael Davidson's *Guys Like Us: Citing Masculinity in Cold War Poetics* (Chicago: University of Chicago Press, 2004), pp. 234–35, n. 11, for a similar interpretation of 'containment' in this poem.
35 O'Hara's love of French poetry is well known. He immersed himself in Rimbaud's work in summer 1949 (Gooch, *City Poet*, p. 141); 'Louise', written six weeks after 'Wind', refers to Lautréamont's *Maldoror*.
36 As John Wilkinson remarks in his discussion of the 'Ode to Joy' in this volume, the 'pretty plains' (*CP*, 281), may allude to the biblical 'cities of the plain'.

The poem can also be read as a discussion of distinct modes of creativity. Understood this way, it might urge the reader, through an embrace of the unpredictable, aleatory energies of the falling snow, to break down the barrier between world and representation, snow and snow ornament. If the 'glass ball' is understood as something akin to the autonomous artwork of Greenbergian modernism, then the snow whirling in fatal winds gives us a form of aesthetic practice into which the world and temporality itself can enter. This is not the experience of transcendent 'presentness' or 'grace' (to use terms famously employed by Greenberg's follower Michael Fried) but one that is time-bound, caught up in the violence of experience, and finite. 'Wind' appears to embrace the worldliness of desire, decay and death. In this it gives force to Feldman's apparently obscure observation, of O'Hara's work, that '[o]nly the artist who is close to his own life gives us an art that is like death'.[37]

What is O'Hara endorsing in this poem dedicated to a composer? Certainly not a version of freedom as a uncomplicated liberation from the fetters of convention, formal or otherwise. And certainly not a rhetoric of rapturous quasi-spiritual revelation. Rather, O'Hara suggests an ambivalent materialization of the poem's spirit-wind. His alternative to the stasis of imprisonment is a highly attenuated vision of freedom, a liberation that could not possibly be co-opted by an ideology of individual freedom, whether existential or political in nature. Indeed, rather than freedom, its operations might better be described by what John Wilkinson, writing of 'In Memory of my Feelings', has called the 'interrogative resistance to the delusions of autonomy in selfhood and in poetic text'.[38] In 'Wind' we can detect just such a resistance, as the poem's apparently liberatory ending is undercut by the mortality it aspires to reject. These ideas are more fully explored in O'Hara's 'Ode to Michael Goldberg ('s Birth and Other Births)' which I read as a wide-screen version of the ideas tested in compressed fashion in 'Wind'. I will devote some attention to this text in due course but I first wish to discuss Feldman's treatments of O'Hara's poem.

Feldman's Settings of 'Wind'

'The O'Hara Songs' consist of two different settings of the complete text of 'Wind' and a version which sets only the poem's first two lines.[39] As the note to the Barton Workshop recording indicates, the composition 'utilises Feldman's compositional/notational system in which each instrument begins simultaneously but performs their own part independently of the others' (in this it is similar to 'Piece for Four Pianos' on *New Directions in Music 2*). In every case, the words are sung with a downward-tending melody that amplifies the word 'falls'. The musical settings are sparse: the first and third versions are scored for a string trio and the second for a

37 Feldman, 'Frank O'Hara: Lost Times and Future Hopes', p. 107.
38 John Wilkinson, 'Tenter Ground', in *The Lyric Touch* (Cambridge: Salt, 2007), pp. 21–32, at p. 25.
39 Both the versions by the the Barton Workshop (Mode Records, MODE 107) and the Ensemble Avantgarde (Wergo, WER 6273) are recommended, though on the latter the German bass-baritone's rendering of O'Hara's 'little bear' as 'little beer' can stall the listener.

piano and chimes. The scope for variation in performance of even such short pieces is evident in the widely differing timings of the Barton Workshop and Ensemble Avantgarde versions.[40]

Feldman uses the instrumentation in each of the songs, as with much of his work, to provide a particular acoustic colour or ambience. Precisely what happens alongside particular words is not of great significance, making the 'Songs' highly unusual as 'settings'. There is no joint articulation of themes – the pieces are open-ended, unresolved and without development. This scepticism about narrative might be read as a realization of Feldman's interest in painterly analogies: 'Stasis, as it is utilised in painting, is not traditionally part of the apparatus of music. Music can achieve aspects of immobility, of the illusion of it: the Magritte-like world Satie evokes, or the "floating sculpture" of Varèse. The degrees of stasis, found in a Rothko or a Guston, were perhaps the most significant elements that I brought to my music from painting.'[41] Feldman thus, in a sense, takes up the challenge offered by 'Wind' – the Songs strive to escape the glass prison of temporality. Yet, as a composer, working in the time-bound medium of music, Feldman can only ever aspire to the *effect* of stasis. The sung text continues its drive towards its own conclusion. The musical realizations evince a desire for painterly stasis but at the same time enact its impossibility.

Three Voices (for Joan La Barbara), composed in 1982, is a more radical work altogether.[42] Conceived as a joint elegy for O'Hara and Philip Guston, the piece is performed by a soprano singer standing in front of two loudspeakers. Feldman remarks, 'There is something kind of "tombstoney" about the look of loudspeakers. I thought of the piece as an exchange of the live voice with the dead ones – a mixture of the living and the dead.'[43] Clearly any performance of the piece has to be exactly timed if the intricate overlaps between tape and voice are to be observed. Much of the performance is wordless, sung in 'vocalese'. When the words arrive, just the first two lines of 'Wind' – 'Who'd have thought/ that snow falls' – are sung (as in the second of the 'Songs'). The verbal lines are sometimes sung in unison but more often broken up and distributed between the three voices.

The elegiac ambitions of the work, which circles around the resonances of 'falling', give it a quality of interruptedness and this informs its organization. The simple, somewhat Beckettian device of the loudspeakers has a direct effect: instead of three soprano voices there is only one, but each utterance of the three vocal lines

---

40 3'09", 2'32" and 2'41" (Barton Workshop) as against 4'53", 1'45" and 3'49" (Ensemble Avantgarde).

41 Morton Feldman, 'Crippled Symmetry', in *Give My Regards*, pp. 134–49, at p. 149. The poet Clark Coolidge approaches this issue from the opposite direction: 'Sometimes I just want to say: Stop, Morty, music is not painting. But he can't forget. That painting is also a time-art'; *Sulfur*, 22 (Spring 1988), pp. 123–29, at p. 125.

42 A version performed by the dedicatee is available on New Albion, NA018; Marianne Schuppe's version (Col legno, WWE1CD 20249) is a strong alternative.

43 Feldman, cited in 'A Feldman Chronology', in Chris Villars (ed.), *Morton Feldman Says: Selected Interviews and Lectures* (London: Hyphen, 2006), p. 272.

is distinct (this is made clear with the panning of CD versions of the piece). The two 'dead' voices issuing from the 'tombstones' are accompanied by the living breath of the central voice. Wind – breath – has become a kind of self-reflexive metaphor for the workings of the piece. 'Three Voices', like many elegies, is engaged in a hopeless attempt to reanimate its subjects. The question-markless question 'Who'd have thought that snow falls' leaves the possibility of reaching an ending – of finitude, that is – in the balance, a hypothetical half-question that the piece cannot answer.

'Ode to Michael Goldberg ('s Birth and Other Births)'

I want to conclude with some brief observations about the role of wind in 'Ode to Michael Goldberg ('s Birth and Other Births)', which was completed in March 1958, about a year after 'Wind'. The Ode is, like 'Wind', ostensibly an autobiographical piece and it also narrates an awakening to a hazardous inversion of values, figured in the poem's last line as 'an extraordinary liberty'. The figure of wind occurs at several key moments in the poem, coinciding with the poem's discussions of the aesthetic and suggesting, perhaps, why O'Hara's poem for Feldman might have been called 'Wind' and not 'Snow'.

The first of these moments is in a short-lined section of the poem that describes schoolboy visits to a 'mountainous hill' behind O'Hara's house, where he scales a water tower.[44] For the boy atop the tower, wind is the vehicle for a thrilling aesthetic encounter:

> the wind sounded exactly like
> Stravinsky
>   I first recognised art
> as wildness, and it seemed right,
>   I mean rite to me
>
> climbing the water tower I'd
> look out for hours in wind
> and the world seemed rounder
> and fiercer and I was happier
> because I wasn't scared of falling off (*CP*, 292)

Folded into this reflection on 'wildness' and art is a parodic version of Wallace Stevens's 'Anecdote of the Jar': 'I placed a jar in Tennessee, / and round it was, / upon a hill. / It made the slovenly wilderness / Surround that hill'.[45] While Stevens meditates on the incommensurability of natural beauty and art, O'Hara locates an enlivening wildness in the experience of wind in a high place, as a naïve but life-changing revisitation of the archetypal modernist jolt of Stravinsky's *Rite of*

---

44 Gooch (*City Poet*, p. 49) identifies the setting as a 'cylindrical, open-topped water tower on Pigeon Hill behind [O'Hara's] house'.
45 Wallace Stevens, *Collected Poems* (London: Faber, 1955), p. 76.

Spring. This is a version of art that can be aligned more with 'fatal winds' than with 'containment'.

Later in the poem, wind is framed in the linked vocabularies of the Holy Spirit and poetic inspiration:

> the wind soars, keening overhead
> and the vestments of unnatural safety
> part to reveal a foreign land
> toward whom I have been selected to bear
> the gift of fire
> the temporary place of light, the land of air
>
> down where a flame illumines gravity and means warmth and insight,
> where air is flesh, where speed is darkness
> and
> things can suddenly be reached, held, dropped and known
> where a not totally imaginary ascent can begin all over again in tears (*CP*, 293)

Wind now ushers in a poet of Promethean powers, whose errand is only partially deflated by the mock pomposity of lines such as 'toward whom I have been selected to bear'.[46] As in 'Wind', the language of illumination carries an entanglement of values – the 'warmth and insight' afforded by the flame are offset by 'speed is darkness', which echoes the words 'there is a glistening/ blackness in the center/ if you seek it' a few lines earlier. Yet, at the same time, an ability to effect creative change on the material of the world is clearly imagined, with 'things can suddenly be reached, held, dropped and known'.

As the poem moves towards its subversively democratic close, wind appears as an agent of dispersal:

> from round the window, you can't
> see the street!
> you let the cold wind course through
> and let the heart pump and gurgle
> in febrile astonishment,
> a cruel world
> to which you've led it by your mind,
> bicycling no-hands
> leaving it gasping
> there, wondering where you are and how to get back,
> although you'll never let
> it go
>
> while somewhere everything's dispersed (*CP*, 297)

---

46 See the current volume's essay by John Wilkinson for discussion of O'Hara's use of the figure of Prometheus.

Wind again occasions an awakening, this time to a world of such cruelty that the 'heart' is left nakedly pumping and gurgling in its presence. This 'cold wind' seems to be aligned with the 'mind' that, wrongly perhaps, leads the 'heart'. In the face of this cruelty, darkness is again given an equivocal value: 'it's not/ a flickering light for us, but the glare of the dark/ too much endlessness,/ stored up, and in store'. Wind as an emblem of dispersal confronts the poet with the uncontainable incoherence of the world, the sickly double of the multiplicity celebrated elsewhere in O'Hara's work. This dispersal, rather like the swirling snow of 'Wind', cannot easily be assigned a moral or aesthetic value.

Wind, then, is associated with three intense moments of artistic encounter in the poem: awe in the presence of nature; an ironic gift of fire; and a moment of psychotic collapse. Each of these moments is a form of wildness that prepares the reader for the equivocal treatment of 'liberty' of the end of the poem. On one hand this freedom is predicated on the new city founded after the revolt of a 'barque of slaves' – a vision of liberty secured through the overthrow of the tyranny. Yet the word 'liberty' is actually assigned to the outsider, who, 'like a pinto', 'alone will speak of being/ born in pain/ and he will be the wings of an extraordinary liberty'.[47] A depiction of collective freedom is thus placed alongside and perhaps even supplanted by a form of messianic deliverance.

In the Ode, then, various forms of 'freedom' are tested. None of these corresponds to the heroic individualism of either Abstract Expressionism or Cold War ideology. The liberty that O'Hara is envisaging is barely even self-directed. Rather it is a form of openness to multiplicity that, at times, recoils painfully from the risky implications of what might instead be experienced as psychotic dispersal. As in 'Wind', liberty is couched in the commonly negative terms of death and darkness. If the alternative to 'containment' in 'Wind' is a 'fatal' finitude, in the Ode it is the terrifying immensity of 'endlessness'. Neither a securely bounded autonomous self nor its polyphonic obverse seems entirely viable.

Returning to Feldman, it can be argued that while both artists occasionally subscribed to a vocabulary of liberating immediacy and freeing personal 'expression' in their writings both held back from the implications of 'endlessness' and acknowledged a form of 'containment'. Feldman insists, 'to make something is to constrain it'.[48] Pattern, as with O'Hara's 'design', was as valuable to each of them, in their different ways, as a commitment to this or that conception of freedom. Each sought to enable his work to unfold without 'clergy'. Yet there is also in each a countervailing commitment to agency and singularity. Various kinds of liberty are invoked by both but these are invariably qualified, undermined or redirected. While a commonplace vocabulary of transcendence appears to propel O'Hara's account of Feldman towards a 'metaphysical place' of 'spiritual growth', a place beyond

47 The 'pinto' is a piebald horse but it also recalls Columbus's second ship. See 'In Memory of My Feelings' for another reference to the *Pinta* and related explorations of democracy and subjectivity.
48 Morton Feldman, 'A Compositional Problem', in *Give My Regards*, pp. 109–11, at p. 111.

language and representation, in O'Hara's poetry a dangerous spirit-wind doubles back on itself, immersing the writer not in higher things but in the material, a giddy upending of values that is ultimately driven by sexual delight and thoroughly wary of the perils of freedom.

'Footprints of a Wild Ballet': The *Poem-Paintings* of Frank O'Hara and Norman Bluhm

Brian Reed

During the past decade, academic interest in the area of intermediality has intensified. Humanities faculties have conventionally been organized according to the doctrine of medium-specificity. Literature, painting, dance, music, film, theatre, photography, and architecture have all been treated as separate specialities. Yet, as Jürgen Müller points out, artistic media never develop in isolation: 'there are various relations among media', and 'their functions arise, among other causes, from the historical evolution of these relations'.[1] Scholarship on intermediality explores how over time media have intersected, diverged, influenced each other, and worked at cross-purposes. Instead of talking about 'simple addition' – conceiving, for example, opera, masques, and Happenings as mixed forms of expression in which different arts independently pursue their own proper ends – the study of intermediality requires one to speak about 'processes in which there are constant interactions between media-related concepts'.[2] Exchanges between and combinations of media can result in shifts in their nature and function as well as revealing avenues for future experimentation.

For scholars interested in intermediality, Frank O'Hara's career offers innumerable opportunities for research. He lived in Manhattan during an era truly remarkable for interchange among the arts. Poets, playwrights, choreographers, composers, painters, sculptors, and filmmakers lived in close proximity, attended many of the same events, and in many cases worked together. O'Hara was enthusiastically at home in this milieu. He knew everyone from Leonard Bernstein to Tennessee Williams to W. H. Auden. A typical week included 'a dizzying series of gallery openings and plays' as well as 'movies, concerts, operas, [and] ballet.[3] His greatest involvement, of course, was in the visual arts. The exhibition *In Memory of My Feelings: Frank O'Hara and American Art* (1999), curated by Russell Ferguson,

---

1 Jürgen Müller, 'L'intermédialité, une nouvelle approche interdisciplinaire: perspectives théoriques et practiques à l'exemple de la vision de télévision', *Cinémas* 10.2–3 (Spring 2000), pp. 112–13. All translations mine.
2 Müller, 'L'intermédialité', p. 113.
3 Marjorie Perloff, *Frank O'Hara: Poet Among Painters* (Chicago: University of Chicago Press, rev. edn, 1998 [1977]), p. 114.

featured an astonishing roll call of artists whom he had befriended, whose work he had promoted, or whose lives he had otherwise touched. Included were Elaine and Willem de Kooning, Jane Freilicher, Philip Guston, Jasper Johns, Alex Katz, Franz Kline, Lee Krasner, Joan Mitchell, Robert Motherwell, Claes Oldenburg, and Jackson Pollock. O'Hara, too, had opportunities to participate in the art world in a number of capacities. Besides serving as an assistant curator of painting at the Museum of Modern Art, he published catalogues and reviews, took part in pitched arguments at The Club (an artists' discussion group), visited studios, wrote poetry about and influenced by art, and even tried his own hand at painting and collage. Artists incorporated his poems into their work, illustrated his poems, and, on occasion, collaborated with him. In sum, O'Hara 'live[d] as variously as possible' at the crossroads between visual and verbal media (*CP*, 256).

O'Hara's collaborations are his most intriguing forays into this interzone. They represent conscious efforts at 'a real fusion of poetry and art'.[4] He preferred to 'work simultaneously' with his collaborators in order to 'play words off images' and generate 'new forms'.[5] He wanted to probe the boundaries between media to discover how they deformed and reformed in the heat of creation. O'Hara's and Larry Rivers's lithograph series *Stones* (1957–60) has drawn the most academic attention, but the other collaborations, too, repay close analysis.[6] This chapter focuses on the 26 *Poem-Paintings* that O'Hara and the abstract painter Norman Bluhm produced over the course of several Sundays in October 1960.[7] Bluhm hung pieces of brown butcher block paper on the walls of his apartment and the two men alternated taking charge. 'Sometimes Bluhm would do a drawing and O'Hara would invent an appropriate set of words; sometimes the procedure was reversed'.[8] Only two colours were used, black and white, and the relatively anti-absorptive support ensured that both the quickly applied paint and the poet's handwriting smudged, blurred, and dripped.

For all O'Hara's fame as an 'action poet' akin to the so-called action painters of the period, these poem-paintings number among the very few examples of direct collaboration with a painter committed to working principally in the mode

---

4 Tatyana Grossman, quoted. in Perloff, *Poet Among Painters*, p. 100.

5 Perloff, *Poet Among Painters*, p. 99. Compare Lytle Shaw, *Frank O'Hara: The Poetics of Coterie* (Iowa City: University of Iowa Press, 2006), pp. 57–58.

6 For readings of *Stones*, see Perloff, *Poet Among Painters*, pp. 99–105; Russell Ferguson, *In Memory of My Feelings: Frank O'Hara and American Art* (Los Angeles: The Museum of Contemporary Art, 1999), pp. 50–59; and Hazel Smith, *Hyperscapes in the Poetry of Frank O'Hara: Difference/Homosexuality/Topography* (Liverpool: Liverpool University Press, 2000), pp. 191–94.

7 Perloff, *Poet Among Painters*, p. 106. Twelve of the *Poem-Paintings* are reproduced in Ferguson, *In Memory of My Feelings*, pp. 59–67. Five appear in Bill Berkson and Joe LeSueur (eds.), *Homage to Frank O'Hara* (Berkeley: Creative Arts, 1980), pp. 124–27. Eight are in *Lingo* no. 7 (December 1997), of which four appear online. See http://www.cultureport.com/newhp/lingo/authors/bluhm01.html.

8 Perloff, *Poet Among Painters*, p. 107.

of high modernist abstraction.[9] Most of his other collaborations would qualify as significantly-to-predominantly representational. In those cases, the visual artists typically explore figuration, as well as iconicity more generally, in response to the poet's puckish wordplay. Bluhm's and O'Hara's poem-paintings, I argue, attempt something different. They test whether paint and language can both be used *gesturally*. That is, they propose a formal and functional homology between particular methods of applying pigment to paper and words to a page. The point is not so much to convey paraphrasable content. Rather, the goal is to mark a moment and a place as constituting embodied expression. Here, Bluhm and O'Hara imply, were bodies that breathed, moved, and thrived: bodies that danced.

When talking about Bluhm's and O'Hara's *Poem-Paintings*, one runs into an immediate methodological obstacle. What is the best framework to employ when talking about a peculiar piece such as *Noël* (1960) (Figure 1)? Does one proceed as a poetry critic, an art historian, or some blend of the two? In the upper-left corner one sees an exclamation mark followed by the word 'noël' in black cursive. A thick white brushstroke begins beneath the 'n' and angles upward toward the right corner. Profuse long drips of white paint, extending to the bottom of the sheet, link the top and bottom halves of the piece. In the lower-right corner appears a vertical list of words, again in black cursive, apparently, too, in the same handwriting: 'apples/ light/ fires/ dances'. The first three words have all been crossed out by white lines. Paired with the list is a blob of black paint that looks as if it were applied downward and to the right. While one can see traces of the paintbrush's bristles, the total effect is not calligraphic. It is as if mid-stroke a sweeping gesture turned into a stabbing or slamming one, scattering paint like a small contained explosion. Overall, the mass resembles the impression of a hot iron, angled to point to the word 'dances'. Five of the long white drips from the top of the piece traverse the black shape, four of them blending with the colour and exiting at its bottom, now grey, amidst many narrow black rivulets.

Conceiving of *Noël* as a slapped-together poem-*cum*-painting does not seem like a promising place to begin. Printed separately, its text is not especially lyrical:

!noël
~~apples~~
~~light~~
~~fires~~
dances

---

9 Harold Rosenberg's article 'The American Action Painters' (1952), reprinted in *The Tradition of the New* (New York: Da Capo Press, 1960), was an influential analysis of Abstract Expressionism. By analogy, O'Hara fairly early on began to be referred to as an 'action poet'. See, e.g., Anthony Libby, 'O'Hara on the Silver Range', *Contemporary Literature* 17.2 (Spring 1976), p. 256.

Figure 1 Norman Bluhm and Frank O'Hara, *Noël*, 1960

One might encounter similarly telegraphic, self-cancelling lines in contemporary works such as Susan Howe's *Articulations of Sound Forms in Time* (1987) and *Eikon Basilike* (1989). Howe, though, almost always embeds such gnomic fragments within larger sequences of verse, prose, and reproduced images. Without such illuminating contexts, O'Hara's effort reads like notes towards a description of a Christmas party. What was memorable about 'noël' this year? Not the food ('apples') and not the festive atmosphere ('light', 'fires'). The 'dances' though were fabulous!

Noël is underwhelming, too, when judged purely as a painting. The two large brushstrokes might be vivid and visually complex, but despite the push-pull of white-versus-black and despite lying on near-perpendicular diagonals, they do not fully establish a lively, dynamic relationship. The distance between them seems a little arbitrary, for example. It could be increased or decreased by several centimeters without destroying the composition. One only has to glance at a large-scale work from the same period such as Bluhm's backdrop sketch for O'Hara's play *Love's Labor* (1958) to perceive traits not on display in *Noël*: bold formal invention and a command of all-over rhythm and structure.[10] A bamboo forest of vertical drips overlays black and red webs of fat wandering oblique brushstrokes. It is an arresting design, legible as a new departure at a moment when many second-generation Abstract Expressionists were drably churning out Willem de Kooning knock-offs.[11]

Marjorie Perloff has argued that many of the *Poem-Paintings* would qualify as 'trivial' and 'negligible' except for the unique 'combination' of text and image that O'Hara and Bluhm achieve. When approached as a hybrid of visual and verbal strategies – that is, not as a poem-plus-a-painting but as an in-between *tertium quid* – they prove to be 'real works of art' that possess 'wit' and 'charm'.[12] Among O'Hara's critics, Hazel Smith has provided the most extensive theoretical treatment of his proclivity to create intermedial art 'in which verbal and non-verbal semiotic systems become intertwined in a non-hierarchical relationship'.[13] In his collaborations, she argues, 'each medium loses its autonomy and becomes merged with the other'.[14] This merger is possible because arts such as poetry and painting are complexly heterogeneous and communicate via a range of different semiotic resources. Moreover, while it might be true that 'painting is richer in iconic signs (that is, signs that resemble their referents) and poetry in symbolic signs (signs which are distinct from their referents) […] all sign types have a common basis in convention (iconicity is relative), and both poetry and painting consist of mixed signs'.[15] In other words, conceived as sign-systems, poetry and painting overlap.

10 See Ferguson, *In Memory of My Feelings*, p. 48, for a colour reproduction.
11 Barry Schwabsky, *The Widening Circle: The Consequences of Modernism in Contemporary Art* (Cambridge: Cambridge University Press, 1997), pp. 22–23.
12 Perloff, *Poet Among Painters*, pp. 108–109.
13 Smith, *Hyperscapes*, pp. 166–67.
14 Smith, *Hyperscapes*, p. 191.
15 Smith, *Hyperscapes*, p. 168.

For instance, the words 'red dog' and a watercolour of a rust-coloured canine can both refer to the same Saussurean sound-image. The word 'wind' printed as *WIND* gives a sense of how fast and strong a breeze is, much like swirling lines in a comic strip. 'A consequence of the shared properties of text and image,' writes Smith, 'is the possibility for semiotic exchange between the two, so that each develops some characteristics of the other.'[16]

While Smith does not dwell at length on the Bluhm–O'Hara collaboration, her analysis of the lithograph series *Stones* illustrates the aesthetic and intellectual pay-off of her semiotic approach. She shows that Larry Rivers and O'Hara defy expectations of 'hierarchical and fixed relationships between text and image in which image illustrates text, or text explains image'.[17] Writing blunders across image boundaries, and, denotatively and connotatively, words relate peculiarly and non-linearly with the visuals both nearby and distant. Above all, text and image begin to resemble each other:

> The iconicity of the text is increased by the use of handwriting, underlining, capital letters, blackened emphasis and smudging, which strengthens its visual impact; and through the brevity, simplicity and ideogrammatic nature of the verbal messages which are text-insertions and more like aphoristic [textual nodes] [...] than complete poems. Similarly, at certain points in the lithograph[s], the iconicity of the images is reduced, so that they draw attention to themselves as structural elements of the design, although they are often images of a particular thing.[18]

In other words, succinct texts with 'visual impact' capture language on its way towards becoming image-like. Images that highlight their 'structural' role in a 'design' are beginning to operate syntactically, that is, like words in a sentence. Smith goes on to claim that this blurring of distinction between sign-systems has an important psychological parallel. The two creators' 'identities' 'fuse' in a quasi-'sexual union', a state which in turn enables them to produce art by means of a 'shared subjectivity'.[19]

Do these generalizations also hold true for the 1960 *Poem-Paintings*? Perloff does partly justify their value as 'real works of art' based on one instance of convergence, the visual similarity between 'O'Hara's rounded letters and Bluhm's curling horse-shoe shapes'. She also cites, however, the painter's 'thick white paint flecks' and 'suggestive, fleeting gestures', characteristics with no immediately obvious verbal counterpart.[20] She wraps up her discussion by extolling the merits of all 26 *Poem-Paintings* viewed as a group. Their 'inventiveness' becomes 'increasingly apparent as we study the relation of gesture to gesture, footmark to handprint, lyric phrase to

16 Smith, *Hyperscapes*, p. 169.
17 Smith, *Hyperscapes*, p. 192.
18 Smith, *Hyperscapes*, p. 193.
19 Smith, *Hyperscapes*, p. 192.
20 Perloff, *Poet Among Painters*, p. 108.

four-letter word, proverb to sexy innuendo, white drop to black letter, and so on'.[21] One cannot, therefore, say that she finds them meaningful because they engage in what Smith calls visual-verbal 'cross-dressing'.[22] Rather, she is struck by the intricate interplay between the many different kinds of marks and inscriptions. Moreover, in her list O'Hara's contributions, while mixed in with Bluhm's, nevertheless remain identifiable and separable. Contrast between compositional elements intrigues her more than any overlap between verse and painting as semiotic systems.

Perloff's analysis dovetails well with Andrew Epstein's critique of Smith as overly 'idealistic'. In *Beautiful Enemies* he demonstrates that O'Hara and his friends, regardless of their intent, in practice proved 'quite unable to give themselves fully over to [an] idealized loss of selfhood' while working collaboratively.[23] Individual efforts were as likely to clash as fit together, occasionally creating as a by-product the lively give-and-take that Perloff highlights. There is a deeper issue at stake here, however. Smith's argument rests on 1990s' hypertextual theory. She posits that O'Hara's collaborations are instances of 'hypermedia' comparable to 'contemporary multimedia work' that feature an aggressive 'hybridization' of 'visual and verbal' registers of communication.[24] She also claims that they function like hypertext webs. When looked at closely, they can be shown to exhibit 'hypertextual links between the visual and verbal' elements of their compositions.[25] That is, a viewer can readily follow implicit but hyperlink-like associations between particular words or phrases and images. '[M]ultidirectional' in orientation, these connections 'allows us to read [them] in a way which is "unfixed", and to "walk" through [them] taking a different route each time'.[26]

Describing intermedial art as 'hypermedia' is designedly reductive. It allows Smith to treat images and texts indiscriminately as *nodes* and to lump all forms of association into the category of *links*. Furthermore, she firmly believes that hypermedia, as webs of non-hierarchically linked nodes, represent a politically progressive mode of cultural production. They decentre the positions of author and reader/viewer while also 'perturbing conventional sign systems' by scrambling them together.[27] In a survey of the last two decades of new media theory, David Ciccoricco credits these characteristically 1990s' assumptions to a misplaced excitement over the ability of 'a network environment' to 'literalize' poststructuralist theory. Deconstruction taught that texts consisted of 'dispersed and boundless' signs; voilà, here was a text ready-dispersed, no analytic scrutiny required![28]

21 Perloff, *Poet Among Painters*, p. 109.

22 Smith, *Hyperscapes*, p. 192.

23 Andrew Epstein, *Beautiful Enemies: Friendship and Postwar American Poetry* (New York: Oxford University Press, 2006), pp. 36–37.

24 Smith, *Hyperscapes*, p. 166.

25 Smith, *Hyperscapes*, p. 193.

26 Smith, *Hyperscapes*, p. 194.

27 Smith, *Hyperscapes*, p. 170.

28 David Ciccoricco, *Reading Network Fiction* (Tuscaloosa, AL: University of Alabama Press, 2007), p. 26.

There was no need, either, to demonstrate 'the death of the author' à la Roland Barthes. Hypertexts promised to reduce authorial control over what contents readers encounter in works of literature and how they progress through them. Moreover, hypertext seemed to encourage plurivocality. Any number of authors could collaborate on hyperwebs, and pre-existing texts, images, and videos could be easily incorporated into them. In short, many young scholars were eager to laud a new mode of knowledge production that appeared to exemplify academically fashionable theories of textuality in its very warp and woof.

A decade later, hypertextuality is no longer a central concept within new media studies. Hypertext continues to exist, of course – the World Wide Web itself still largely relies on a page-based, link-and-node model for its operation – but theorists no longer consider it a fundamental paradigm for understanding how media function. Preferred today is a phenomenological model. Three-dimensional, static network-structures are far from the only way to 'conceptualize [...] embodied movement within and in relation to' virtual (and real) spaces.[29] To grasp this point, one has to stop thinking in terms of topography and embrace topology. Actual bodies, as people inhabit and experience them, do not move through a 'fixed landscape' mappable with a Cartesian 'coordinate grid'.[30] Indeed, there exists no unobstructed 'celestial viewpoint' that would enable a 'disembodied' subject, that is, one 'wholly detached from what it sees', to provide an objective cartography of a space.[31] Bodies are caught up in, cannot be extricated from, 'the movement of points in a dynamic field'. Exact measures of distance matter less than 'connectivity', that is, how and why one travels between different locations.[32] To navigate such a shifting environment one must rely on 'proprioception', an awareness of the disposition and motion of one's body.[33]

Proponents of the phenomenological turn within new media studies would ask whether semiotics provides the best means for conceptualizing intermediality. They would say that, whether a critic relies on C. S. Peirce or Ferdinand de Saussure as a starting point, defining art forms as sign-systems is over-hasty. As Brian Massumi explains, 'cognitive functions' including sign-making and sign-attribution arise from a prior 'multi-dimensioned, shifting surface of experience'.[34] Art does not only communicate via kinds of inscription (icons, symbols and indices). It also, in a pre-rational manner, emerges from and appeals to what Mark B. N. Hansen calls *tactility*, the direct immediate affective contact between a body and the spaces around it.[35] Tactility, one must understand, is not the same thing as the sense of

29 Ciccoricco, *Reading Network Fiction*, p. 92.
30 Ciccoricco, *Reading Network Fiction*, p. 45.
31 Ciccoricco, *Reading Network Fiction*, p. 59.
32 Ciccoricco, *Reading Network Fiction*, p. 45.
33 Ciccoricco, *Reading Network Fiction*, pp. 60–61.
34 Brian Massumi quoted in Mark B. N. Hansen, 'Seeing with the Body: The Digital Image in Postphotography', *Diacritics* 31.4 (Winter 2001), p. 67.
35 Hansen, 'Seeing with the Body', pp. 60–61.

touch. It is a more general term for the interface between self and world, and it is inherently 'synaesthetic' and 'cross-modal', that is, it makes use of and fuses information coming from various kinds of sense-receptors.[36] In this view, 'human perception takes place in a rich and evolving field', and over time a viewer takes in an artwork in many different ways – sensually, emotively, kinaesthetically, and semiotically.[37]

This line of argument does not invalidate Smith's interpretation of *Stones*. It does, however, render it a special case. There is no guarantee that a similarly sign-focused approach would be appropriate when analysing any other inter-medial artwork. A critic does not have to presume that Bluhm's and O'Hara's *Poem-Paintings* are calculated, in the name of a utopian-postmodernist politics, to interrogate and collapse boundaries between the arts. Instead one ought to ask: What sorts of perception and cognition do these artworks solicit and reward? How do they occupy space? What spaces, virtual or actual, do they generate or suggest as one interacts with them?

In an interview with Marjorie Perloff, Norman Bluhm recollects the setting in which the *Poem-Paintings* were created. Significantly, they were not products of a studio, that is, a workplace. They originated in a domestic space:

> Frank and I enjoyed music. We used to meet Sunday mornings at my studio, listen to music and talk and look at the paintings, and then go to my home and listen to records. One time, listening to opera (Toti dal Monte, the famous 300-pound soprano, singing *Madame Butterfly*), I said to Frank: 'I have all this paper, let's put it on the wall.' And we decided we'd like listening to the music and playing around with words and paint. It wasn't a serious art project. We just wanted to do something while the music was going on.[38]

Bluhm carefully distances the *Poem-Paintings* from his 'serious art', the 'paintings' that are not only spatially but also temporally removed from the O'Hara collaborations (which happen only on Sundays, the proverbial day of rest, not during the work week). He claims that the collaborations represent no more than 'playing around', a semi-productive alternative to utterly wasting time ('just wanted to do something'). These disclaimers seem to express a vocation-related anxiety. He wasn't painting, as he understood the art form, though he was adding pigment to a surface. He struggles to find an alternative term. He tests 'Happening', 'theatrical event', and 'opera buffa'.[39] Curiously, each of these words de-emphasizes the *Poem-Paintings* as finished products and locates aesthetic importance in the act of composition, which is compared to a mixed-media performance. He stresses the spectacle

36 Hansen, 'Seeing with the Body', p. 72.
37 Hansen, 'Seeing with the Body', p. 61.
38 Quoted in Perloff, *Poet Among Painters*, p. 106.
39 Quoted in Perloff, *Poet Among Painters*, pp. 106–107.

of two men, moving from sheet to sheet of paper, accompanied by a soundtrack.

When he is drawn into discussing the completed *Poem-Paintings*, Bluhm again belittles his contribution. He insists that 'the words are more important than gesture'. He also proves unhelpfully vague. 'The idea,' he says, 'was to make the gesture relate, in an abstract way, to the poem,' while avoiding any sense that the 'gesture' serves as an 'illustration of the poem'. A few of the pieces, such as *May!* (Figure 2), could perhaps be explained this way. At the top appear the cursive words 'May! Am I/ a pole?' At the bottom are an overlapping, interlocking series of black brushstrokes. Two inverted horseshoes, tilted left, overlay two inverted Vs tilted right. Lastly, a single thick line, roughly parallel to the upstroke of the inverted Vs, turns the lower-right corner into a triangle. Unifying the whole work is a giant 7 in white paint that begins as a solid line cutting across the top of the paper; when it reaches the upper-right corner, it suddenly turns into a sequence of discrete dabs that extends down toward the mid-point of the bottom edge. O'Hara's words are, of course, suggestively sexual. Maypoles have been considered dodgy since Elizabethan times because of their close association with mixed-gender pagan rites of summer. The poet addresses the month of May – or a woman named May – and disingenuously asks 'am I/ a pole', as if an erection (perhaps one he is showing off?) groups him with a new nationality composed of the few, the proud, the ithyphallic (pole/Pole). 'May' also carries overtones of permission: may I be your pole tonight? Bluhm's brushstrokes evoke the spatter and spurt of bodily fluids, or perhaps the energetic spinning and weaving of ribbons around a maypole. Through the contours, clustering, and shape of his applications of paint, he conveys an erotic energy comparable to O'Hara's words.

May!, however, is representative of only one type of *Poem-Painting*. *I'm So Tired* exemplifies a different kind, one that would also include *Haiku* and *Chicago*. It consists of a longer text with an unobtrusive vertical scattering of white dots mostly on the left-hand side:

> I'm so tired from
> all the parties, it's
> like January! and
> the hangovers on
> the beach – they're
> fun too – and you
> at last get to wear
> your Christmas
> presents.[40]

It is not immediately obvious how the white dots mime what O'Hara describes, a crash after a prolonged bender. Do they suggest sea spray at 'the beach'? Snow, to

---

40 Ferguson, *In Memory of My Feelings*, p. 63.

Figure 2 Norman Bluhm and Frank O'Hara, *May!*, 1960

suggest 'January' and 'Christmas'? An indication that the painter, too, is too 'tired' to do much? In pieces such as *I'm So Tired*, the relation between text and image is not merely 'abstract' but indeterminate.

A third set of *Poem-Paintings* displays visual-verbal interaction so straightforward that it appears to contradict Bluhm's assertion that he was avoiding 'illustration'. *Bang*, for instance, has one letter in each of its corners, clockwise spelling out B-A-N-G. In the centre appears a large inverted black V that scatters drops and fine lines of paint every which way. One sees either an explosion or, perhaps, a spray of blood after a bullet's impact. A later, more complex piece, *Hand*, consists of a cartoonish outline of four fingers and a thumb. Lines of verse have been written across each digit in a thin slight cursive:

> You eat all the time
> you even know how to use   chopsticks
> So why don't you write me
> a letter
> forget it[41]

While technically Bluhm's hand does not illustrate O'Hara's text – it came first, meaning that one would probably have to call the poem a caption – regardless, *Hand* consists of an iconic representation of a body-part paired with a text addressing the same referent. Visual and verbal registers of communication are working together in an instantly recognizable fashion.

Finally, a couple of *Poem-Paintings* integrate images into the texts almost in the manner of block quotations. *There I Was* places three lines at the top – 'there I was/ minding my own/ business when' – and two more at the bottom – 'buses always/ do that to me'.[42] In between appears a number of white brushstrokes and a partial black circle that together resemble a squashed top hat. Conceivably one could also interpret it as a prone stick figure beneath a squarish mass leaning to the right. The general idea, though, is intelligible. Bluhm has provided if not an illustration in the realist sense then certainly an energetic free rendering of O'Hara's scenario of man-meets-bus. *This Is the First* is even more blunt. At the top O'Hara has written, 'this is the first person/ I ever went to bed/ with'. In the lower-left corner appears the interjection, 'wow!'.[43] In the middle and to the right Bluhm has added two black curves and a short connecting line. A dot of paint turns the first curve into a crude sketch of a breast with a nipple. The second curve is more ambiguous – is it a thigh or a buttock? – but Bluhm, a straight-identified artist, has clearly read himself into O'Hara's 'I' and painted accordingly. A narrow horseshoe-like white brushstroke pointed upward toward the breast-shape is almost embarrassingly phallic, and the accompanying explosion of white dabs and drips is unmistakably ejaculatory.

41 Ferguson, *In Memory of My Feelings*, pp. 60–61.
42 Ferguson, *In Memory of My Feelings*, p. 66.
43 Ferguson, *In Memory of My Feelings*, p. 67.

O'Hara's 'wow!' could be commenting on any aspect of the painter's tasteless but energetic response to the invitation to fill-in-a-blank.

Bluhm's description of the *Poem-Paintings* does prove revealing in one important respect. He repeatedly refers to his contribution as 'gesture'. The word carries special weight in his lexicon. From 1947 to 1955, he lived in Paris, and he studied such French masters as Corot, Matisse, and Monet. Initially, he was absorbed in landscape painting, and, often working *en plein air*, he produced 'horizonless' canvases that captured 'light without articulation and definition'.[44] 'Parisian exhibitions of Pollock and other abstract expressionists', however, as well as sharing a studio with the expatriate Sam Francis, prompted Bluhm to explore 'allover field painting'. He experimented with 'veils and sweeps of colour', and his style became not only more 'direct' and 'raw' but, as Paul Schimmel puts it, also more 'gestural'.[45] After Bluhm moved to New York in 1955, his paintings took on a distinctly 'Pollock-like quality', 'filling the canvas close to the edge with active gestural motion'.[46] By the end of the decade, in such landmark works as *Chicago 1920* (1959) and *Winter Nights* (1959), his brushwork had become positively 'baroque', often taking the form of a 'sensuous, S-shaped twisting line' accompanied by 'explosive bursts and rivers' of pigment.[47] First-generation Abstract Expressionists had already devised a battery of techniques for showcasing an artist's handling of paint; Bluhm distinguished himself by exaggerating those techniques to unprecedented extremes. His use of 'gesture' as a shorthand reference to his work with O'Hara makes perfect sense. His audacious manner of handling paint had long since become his trademark.

Moreover, within the New York art world of 1960, 'gesture' could no longer be seen, as Harold Rosenberg once presented it, as a wholly intuitive natural extension of an artist's psyche or personality.[48] In the wake of such well-publicized pieces as Robert Rauschenberg's *Factum I* and *Factum II* (1957) – uncannily identical canvases that include the same drips, blots, and other 'accidents' – and Jasper Johns's *False Start* (1959) and *Jubilee* (1959) – paintings that employ exactly the same mock-Abstract Expressionist brushwork, once in colour and once in black, white, and grey – gesture had been, as a Russian Formalist would put it, laid bare as a device. Part of the notoriously 'mannered' feel to Bluhm's late 1950s paintings stems from his awareness that gesture can be an end in itself, an arena for aesthetic exploration apart from any signifying intent.[49] Accordingly, he puts a spotlight on, he theatricalizes, what his older colleagues had often considered to be primarily instrumental, a route into the unconscious or the primal past.[50] The link between the artist's hand

44 Paul Schimmel, 'The Lost Generation', in Paul Schimmel et al. (eds.), *Action Precision: The New Direction in New York, 1955–60* (Newport Beach, CA: Newport Harbor Art Museum, 1984), p. 28.
45 Schimmel, 'The Lost Generation', p. 28.
46 Schimmel, 'The Lost Generation', p. 29.
47 Schimmel, 'The Lost Generation', p. 29.
48 Rosenberg, 'The American Action Painters', p. 29.
49 Schimmel, 'The Lost Generation', p. 29.
50 See, e.g., Mark Rothko and Adolph Gottlieb, 'The Portrait and the Modern Artist', in Mark Rothko,

and the canvas, too, had become newly available for centre-ring showmanship. In 1961 Fred McDarrah published a celebrated photograph of Bluhm painting.[51] He perches precariously in profile on a stepladder, one leg stuck out behind him for balance, his arms spread out, and his torso inclined drunkenly forward. It looks for all the world as if he is a crazed ballet dancer attempting an arabesque under impossible circumstances.

This pose conveys something crucial about Bluhm's work circa 1960: his dramatic gestures appear to blur the line between an art that produces autonomous objects (painting) and a kinaesthetic art 'integrally situated in the body' (dance).[52] Brushstrokes might have ceased to grant reliable access to artists' interior lives, but they did retain their ability to refer indexically to the presence and movement of a body. By exaggerating and stylizing how he applied paint to canvas, Bluhm foregrounded his brushwork's function as a trace of embodied performance. The *Poem-Paintings*, too, seem to draw attention to this feature of his creative process. The word 'dances' appears in *Noël*, for instance, and Bluhm describes the creation of the whole series as if he and O'Hara were involved in an improvised *pas de deux*. And, when the works were first exhibited in January–February 1967, John Perrault, in a review in *ARTnews*, referred to them as a 'zany dance of the seasons' and 'footprints of a wild ballet'.[53]

Did O'Hara also consider the *Poem-Paintings* dance-like? They belong to the years 1959–61 when his romance with Vincent Warren, a dancer with the New York Metropolitan Opera Ballet, was at its height. During this period the names of friends such as the dance critic Edwin Denby and the choreographer George Balanchine make frequent appearances in his verse, and he casually refers to avant-garde performances such as James Waring's *Dances Before the Wall* (1958).[54] He also regularly cites such aesthetic touchstones as Busby Berkeley, Sergei Diaghilev, Ginger Rogers, and *Swan Lake*.[55] In lyrics such as 'Mary Desti's Ass' (1961), he even casts himself as a dancer. The poem's 'I' is both factually autobiographical ('I met Kenneth Koch's mother') and, more whimsically, *une première danseuse* ('I stepped in once/ for Isadora [Duncan] so perfectly/ she would never allow me to dance again' [*CP*, 401]).

O'Hara's inveterate habit of identifying with glamorous female performers – most famously Judy Garland, Billie Holiday, and Lana Turner – renders especially significant a pair of poems that he wrote in the summer of 1960. The first, 'Glazunoviana, or Memorial Day', contains a fantasy sequence centring around the balle-

Writings about Art (New Haven: Yale University Press, 2006), pp. 37–40.

51 Fred McDarrah, *The Artist's World in Pictures* (New York: E. P. Dutton, 1961), cover.

52 Leslie Satin, 'Sally Gross, Suddenly', *PAJ: A Journal of Performance and Art* 22.1 (January 2000), p. 11.

53 Quoted in Perloff, *Poet Among Painters*, pp. 106 and 108.

54 For Denby, see *CP*, 345 and 393. For Balanchine, see *CP*, 339. For Waring, see *CP*, 344.

55 For Berkeley, see *CP*, 354 and 390. For Rogers, see *CP*, 370. For Diaghilev and *Swan Lake*, see *CP*, 377.

rina Maria Tallchief. In 1955, Tallchief had danced lead in Balanchine's *Pas de Dix* (1955), a piece which borrowed music from the last act of Alexander Glazunov's *Raymonda* (1898). Now O'Hara imagines her 'return[ing] to City Center' for an even grander Glazunov event, a 'full-length' revival of his storied ballet *The Seasons* (1900):

> escaping from my heart the vision
> hovers in the air like a cyclone over sordid Kansas
> as her breathing limbs tear ugliness out of our lives
> and cast it into the air like snowflakes. (*CP*, 363)

O'Hara, significantly, does not describe Tallchief's appearance. She appears only as a body in motion, 'limbs' that 'breath[e]', 'tear', and 'cast'. She is awhirl, like a 'cyclone'. For the poet, the art of dance seems to boil down to grandly significant corporeal gestures.

A second poem, 'Ode to Tanaquil Leclerq', seems calculated as a companion piece. Tallchief was Balanchine's third wife, and Leclerq his fourth. Both were principal dancers with the New York Ballet. Moreover, although O'Hara again focuses on movement and breath, this time he is loth to interpret what he sees. Instead of a decisive act such as 'tear[ing] ugliness out of our lives', Leclerq's 'superb' gestures prove to be a 'window' on to 'something' so ineffable that it exceeds language:

> [...] everything you do
> repeats yourself simultaneously and simply
> as a window 'gives' on something
>
> it seems sometimes as if you were only breathing
> and everything happened around you
> because when you disappeared in the wings nothing was there
> but the motion of some extraordinary happening I hadn't understood
> the superb arc of a question (*CP*, 364)

O'Hara here revises his depiction of Tallchief. A skilled dancer such as Leclerq does not make one think of cyclones and snowflakes; she offers 'the motion of some extraordinary happening' but leaves behind not a message but the 'arc of a question'.

Can one read this passage as self-reflexive? 'Mary Desti's Ass' suggests that the answer is yes. In addition to Isadora Duncan, the 'I' in that poem disses yet another ballerina closely associated with Balanchine, Tamara Toumanova ('she looked like a cow' [*CP*, 402]). In other words, O'Hara suggests that he can beat the Balanchine crew – implicitly including Tallchief and Leclerq – at their own game. This declaration of rivalry has important resonances for any reading of the *Poem-Paintings*. The Leclerq ode dates from June 1960. On 18 October, during the same month in which he collaborates with Bluhm, he also wrote 'Steps', which mentions that 'the park's full of dancers with their tights and shoes/ in little bags' (*CP*, 371). In November, Balanchine premiered *Liebeslieder Walzer*, a piece that almost immediately showed up in O'Hara's 'Variations on Saturday', a poem dated 10 December (*CP*, 378). Roughly a week later, he ended the lyric 'Lines During Certain Pieces of Music' by referring to 'a performance of *The Fairy's Buss* at the City Center' – an allusion to Balanchine's 1950 revival of Igor Stravinsky's *Le Baiser de la Fée* (1937), featuring none other than Maria Tallchief (*CP*, 384). Hence, it is safe to say that bodies, gestures, and movement to music were all on O'Hara's mind in autumn 1960 and winter 1961. The decision in October not to sit passively while listening to music was a logical extension of aesthetic questions that he was exploring elsewhere.

How, though, might the poet's interest in dance give one concrete insights into the *Poem-Paintings*? A recent article, Rachel Duerden's 'Dancing in the Imagined Space of Music' (2007), provides a possible response. Duerden concentrates on the concept of gesture as a way to explore inter-art collaboration, and she builds her argument around an analysis of a work that O'Hara knew well, Balanchine's and Stravinsky's ballet *Agon* (1957).[56] She defines a gesture as a bodily movement that has been 'abstracted' or 'estranged' such that it stands out from movement-in-general as especially significant, that is, as 'meaning-bearing'.[57] The 'meaning' that a gesture conveys, however, is not always referential. Indeed, during a dance gestures frequently appear to invite an audience to interpret them only then to frustrate any desire to translate their effects into words. Under such circumstances, gestures function primarily to seduce an audience into attending closely to the here-and-now. The result, she argues, is a heightened awareness of the 'likeness and un-likeness' between the music and the choreography.[58] The space of performance becomes newly perceptible as one that 'music and image [...] inhabit equally' and dynamically, capable in fact of 'commentary' on each other's unfolding.[59] For example, during part of the 'Brasnle Gay' sequence in *Agon*, the female soloist moves her arms in a 'brisk and staccato' rhythm in time to an *ostinato* figure played on the castanets. Because of the synchronicity, one expects to see the dancer either playing the instrument herself or at least miming such a performance. Instead, she de-emphasizes her hands, virtually reducing them to 'after-images' of the chief 'focus of articulation', her wrists.[60] According to Duerden, over the course of any given ballet the accumulation of many such moments of similarity-in-difference tends to affirm the fecund diversity of the creative process. Different media enable disparate opportunities for 'draw[ing] attention to the phenomenon of being alive'.[61]

This argument corresponds well with O'Hara's meditation on gesture in the Leclerq ode. He, too, presents gesture as a 'window' that, instead of revealing

---

56 For O'Hara's familiarity with *Agon*, see Michael Magee, 'Tribes of New York: Frank O'Hara, Amiri Baraka, and the Poetics of the Five Spot', *Contemporary Literature* 42.4 (Winter 2001), pp. 702–703.

57 Rachel S. Chamberlain Duerden, 'Dancing in the Imagined Space of Music', *Dance Research* 25.1 (Summer 2007), pp. 74–75.

58 Duerden, 'Dancing', p. 73.

59 Duerden, 'Dancing', p. 76.

60 Duerden, 'Dancing', p. 77.

61 Duerden, 'Dancing', p. 75.

profound content, encourages one to notice the specifics of what is 'happen[ing] around' a dancer. True, he would be the first to point out that 'draw[ing] attention to [...] being alive' does not lead to unalloyed joy. His poetry is everywhere acutely conscious of life's utter fragility. Leclerq herself contracted polio in 1956 and never danced again. His ode says that she is 'hunted', and he mentions 'death' (*CP*, 364). Regardless, though, he clearly shares Duerden's sense that a gesture interrupts action-as-usual and promotes awareness of a work's unfolding through time. Moreover, Duerden's focus on gesture as a 'point of contact' between art forms enables one to see how O'Hara's reflections on dance could be harnessed to think about a different case of inter-art exchange, the *Poem-Paintings*.[62] Bluhm's painterly gestures and O'Hara's impromptu phrases frame each other. Each man produces 'meaning-bearing' marks on paper, but the specifics of how or what those marks make referential (or indexical or symbolic) sense is secondary to the fact that they open up a phenomenological space in which the audience becomes alternately viewers and readers, exploring, like Marjorie Perloff, the diverse kinds and orders of inscriptive 'gestures' as well as their myriad interplay.

Can one speak of O'Hara's own contributions to the collaboration as 'gestural'? Arguably, yes. Moreover, in contrast to poetry critics from R. P. Blackmur to Hazard Adams who have rather evasively tried to define certain uses of language as 'gesture', one can use 'gesture' here in a fairly specific sense.[63] Just as Bluhm considers his work to be more 'gesture' than bona-fide painting, so too O'Hara's words, as Perloff observes, are rarely capable of standing apart as independent poems. He writes phrases and sentences that are closer to ordinary language than common even in his own highly colloquial *oeuvre*. He supplies mostly lists, anecdotes, exclamations, profanity, and gags. Such speech acts are, however, extracted, 'abstracted' as Duerden puts it, from everyday discourse, and 'estranged'. They are language reborn as gesture; instead of offering profundity, they ask viewers to contemplate what it means to scribble words in a picture plane also occupied by slashing and sloshing paint.

Ever since the publication of Allan Kaprow's article 'Jackson Pollock's Legacy' (1958), art historians have taken it for granted that Pollock's idiosyncratic athletic manner of painting represents a crucial hinge between modernism, which privileged the production of autonomous artworks, and 1960s' and 1970s' postmodernism, which privileged conceptual and process-based works.[64] One should not be terribly surprised, then, to learn that a collaboration between Bluhm, a painter deeply influenced by Pollock, and O'Hara, author of a 1959 monograph on Pollock, places pressure on the question of gesture. Around that same issue, one

---

62 Duerden, 'Dancing', p. 74.
63 For previous theories of poetry and gesture, see Hazard Adams, *The Offense of Poetry* (Seattle: University of Washington Press, 2007), pp. 95–112.
64 Kaprow's essay is reprinted in *Essays on the Blurring of Art and Life* (Berkeley: University of California Press, 2003), pp. 1–9.

might say, the entire New York art world was soon to pivot. It is news, however, to discover a painter and a poet finding common ground in a third art form, dance. Bluhm's and O'Hara's *Poem-Paintings* demonstrate that cross-media collaborations are complex affairs that can proceed in most unexpected ways. W. J. T. Mitchell's use of the term 'imagetext' to cover the terrain of visual-verbal interchange, for example, must be deemed inadequate.[65] It does not take into account the full field of phenomenological possibilities. The whole human sensorium becomes open for artistic inquiry once the 'wild ballet' of intermedial experimentation unsettles conventional divisions between the arts.

---

65 W. J. T. Mitchell, *Picture Theory: Essays on Verbal and Visual Representation* (Chicago: University of Chicago Press, 1994), p. 83.

Memory Pieces: Collage, Memorial and the Poetics of Intimacy in Joe Brainard, Jasper Johns and Frank O'Hara

Nick Selby

I remember the first time I met Frank O'Hara. He was walking down Second Avenue. It was a cool early Spring evening but he was wearing only a white shirt with the sleeves rolled up to his elbows. And blue jeans. And moccasins. I remember that he seemed very sissy to me. Very theatrical. Decadent. I remember that I liked him instantly.[1]

The space of memory. A textual insistence: I remember this, and this, and this. A textual supplement: '*And* blue jeans. *And* moccasins.' A body in a place at a certain time. A self-aware performance courting danger. A touching friendship. A scene of desire and of loss. Thus Joe Brainard remembering his friend Frank O'Hara.

When the first version of Joe Brainard's *I Remember* was published by Angel Hair Books in 1970, Frank O'Hara was already nearly four years dead. Brainard's book is a collage of memories of growing up in America in the '40s and '50s. It depicts the life – inner thoughts and public events – of an artist deeply involved in the 'decadent' avant-garde art scene of New York in the late '50s and '60s. It remembers the trivial and the profound, all with touching intimacy. In those moments where Brainard remembers his friend and occasional artistic collaborator Frank O'Hara, memory becomes a space that is unavoidably drawn into that of elegy:

> I remember Frank O'Hara's walk. Light and sassy. With a beautiful bounce and a slight twist. It was a beautiful walk. Confident. 'I don't care' and sometimes 'I know you are looking.'[2]

Remembering differently, another poet, Michael Palmer, writes of O'Hara as the scene of various, interweaving, occasions of poetic memory. Though Palmer elegizes O'Hara in his 'Notes for Echo Lake 3' (1981) that very act of elegizing is presented as the site of renewed textual energies, as a scene of continuing poetic production. To remember O'Hara is – for Palmer – to turn him (by returning to him) both in to and into the poem. O'Hara's broken body, lying in hospital after his

---

1 Joe Brainard, *I Remember* (New York: Granary Books, rev. edn, 2001 [1975]), p. 15.

2 Brainard, *I Remember*, p. 20.

beach accident, becomes textual matter, a thing that is stitched together from other texts and from the play of the line in the poem before us. It is collaged together from accounts of O'Hara's place in the circle of friendships and literary, artistic and poetic connections which he has come to signify:

> As Robert's [i.e. Robert Duncan's] call on Tuesday asking whether I knew that Zukofsky had died a couple of days before. The call came as I was reading a copy of Larry Rivers' talk at Frank O'Hara's funeral (July, 1966), 'He was a quarter larger than usual. Every few inches there was some sewing composed of dark blue thread. Some stitching was straight and three or four inches long, others were longer and semi-circular…'

> As Robert's call on Tuesday a quarter larger than usual asking whether I knew whether I knew. Blue thread every few inches, straight and semi-circular, and sand and wet snow. Blue snow a couple of days before. Whether I know whatever I know.[3]

These opening examples help to reveal some of the ways in which O'Hara is a poetic presence in avant-garde American poetics of the latter part of the twentieth century. This is not because he represents a poetics of authenticity, one of assured selfhood and affective subjectivity, but rather because such examples recognize that any reading of O'Hara cannot escape the implication that his selfhood is a carefully choreographed textual performance, light and sassy, knowing we are looking. Such a performance, underpinning as it does the breathless and bravura excitement of O'Hara's most famous poems as they 'go on [their] nerve' (*CP*, 498), also challenges us to confront its own textual constructedness. In some senses this accounts for the campy superficiality, the seeming irreverence, of his work. Indeed, his is a poetics in which the poet is larger than life. But in other senses this means that O'Hara's poetic selfhood – both through and in its play of memory and elegy – continually discovers to us the textual mechanics from which it is made.

What I want to suggest in this essay, by reading O'Hara alongside examples of work by his artist friends and collaborators Joe Brainard and Jasper Johns, is that O'Hara's sense of his poetry – and indeed his body – as a self-aware performance unpicks, as it were, the textual stitches in which authenticity and feelingness might be located. The essay will therefore examine O'Hara's, Brainard's and Johns' work in terms of a poetics of collage and how such a poetics might be seen to open out questions of what – literally – to put in the picture. If, for Brainard, memory and feelingness are key elements to his art and writing, this is also true of the elegiac pieces made by Johns that reflect upon his friendship with O'Hara. What unites these works is their questioning of the efficacy of a poetics of elegy and of touch.

Collage-work is crucial to this questioning. For it is in collage-work, because of the attention it draws to the ways in which an artist has organized her or his

---

3 Michael Palmer, 'Notes for Echo Lake 3', in *Notes for Echo Lake* (San Francisco: North Point Press, 1981), p. 16.

materials, because it so clearly is the aesthetic trace of the process by which the artist has (often very literally) had a hand in the composition, that artists such as O'Hara, Brainard and Johns might find a means to challenge traditional ideas of poetic space, subjectivity, and a poetics of affect. As the anonymous author of the biographical statement about Brainard for the Academy of American Poets puts it, collage is an artistic means to reveal 'the process and materials rather than any will of the artist, reflecting style over content and a refusal on the artist's part to take the art, or himself, too seriously'.[4] Certainly an attention to processes and materials is one of the effects of work by Brainard, Johns or O'Hara. What I'm hoping to suggest, however, is that in their respective poetics of collage, these three *do* take their art seriously: their work, considered as art, as a made object, becomes the space of memory and elegy. Or more properly, as self-aware aesthetic perform- ances their work explores the terms under which a poet or a painter might be the expressive origin of the work.

The main focus for my exploration of these issues will be O'Hara's poem 'In Memory of My Feelings', which he wrote in late June and early July 1956 (see *CP*, 538). Famously, near the close of the poem, O'Hara describes his collaged poetic surface, and its surreally juxtaposed imagery, as 'the scene of my selves' (*CP*, 257). O'Hara's insistence on the poem as a dramatic setting, a scene, in which elegy and memory are seen to be acted out raises interesting and, I think, quite complicated questions about how the poet might be felt to be 'in' the poem, about how intimacy can be read as the origin of a poem. The appeal to intimacy in O'Hara, Brainard and Johns, in turn, comes to depict masculinity as a deeply conflicted aesthetic site. Manliness in their work – as a scene of memory and elegy, of desire and loss; as, especially, a *made* place, consciously acted out – becomes a poetic ruse, a means of debating the cultural effects of literary and artistic friendship and collaboration.

The final two sections of 'In Memory of My Feelings' dramatize what feel like increasingly desperate attempts to salvage a sense of identity from amidst the welter of materials that bombard the poem. The disturbingly jagged energies of these closing stages of the poem issue from its sense of itself as textual collage. Indeed, its technique of startling and surreal jump-cuts between private and public personae, along with its attention to the terms of its own textual composition, relates it clearly to a poetics of collage in which, according to Eddie Wolfram's *History of Collage*, the 'sticking together [of] bits and pieces of random and miscellaneous bric-a-brac [can] stir the imagination to release hidden associations'.[5] In these moments, the poem certainly becomes alive to the possibilities of its hidden associations. Its very textual techniques, though dissociative and disruptive of any notion of a unified self, discover the poem's reliance upon a poetics of touch, a lyrical, as it were,

---

4 Anonymous, 'Joe Brainard: "I Remember"', Academy of American Poets website, http://www. poets.org/viewmedia.php/prmMID/5945.

5 Eddie Wolfram, *History of Collage: An Anthology of Collage, Assemblage and Event Structures* (New York: Macmillan, 1975), p. 7.

phenomenology of feelings. In Section 4 of the poem this discourse of feelings (alongside the repeated 'I am' that catalogues the various selves assumed by the poet) specifically recalls Whitman's 'is this then a touch? quivering me to a new identity' in his 'Song of Myself'.[6] And the playful reference to O'Hara's friend the artist Grace Hartigan also initiates a poignant meditation on friendship, intimacy and the depth of feeling that becomes available when textual, or indeed real, bodies are juxtaposed:

> Grace
> to be born and live as variously as possible. The conception
> of the masque barely suggests the sordid identifications.
> I am a Hittite in love with a horse. I don't know what blood's
> in me I feel like an African prince I am a girl walking downstairs
> in a red pleated dress with heels I am a champion taking a fall
> I am a jockey with a sprained ass-hole I am the light mist
> in which a face appears
> and it is another face of blonde I am a baboon eating a banana
> I am a dictator looking at his wife I am a doctor eating a child
> and the child's mother smiling I am a Chinaman climbing a mountain
> I am a child smelling his father's underwear I am an Indian
> sleeping on a scalp
> and my pony is stamping in the birches,
> and I've just caught sight of the *Niña*, the *Pinta* and the *Santa Maria*.
> What land is this, so free? (*CP*, 256)

Surreal and darkly funny as these identifications strike us, they are also underscored by mounting speculation about the nature of contact between figures of power and those without power – a dictator and his wife, for example, a doctor and a child, and another child portrayed in a frankly abject relation to her or his father's underwear. It is in the poem's acting out – its masque – of these various selves that the mask of poetic identity might be felt to slip and that the poem might therefore begin to reveal the hidden associations – ideological and political – that haunt its 'sordid identifications'. The histories of various acts of imperial expansion seem embedded, therefore, in the poem's collage technique, in its portrayal of various figures of intercultural contact, from Hittites conquering Asia through their horsemanship, to African princes and their role in the slave-trade, to Columbus 'discovering' the New World. O'Hara's poetics of collage inevitably leads to a disruption of notions of individual identity, a disruption that makes apparent the ways in which selfhood, lyric voice, and expressive subjectivity are inescapably bound-in to discourses of Americanness. Because of his disruptive collage techniques, then, O'Hara is able genuinely to ask 'What land is this, so free?', a question that cuts to the heart of his aesthetic and social concerns as a poet and central figure of the

6 Walt Whitman, *The Complete Poems*, ed. Francis Murphy (London: Penguin, 1986), p. 91.

New York artistic scene in the mid-1950s.

Another effect of O'Hara's collage technique throughout 'In Memory of My Feelings' is that it expressly sets up an engagement between poetic surface and bodily interiority. Such looking inwards, the felt intimacy of this poem, allows for a blurring of the boundaries between the personal and the ideological. Repeatedly throughout the poem O'Hara dramatizes the space he occupies, as poet, in the poem. In some senses his insistence on putting himself in the poem, and on examining the compositional strategies and energies that allow him to do this, parallels a similar desire of Abstract Expressionist painters to be, literally, 'in the picture'. Most notably, Jackson Pollock, a painter immensely admired by O'Hara, stated 'When I am *in* my painting, I'm not aware of what I'm doing', thus privileging, as a freeing up of technique, the gestural energies of the artist's body *in the work.*[7] In lines near the close of the poem, the locus for O'Hara's efforts to make transparent his various selves – personal and ideological – is his body. Here O'Hara describes himself in terms that mark the body as, simultaneously, the site of abjection and the scene of a superficial melodrama of selfhood:

> When you turn your head
> Can you feel your heels, undulating? that's what it is
> to be a serpent. I haven't told you of the most beautiful things
> in my lives, and watching the ripple of their loss disappear
> along the shore, underneath ferns,
>   face downward in the ferns
> my body, the naked host to my many selves, shot
> by a guerilla warrior or dumped from a car into ferns
> which are themselves *journalières.*
>   The hero, trying to unhitch his parachute,
> stumbles over me. It is our last embrace. (*CP*, 256)

Like the hero described here, O'Hara is a body parachuted into the poem's drama of many selves, naked and vulnerable. The sense of bodily threat that comes to dominate the poem's closing moments thus registers its overarching themes of loss, disappearance and elegy. If the body is the site of feeling, then collaged descriptions of the poet's body being shot by a guerrilla and dumped from a car merely emphasize the extent to which the poem's textual body too is shot through with feelingness. Such juxtapositions enable the poem to stand *in* memory of O'Hara's feelings.

I want to develop this investigation of the qualities of inwardness in O'Hara's poetics of collage, now, by thinking briefly about some of Joe Brainard's collage-works. Firstly, I'm going to look at a collage that Brainard made in collaboration with O'Hara in 1964. Though seemingly jokey, irreverent and campily light-hearted, this is a work that (along with others he made with O'Hara at this time) challenges

---

7 Pollock is cited in David Anfam, *Abstract Expressionism* (London: Thames & Hudson, 1990), p. 125.

the ways in which masculinity and the figure of the male body are placed at the heart of American ideology. I'll then look at another Brainard piece, from 1968, in order to think about how, like O'Hara's, Brainard's work raises explicit questions about how an artist might put herself or himself *in* the picture. These examples raise important questions about the efficacy of a poetics of touch within an idea of collage because of the attention they demand to the work of the artist's hand among her or his materials. What is striking about these examples, as well as what marks their relationship to O'Hara's work, is that the emphasis they place on their own tactile qualities is part and parcel of their questioning of the meanings of masculinity.

This can be seen in the example of the collage, *I Grew this Mustache...* (1964) (Figure 1), on which Brainard and O'Hara collaborated. O'Hara's contribution to this piece – the text written in the speech bubble, his hand in the work – was added quickly, in an improvisatory way, according to Brainard. The lightness of touch and crisp wit of this collaboration serves a serious purpose, however, bursting as it does the bubble of high-art seriousness associated with Abstract Expressionism. Also, as Russell Ferguson has pointed out, Brainard's and O'Hara's collage collaborations 'display a sharp consciousness of an emerging sexual politics'.[8] This particular collage consists of a border of Ghanaian postage stamps of alternating 2d and 3d value. Within the frame of stamps is laid what looks like a rectangular fragment from a wallpaper design book, in the style of Japanese flower painting. Inside this frame is a pasted black-and-white photograph of a muscular sportsman who is holding, in an aggressively suave male posture, a fencing foil. However, this picture is almost totally covered by another, slightly smaller, rectangular picture. The figure in this second picture is clearly naked, or nearly so, and is an image that has apparently been cut and pasted into the collage from a faintly erotic male sports-star magazine. Pasted on top of this image is a red-tinted picture of a man in a suit and tie, wearing a moustache, every bit the stereotype of a male screen idol, with Clark Gable good looks. Semi-obscured Spanish text beneath the image reads 'Charro boricua' (roughly, 'the Puerto Rican cowboy').[9] In the speech bubble drawn over this figure, O'Hara has written 'I grew this mustache because my girl has one and I think mustaches are pretty sexy'.

The effect of such layering in this collage is to focus attention upon the cultural frames through which maleness is both obscured and made apparent, and upon men's masks and masques. That masculinity – and male power – is subject to processes of cultural performance, negotiation and negation is implicit in the collage's use of stamps from Ghana (not only does this intimate the writing back

---

8 Russell Ferguson, *In Memory of My Feelings: Frank O'Hara and American Art* (Berkeley: University of California Press, 1999), p. 103.

9 The image may come from the album of this title (or promotional material relating to it) by a Latin American musician or singer named Gerardo Molina. This appears to be confirmed by the signature on the image.

Figure 1 Joe Brainard and Frank O'Hara, *I Grew this Mustache…*, 1964

of the colonized to the colonial centre, but remembers for us O'Hara's interest in 'what the poets/ in Ghana are doing these days' ('The Day Lady Died' [*CP*, 325]) in the attention it gives to competing styles of the exotic and the erotic (Japanese flowers, body building, a Latin-lover hero), and in the seemingly absurd gender politics of O'Hara's text. Such techniques of layering, overlapping, cutting and pasting further expose the ruses of male agency by suggesting that beneath the surface effects of maleness, the stylistics of living as variously as possible, is a deep-seated desire for contact, intimacy and feelingness. Although collage as an artistic technique can be seen to emerge from modern forms of mass reproduction, its address is very often to intimate senses of the self and the body.[10] Brandon Taylor has noted that because of collage's 'experimental quality and [...] the marginality of its status', its 'relative *privacy*' makes our encounter with it 'a paradox'.[11] What this suggests is that the 'new relationship between the "low" culture of stamps and two-penny song, and the "high" culture of professional art' that Taylor describes as one of the important effects of collage as modern art provides Brainard and O'Hara with a means of engaging the paradoxes of expressivity and privacy.[12] Their collaborative work, therefore, seems to lay bare the ways in which a discourse of male feelings – both literally, in the touch of the hands in manipulating artistic materials, and figuratively in terms of the inner lives of the two artists working together on it – might emerge from apparently playful and irreverent procedures.

If one of the effects of *I Grew this Mustache...* is a renewed sense of the power of a poetics of collage and collaboration, it also shows how an examination and a critique of maleness in the mid-1960s might be seen to be fused with an opening out of questions of interiority. Its inward turn is both a result of its dealings with the materials of its composition, and its consciousness of the sexual and gender politics from which it emerges. According to Peter Middleton, the difficulties of negotiating inwardness are central to an understanding of the masculinity of twentieth-century modernity. To be male, he argues, is to feel oneself divorced from one's feelings, lacking a language for emotional self-reflection.[13] This has been especially true, remarks Middleton, for the male artist in modern culture: 'The artist's problem is that his kind of inwardness is no longer respected and all he can blame is a modern state of emasculation'.[14] For US males in the 1950s and 1960s, the notions of masculinity promulgated by the culture meant a divorce from one's feelings and the lack of a language for self-reflection. In mid-century America, it would seem, a growing recourse to modes of inwardness and of feelingness was a means of challenging the sorts of 'hegemonic masculinity' implied by Middleton (and defined by Robert Connell).[15] If, as Michael Kimmel puts it, 'loneliness, emptiness [...] became the dominant terms in the era's [i.e. the 1960s'] cultural analysis of masculinity', then this does seems to mark such an inward turn, and a recognition of the troubled nature of both being male and having feelings.[16] This seems confirmed by David Savran's analysis of the changing nature of American masculinity in the 1960s and 1970s in which, he notes, there emerges 'a new, more feminized [...] masculinity [occupying] positions marked

10 See Wolfram, *History of Collage*, pp. 15–22; and Brandon Taylor, *Collage: The Making of Modern Art* (London: Thames & Hudson, 2004, p. 8.
11 Taylor, *Collage*, p. 9.
12 Taylor, *Collage*, p. 8.
13 Peter Middleton, *The Inward Gaze: Masculinity and Subjectivity in Modern Culture* (London: Routledge, 1992), p. 3.
14 Middleton, *The Inward Gaze*, p. 10.
15 Robert W. Connell, *Masculinities* (London: Polity, 1995).
16 Michael Kimmel, *Manhood in America: A Cultural History* (New York: The Free Press, 1996), p. 265.

historically as both masculine and feminine'.[17] Both Brainard and O'Hara, here, seem to partake of this kind of re-negotiation (it is key, as I shall argue later, to their sense of being both male *and* gay) by satirizing the male heroics of growing a moustache or of disentangling oneself from a parachute. It is at such moments that we encounter their struggles to negotiate a language of inwardness, to feel how they might be in the picture.

The relationship between aesthetic surface and bodily interiority seen here (and in other Brainard/O'Hara collaborations), can also be seen in one of O'Hara's most famous poems, 'Why I Am Not a Painter'. Much like the *I Grew this Mustache...* piece, this is a poem that expressly sets up an engagement between 'low' and 'high' art, and between aesthetic surface and bodily interiority in terms of a nervy, anxious restlessness. But what such restlessness discloses is a questioning of the regulatory systems of art and the ideological frames that define us. The poem moves, that is, from surface to interior, from a questioning of the superficiality of how we are labelled – am I a 'painter' or 'poet' – to an investigation of what such acts of naming contain. O'Hara's anxious comings and goings in the poem, which mark a movement through a city that is mere surface, gradually succumb to a discourse of interiors: of male friendship, of what it feels like to be a poet or a painter, of time and things passing. We realize that O'Hara is dropping *in* to see Mike Goldberg, and the poem turns on what is included in a work of art:

> [...] Mike Goldberg is
> starting a painting. I drop in.
> 'Sit down and have a drink' he
> says. I drink; we drink. I look
> up. 'You have SARDINES in it.'
> 'Yes, it needed something there.'
> 'Oh.' I go and the days go by
> and I drop in again. The painting
> is going on, and I go, and the days
> go by. I drop in. The painting is
> finished. 'Where's SARDINES?'
> All that's left is just
> letters, 'It was too much,' Mike says. (*CP*, 261–62)

Jokily, but also in line with the poem's investigation of interior aesthetic space, at the poem's conclusion O'Hara announces 'I am a real poet' because the poem he has written 'is even/ *in* prose' (my emphasis).

I want to suggest that this poetic restlessness, this anxious coming and going over cultural surfaces and the disguised attention to interiority, encapsulates precisely those conflicting discourses of American masculinity at the heart of what I'm

17 David Savran, *Taking it Like a Man: White Masculinity, Masochism and Contemporary American Culture* (Princeton: Princeton University Press, 1998), p. 37.

calling O'Hara's and Brainard's poetics of collage. As Margaret Mead has pointed out, the restless anxiety of American men in the post-war years stems from 'the contradictory cultural messages that form the backbone of male socialization'.[18] In this view, traits such as aggression are simultaneously endorsed and suppressed by the discourses surrounding masculinity. Manhood itself, then, is located on anxiously ambivalent and dissolving boundaries between body and text, and as we have already seen, it is just such boundaries that Brainard's collages and O'Hara's poetry interrogate, through their attention to margins, frames and interiors. In this context, it should be noted that the body itself, according to Mary Douglas, provides the model for an imagery of limits, boundaries and transgressions: 'The body is a model which can stand for any bounded system. Its boundaries can represent any boundaries which are threatened or precarious.'[19]

Precarious boundaries and issues of the body and of touch certainly seem to be at play in another Brainard collage, his *Untitled (Good'n Fruity Madonna)* of 1968 (Figure 2). This piece also presents a clear challenge to conceptions of the relationship between modes of popular and high art. While the iconography of the Virgin Mary specifically recalls a long art history, the collage technique here sees her become (irreverently) a figure of reproduction, thus suggesting the place of her image within popular consciousness. The juxtaposition of the image of the Madonna alongside pieces from packets of Good'n Fruity candy not only suggests that religious and commercial imagery are equally reproducible and consumable parts of a mass culture, but it also implies that the apparent paradoxes of such juxtapositions might enable a reading that looks beyond the bright and glittering surface of such connections to a rather more urgent set of inner tensions shaping this piece. That the Madonna is here seen as both 'good' and 'fruity' certainly suggests that her iconic cultural power is – to say the least – ambiguous. Morally good, a model of chastity and obedience, she is also sexually enticing, deliciously fruitful. As with imagery of a similarly iconic (and camp) heroine of Pop Art, Marilyn Monroe (which Brainard, I think, parodies here), such ambiguities rest in issues of the body and of sexuality.

Like *I Grew this Mustache...*, this later collage draws attention to the bodily in terms of the tactile qualities at the heart of its composition. But the body is also thematized here. As the site of feeling – of desire, of touch, of hunger – it places us at the centre of a culture of anxious consumption. This means that the body seems always at a point of perilous threat in the collage. If collage is based in techniques of cutting and splicing, of fragmentation and replacement, then here it is the body (as flesh made text) that is continually imaged as torn apart. On a simple level this is apparent in the fact of the image's repetition, the fact that it has been

18 Cited in Kimmel, *Manhood in America*, p. 230.
19 Mary Douglas, *Purity and Danger: An Analysis of the Concepts of of Pollution and Taboo* (London: Routledge, 1991 [1966]), p. 115; and Anthony Synnott, *The Body Social: Symbolism, Self and Society* (London: Routledge, 1993), p. 229.

Figure 2 Joe Brainard, *Good 'n Fruity Madonna*, 1968

cut and pasted into the picture from elsewhere. One of the pressing questions of this collage becomes, thus, 'which body is the true body, the original?' Most noticeably this sense of bodily rupture portrayed in and through the physically ruptured material of the collaged surface itself occurs in the top left-hand panel of the piece, where one of the Madonna's hands, one of the feet, and part of the face of the Christ-child are absent, torn out of the picture. Paradoxically, the absence here of the instruments of touch and personal identity (hands and face) forces feelingness back into the picture: these gaps register powerfully because they gesture inwards, to more than the dependencies of colour and shape within the overall design.

I have already suggested that one reason why this inward turn is especially marked in O'Hara's and Brainard's work is that their investigation of masculinity is freighted by their own homosexuality, by the 'sharp consciousness of an emerging sexual politics' noted by Russell Ferguson (see above). Indeed, as Marjorie Perloff pointed out in the 1997 introduction to the new edition of her *Frank O'Hara: Poet Among Painters*, what is obvious about O'Hara's style is that it is 'a style recognizably gay'.[20] This is no less true of Brainard's work, in which tropes of inwardness and

20 Marjorie Perloff, *Frank O'Hara: Poet Among Painters* (Chicago and London: University of Chicago Press, rev. edn, 1998 [1977]), p. xi.

friendship, of the body and desire, and questions of design and technique all perform a masculine identity that is markedly gay. Whether writing a poem about oranges, or making a collage of the Madonna and child, O'Hara's and Brainard's work is playfully fruity.

Much has been written about gay aesthetics in relation to O'Hara's work, and it is not my intention to add to this.[21] My point is, rather, that for Brainard and O'Hara, the importance of a poetics of collage lies in its ability to assert and investigate strategies of inwardness, and of aesthetic feeling, in ways that challenge the superficial and defensive masculinity promulgated in post-war American society. Most especially, their collage techniques require a reimagining of how an actual body might come to be figured within the body of a text or a picture.

With this in mind I want to turn very briefly to the work of another of O'Hara's friends, the painter Jasper Johns, before returning to the poem 'In Memory of My Feelings'. In terms of a poetics of touch and feelingness, Johns' painting *In Memory of My Feelings – Frank O'Hara* (1961) (Figure 3) is especially arresting. From the two canvas panels which are hinged together and comprise the painting's surface, to the spoon and fork that dangle together on a piece of straightened out clothes-hanger wire at the left of the canvas, to the overall design, which is reminiscent of Johns' famous Flag paintings of a few years earlier, and to the O'Hara poem to which the painting alludes in its title, this is a painting that emerges from a consideration of various sets of dependencies. Like O'Hara's 'Why I Am Not a Painter', the relationship of paint to text is here engaged in the stencilled words 'In Memory of My Feelings – Frank O'Hara Johns 61' that appear – partly obscured by over-painted brushstrokes – across the bottom of the canvas. Johns, that is, makes material (out of) his friendship with O'Hara. In this sense the painting, though abstract and scrupulously non-figural, is personal. This is not to say, though, that it declares feelings that are simply intimate and personal. By quoting the title of O'Hara's poem within the painting, Johns is constructing feelings themselves as dependent upon artistic ruses as much as they are expressive of individual emotions. Indeed, Johns himself noted, in conversation in 1973, that in his work he attempted 'not to confuse my feelings with what I produced. I didn't want my work to be an exposure of my feelings'.[22] What the painting *does* expose, though, is feelingness. And this results from the tactile sense with which we weigh the relationships of dependency set out on the canvas before us: what literal and figurative weight should we give to the dangling cutlery? What relationship is there between the words 'Dead Man',

---

21 See, for example, Bruce Boone, 'Gay Language and Political Praxis: The Poetry of Frank O'Hara', *Social Text* 1 (Winter 1979), pp. 55–92; Terrell Scott Herring, 'Frank O'Hara's Open Closet', *PMLA* 117.3 (May 2002), pp. 414–27; Hazel Smith, *Hyperscapes in the Poetry of Frank O'Hara: Difference/ Homoxexuality/Topography* (Liverpool: Liverpool University Press, 2000); and Michael Davidson, who notes of 'In Memory of My Feelings' that 'O'Hara suggests that, like sexuality itself, nationhood is an unstable category' (*Guys Like Us: Citing Masculinity in Cold War Poetics* [Chicago and London: University of Chicago Press, 2004], p. 112).

22 Michael Crichton, *Jasper Johns* (London: Thames & Hudson, 1977), p. 20.

Figure 3 Jasper Johns, *In Memory of My Feelings – Frank O'Hara*, 1961

stencilled in big letters on the canvas in its bottom right-hand section, and the bold brushstrokes of blue paint that nearly obscure these words?[23] What sort of relationship *hinges* on the division of the canvas into two halves?

Such questions are ones that confuse, quite deliberately, ideas of the literal and metaphorical touch of the artist in his work. This painting, which touches upon O'Hara's poetry in peculiarly fitting ways, also depends upon it. Yet it proceeds from concerns that are very much embedded in Johns' own work, most especially in the ways that his paintings confront the viewer with what Fred Orton describes as 'a play of hermeneutic intrigue'.[24] At the heart of such intrigue is, according to Orton, an examination of touch. 'Johns' art', he notes, 'operates in the mode of touch, continually reorienting whatever localised physical connection to his works the viewer may succeed in establishing'.[25] In connection with O'Hara's work, though, such a poetics of touch connects to a negotiation of masculinity. Again, Orton has noted that 'masculinity is there in Johns' touch, not as a securely established self but as a disavowed self'.[26]

In a work that Johns began during O'Hara's lifetime, but finished four years

---

23 See Perloff, *Poet Among Painters*, pp. xxi–xxii; and Fred Orton, *Figuring Jasper Johns* (London: Reaktion Books, 1994), pp. 64–65.

24 Fred Orton, *Jasper Johns: The Sculptures* (Leeds: The Henry Moore Institute, 1996), p. 16.

25 Orton, *Jasper Johns: The Sculptures*, p. 27.

26 Orton, *Jasper Johns: The Sculptures*, p. 28.

Figure 4 Jasper Johns, *Memory Piece (Frank O'Hara)*, 1961–70

after his death, Johns questions such a disavowal. His *Memory Piece (Frank O'Hara)* (1961–70) (Figure 4) elegizes O'Hara by expressly making the poet's lost body and touch, the memory of his feelings, the scene of its aesthetics of self. This sculpture consists of a box, containing three drawers of sand. The sand was taken from Edisto beach, South Carolina, where Johns had a studio and where O'Hara had visited him in the summer of 1961. On the inside lid of the box is a cast of O'Hara's left foot, made in rubber from an impression of his foot in the sand of the beach. When the lid is closed, O'Hara's footprint is impressed into the sand contained in the top drawer. As in the earlier *In Memory of My Feelings – Frank O'Hara*, this is a work expressly concerned with memory and feelingness.

Russell Ferguson describes the piece as 'an intimate kind of memorial', but its unsettling elegiac effect seems to be a consequence of its attempt to question the mutual dependency of intimacy and memorial.[27] Here, indeed, an aesthetics of intimacy, touch and bodiliness depends on the physical absence of O'Hara's actual

27 Ferguson, *In Memory of My Feelings*, p. 133.

body. The impression of O'Hara's foot in the sand (and by extension the very act of memory and the art of memorial) depends upon a substitution of the poet's actual body by that which it is not, the artwork itself. Though, of course, this piece has a particular potency given the circumstances of O'Hara's premature death, it seems fully aware of the sorts of difficulties with intimacy, selfhood and feelingness that O'Hara's poem (and Brainard's work) explores. Here are no masculine heroics. In Larry Rivers' words spoken at O'Hara's funeral and quoted in Michael Palmer's poem at the start of this essay, O'Hara's wounded body is larger than life, 'a quarter larger than usual'. But here we see that that is not the case, merely a poetic ruse, a stitching of him into the text of his own poetic memorialization. Here the impression of O'Hara's foot in the sand, his body printed in time, is exactly the same shape and size as his actual foot. Intimate, that is, with his body, but expressing its final absence.

To move towards my conclusion I want to return to a discussion of O'Hara's 'In Memory of My Feelings'. It is the pressure of such a reimagining of the poet's body that we have seen in relation to the work of Joe Brainard and Jasper Johns that is, I want to argue, absolutely crucial to the power and affectivity of 'In Memory of My Feelings'. By continually renegotiating its relationship to the poet's actual body this is a poem that courts ambiguity, and juxtaposition, in order to discover the poetic possibilities of living as variously as possible. The closing lines of the poem resonate powerfully because of their ability to demonstrate *feelingly* how O'Hara's sense of being in the poem is subject to his exploration of a complex set of relationships between performative positions available to him as poet. While sounding sincere, authentically troubled by the sense of lost feelings and the poetic occasion that calls for their memorializing, the poem's closing moments also announce that its nostalgia for a lost self is a mere performance, a ruse in which intimacy and feeling-ness, even the body itself, are exposed as effects of the poet's textual negotiations:

> and I have lost what is always and everywhere
> present, the scene of my selves, the occasion of these ruses,
> which I myself and singly must now kill
> and save the serpent in their midst. (*CP*, 257)

Because of its playful and powerful articulation (indeed, deconstruction) of the heroic dramas of a seemingly beleaguered sense of American identity, 'In Memory of My Feelings' is commonly seen as one of O'Hara's most important poems: Geoff Ward describes it as 'O'Hara's first incontrovertibly major poem';[28] for Marjorie Perloff it is 'not only O'Hara's best autobiographical poem, but one of the great poems of our time';[29] and more recently, Andrew Epstein describes it as 'one of the most important and influential postwar American poems'. It is, he notes, 'a

28 Geoff Ward, *Statutes of Liberty: The New York School of Poets* (Basingstoke and New York: Polity, 2nd edn, 2001), p. 70.
29 Perloff, *Poet Among Painters*, p. 141.

poem that stands – or perhaps flickers or dances [...] – at the center of [O'Hara's] poetry' because of its display of what he terms O'Hara's 'pragmatist conception of the self'.[30] Here Epstein evokes what he takes to be O'Hara's concern that the poem gets things done in terms of interpersonal communication, as an instrument of friendship and intimacy. Epstein thus reads 'In Memory of My Feelings' as a poem exercised by its attempt to make its scenes of the self intimate with a kind of cultural force of communicative efficiency. He shares, that is, with Michael Magee a sense 'that O'Hara draws much of his aesthetic disposition from pragmatism'.[31] Indeed, like Magee, Epstein turns to O'Hara's concept of 'Personism' to delineate this pragmatist idea of O'Hara's uses of poetic intimacy. (Unlike Magee, though, Epstein does not specifically evoke the philosophical legacy of Emerson's pragmatism, and is thus less able to claim, as Magee does, that O'Hara's poetics represents 'a kind of democratic symbolic action'.)[32] What O'Hara's poem, then, seems to trace is the pragmatic struggle of its poetic economy (much like Emerson's philosophy of emergent nationhood) to accommodate intimacy and expressivity to its action within a democracy of feelings. It would seem, then, that claims to the poem's greatness rest largely in its self-conscious efforts to delineate – or figure out – a language and poetics of expressive intimacy. But to acknowledge this, I would argue, is to acknowledge a difficulty around inwardness and collectivity at the heart of the very idea of a poetics of American identity. The intimacy and affectivity of engagement with an individual – feeling – self in 'In Memory of My Feelings', and indeed O'Hara's work more generally, thus becomes an index of its claim to public attention, of its place within an idea of American poetry.

For O'Hara, too, the memorializing of his feelings throughout the poem makes clear the paradoxical and contested nature of identity. But for O'Hara this is less an effect of a relation to (American) literary ideologies, and more to do with the ways in which the poem foregrounds the poet's relationship to the process and materials of its composition. It is because of the poem's collaged textual surface that its poetic self is seen continually to erase itself even as it is asserted. Ideas of intimacy, masculinity and the trope of transparency that sustains them in the poem – whether in terms of Perloff's notion of the 'autobiographical' or Epstein's rather more sceptical and pragmatist sense of O'Hara's poetic self as a precursor to the play of decentred subjectivity within postmodernity – are functions of O'Hara's poetics of collage, rather than tactics of intimacy in a confessional poetics. It is in these terms, then, that O'Hara can enact his poem's wider cultural and ideological engagements. The opening lines of the poem make clear the textual means by which O'Hara puts himself, and his feelings, *in* the poem:

30 Andrew Epstein, *Beautiful Enemies: Friendship and Postwar American Poetry* (Oxford and New York: Oxford University Press, 2006), p. 99.
31 Michael Magee, *Emancipating Pragmatism: Emerson, Jazz, and Experimental Writing* (Tuscaloosa: University of Alabama Press, 2004), p. 131.
32 Magee, *Emancipating Pragmatism*, p. 131.

> My quietness has a man in it, he is transparent
> and he carries me quietly, like a gondola, through the streets.
> He has several likenesses, like stars and years, like numerals.
>
> My quietness has a number of naked selves,
> so many pistols I have borrowed to protect myselves
> from creatures who too readily recognize my weapons
> and have murder in their heart! (*CP*, 252–53)

Though these lines propose various ways in which the poet's feelings – and, by extension, poetic feelingness – might be contained within the poem, they also attest to the ways in which its act of poetic self-investigation slips away from such containment.

For a start, those very feelings, the ostensible subject of the poem, have, it would seem, already slipped away. The poem is, after all, an elegy to them, written in their memory. But if such feelings are dead at the poem's outset, they also figure curiously in its imagery of containment, as though the poem has become their textual coffin, carrying them through its poetic streets, gondola-like. This plays into the suggestion in these lines that to be a man is to struggle with, but barely to contain one's feelings and expressive capabilities. What I'm suggesting here is that the poem makes apparent from the outset the contested and paradoxical nature of masculinity, and that it does this because of the attention it gives to the slipperiness of its textual surfaces. On the one hand, that is, the poet's presence in the poem as 'a man' is defined by his containment within a sort of emotional diffidence: 'My quietness has a man in it'. This man seems traditionally reserved, reluctant to display feelings, quietly guarded on the potentially dangerous streets. On the other hand, though, the poem announces that one of its principal investigations will be what it feels like to be a man in 1950s America; it declares that at the heart of its sense of self is 'a man'. Effectively this means that the apparent transparency of selfhood that is presented here sits uncomfortably within those frames that define and express it. Most especially we begin to see through the ruses of this poetic identity when we notice how conditioned they are by an evasive syntax. It is not at all clear whether the male pronoun 'he' in the second half of the opening line refers to 'quietness' or to 'man'. If the former case, then the gendering of 'quietness' as male is surely significant in an understanding of how the poem's sense of transparency might operate. In this case the poet is the strong, silent type: keeping feelings under wraps. If, however, we opt for the latter case, then, we are presented with a very different model of manhood. Here the man is transparent, with the implication that his feelings can be read, that his selfhood is genuine, and his 'authenticity' marked by such transparency.

As if this weren't complicated enough, the second line continues – syntactically – to undermine the poem's articulation of transparency and maleness. To what does the repeated 'he' ('he carries me quietly') in line two refer? Depending, of course, on how we have read the first line, it could refer to either 'quietness' or 'man'. Such determined readings, though, risk tautology (quietness carries the self quietly) or produce a faintly paradoxical reading of manhood's transparencies (in which a man is inside quietness, and yet carries 'me' quietly). However, following the logic of a sort of syntactical paralleling between the poem's first two clauses (and this is supported by the line break and the consequently strong emphasis on the copula 'and'), it is perfectly possible to read the first 'he' as referring to 'quietness' and the second one to 'man'. In this case questions of quietness and of maleness are kept separate, yet in tandem, by the poem. They circulate around each other, each contained by and containing the other, but never quite becoming absorbed into the other.

This image of the poem's sense of its own circulating textual economy of selfhood brings me to my conclusion. The apparent inward turn towards the poet's 'true' inner self is playfully imaged throughout the poem in terms of a battle between the poet's various selves and a deceiving 'serpent', a sort of 'snake in the grass' of poetic subjectivity.[33] We have already seen the (melodramatic?) killing of the serpent in the last line of the poem. At another point the poet announces that his 'transparent selves/ flail about like vipers in a pail' (*CP*, 253), and at another we are told:

And now it is the serpent's turn,
I am not quite you, but almost, the opposite of visionary.
You are coiled around the central figure,
                            the heart (*CP*, 256)

The undulating, flailing turns of the serpent in the poem are not only carefully plotted against the poem's sense of selfhood as a lost paradise, an edenic myth of originary feelings, but they also image the inward turn of the poem, its coiling around the central figure of feeling, the heart. With this figure of the poem as a turning back on, and into, the heart of O'Hara's memory of his feelings, I can now turn back to another poet, Michael Palmer, whose elegizing of O'Hara I quoted at the beginning of this essay. Palmer's 'Notes for Echo Lake 3' ends by speculating on the conditions of a poetic engagement with the world. Poetic feelingness, he suggests, is about a continual re-engagement with, and re-turning to, the world and its texts: 'In the poem he learns to turn and turn, and prose seems always/ a sentence long'.[34] Prints in the sand, pages of text that return to us: this strikes me as a fitting way to elegize O'Hara.

33 See Ward, *Statutes of Liberty*, p. 75.
34 Palmer, 'Notes for Echo Lake 3', p. 17.

Index of Works by Frank O'Hara

General Index